Poetry in Pieces

FLASHPOINTS

The series solicits books that consider literature beyond strictly national and disciplinary frameworks, distinguished both by their historical grounding and their theoretical and conceptual strength. We seek studies that engage theory without losing touch with history, and work historically without falling into uncritical positivism. FlashPoints will aim for a broad audience within the humanities and the social sciences concerned with moments of cultural emergence and transformation. In a Benjaminian mode, FlashPoints is interested in how literature contributes to forming new constellations of culture and history, and in how such formations function critically and politically in the present. Available online at http://repositories.cdlib.org/ucpress

Series Editors: Ali Behdad (Comparative Literature and English, UCLA); Judith Butler (Rhetoric and Comparative Literature, UC Berkeley), Founding Editor; Edward Dimendberg (Film & Media Studies, UC Irvine), Coordinator; Catherine Gallagher (English, UC Berkeley), Founding Editor; Jody Greene (Literature, UC Santa Cruz); Susan Gillman (Literature, UC Santa Cruz); Richard Terdiman (Literature, UC Santa Cruz)

Poetry in Pieces

César Vallejo and Lyric Modernity

Michelle Clayton

UNIVERSITY OF CALIFORNIA PRESS

Berkeley · Los Angeles · London

University of California Press, one of the most distinguished university presses in the United States, enriches
lives around the world by advancing scholarship in the
humanities, social sciences, and natural sciences. Its activities are supported by the UC Press Foundation and by
philanthropic contributions from individuals and institutions. For more information, visit www.ucpress.edu.

University of California Press
Berkeley and Los Angeles, California

University of California Press, Ltd.
London, England

Library of Congress Cataloging-in-Publication Data

Clayton, Michelle, 1974–
    Poetry in pieces : César Vallejo and lyric modernity /
Michelle Clayton.
        p. cm.—(FlashPoints ; 4)
    Includes bibliographical references and index.
    ISBN 978-0-520-26229-4 (pbk. : alk. paper)
    1. Vallejo, César, 1892–1938—Criticism and
interpretation. I. Title.
    PQ8497.V35Z616   2011
    861'.62—dc22

                                    2010020042

Manufactured in the United States of America

20   19   18   17   16   15   14   13   12   11
10   9   8   7   6   5   4   3   2   1

This book is printed on Cascades Enviro 100, a 100%
post consumer waste, recycled, de-inked fiber. FSC recycled certified and processed chlorine free. It is acid free,
Ecologo certified, and manufactured by BioGas energy.

Contents

Acknowledgments

My thanks to the FlashPoints editorial committee at the University of California Press and to the Modern Language Initiative, for their support of this book. I have had the extraordinary luck to work with an extraordinary editor, Ed Dimendberg, whose wit, good sense, and German references kept me lively and often laughing during the final stages of revision. Hannah Love, Lynne Withey, and Emily Park have been very helpful through the editorial phase, as has my copy editor, Sheila Berg, who has patiently removed many Irishisms; any remaining are the product of my own stubbornness. I owe a special debt of gratitude to the two manuscript reviewers, Christina Karageorgou-Bastea and Gwen Kirkpatrick, both fine readers of Spanish-language poetry, who gave me enormously useful suggestions for local and conceptual revisions. I am also grateful for comments from other anonymous readers who helped me to fine-tune certain points of the argument.

This book is the product of many conversations. Not all of them had to do with Vallejo, but they all helped to trace out the broad contours of this book, reminding me constantly of the need to read widely and with an openness to unexpected connections. My most immediate debt is to my wonderful adviser at Princeton, Jim Irby, who first introduced me to Vallejo's poetry; Jim's rigor as a critic and his encouragement and patience as a mentor through and beyond my graduate years have given me a model not only for poetry criticism but for academic generosity as well. Many other faculty members at Princeton gave depth and breadth to my thinking about poetry's forms, contents, and contexts: Arcadio Díaz-Quiñones, Ricardo Piglia, Lucía Melgar, Ricardo Krauel, Michael Wood, Eduardo Cadava, and Doug Mao. Behind them are a line of teachers who introduced me to poetry and the pleasures of Latin American literature: Charmian Arbuckle and Hilda Quinn in Ireland and Clive Griffin, Robin Fiddian, and David Constantine at Oxford.

In my professional life at UCLA I have had the support of a lovely community of scholars. Colleagues in my two home departments, Comparative Literature and Spanish & Portuguese, in English, and across the city in departments at the University of Southern California, helped to keep this project in motion, through timely encouragement or suggestions for further reading and thought. My special thanks go to a number of colleagues whose support went above and beyond the call of duty: Ali Behdad, Veronica Cortínez, Marzena Grzegorczyk, Michael Heim, Roberta Johnson, Kathy Komar, Katherine King, Efraín Kristal, Beth Marchant, Mark Seltzer, Ross Shideler, Shu-mei Shih, and Andrés Soria Olmedo. Staff members at UCLA—in Rolfe, Royce, and Humanities—provided practical support for various aspects of my research. Whatever freshness this book has is also due to the undergraduate and graduate students at UCLA who have struggled with Vallejo alongside me, energetically disproving a colleague's early warning that "Vallejo depresses the students." And this project also owes much to the quick-witted capabilities of research assistants at various moments in my writing: Vanessa Fernández, Peter Lehman, and Román Luján.

I have presented sections of this book to audiences at a variety of universities and conferences; I thank those audiences for suggestions about how to frame Vallejo for different groups and for steering me in the direction of some unsuspected connections. Conferences have always reenergized my take on Vallejo, largely through surprising conversations with colleagues in close or distant fields. For keeping me aware of the possibilities and excitements of cross-cultural poetics, I thank Chris Bush, Eric Hayot, John Marx, Barrett Watten, and Steve Yao. Within Latin American studies, I have found some remarkable models and interlocutors in Jorge Coronado, Robert Kaufman, Justin Read, Fernando Rosenberg, Gonzalo Aguilar and, right at the finish line, Anna Deeny. Gene Bell-Villada, José Antonio Mazzotti, Guido Podestá, and Dan Balderston have been supporters of the project from its earliest days; the latter two have also pulled me onto different and fruitful critical tracks at opportune times. Jean Franco and Julio Ortega generously read sections of this book while it was in preparation, as did David Lloyd, whose enthusiasm for Vallejo and careful critical eye gave me an intellectual boost at exactly the right moment. A conference on Vallejo's poetry that I organized in 2007 led to wonderful conversations with the critic Stephen Hart, whose work has been so important for my own thinking, and the translator Clayton Eshleman, who has generously allowed me to use his translations in this book. Finally, I am grateful to the *Revista de Estudios Hispánicos* for publishing my article "*Trilce*'s Lyric Matters" and for giving me permission to reproduce its contents in chapter 3.

Various institutions provided funding for my research in libraries in the United States and abroad. The Princeton Program in Latin American Studies helped me get the project off the ground, supplemented later by several UCLA Senate Research Enabling Grants and by a UCLA Latin American Institute Faculty Fellowship during my sabbatical leave. Jorge Puccinelli, José Antonio Rodríguez Garrido, Fernando Velázquez, and Victor Vich showed me great intellectual generosity and hospitality in Lima, as did Jorge Fondebrider, Florencia Garramuño, and Alvaro Fernández-Bravo in Buenos Aires.

This book has been a long time coming. My thanks to friends who kept this project going through dark nights of the soul and white screens of death. At Princeton: Peter Barberie, Laura Bass, Elissa Bell, Paul Firbas, Josh Gold, Andrew Krull, Kati Lovasz, José Antonio Lucero, Noel Luna, Eric Trudel, and Gillian White; in Los Angeles, Kenny Berger, Mat Coleman, Tom Holden, Priya Jaikumar, Alex Purves, and Mary Thomas; in Providence and Boston, Anna Henchman, Leah Price, Kate Ramsay, Ravit Reichman, Zach Sng, Tim Watson, and Esther Whitfield; and in a bewildering variety of locations, Alessandra Perna. And to my parents, Christopher and Maureen Clayton, who early encouraged me to follow unlikely interests, and who have been a supportive presence for me throughout the writing. Some of the best preparation for this book involved hours spent laughing with the brilliant Barry McCrea. Tim Bewes generously listened to far more musings about an unfamiliar poet than he might ever have wished and provided excellent angles for my arguments. I particularly thank Thangam Ravindranathan, with her own words, for finding in my book "what is, but also what is not"; much of what is there is indebted to conversations with her, both on and off topic. Alice the cat provided the book's sound track.

My most important reader is my husband, Stuart Burrows, whom I met long ago in a graduate seminar on English poetry, and who little suspected then that he would have to spend twelve years reading reams of writing on a Peruvian poet, not to mention start learning Spanish himself. His enthusiasm for far-flung reaches of literature, music, film, and art has taken this book and my thinking in countless unexpected directions. With his warmth and his wit, Stuart will always be the greatest spur to writing, and the loveliest distraction from it.

Introduction

"The Whole, the Part!"

One might . . . maintain that modernity is indeed marked by
the will toward totalization as much as it is metaphorized by
the fragment.
—Linda Nochlin, *The Body in Pieces*

We have grown accustomed to conceptualizing the divide between
modernisms and avant-gardes as one between recollection and rupture, epitomized in the ways in which their iconic works deal with increasingly uncontainable contents: a shoring-up of fragments against
ruins, in T. S. Eliot's classic formulation, or a willful scattering of references across the surface of what no longer pretends to hold together,
as in Dada sound poetry. On the one hand, a vertical aesthetic, which
finds meaning for modernity in its recapitulation of the past; on the
other, a horizontal one, which severs itself from the past and recon-
stitutes the present as a man-made constellation. These apparently
opposed aesthetics have in turn divided scholars, requiring them to
declare their allegiance to one mode or another and to declare their
mode the dominant.[1]

But as Tom Gunning has recently argued ("Modernity"), the two
modes—dispersal and containment—necessarily coexisted and played
off one another in early-twentieth-century aesthetics, as disciplines ad-
justed themselves to the proximity of new media and the connected
reshaping of the modern sensorium. Artworks, in other words, could
choose either to open or to close themselves to the effects of modernity
on bodies and language. Or, occasionally, to have it both ways at once,
as Linda Nochlin argued in her now-classic study of modern art history,
The Body in Pieces, which begins by placing its accent on an inconsol-

able nostalgia for the past and a modern dwelling amidst fragments, only to uncover hidden drives toward recuperation in the very works that seemed to most resist it.

For those writers working in two or more cultural zones, it becomes more difficult to delineate their place within modernist or avant-garde aesthetics, for a number of reasons. First, the relationship to the past in a postcolonial setting is more than an issue of simple recuperation as it is for European writers. Second, both the fragment and its organizational opposite, the museum, signify quite differently in metropolitan and colonial contexts, involving in the latter not a violent shaping of a cultural heritage but a mode of precarious knowledge (Aguilar; Rosenberg). And third, the very fact of operating across cultural spheres means that a poet's language potentially changes its meaning in different contexts, whether through the poet's active choosing or the reader's interpretive paradigms. What comes into play, then, in our reading of modern postcolonial writers is the question of frames: deliberately imposed ones that may crop and contort, as in Nochlin's discussion, or delicately superimposed and juxtaposed frames that add nuance to our notion of multiple contexts.

In the study that follows, I explore the writing of the Peruvian poet César Vallejo, whose writing was almost symmetrically divided between Peru and Paris—with two collections of poetry composed in each place—and whose poetry may seem to be split between avant-garde experiment and political commitment. As I argue throughout this book, these two modes are two sides of the same coin, and increasingly so in his Paris years. Although what may come to appear uppermost is the political charge of his later work, it is nowhere entirely free from a formal violence or fragmentation that mediates and mirrors the poetry's contents. And as I demonstrate over the course of the book's six chapters, the coherence of Vallejo's poetics lies in his deployment of what I call "body language"—a conjoined semiotics of word and gesture that develops and takes different forms over the course of his work, but which always foregrounds the activity of bodies attempting to articulate themselves in a shattered context. This often takes unexpected forms: his early Peruvian poetry, for instance, repeatedly stages the performance of a poet already expelled from local traditions, who reaches or calls out to others without managing to make his expressions hit home. And in the poetry he composed in Paris, Vallejo proves himself increasingly aware of the suffering bodies of others, of the violence being done to them by an official language that usurps their speech, but also of his lack of authorization to speak for them. Where he attempts to find a ground of commonality is precisely in the body: the sharing of basic physical processes of suffering and enjoyment, the investment in the possibility of a kinaesthetic empathy, but also the knowledge that we experience our own bodies and the bodies of others only in pieces.

What Vallejo proposes in his poetry, I suggest, is an ethics of the fragment: not a celebration of the fragment on avant-garde terms, but a recognition of its centrality to modes of modern subjectivity and collectivism. Poetry in pieces, in other words, as the most responsible mode of lyric modernity.

PROVINCIAL OF THE WORLD

Todos somos provincianos, don Julio. Provincianos de las naciones y provincianos de lo supranacional.

We are all provincials, Don Julio. Provincials of nations and provincials of the supranational.[2]

—José María Arguedas[3]

I open this study with a retrospective gaze to set the stage for different framings of Latin American writing. In the late 1960s a polemic erupted between the Argentinean Julio Cortázar and the Peruvian José María Arguedas over the question of how to represent Latin America in literature.[4] The exchange took place in a moment that seemed to promise an effective intertwining of local aesthetics and global politics: the spread of international socialism in the aftermath of the Cuban Revolution, coupled with the growing visibility of Latin American writing through the international success of the formally experimental Boom novelists (Gabriel García Márquez, Carlos Fuentes, Mario Vargas Llosa, Cortázar himself). This critically timed exchange, between two of the continent's most prominent writers, offers a remarkable condensation of polemics over relations between the local and the international, immediacy and mediation, aesthetics and politics, which cluster around postcolonial writing in the twentieth century and which provide the backdrop and often the texture of this book.

The opening salvo was Cortázar's response to *Casa de las Américas* director, Roberto Fernández Retamar, who had asked for an essay on the "situation of the Latin American intellectual," clearly hoping for a statement that would underline the nexus between the Cuban Revolution and continental literary experiments. Cortázar responded not with an essay but with an open letter, which allowed him—he insisted—to

make his statements as a particular individual rather than as a representative type or authoritative voice. In this nuanced document, Cortázar
explicitly resisted speaking as a "Latin American intellectual," emphasizing not only the separation of his aesthetic writings from his political
beliefs, but his physical distance from events on the ground, given that
he had been living in France since 1951. That distance, Cortázar suggested polemically, had allowed him to develop a more textured view
of Latin America, through his greater access to a broad range of sources
on what was happening in the world and at home and because in Paris
he had come into contact with forms of international socialism. Writing
and thinking at a distance from Latin America, he claimed, allowed him
to avoid the consuming "challenge-and-response" of local events and
to develop a more "planetary" view of the continent, without thereby
moving in the direction of "diffuse and theoretical universalisms." Paris,
in other words, had given him sufficient distance to see Latin America in
its complexity without becoming bogged down in its details and, in the
process, to develop a personal aesthetic that reached beyond local Argentinean literary concerns to encompass a more broadly international
and humanist-inflected socialism.

Arguedas encountered the letter as he was about to begin writing his
most ambitious novel to date, *El zorro de arriba y el zorro de abajo* (The
Fox from Up Above and the Fox from Down Below). His earlier novels
had charted a progressively swelling terrain, from small towns in the Peruvian sierra through larger provinces to an all-encompassing vision of
national tensions in the 1965 novel, *Todas las sangres* (All the Bloods).
His latest project aimed to take on a categorically new space: the fishery
boomtown of Chimbote, where rapid modernization was being carried
out by local bodies and foreign capital, whose conflicting interests were
resulting in unpredictable clashes.[5] Attempting to capture this event in its
unfolding not only entailed rethinking the ethnic makeup and local segre-
gations of the nation as they re-presented themselves in this new coastal
city but also prompted Arguedas to rethink the relationship between his
work as an ethnographer and his practice as a novelist.

This new novel, written haltingly, is divided between two alternating parts: on the one hand, a fictional narrative involving various representative types as they settle into precarious arrangements and new
conflicts in Chimbote, pressured by the demands of industry, ethnic
and class antagonisms, local politics, and neocolonial entanglements;
on the other, a personal diary, which not only presents an agonizing
self-critique but also assesses the work of contemporary Latin American

novelists. It is in this context that Arguedas broaches the topic of his procedural discrepancy with Cortázar. His first diary counters Cortázar's perceived affront to localist aesthetics, insisting that a close-up focus on a local phenomenon such as Chimbote not only addressed immediate and geographically limited issues but also involved an engagement with the world. One could be a provincial of the nation, Arguedas suggested, without ceasing to be a provincial of the supranational, and a political-aesthetic commentary on the most narrowly circumscribed events in the age of neocolonialism was necessarily a contribution to any understanding of global politics and aesthetics.[6]

This confrontation between Cortázar and Arguedas evokes Walter Benjamin's distinction between two irreconcilable kinds of storyteller: one who remains at home to pass on existing traditions and comment on their transformations, and one who travels abroad in order to send back reports on foreign affairs, pointing to their importance for understanding developing local events ("Storyteller"). Notably, in this discussion of point-of-view framing and articulation, poetry is afforded very little place, which suggests that in the 1960s—just as today—the aesthetic of lyric poetry was thought to have little to say about or contribute to political discourse.[7] However, it does make an oblique appearance in Arguedas's last diary, where he glosses an observation on the closing of a literary cycle in Peru with the elliptical statement "Vallejo era el principio y el fin" (Vallejo was the beginning and the end) (246). What Vallejo appears to represent for Arguedas, here and in comments elsewhere, is the fullest articulation of a critical and historicized local identity at a particularly strained moment, giving voice to a Peru being pushed into modernity while struggling to reconnect with its precolonial past.

Arguedas's reading of Vallejo has had many echoes among later critics, who have understood Vallejo's poetry to be the voice of the local as it enters into tense contact with international modernity. Yet I will be arguing throughout this book, in what may itself be a polemical vein, that Vallejo occupies a position equidistant from both Cortázar's somewhat airy cosmopolitanism and Arguedas's agonizing localism. Vallejo's critical and self-critical perspectives on both the local and the global are far less consistent than one might expect, and they determinedly work against the articulation of a fixed and constrained viewpoint. Rather than aligning himself with either Peru or the West, his commitment is to multiple and constantly shifting attachments, which are those of his reading and experiential horizons—diasporic Peruvianism, the international avant-gardes, Soviet politics, Harlem Renaissance aesthetics, Spanish antifascism, to name just a few. In a gloss on Arguedas's retort to Cortázar—cited as the epigraph to this section—I will be proposing that we consider Vallejo as a "provincial of the world," tethered neither to the local (speaking exclusively to, of, and from Peru) nor to a denationalized universalism (as in Casanova's reading of Beckett [2006]) but rather tied to the world ("atado al globo," as he puts it in the early poem "Huaco"), about and to which he speaks from a localized position which is nonetheless constantly on the move.

Born in 1892, Vallejo was raised as a Spanish speaker in the small Andean town of Santiago de Chuco.[8] He studied literature and then law in the coastal city of Trujillo and in the capital city of Lima, taking up work as a schoolteacher in both cities, eking out an existence among their local bohemias; he famously spent three months in jail for allegedly instigating a skirmish that took place during a visit to his hometown.[9] During this period, he published two collections of poetry—*Los heraldos negros* (The Black Heralds) (1919) and *Trilce* (1922)—which went almost completely ignored, eliciting little more than a few jibes from the cultural establishment. In the face of this apparent failure and chased by a lingering arrest warrant, Vallejo set sail for Paris in 1923, where he lived—with a short period of exile in Madrid in 1932 due to his political activities—until his death in 1938, never returning to Peru, despite sporadic attempts to do so. Through the late 1920s he earned a meager living as Paris correspondent for various Peruvian newspapers—for which he was rarely paid—while supplementing his income by means of a law scholarship, occasional translations, and work as tutor to the children of visiting dignitaries. His connection to Peru reasserted itself momentarily in the mid-1920s, when he found himself alluded to in two intersecting debates at home: the indigenism polemic, which focused on the proper forms of local representation (Aquézolo Castro), and a polemic over the avant-garde, split between politics and aesthetics, involving a broader international dimension (Lauer, *Polémica*). Nonetheless, he resisted inscription in either one, turning his attention instead to artistic debates taking place in Paris, to broader commentaries on modernity and geopolitics, and to a developing interest in Marxism, beginning in the late 1920s and persisting—or fluctuating—through to the Spanish Civil War in 1936–38, until his death from a still-unidentified illness.[10]

Vallejo published only five poems during his Paris years, although we know that he composed at least forty-seven undated poems between

1923 and 1936. A final burst of poetry under the impact of the Spanish Civil War in late 1937 produced sixty-seven more poems, almost all of them carefully dated by month and day. Fifteen of these were shaped by the poet into the collection *España, aparta de mí este cáliz* (Spain, Take This Cup from Me), published by Republican soldiers in 1939. The remainder were organized and published posthumously by subsequent editors under several controversial titles, with *Poemas humanos* (Human Poems) being the first (Paris, 1939; ed. Georgette Philippart de Vallejo and Raúl Porras Barrenechea) and the most durable. During his Paris years, Vallejo also produced a novel, *El Tungsteno* (Tungsten) (1931); a commissioned novella, *Paco Yunque,* rejected as being "too sad"; two "Incan" stories published in Spanish magazines; a series of reports on his visits to the Soviet Union, some of which were published—to great success—as *Rusia en 1931,* while others remained unpublished under the title *Rusia ante el segundo plan quinquenal* (Russia before the Second Five-Year Plan); two notebooks containing jottings on aesthetics, *Contra el secreto profesional* (Against the Professional Secret) and *El arte y la revolución* (Art and Revolution); a series of never-staged plays; and two screenplays, also never produced.

My focus in this book is restricted to Vallejo's lyric and journalistic writings, treating the latter as a hinge between his earlier and later poetry. As I will argue, Vallejo's poetry and journalism both offer an agonizingly tense but also exhilarating performance of an ongoing struggle with the central and the marginal questions of modernity, influenced by his readings and eventually his residence in two markedly different contexts: Peru and Paris. The diverse makeup of the different towns and cities in which Vallejo lived in Peru, the time it took for texts to arrive from abroad, and his ongoing fraught relationships with contemporary writers and critics of conservative, avant-garde, and indigenist stripes mean that to read his poetry and prose in a Peruvian context already imposes a prismatic frame. Similarly, Vallejo's residence in Paris in the 1920s and 1930s—heyday of international modernism in its passage from aesthetic experiment to political commitment—must be measured against more familiar narratives of writers' lives in the capital of literary modernity. Vallejo moved to Paris only to take up a marginal position at the center: writing poetry that went unpublished and chronicles for Peruvian newspapers that he feared were going largely unread, about experiences that were most likely secondhand, derived from his own readings of Parisian newspapers and his eavesdropping in cafés. In this sense, as both poet and journalist, he was folded into metropolitan modernity while remaining invisible within it. Attending to that inside-outside position, which is paradigmatic for many modern writers, allows us to expose the gaps in usual narratives of international modernism while adding nuance to readings of those writers who operate—to follow Pascale Casanova's valuable point ("Literature" 81)—in two different cultural panoramas at once.

One of the driving forces behind this book is my conviction that Vallejo deserves to be—indeed must be—read in relation to the multiple contexts in which he lived, read, thought, and wrote; contexts that place important constraints on his writing but that also give it its peculiar and volatile texture. Vallejo's sense of being out of place both at home and abroad, of appealing to different and potentially indifferent audiences, sometimes produces uncomfortable—even discomforting—shifts in his writing. But rather than smoothing these out to provide a cohesive narrative of ideological or aesthetic consistency, we should ask what they might mean for broader theoretical questions about the relation between politics and aesthetics, between history and literary genres, in the modernist period.[11] In Vallejo's case, as I hope will become clear, it is helpful to think about affiliations rather than filiations (Said, *World* 174–75), paying attention to what he connects his own writing to rather than what it directly descends from, and tracing the tensions that these affiliations entail. We also need to recognize the debates in which he resisted participating—in other words, listen to the silences as well as the sounds of his writing. The writer and modern subject, as Vallejo intimates throughout his poetry and prose, cannot simply adopt a position or take one as a given—with an unquestioned grounding in ethnicity, heritage, gender, class, and so on—but rather works and lives in situated conditions of self-critique and self-correction. This commitment to momentary yet full-bodied attachment renders the writer's position precarious but also productive: it may be difficult to speak of a program in Vallejo's poetry, yet its lack of a coherent agenda is, paradoxically, a sign of its sustained commitment to critical thought. I will be arguing that Vallejo's poetry is most theoretically, politically, and aesthetically challenging at the moments when it seems most intransigent, when it slips our—and sometimes its own—grasp.

Occasionally, coherence is to be found where we least expect it. In the late 1920s Vallejo produced three separate articles that appear to be on unconnected, even incompatible topics: the avant-gardes ("Poesía nueva" [New Poetry], 1926; *ACC* I: 300–301), indigenism ("Los escollos de siempre" [The Usual Stumbling Blocks], 1927;

ACC I: 495–96), and socialism ("Ejecutoria del arte socialista" [Final Judgment on Socialist Art], 1928; *ACC* II: 652–53). All three of these articles, however, are articulated around the same central axis: the openness of the body to historical experience and the production of responsive gestures through a sensorium subjected to constant retraining. Rather than rejecting modernity—as the "new poetry" article in particular has been read—Vallejo offers images for its incorporation; modern subjectivity and self-positioning are here less a question of lip service than of bodily processing. This is at once a physiological and a radically historicist argument, and it implies a continuity between all three concerns—indigenism, socialism, the avant-garde—in Vallejo's writing: a self-positioning that entails an alignment of body and mind, an aesthetics and politics of full-bodied adhesion, within an enfolding panorama of contemporary urgencies, dictates, and constraints. As I will argue throughout this book, Vallejo's concern is to give poetry and politics back their bodies, and thereby to extend the sense and reach of the lyric.

These three topics, moreover, correspond to the three frames through which Vallejo's poetry tends to be read, often mapped onto the three distinct blocks of his lyric writing: indigenism and *Los heraldos negros* (1919), the avant-garde and *Trilce* (1922), socialism and the posthumous poetry (composed between 1923 and 1938). First-time readers may associate Vallejo in advance with avant-garde experimentation, which has been the focus of some dazzling close readings (Coyné; Paoli; Ortega); others likely have a sense of his ideological connection to either indigenism or international Marxism. The interest in reading Vallejo as a localist or indigenist poet, which began with his contemporaries (Orrego; Mariátegui), has proven markedly resilient; in recent years it has led to highly nuanced commentaries on his relation to Peruvian history (Cornejo Polar; Mazzotti). More recently still, Vallejo's iconicity as a Marxist poet has gained particular traction with his international readers, as a new exemplar for political poetry in the fraught moment of the 1930s (Lambie; Dawes). Both of these latter readings have great power and merit, but both occasionally run the risk of oversimplifying Vallejo's own historically shifting positions—which, moreover, take markedly different forms in his poetry and prose—not to mention side-stepping the deliberate difficulty of his poetry. I will be arguing that Vallejo offers a more complicated take on the writer's relation to history—local and international—and on the lyric's relation to politics than either of these perspectives allow.

I want to tease out this question from the outset by looking at a poem that ostensibly weaves the two concerns together. "Telúrica y magnética" (Telluric and Magnetic) is one of a series of poems that Vallejo wrote in the early 1930s, at the apex of his commitment to Marxism. Those poems focus on what we might call "local universals"—figures linked to specific geopolitical economies, presented as exemplars for a new transnational historical agency—and they emblematize Vallejo's faith in the capacity of the working classes to seize hold of their own destiny and set off a revolutionary chain reaction of revolution, "con efecto mundial de vela que se enciende" (with the universal effect of a candle that catches fire), as he puts it in "Gleba" (Glebe). Among these figures were—unsurprisingly—Bolsheviks but also industrial and agricultural workers of indeterminate nationality, the unemployed (physically located in Europe but abandoned by their national systems), and miners, linked to the neocolonial sites of extraction with which Vallejo was familiar from Peru.[12] Although all of these figures are related to labor and hence to the body, the poems in which they appear restore an immense and immediate power to speech—but not, significantly, to the speech of the poet. As Jean Franco noted in her pioneering study of Vallejo (*Dialectics* 172), the poet's own words in these poems are halting, self-questioning, self-ironizing; conversely, the laboring figures he apostrophizes "hablan como les vienen las palabras" (speak as the words come; "Gleba"), suggesting that unmediated access to language comes through the body, in a rehearsal of the ongoing debate about the virtues of manual over intellectual labor.[13]

In 1931 or 1932—after his third trip to the Soviet Union—Vallejo began work on "Telúrica y magnética," which explicitly conjoins Marxism and Peru and, as a partial corollary, theory and practice. Here is the poem:[14]

¡Mecánica sincera y peruanísima
la del cerro colorado!
¡Suelo teórico y práctico!
¡Surcos inteligentes; ejemplo: el monolito y su cortejo!
¡Papales, cebadales, alfalfares, cosa buena!
¡Cultivos que integra una asombrosa jerarquía de útiles
y que integran con viento los mujidos,
las aguas con su sorda antigüedad!

¡Cuaternarios maíces, de opuestos natalicios,
los oigo por los pies cómo se alejan,

los huelo retornar cuando la tierra
tropieza con la técnica del cielo!
¡Molécula exabrupto! ¡Atomo terso!

   ¡Oh campos humanos!
¡Solar y nutricia ausencia de la mar,
y sentimiento oceánico de todo!
¡Oh climas encontrados dentro del oro, listos!
¡Oh campo intelectual de cordillera,
con religión, con campo, con patitos!
¡Paquidermos en prosa cuando pasan
y en verso cuando páranse!
¡Roedores que miran con sentimiento judicial en torno!
¡Oh patrióticos asnos de mi vida!
¡Vicuña, descendiente
nacional y graciosa de mi mono!
¡Oh luz que dista apenas un espejo de la sombra,
que es vida con el punto y, con la línea, polvo
y que por eso acato, subiendo por la idea a mi osamenta!

   ¡Siega en época del dilatado molle,
del farol que colgaron de la sien
y del que descolgaron de la barreta espléndida!
¡Angeles de corral,
aves por un descuido de la cresta!
¡Cuya o cuy para comerlos fritos
con el bravo rocoto de los temples!
(¿Cóndores? ¡Me friegan los cóndores!)

¡Leños cristianos en gracia
al tronco feliz y al tallo competente!
¡Familia de los líquenes,
especies en formación basáltica que yo
respeto
desde este modestísimo papel!
¡Cuatro operaciones, os sustraigo
para salvar al roble y hundirlo en buena ley!
¡Cuestas in infraganti!
¡Auquénidos llorosos, almas mías!
¡Sierra de mi Perú, Perú del mundo,
y Perú al pie del orbe; yo me adhiero!
¡Estrellas matutinas si os aromo
quemando hojas de coca en este cráneo,
y cenitales, si destapo,
de un solo sombrerazo, mis diez templos!
¡Brazo de siembra, bájate, y a pie!
¡Lluvia a base del mediodía,
bajo el techo de tejas donde muerde

la infatigable altura
y la tórtola corta en tres su trino!
¡Rotación de tardes modernas
y finas madrugadas arqueológicas!
¡Indio después del hombre y antes de él!
¡Lo entiendo todo en dos flautas
y me doy a entender en una quena!
¡Y lo demás, me las pelan! . . .

As Franco notes (173), this poem originally began as a lyric engagement with Marxism, an attempt to deal poetically with abstract questions of theory and praxis by applying them to rural labor (the original title was to be "Meditación agrícola," "Agricultural Meditation"). When Vallejo revisited the poem, most likely in 1937, he reworked and radically expanded it to include Peruvian elements, which has led to its consecration as one of the most explicit meditations in his work on Peru.[15] Not locally circumscribed, however, but connected to the world—"Perú del mundo, / y Perú al pie del orbe" (Peru of the world, / and Peru at the foot of the globe)—and to which the poet significantly *declares* his allegiance instead of taking or presenting it as a given.

In its final form, the poem offers a catalog of elements populating or constituting the Peruvian soil and national sense; its constant exclamations (a total of thirty-four that make up the poem's sixty-three lines) create an effect of celebration, directly mimicking the modes of nineteenth-century neoclassical poems, which listed the contents of Latin America for locals and foreigners alike, such as Andrés Bello's 1826 "Silva a la agricultura de la zona tórrida" (Silva to the Agriculture of the Torrid Zone). The only line that deviates from this grammatical structure is a question encased in a parenthesis halfway through the poem: ("¿Cóndores? ¡Me friegan los cóndores!" [Condors? Screw the condors!]).[16] But why the parenthesis? To whom is the speaker implicitly responding? And why would his interlocutor have questioned the absence of condors? This sudden and parenthetical self-interruption shifts the poem in a direction other than that of simple celebration: instead, it points to the pressure to produce recognizable stereotypes, whether for a local or a foreign eye, and this almost imperceptibly turns the poem into a kind of anti-Baedeker, frustrating the expectations of tourist and nationalist alike.[17]

We may therefore be tempted to read these unfurling exclamations as underwritten by irony. Yet as this poem suggests, there are differing degrees of irony, and "Telúrica y magnética" is filled with many moments that look utterly sincere: declaring allegiance to both Peru and the world, proffering the indigenous native as universal man. These, in turn, are either undercut or intensified by moments of humor, whether tender (accompanying ideological systems with ducklings) or vulgar ("Screw the condors!"). At the same time, the poet's position in the poem is peculiar, to say the least: if he appears in the exclamations themselves as the source that underwrites their effect, he also presents himself in contingent relation to the Peruvian emblems he celebrates— whether linked to them through a kind of heraldry (patriotic asses and vicuñas) or through his own respectful inclination toward them. By the end of the poem, what seems uppermost is not the poet's ability to represent local elements for a reader, but to understand them *himself,* and to turn that understanding into expression: an expression that is itself decidedly unlocatable—using both national and international instruments—and that, stranger still, feigns an utter nonchalance as to how it will be received:

¡Lo entiendo todo en dos flautas
y me doy a entender en una quena!
¡Y lo demás, me las pelan! . . .

I understand it all on two flutes,
and I make myself understood on a quena!
As for the rest, they can jerk me off! . . .

As part of this by turns feckless and focused lyric treatise on the local-global, the poem works together lists of recognizable words from political discourse and from Peruvian scenery, blending elevated tones and terms with bathetic emotions and language, inflecting Romantic discourses on the sublime with some of the buzzwords of contemporary discussion ("occ-anic feeling" is taken from Freud's 1930 *Civilization and Its Discontents*). But rather than enfolding the reader in a harmonic performance of Peru's consonance with the world and poetry's consonance with political imperatives, these dissonances send the reader lurching through a sequence of clashing chords. What at first sight seemed like a successful meshing of Marxism and indigenism becomes a much more unstable performance of a meditation on the local and the poet's responsibility to it, involving tensions not only between the individual elements of its catalog but also between those elements and the poem's overarching tone. If we pay sufficient heed to the charge of those exclamations, they end up ironizing themselves and exhausting our attention; but if we bypass the question of tone, we miss the complications of the poem's "statements."

This quandary, I will suggest, is emblematic of Vallejo's poetry. His writing requires that we pay inordinate attention not only to the contents of poems but also to their form and tone, and to the possible disharmonies between them; and these disharmonies offer a much richer and more demanding image of the relation between the poet, his subjects and objects, and history. Vallejo's poems, as I argue throughout this book, never cease to reach toward their surrounding situations, but at the same time they incessantly question the reach of poetry, and they resist offering compensatory aesthetic images to counterbalance the violence of their social environments; his poems are always more attentive to parts than to wholes, to broken metonymies than to integrative metaphors. While this might seem a primarily aesthetic question, it is related to much larger questions of political representation. In his early poetry, as I argue in chapters 2 and 3, Vallejo relentlessly breaks discourses and bodies down into their constituent parts, bringing discussions of proper language (whether lyric or political) and of adequate representation back to their material bases while undercutting the demand that poetic discourse or national landscapes easily yield up their contents. And in his later poetry, as I discuss in chapter 6, this question becomes more directly related to the constituency of political subjectivities. Vallejo's Paris poems, I will suggest, attempt to hold the individual (the part) and the collective (the whole) in view simultaneously, and to consider them in their enmeshment, offering a willfully excessive lyric supplement to reductive political discourse. The relation between parts and wholes that structures this poetry is therefore a concern of the lyric—the elements that make it up, but which, in their interplay, can undermine its utterances—but also of politics, as Vallejo's poetry enacts its own deliberately difficult inscription in local and international history.

If in his Paris years Vallejo began to sense that the subjective nature of the lyric no longer lent itself to public address, he was not completely prepared to accept the extinction of the lyric subject—and with it, of subjectivity *tout court*. He held out a lingering hope that poetry might find a way to coexist with politics, without fully extinguishing the peculiarities of its own voice. He therefore continued to compose poems sporadically through the late 1920s and early 1930s, although he refrained from publishing them, for reasons I explore in chapter 4. And as he mapped out various ways for the lyric to harness the voices of its time without losing its own, Vallejo's poetry stood as a contrapuntal private discourse to his prose writings—journalistic articles in Latin American and European newspapers, discussed in chapter 5—meant for a public. Vallejo alluded to this implicit dialogue through his revision of "Telúrica y magnética." In its first version, the line "Paquidermos en prosa cuando pasan" (Pachyderms in prose when passing) stood alone, but the revised version adds "y en verso cuando páranse" (and in poetry when standing still; my trans.). If prose walks alongside history, poetry attempts to interrupt it—resisting the march of history, yet still consciously inscribed within it.

Vallejo wrote throughout his career from a position of marginality: first in a Peruvian context that tended to sideline poetry in favor of more aggressive prose and later as a Latin American in Paris, writing newspaper chronicles in Spanish with three different audiences in mind—Peruvian readers at home, his avant-garde contemporaries in Paris, and the man on the street. This triptych performance, coupled with the radical difficulties of his poetry, makes him a particularly compelling case for rethinking the modes of international modernism in the interwar years.[18] But it also keeps him current. The growing sense of Vallejo's significance for contemporary relations between poetry and politics was signaled in Garrett Keizer's October 2007 lead article in *Harper's Magazine,* which quite remarkably used Vallejo's work—and specifically the line "Hay, hermanos, muchísimo que hacer" (There is, brothers, much too much to do) from the poem "Los nueve monstruos" (The Nine Monsters)—to present a call to action in a moment of political suspension.

But how do we do justice to a poet who was rarely read and little understood in his own lifetime, who has been read too easily in the intervening years as an exemplar of Peruvian representational aesthetics and politics, and who is just beginning to emerge in Anglophone and other contexts as shedding new light on international modernism while connecting to contemporary reflections on the lyric? In Latin America Vallejo has long been considered one of the most significant poets of the past century; nonetheless, the difficulty of his writing and his appropriation for Peruvian cultural politics have meant that studies of his work have largely appeared in Spanish and restricted him to a bounded local context. Moreover, formalist exegeses of his work over the past half century have only sporadically connected Vallejo's writing to larger modernist or avant-garde debates. Despite many nuanced considerations of his recasting of Spanish-language poetry, there has been little reflection on his importance for the broader panorama of lyric theory and practice in the West.

In general, the major tendency in Vallejo criticism has been to view him as exceptional, cut off from any context that might explain his development. In this book, conversely, I aim to open a new paradigm for reading his poetry and journalism by relating them directly to the work of other Peruvian, Latin American, and European writers and theorists, showing Vallejo's constant and conscientious dialogue with a broad discursive and material context. Examining his convergence and divergence with some of the central tenets of the international avant-gardes, while underlining his coincidence with better-known writers such as Walter Benjamin, James Joyce, and Georges Bataille, I hope to make Vallejo available to a wider audience and to foreground the potential of his poetic thought on politics and aesthetics in modernity. Vallejo's poetry and prose, as I demonstrate through close reading, cultural-historical analysis, and theoretical inquiry, is critically connected to debates within the Latin American and international avant-gardes, on which it sheds important new lights; but it also opens itself up to the present, to current theoretical investigations of the relation between aesthetics and politics, offering new angles for viewing the place and reach of the lyric. My six chapters probe the range of interlocking reflections in Vallejo's writings on the lyric, local and international history, and the ethics of bodies and languages; they aim to explain and expand the historical and theoretical contexts in which Vallejo can be read, arguing through his example for poetry's capacity to grapple with questions of absolute contemporaneity.

Poetry in Pieces follows a chronological trajectory through Vallejo's writings: from his two Peruvian poetry collections, the modernist/indigenist *Los heraldos negros* and the intransigently avant-garde *Trilce*, to his two posthumous collections, *Poemas humanos* and *España, aparta de mí este cáliz*. The hinge between the two periods is formed by Vallejo's newspaper chronicles of 1923–36, written in Paris for a Peruvian audience. These chronicles have received very little critical attention and have rarely been used to shed light on his poetry, despite the fact that they map a crucial passage in Vallejo's thought from an emphasis on language to a focus on bodies, moving into a full-blown analysis of capitalism as a time-out-of-joint. Moreover, Vallejo's account of Paris in the 1920s and 1930s offers a crucial corrective to triumphalist narratives of modernist or avant-garde developments in the capital of cosmopolitan culture. Taken together, his poetry and prose can be seen not only to explore and go beyond the options available to a writer from a peripheral location in a moment of high modernism and avant-garde dislocations; they also elaborate reflections on transnational culture—and the relation within it of poetry and politics—during a period of geopolitical reconfiguration, striated by hierarchies of race, class, and language. Vallejo's insistent positioning of the lyric subject as a contingently located social subject produces a self-critical poetics of resistance, transformation, and potentiality. His poetry and prose, in short, are crucial for rethinking modernism from the outside and from below; their defiant cultural and class marginality operate not as a restriction but as an opening to new views of the modern.

My first chapter, "Pachyderms in Poetry and Prose," tracks the emergence of Vallejo's early poetry from a series of debates in turn-of-the-century Peru between poetry and prose, conservative and critical nationalisms, localism and internationalism. Vallejo's work, like that of many of his fellow Peruvian writers, can be read as a projection of willed contemporaneity with the West, his aim being to produce not *modern* but *contemporary* writing, as a mode of transcending uneven modernization in Latin America. And in practical terms, what was contemporary with his writing were not just local politics but the international avant-gardes, which circulated rapidly through Latin America. By examining the different forms of temporality and spatiality offered by those avant-gardes, and the responses they generated among a variety of poets and critics up to Vallejo, I track Latin American poetry's shift early in the century from anachronism or timelessness toward a committed contemporaneity.

In my second chapter, "Invasion of the Lyric," I examine the contortions of language in Vallejo's first two collections of poetry, *Los heraldos negros* and *Trilce*. What both collections present, I suggest, is the corrosion of the lyric by a growing sense of linguistic estrangement and its invasion by the heterogeneous voices and discourses of modernity. Vallejo initially emphasizes the degradation of the language used to capture public and private feelings, but what gradually takes the place of lyric refinement in his poetry is an aesthetic of the robustly material, of the sensorial bases of experience. And where Vallejo crucially diverges from other Latin American and international avant-gardes is in his shift away from sight toward sound, smell, taste, and touch. This radical recasting of the poet's relation to the outside world ushers in a productively estranged relation to lyric language; the movement from *Los heraldos negros* to *Trilce* can be seen as Vallejo's process of unlearning language in order to revitalize the poetic utterance. Vallejo's early poetry deliberately incorporates orality, colloquialisms, and linguistic mistakes; it reconciles indigenism and the avant-garde, both of which sought to make room for new utterances; and it profits from being read alongside statements and practices by a range of Peruvian and Western writers—from Cubist poetry and Dada performances to Latin American experiments with vernacular culture. Further, Vallejo's poetry increasingly unveils the extent to which lyric and social subjects alike are spoken through by other voices; poetry is here not the private utterance of a reflective lyric voice but a response and an address to an outside. His poetry, I argue, takes conversation as its covert model, ushering in a new conception of the lyric: no longer the self-contained statement of an individual speaker, but an opening up to the world's voices, which implode into the poetry's fragmented utterances. And as I argue at the close of this chapter, Vallejo's project is not just the incorporation of multiple voices into poetry; it is the full installation of the body in the lyric, a reconnection of language to sensory experience.

In *Trilce,* everything moves through the body, and the body itself is constantly irrupting into the poetry, interrupting the lyric with cries of pleasure or pain, images of physical abasement and excitement. My third chapter, "Lyric Matters," explores the representational practices of Vallejo's second collection of poetry. *Trilce,* I suggest, offers a simultaneous dismantling and recasting of representation, following three distinct yet interwoven modes. The first involves an onslaught on symbolist modes of representation, rejecting conventional practices of metaphorical transubstantiation in favor of a metonymic poetics of contiguity, in which the figurative is frequently displaced by the literal, metaphors are brought back to their material bases, and elements rub up against one another, exchanging some of their properties in the process. The second mode agilely parries the demand that Latin American poetry yield up its local referents in an easily usable form, presenting instead a transformed poetics of the oblique, the mixed, and the fragmentary. The third undertakes the incorporation of waste, of absence, of nonvalue and negativity into a lyrical rethinking of presence and potentiality. All three approaches involve techniques of fragmentation, of circulation, and of transformation, and all three resist the temptation to mimic economic practices of producing raw materials for consumption abroad. At the same time, they upset even the most radical European and Latin American practices of fragmented representation; displaying no nostalgia for wholeness, *Trilce* proposes a peculiar poetics of matter that condenses a new kind of lyric investment in history, as well as an oblique inscription of history in the lyric. The connection to history appears on one level through the representation of even the most humdrum or grotesque of bodily activities, which finds important analogues in writings by Joyce and Bataille. But the question of representation is given an extra charge in Vallejo's poetry by reference to the primitivist exploits of the international avant-gardes, to cultural and socioeconomic plundering by Western powers, and to mismanagement of national resources. The key element that condenses these reflections is guano: at once material and metaphorical, it ties together a national past and the present remnants of its bankruptcy, alluding to the most ignominious productions of the body and functioning as matter given over to a future, producing new elements from the soil in which it is invested. By referencing guano in an avant-garde collection often read as hermetically sealed, Vallejo formally works history into the lyric, exploiting poetry's untapped potential for mining socioeconomic matter while resisting the temptation to produce facilely reflective writing.

In 1923 Vallejo moved to Paris, partly to escape an arrest warrant, partly to experience metropolitan modernity. While acquainting himself with European debates over aesthetics and politics, he remained attentive to debates developing back in Peru. These latter debates became condensed in a mid-1920s polemic setting indigenism (a project of local recovery and representation) against the avant-garde (connected to contemporary international experiment). My fourth chapter, "Lyric Technique, Aesthetic Politics," reads Vallejo's reluctance to continue publishing poetry against the backdrop of these interlocking debates. The answer, I contend, lies in his failed attempts to produce a theory of his own poetic technique that would satisfactorily entwine his aesthetic practice with his growing political commitment. This dilemma comes into sharper relief when his sporadic theoretical writings are compared with those of his contemporary José Carlos Mariátegui, who in those same years was producing provocative readings of the international and local avant-gardes but also problematically restrictive readings of Vallejo's poetry. This chapter therefore reads these two writers contrapuntally, comparing their responses to one another, to the unfolding panorama of interwar aesthetic politics, and to the increasingly attractive medium of film, whose redemptive promise was epitomized for both in the figure of Charlie Chaplin.

My fifth chapter, "Literature Under Pressure," studies Vallejo's wide-ranging journalistic articles, written from Paris for newspapers in Peru between 1923 and 1930. These articles offer critical reflections on modernity and its explanatory discourses, unveiling the breakdown of physical and linguistic communication across classes, races, cultures, and nations within a rapidly transforming geopolitical scene. Lacking the means and the language skills to participate fully in cosmopolitan culture, Vallejo inhabited Paris as an anti-flâneur, using his chronicles to foreground the material bases of cultural and political praxis that denied a variety of potential participants—himself included—full access to modernity; his prose writings thus expose the underbelly of what we tend to think of as the apotheosis of transnational modernism in inter-war Paris, demanding that we consider its submerged layers alongside its surface flourishes. Finding himself excluded from the Parisian feast, Vallejo produces parodic ethnographic reports on international moder-nity, revealing the pressures placed on both bodies and languages by interwar geopolitics and by cultural and social striation.

This chapter charts the ways in which Vallejo shifts from speaking as a Peruvian and/or Latin American viewing Paris and broader inter-national culture and politics from the outside, to a series of temporary affiliations with oppositional models of culture: black theater in Paris, Soviet experiments, and the common passerby or *transeúnte*. I trace his zigzagging commentary on the semiotics of modernity and its structur-ing discourses, a commentary that provides a crucial counterpart to writings by the Frankfurt school and by the surrealists; Vallejo's reflec-tions on fashion, sport, science, theater, and film cut their way through international modern culture from outside and from below. His cri-tique, I argue, takes place not just through content but also through form. Parodically mimicking the journalistic modes of the period, which knitted together all aspects of the modern to provide an image of interlocking coherence, Vallejo's chronicles press the jaggedness of montage into the service of ironic contrast; his virtually filmic writings set clashing images from the modern scene alongside one another to reveal the divergent ways in which urban modernity is experienced by subjects from different classes and cultures. It is unsurprising, then, that Vallejo should have found one of the only possibilities of redemption in silent film: in the playful movements of Chaplin, and in the interplay be-tween different filmic techniques, he located glimmers of new represen-tational practices, with the potential to reach across classes and cultures to produce a critical spectator—and ultimately an actor or agent—of the modern.

Vallejo's exile in the capital of avant-garde culture undercut his own avant-garde leanings, moving him toward an awareness of the need for communication, critique, empathy, and resistance—concerns that threw the notion of poetry's reach into crisis. My sixth chapter, "Mak-ing Poetry History," examines Vallejo's posthumously published and

tentatively titled collection *Poemas humanos,* composed sporadically
from the mid-1920s to 1936 and completed in a final burst of poetic
activity in late 1937. If Vallejo's prose insisted on taking note of the
economic underpinnings and exclusions of culture, his poetry reat-
taches economics to subjectivity, emphatically focusing on the place of
the individual within collectivities. It thereby offers a critique of modern
political modes but also of systems of civil discourse, which attempted
to organize individuals into productive political bodies while canceling
their residual needs and desires. And while parodying these nonlyric
discourses, Vallejo undercuts the presumptions of poetry itself, resisting
the temptation to offer facile representations of modernity's mass subjects. But in attempting to make room for the bodies and voices of his
fellow modern men, Vallejo also registers his anxiety over the potential
erasure of the lyric voice; this late poetry offers a relentlessly self-critical
analysis of the possibilities of lyric engagement, without entirely canceling out the category or possibilities of poetry. And it does all this with
a remarkably light but also formally complex touch, in the interminable
and chaotic lists that tend to structure these late poems, which are more
heterogeneous and often flat-out funnier than critics have suggested.
Vallejo's model in this respect, I argue, was not contemporary poetry
but film, and his teeming, haywire poems draw insistently on the latter's
dual techniques of montage and slapstick.

Folded into *Poemas humanos* is the self-contained Spanish Civil War
sequence *España, aparta de mí este cáliz,* written in the last three months
of 1937; its composition alternated with that of poems which remained
part of the larger volume. *Poemas humanos* and *España, aparta de mí
este cáliz* have always been treated in isolation, due to the apparent universalism of the first and the radically historical and located utterances
of the second. Nonetheless, the unusually careful dating of each composition (Vallejo sometimes produced a poem for each collection on a
single day) signals a conscious experimentation with different forms of
the lyric; not only does Vallejo unexpectedly return to poetry in order to
engage with contemporary historical events, but in that return, he maps
out two critically divergent modes of poetry's engagement with history.
I therefore consider the two collections in their interrelations, exploring
their new configurations of bodies and voices in contingent connection
to specific historical moments, and tracing the interplay of aesthetics
and politics in Vallejo's evolving sense of the reach of the lyric.

This late poetry pushes Vallejo's earlier contrast between metaphor
and metonymy into a reflection on politics and the material bases of

modern collective life; his play with fragmented bodies issues into a large-scale commentary on the striation of the body politic, and on the strivings of language within it to articulate new possibilities of individual and collective utterance. At the same time, *España, aparta de mí este cáliz* sets the utterances of the poet against both the incommensurability of a critical geopolitical juncture and the popular articulations of struggling bodies in the Spanish Civil War, implicitly repeating Friedrich Hölderlin's question, "what are poets for in a time of dearth?" This question, I suggest, subtends Vallejo's entire body of work, and its varying articulations—organized around the place of bodies and language in poetry—makes him a crucial addition to our understanding of the modern lyric.

CHAPTER 1

Pachyderms in Poetry and Prose

¡Paquidermos en prosa cuando pasan,
y en verso cuando páranse!

*Pachyderms in prose when passing by,
and in verse when standing still!*

—Vallejo, "Telúrica y magnética"

PORTRAITS OF THE ARTIST

Vallejo's poetry, from the earliest to the latest, contains unflinching portraits of an artist: struggling with his own body and language, with his responsibility to the figures and landscapes that surround him, and with the history of poetry. Yet for all this self-figuration, we have very little sense of what Vallejo the man was like. There is, as yet, no authoritative biography.[1] Accounts by Juan Espejo Asturrizaga and Antenor Orrego focus only on Vallejo's Peruvian years (1892–1923). Juan Domingo Córdoba Vargas, Ernesto More, and Armando Bazán offer glimpses of Vallejo during their short associations with him in Paris, but their narratives suffer from the blindnesses of hindsight, and they frequently contradict one another as regards dates. Vallejo's widow Georgette's voluble account of his later years in Paris—written expressly to underline his political commitment but more covertly to contradict other versions—is riddled with errors, overstatements, and omissions. And Vallejo rarely appears in memoirs by or about better-known figures he associated with in France and Spain, such as Pablo Neruda, Rafael Alberti, or Federico García Lorca. Meanwhile, Vallejo's own utterances in poetry and prose are so shifty and fragmentary as to give us only very momentary glimpses of biographical facts behind the writing—intermittent references to real names and places, often attached to unlikely details (such as the claim, in *Trilce*

XIV, that his salary as teacher in Lima earned him the absurdly small salary of five *soles*).

Nor do we have any defining statement of poetics. Vallejo's few prose statements on his procedure and principles work in the direction of negation or complication rather than clarification; in a 1925 chronicle, for instance, he tantalizingly disavows any connection between his work and Harlem Renaissance aesthetics, although he of course opens this as a possibility simply by mentioning it (*ACC* I: 170).[2] Vallejo's self-positioning is often available only as a negative impression: in his reticence with regard to his own poetics, his silence in certain debates, and his refusal to provide a definitive statement of the relation between his poetry and political questions. Nicola Miller's brief portrait of Vallejo speaks volumes in this respect. Commenting that "Vallejo must have been an interviewer's nightmare," she notes that "he was cursory or enigmatic even in response to unexceptionable questions," coming across in his prose statements as "irascible," "curmudgeonly," and occasionally even "cadaverous" ("To Interpret" 174). Yet his poetry, by contrast, repeatedly stages intensely self-critical self-reflections, and it is in the poems that we find a performance—if never quite an explicit elucidation—of the relationship between the lyric and history.

Vallejo frequently insisted that his statements could not be separated from the contexts in which they were uttered—that the full meaning of statements and contents alike might only be fully discerned in hindsight. Quoting, for example, his declaration to an interviewer that he had no desire to align himself with any modern aesthetic movement, Vallejo remarked, "Siempre gusté de no discutirme ni explicarme, pues creo que hay cosas o momentos en la vida de las cosas que únicamente el tiempo revela y define" (I have always preferred not to discuss or explain myself, because I think that there are things or moments in the life of things which only time will reveal and define) (*ACC* I: 170). This comment condenses two central modes of Vallejo's poetry. On the one hand, a belief in the historical situatedness of any statement, mirrored in the relentless present tense of a poetics that reassesses itself and starts afresh with every new poem, knowing itself to be fully comprehensible only in the future (*ACC* II: 734–36);[3] on the other, an evasion of direct statement. As he argued in the 1926 essay, "Poesía nueva" (New Poetry) (*ACC* I: 300–301), the attempt to render a contemporary context simply by naming its elements amounted to a false reification of the experience of history, which should appear as form rather than content. These two modes can be gathered under the concept of *historical indirection*.

What is central to Vallejo's poetics, as I suggest throughout this book, is an evolving sense of the critical importance of spontaneity, of adaptation to a situation, which makes his poetry the scene of constant movement—for the writer but also for the reader. Vallejo's writings eschew anything that looks like fixity, anything that would allow himself or his reader to settle into complacency. In part this is a corollary of his own constant movement: from the sierra to the cities of Peru, and later to Paris, Russia, and Madrid; from readings in Spanish Golden Age poetry through Romanticism to the international avant-gardes and into the plastic and visual arts; from poetry into prose and back out again. But it is more closely connected to his refusal to offer a comfortingly coherent poetics. Vallejo instead presents his own work as a "horizontalizing" aesthetic (*ACC* I: 46) that attempts to connect lyric poetry and the modern subject with their momentary backdrops, exploring the effects of the latter on the former. And those backdrops, as Vallejo's poetry and prose insistently register, were themselves undergoing processes of constant change. It is not only plants that grow in the spaces of Vallejo's writing (such as the mosses collecting around a lover's refusals in *Trilce* LXII), but machines, economics, and political ideologies, all of which bear witness to the inroads and the traumas of modernity, in Peru as much as in Paris.

I hope to preserve some sense of this contradictoriness in the chapters that follow, reading Vallejo's apparent lack of coherence as the result of a shifting attachment to various local contexts while remaining always alive to the changes of modernity. As I map out in this opening chapter, Vallejo's writing emerges at the crossroads of different aesthetic possibilities—the waning of a cosmopolitanist and symbolism-inflected *modernismo* in Latin America, the development of new ways to articulate local concerns while engaging with the contemporary international avant-gardes—and of warring political ideologies in the context of shifting geopolitical configurations. His concern at each one of these junctures is with the possible reach of poetry, understanding the lyric not as a solipsistic aesthetic form providing a refuge from history, but as a mode of processing the most pressing contemporary problems, and subject to constant self-critique. By putting poetry on trial—to paraphrase an expression by his contemporary José Carlos Mariátegui— Vallejo offers us a critical example of the ways in which the modern lyric can submit itself to history and survive the encounter.

LYRIC HISTORY

Poetry can seem a profoundly paradoxical genre: at once a mask and a voice, a momentary outburst and a durable document, pure subjective expression and the most convention-bound utterance. And as a genre that theoretically speaks for the individual and exhausts itself in its enunciation, poetry has often been deemed incapable of engaging with a collectivity and generating either immediate or lingering effects. Academic literary studies have for the most part clung to the relation between nation and narration—not nation and lyric—as the place where reflection on history happens. And as Auden famously put it in his "In Memory of W. B. Yeats," "poetry makes nothing happen." But as he less famously continued, "it survives, / a way of happening, a mouth."

That mouth has too often been viewed as ahistorical and disembodied. To paraphrase Yeats's poem "Byzantium," poetry in theory remains "a mouth which has no moisture and no breath," contorted in the gesture of its voicing, with no capacity to summon equally "breathless mouths" or to be summoned by them. In Anglophone criticism, poetry has had its strongest defenders among New Criticism–trained critics, who have tended to present it as an utterance set outside history, insulated from real-world reference. Politically inflected Anglophone literary criticism has also been disinclined to press poetry for its connection to history but for a different reason: a sense that the lyric fails to render a significant image of the individual's relation to a multidimensional sociopolitical environment.[4] Marxist criticism, in its commitment to a critique of aesthetic ideology, has viewed the lyric with enormous suspicion—as Robert Kaufman has repeatedly signaled—despite ostensibly building on Adorno's and Benjamin's probings of poetry's relation to specific political questions and to a broader historical environment.[5] And the historicist turn in Americanist literary studies has generally continued to sideline poetry in its focus on prose, as Joseph Harrington points out (159–60).[6] Meanwhile, postcolonial criticism— as Jahan Ramazani and Brent Edwards ("Genres") have both recently argued—shows a marked reluctance to engage with the lyric.[7] Ramazani's analyses of postcolonial poetry are an important contribution to the debate; yet in their restriction to Anglophone poetry, they raise a second question, involving hierarchies not of genres but of languages. Hispanophone or Lusophone poets present the extra obstacle of speaking a language that is not-quite European but also not-quite indigenous, and in their engagement with foreign models they moreover tend to write back to the wrong empire—the French symbolist rather than the Spanish colonialist (Molloy 372).[8]

Recent criticism, however, has begun to connect poetry in more productive ways to broader historical and theoretical contexts. A 2008 *PMLA* section, "New Lyric Studies," took issue with the compartmentalization of the genre, reassessing the question of the lyric voice, of poetry's connection to prose in periods of historical duress, and of the lyric's contribution to understandings of transnationalism. Meanwhile, a new anthology of critical and theoretical writings, *Poetry and Cultural Studies* (2009), which foregrounds the sidelining of poetry in studies of national literatures, further aims to undo any notion that poetry is necessarily trapped in the domain of high culture. Approaching poetry from diverse angles—ethnicity, mass culture, Frankfurt school critical theory—it attempts to recover the historical role of the lyric in processing various forms of culture: national, regional, popular, socioeconomic, ethnic.

But we need also to retain a sense of the tensed relation between poetry and history, which we can trace in its forms and tones even more than in its contents. Texts are necessarily worldly, as Edward Said relentlessly reminded us, enmeshed in the conditions from which they spring. But a lyric voice is constitutively caught between the public and the private, between an utterance that captures the internal or intimate and one that reaches out to a community; the challenge of the lyric, as Kaufman glosses Adorno's "Lyric Poetry and Society," is therefore to think subjectivity and objectivity simultaneously (363). Poetry's codes are structured in large measure by the possibilities of a historical moment, inflected by a sense of local urgencies; but the lyric also aims to reach beyond them, opening itself up to interpretations that go beyond the purely local or contemporary, unfurling through history.

Over the course of this book, I follow this call to hear poetry as a voice for history by reconnecting Vallejo's writing to its diverse contexts: Peruvian political and artistic debates, a generational shift in Latin American poetics, the broader panorama of the international avant-gardes, and interwar Europe. These contexts naturally involve their own questions and circuits, although they frequently overlap; each one is structured and striated by new local political imperatives and changing understandings of culture's relation to the social, to economics, and to geopolitics. I am equally concerned to trace the ways in which poetry harnesses contemporary voices precisely in order to move beyond them; as the next chapter examines, Vallejo's Peruvian poetry sets its own voice alongside and in competition with past and present voices—literary, political, popular. But I want to begin by dwelling on Vallejo's initial contexts to give a sense of the background of his first collections. This chapter therefore tracks the dominant modes of poetry in postindependence Latin America, its specific modulations and shifting place in turn-of-the-century Peru, and its gradual enmeshment with local political-cultural debates, against the backdrop of the avant-garde's circulation through the continent. This condensed and crisscrossed panorama prepares for the appearance of Vallejo's two Peruvian poetry collections, *Los heraldos negros* and *Trilce*.

THE LYRIC AND THE CONTEMPORARY

In the aftermath of military defeat by Chile in the War of the Pacific (1879–83), Peru faced an acute representational crisis that unsettled both its politics and its literature. Forging a newly solid image of the nation entailed radically rethinking its relation to its pre-Columbian and colonial pasts, while also confronting the present-day imbalance between the capital and the provinces. After independence in the early 1820s, the country's power base had remained in Lima, its virtually feudal supporting structures spreading like tentacles through the countryside, which continued to funnel funds to the capital. Meanwhile, expanded neocolonial arrangements handed over control of road-building projects, mining, and commerce to Britain and subsequently to the United States. All these conditions solidified a situation that Vallejo himself referred to as "semicolonial" (*ACC* II: 904), and that Adam Sharman has recast as "colonial postcolonial" ("Semicolonial" 192). In Sharman's blunt assessment, "Decolonization did not take place, post-colonialism never happened, and Quechua never became the official language of any of those new nation-states. Indigenous groups continued both in the nineteenth century and in Vallejo's day to be colonized subjects of a political, economic, and cultural order that was manifestly not their own" (194).

Peru's postindependence fault lines ran between creoles, mestizos, and indigenous groups, between the ruling and working classes, and within those groups themselves, split along lines of ethnicity and economic interest and allegiances, all of which were complicated by the importation of black and Chinese forced labor and by new neocolonial alliances throughout the modern period.[9] Many intellectuals pointed to this rampant fragmentation as a major factor in Peru's military defeat: the inability to foster a strong sense of patriotism, it was argued, had resulted in an undermotivated army comprising largely mestizo and indigenous soldiers, whose union easily crumbled under the Chilean onslaught.[10] The immediate postwar issue, then, which remained at the center of national debate over the next forty years, was the following: how to create and sustain a representative image of the nation that would incorporate all its inhabitants and earn their allegiance.

The early twentieth century therefore witnessed a series of struggles over forms and contents of national representation, as both politics and aesthetics began to grapple with past and present omissions and repressions. This period saw a striking increase in the number of newspapers produced, linked to the mass migration of representatives of the provincial and Andean middle and working classes—often of mestizo origin—into the cities.[11] These new journalists set themselves against a university system dominated by the oligarchy; the prose they forged in their newspaper articles served to elaborate a polemical critical nationalism, taking as its target a conservative nationalism with its roots sunk deep in colonial structures. At stake in these broad debates were not only internal issues of regionalism and nationalism but also Peru's representation before the world: the concern of the area's major writers in this period was to bring local politics and literature up to date with the international scene. The aim of Peru's most radical intellectuals, however, was not simply to emulate Western-shaped forms of the modern, but to map out the country's own options, setting its productions *alongside* Western forms rather than following after them. This was less a question of projected modernity than of willed contemporaneity.[12] Images of contemporaneity, when projected from a space that saw itself as both peripheral and suffering from time lag, risked reifying hierarchies of global culture; but they could also highlight alternative options that dismantled those hierarchies. Forms of the modern that drew upon European models—such as the literary bohemia that developed in Peru's major cities in the early 1910s—could themselves seem outdated alongside modes of everyday life in parts of the country less overtly inflected by modernity.

The poem "Idilio muerto" (Dead Idyll) from Vallejo's first collection, *Los heraldos negros,* throws a spotlight on this contradictory contemporaneity. Positioning his own present-tense unproductiveness—in a literary bohemia in the city of Trujillo—against the daily activities of a lover in his sierra hometown, the poet muses aloud on what "mi andina y dulce Rita" (my Andean and sweet Rita) is currently doing outside the space of modernity, and his language points to a surprising disjunction between conceptions of time in both sites. Setting the poet's timeless "ahora" (now) in the city against the deictically temporalized "esta hora" (at this hour) in the countryside, the poem suggests that it is not urban modernity but the Andean region that is more alive to change. Moreover, the hypothetical imagining of Rita's activities brings in an implicit future tense ("¿qué estará haciendo esta hora . . . ?"; what could [she] be doing at this hour [my trans.]) that projects her activities forward in a moving temporality from which the poet is excluded. The poem's two figures also occupy importantly differing positions: while he, bohemian poet, sits pickling in cognac—his only movement located in the blood that drunkenly dozes inside him—Rita is instead exposed to the world, on the threshold ("ha de estarse a la puerta"; she must be at the door), receptive to what is outside her. Rita's position points to an openness to time and space, routine and change; the poet's position marks a stagnating self-enclosure.

As Paul de Man signaled, this kind of disparaging of literary modernity—figured as the desire to abandon literature and reenter the real—generally does the opposite of what it pretends; rather than cancel literary modernity, it aims to guarantee the survival of modern literature (*Blindness* 161). And it does so by turning the space of production into a space of productive crisis, a self-critical site for rewriting the figure of the poet and his relationship to his surrounding discursive and material environment. Vallejo's early writings repeatedly stage an attempted return to the lost idyll of home and Andean ritual, only to discover that the lyric subject is unrelentingly excluded from both, restricted to describing what he witnesses and his own externality to it. This is already suggested in the title of the poem just quoted, "Dead Idyll," although what is dead—as the poem goes on to explain—is not the Andean idyll itself but the possibility of the poet's idyllic reinsertion in it. Ultimately, however, this logic doubles back on itself: the exclusion of the modern poet from that world is revealed as a consequence of the latter's own stagnation within ritual. Indeed it is striking just how many of the poems in *Los heraldos negros* are structured around images of petrification, paralysis, or emptiness, particularly when they refer to poetic reconstructions of Andean culture; and indeed, those many poems that have been taken as celebrations of the vitality of traditional culture can more pointedly be read—as Sharman (*Tradition*) and Hart ("Vallejo in Between") suggest—as a veiled critique of that culture, of the rituals that made it as static as the urban literary bohemia that implicitly rejected it.

The modern sense that the lyric as a genre was both out of time and out of place, and that the times and places on which it turned its eye were themselves stagnating, led to various meditations on the concept of the "meanwhile." The notion of a suspended temporality into which poetry might cut reaches back to German Romanticism, most clearly articulated in Friedrich Hölderlin's ode "Brot und Wein" (Bread and Wine) (ca. 1800), which questions the point of poetry in the unfolding moment of modernity:

> So zu harren, und was zu tun indes und zu sagen
> Weiss ich nicht, und wozu Dichter in dürftiger Zeit.
>
> *So to wait, and what to do meanwhile and to say*
> *I know not, nor what are poets for in a time of dearth.*

In the period of the nascent international avant-gardes, the "meanwhile" had shrunk into the self-consuming moment of modernity, a condensation of experience into the split second of its duration, inaugurated by the poetry of Baudelaire—in which the experience of the city, as Benjamin puts it, is that of "love at last sight" (*Writer* 77). But it could also be reconceived as a period of transition, holding a place while thought was being worked out. The duration of the present may have been calculated scientifically in these years as lasting between five and twelve seconds (Kern 82), but as the Peruvian sociocultural theorist Mariátegui argued, the entire avant-garde period needed to be understood as a dilated present, held open as a bracket for experimentation. In a series of articles in the 1920s, Mariátegui insisted on the need to work time for reflection into the contemporary moment rather than simply thinking about immediate goals; he argued that the experimental moment of the avant-gardes was not simply a dilettantish evasion of historical urgencies, but the opening of a space and time for critical thought which allowed for a strategic separation of aesthetics and politics, freeing the former from the practical considerations of the latter (*Artista* 60–69).

It was an enormously resonant theoretical move to cast this period as a battle for contemporaneity rather than a struggle over modernization. To project a Peru contemporary with the rest of the western hemisphere meant viewing the *entirety* of the West as passing through an open period of experimentation, rather than reinforcing the impression of a peripheral nation rushing to catch up with metropolitan advances. The two most promising formal vehicles for these experiments, as Mariátegui mapped out in his own writing and criticism, were the essay (in its etymological sense of sketch or practice, drawing on Montaigne) and the lyric (as a genre that registers the momentary and can therefore be revolutionary). The entanglement of poetry and prose becomes central to engagements with the national and the international, mapped out in a debate over respective lyric and journalistic capacities to capture the contemporary.

POETRY'S ANACHRONISMS

Before delving into the specific modulations of this question in Peru, it is helpful to consider the larger panorama of Latin American writing in the preceding years and the place of poetry within it. In the postindependence decades of the early nineteenth century, poets from various parts of Latin America were intimately involved in the project of forging a new continental consciousness. Their contributions often took the form of long narrative poems, which aimed to frame views of Latin America for local readers; these poems were written not only against the colonial legacy of the past, but against the numerous travel narratives and visual images being produced by contemporary visitors to the continent, from the naturalist Alexander von Humboldt and the painter Johann Moritz Rugendas to various neocolonialist adventurers such as Francis Bond Head.[13] There were often clear ideological differences between these local and foreign renditions. If the former attempted to generate authochthonous voices and viewpoints and a sense of entitlement to local matters, the latter's projects ranged from the scientific through the cultural to the neocolonial, with frequent overlaps between these concerns. Yet as Jennifer French points out, to posit a strict separation between local and foreign accounts is an oversimplification. Many of what we now recognize as "foundational creole text[s]" were themselves "heavily mediated by European discourse" (3)—occasionally Spanish but more frequently British, French, or German.

All of these writers, artists, scientists, and explorers were looking at the same nature; all of their sights, for their own specific reasons, converge on the usable raw materials of the continent. But their view of this nature, naturally, varies radically. One area where they diverge is in their sensitivity to the presence of the past in that landscape. Foreign travelers continued to posit Latin America as a New World, a tabula rasa to be mined by new powers, and in the process, they showed themselves oblivious to any pre-Columbian traces in the landscape. As Mary Louise Pratt demonstrates, Humboldt's narratives blot out not only the indigenous "helpers" who accompanied him on his journeys but also the routes beaten out by previous generations across the countryside (115–17, 125). And as Jean Franco has shown, other travelers were almost comically blind to traces of the civilizational past in the landscape. One Captain Andrews, happening upon a forest of enormous mossy trees, remarked that "they seemed coeval with old time, and supplied associations of age which the castled ruin inspires in Europe, but which would be looked for in vain here" (quoted in *Critical Passions* 137). Like many of his contemporaries, Andrews cannot see local history for the trees.

Local writers, by contrast, saw everywhere forests of signs which were sometimes literal temples and which handily pointed to both the future and the past. In the 1820 poem "En el Teocalli de Cholula," the Cuban poet José María Heredia mimics the European trope of a walk through the landscape to a high vantage point: in this case not a Schillerian mountain path but a Mesoamerican pyramid. While resting, he scans the surrounding landscape in a reverie of new beginnings, only to find himself overwhelmed and alarmed by its pre-Columbian energies; that sense of the past, however, gradually changes its sign, reanimating the poet's faith in local possibilities (Hills 85–91). In 1825 the ghostly apparition of the last Inca emperor, Huayna Capac, seals an important battleground victory in *Victoria de Junín: canto a Bolívar,* by the Ecuadorian poet José Joaquín Olmedo (Hills 45–82). As Antonio Cussen notes (130), the poem was very favorably reviewed the following year by the Chilean poet and statesman Andrés Bello, who celebrated both its Latinate grounding and its suturing of the independence process to the pre-Columbian past. Bello published his own immensely influential poem, "Silva a la agricultura de la zona tórrida," that same year (Hills 27–41). Presenting a neoclassical catalog of Latin American matters, it highlights the usefulness and uniqueness of the continent's present-day raw materials, appealing to their past and future agricultural worth, aiming to turn Latin American nature into history (Kaempfer 273).[14]

In the subsequent decades, however, it was usually not poets but prose writers—frequently playing a dual role as politicians—who represented newly independent nations to themselves, through a range of hybrid novels which, like Domingo F. Sarmiento's *Facundo,* combined travelogues and reportage with fiction and anecdote to give their constituents a sense of the contours, contents, and possibilities of the Latin American space.[15] By the last decades of the century, poets had largely retreated to the sidelines, focusing on asserting the autonomy of po-

etry—not from political commitment, which was apparently no longer a real issue, but from marketplace concerns (Rama, *Poetas;* Jrade,
Modernismo). With some notable exceptions—such as the Cuban José
Martí—strategies for poetry centered on engaging with European tastes
(neoclassicism, Romanticism, and symbolism) rather than explicitly
forging new local voices of political critique, and poetry itself remained
associated with oligarchic forms of leisure, "intended to enhance civilized life, not to shake its foundations" (Franco, *Dialectics* vii). By the
late nineteenth century, it seemed at best an aestheticist pursuit, at worst
an anachronism, and many of those writers who wanted to intervene in
debates put their poems in drawers while sending their prose out into
the streets.[16]

This split between poetry and prose is most clearly emblematized
in the works of Manuel González Prada, who carved out a polemical
space for himself in discussions of the nation-state in the aftermath of
Peru's defeat in the War of the Pacific, in which he had fought. While
many of his contemporary intellectuals argued for the need to reem-
phasize Peru's Hispanic heritage in order to buttress a fractured nation-
state, Prada insisted in his numerous lectures and essays on the need to
incorporate the indigenous majority into the national imaginary and
practice, which meant radically recasting the meaning, reach, and representational politics of the nation. What has been less discussed is the
fact that in those same years, Prada was also ceaselessly experimenting
with foreign lyric forms—working on translations and transpositions of
Goethe, Lessing, Heine, Hugo, and others, offering a mode of relating
to Europe that bypassed both a Spanish-derived Romanticism and a
modernista subscription to French symbolist aesthetics. Throughout the
period of his critical and political activism, from the late 1860s until the
early 1900s, Prada was also busy composing volumes of proto-*modernista* poetry and composing a treatise on meter, *Ortometría* (Orthomet-
rics), which directly paralleled theoretical work being undertaken at the
same time in Germany and France.

This fact, however, tends to disappear behind a general emphasis on
his political writings—an emphasis encouraged by Prada himself, who
did not publish his two collections of poetry (*Minúsculas* and *Exóticas*)
until 1901 and 1911, respectively, long after their composition, leaving
his *Ortometría* entirely unpublished. Had any of these been published
on time, they would have made him an important Peruvian progenitor
of *modernismo,* contemporary with—or indeed preceding—the movement's putative founders, Rubén Darío and José Martí. This tells us

much about a local lack of faith in poetry's ability to grapple with contemporary problems: in turn-of-the-century Peru, aesthetic concerns and experiments were not just subordinated but actively suppressed in favor of a focus on political matters apparently best dealt with in prose. Without the War of the Pacific, as Luis Alberto Sánchez hypothesizes, Prada might have focused more of his energies on publishing his poetry rather than pouring his energies into political writings on the current state of Peru (*Chocano* 42). Prada's strategic separation of his poetry and prose shares in a widespread feeling that poetry was an atemporal genre, unsuited to engaging directly with the contemporary.

Prada himself revealed an acute awareness of this quandary in a 1902 newspaper article on poetry in the Buenos Aires daily *La Nación*. Referencing European anxieties about poetry's possible disappearance in the face of burgeoning industry and science, he mapped the increasing importance of prose over poetry onto images of progressive modernization ("la prosa tiende a eliminar al verso, como el gas eliminó a la bujía, como la luz eléctrica va eliminando al gas"; prose tends to replace poetry, just as gaslight replaced the candle, and electric light is beginning to replace gaslight; *Obras* I: 334). But he also contended that poetry's decline stemmed from its failure to keep up with what was most exciting and mobile in modernity—from the fact that poets were modeling their writing on the fixed formulas of bureaucratese rather than on the risks of science. True poetic thought at the turn of the century, Prada argued, was found in science rather than in poetry, because poets were still reluctant to open the lyric up to experiment (335).[17] Spanish-language poets, in particular, he claimed, were guilty of taking refuge in "medieval" questions of religion and patriotism, turning themselves into "living anachronisms" (336). And while severing themselves temporally from the present, they further restricted their range in space; instead of directing themselves to humanity at large, Latin American poets spoke only to themselves and their local concerns. Far from being "in advance" of action, as Rimbaud had demanded thirty years earlier, or allying itself with science, as Wordsworth had suggested in his 1800 preface to the *Lyrical Ballads*, modern Latin American poetry was almost willfully cutting itself off from the contemporary moment—avoiding risks and possible failures but also the potential gains of experimentation.

Another clear sign of continental poetry's avoidance of the present was found in its trafficking in ghosts, its investment in the local landscape's spirits rather than its matter. At the dawn of the twentieth century, when poets such as Martí or the Mexican Amado Nervo looked at the landscape of postindependence Latin America, what frequently rose up to greet them were its ghosts, and with a less encouraging message than in Olmedo and Heredia. The new apparitions were usually not pre-Columbian figures but the heroes of independence struggles, often voicing their fury at the continent's failure to move beyond semicolonial structures. This Romantically derived aesthetics of spectrality, coinciding with a political desire to found the modern nation on the resuscitated traces of its past (a maneuver Conway provocatively terms *necronacionalismo*), was repeatedly cast as the cornerstone of the modern lyric, restricting poets to media through which the past reincarnates itself.[18] Strikingly, Vallejo's mentor, Antenor Orrego, chooses precisely this frame for recounting performances of *Trilce* (1922) at the Chan-Chan ruins:

> Vallejo recitaba allí algunas de sus más recientes composiciones, trepado sobre el muro carcomido de algún viejo y suntuoso palacio o de alguna huaca, preñada de pávidas consejas de aparecidos, relatadas por los vecinos. Sus palabras tenían resonancias de vetustas lejanías, como si un meteorito de milenios, fascinante por su extraño embrujo, volviera de súbito para montar la guardia de su canto. . . . Desorbitada ya un tanto la imaginación parecíanos, por momentos, que una teoría fantasmal de sombras arcaicas, levantándose de sus tumbas, desfilara ante nosotros desde más allá de la historia y de la vida. (*Mi encuentro* 67–68)

> *Vallejo would recite some of his newest compositions there, standing on the eroded wall of some sumptuous old palace or funeral mound, structures pregnant with the neighbors' fearful reports of ghosts. His words carried resonances of ancient distances, as though a millennia-old meteorite, fascinating and strangely bewitching, had suddenly returned to stand guard over his song. . . . With our imagination already somewhat unsettled, it sometimes seemed to us that a spectral theory of archaic shades, arising from their tombs, were parading before us from beyond history and beyond life.*

If we look at Vallejo's earliest writings, however, what we find is a commitment to a demystificatory materialism that answers Prada's exhortations. In a series of poems published in the children's journal *Cultura infantil* in the early 1910s, Vallejo laid bare the scientific processes underlying what might otherwise seem mystical phenomena—the phosphorescent gas that glimmers at night in graveyards, the sweating of plants. Not simply exercises in lyric pedagogy, these poems temper the prevailing discourses of Romanticism and spiritism with science; they reground nature and culture in matter, in a period that tended to sublate and ideologize both into spiritual explanations. By giving nature back its body in a maneuver that we will see is characteristic of his poetry, Vallejo tries to stop it from turning into second nature, into mystificatory ideology.

OCCASIONAL POETRY

Vallejo made his official debut in front of a larger public through the genre of occasional poetry in 1915 and 1916. As a highly codified genre permitting no real deviation from the norm in order to have the desired effect on a large-scale audience—indeed demanding the production of a recognizable and highly impersonal voice—occasional poetry might seem unpropitious for articulating a new aesthetics. But it did offer a way to enter the public sphere, and Vallejo made his entrance with two long poems, "Primaveral" (Springtime) and "América Latina," declaimed on a city-square balcony and in a university center respectively. Each one was reprinted or glossed in newspapers the following day by friends anxious to herald the emergence of a local poet who would bring a "brisa de modernidad y de renovación" (breeze of modernity and renovation) into Latin American letters (Espejo 41).[19]

Tied to the circumstances of its declamation, occasional poetry is at once ephemeral and institutional, a supplement to a main event while performing the latter's consecration; to accompany civic gestures and events with poetry is to suture the political life of the nation to its culture. In early-twentieth-century Latin America, as celebrations marking the local centenaries of independence began to get off the ground, examples naturally abounded. And in Peru, occasional poetry saw its triumphant apogee in 1922—the year of *Trilce*'s publication—in a baroque ceremony surrounding the "coronation" of the Peruvian poet José Santos Chocano as "Poet of America." Now remembered derogatorily if at all, Chocano in the first quarter of the century was a recognized standard-bearer for transatlantic and trans-American literary relations; as he traveled from city to city on diplomatic missions, befriending writers and politicians of various stripes (often leaving just ahead of criminal allegations), he seemed to offer—or indeed incarnate—a mode of bridging aesthetics and politics, Europe and Latin America, in a New World corrective to Darío's cosmopolitan *modernismo*.

Chocano repeatedly presented himself in his poetry as the embodied voice of a country and a continent, facilely proclaiming his ability to shift between indigenous and Hispanic identities and lyrically do them both justice:

> Cuando me siento Inca, le rindo vasallaje
> Al sol, que me da el cetro de su poder real;
> Cuando me siento hispano y evoco el Coloniaje,
> Parecen mis estrofas trompetas de cristal . . .

When I feel Incan, I honor the Sun
who gives me the scepter of his royal power;
when I feel Spanish and evoke the Empire,
my stanzas sound like crystal trumpets . . .
(Trans. Andrew Rosing, in Tapscott 57)

Chocano's transatlanticism is not just facile but retrograde as well; in the dedicatory poem to *Alma América,* addressed to King Alfonso XIII of Spain, he casts himself not as an independent Latin American subject placing himself on a par with Spanish citizens, but as a new Columbus, recolonizing the continent through language and re-presenting it to its former imperial ruler (elsewhere in the collection he baptizes himself a "Colón del verso," or Columbus of verse). As this suggests, his poetry is undergirded by a "nostalgia de la hazaña" (nostalgia for the great deed), to use Martí's term for the modern poet's quest. But whereas Martí's invocation of the heroes of independence (in his poem "Sueño con claustros de mármol" [I Dream of Marble Cloisters]) subordinates the poetic word to direct action—as James Irby notes, the lyric subject is treated with contempt by the heroes his own words reanimate, and he ultimately disappears from the poem (143–45)—Chocano presents his own voice as the apotheosis of action. And whereas Martí's entire enterprise centers on winning cultural and political independence, Chocano's implicit desire is to overthrow it, to return in poetry to the imagined days when poet-conquerors could bequeath linguistic territories to their rulers. Those rulers, moreover, are not envisioned as local: Chocano's poetry is pointedly addressed to a Spanish audience rather than a reconfigured Peruvian or Latin American sovereignty.

Nonetheless, in the 1910s and early 1920s, Chocano was incongruously acclaimed by both the avant-garde and the government as the voice of Latin America; his success culminated in a grandiose ceremony on November 5, 1922, on the streets of Lima (in front of a monument to the fallen heroes of the War of the Pacific) and in the Teatro Forero, where Chocano declaimed his poetry and received lyric tributes from a wide variety of young and established poets. The paraphernalia and courtly performance of the coronation itself were a careful representation of Peru's reconfigured cultural politics under President Augusto B. Leguía (1919–30). The event followed upon months of careful planning, involving such extensive organization and orchestrated spectacle that it missed its projected October date (scheduled for el Día de la Raza, or Columbus Day). Delegates from each of Peru's provinces were invited to attend the mass event, which could therefore be cast as a gathering of the country around its foremost ambassador of culture. Celebratory speeches were given by the establishment critic Clemente Palma, by the mayor of Lima, by Chocano himself, and by the president of the Republic. The central event's reason for being, in other words, was less the consecration of a poet than the celebration of the cultural efforts of the first years of Leguía's regime—and not just before the eyes of his Peruvian subjects. As the writer who frames the ceremony in the commemorative volume explains, the event marked the success of a Leguía-led Peru "ante todos los pueblos civilizados" (before all civilized peoples); the fact that the country was now in a position to select a representative poet (who, after all, is christened not "Poet of Peru" but "Poet of America," making Peru a glistening metonym for the continent) stood as evidence that its culture, like its industry and commerce, was primed to explode onto the international scene.

This entirely imaginary relationship to an international community—through an internal and state-sponsored spectacle, focused and performed around the figure of a national poet—gives some sense of the pressure being placed on the lyric in these years. Poetry was being asked to represent the country to itself, to form a bridge between the people and their leader through common tastes, but also to forge a link to an outside world, to act as a password of culture that would open the global doors of industry and commerce. Of course, the ceremony itself, as Sánchez elucidates *(Chocano)*, was not the expression of popular will but its negation; Chocano's coronation was a compensatory gesture made to a poet who had been vilified for his excessively close connections to the Leguía regime. His consecration, in other words, marks not the unlikely enthusiasm of a critically aware and continent-wide public for a bombastic poet, but the triumph of a local regime determined to keep a tight rein on cultural politics and lyric representation.

If Chocano was roundly acclaimed by the establishment, his reception by the avant-garde is more bewildering.[20] Chocano was one of the few Peruvian poets championed by the avant-garde of the 1910s, and the affective charge of his easily representational poetry was difficult to resist. Accounts by Vallejo's friends testify that the young poet was in the crowd for the coronation, wiping away tears—more likely indexes of envy over Chocano's success rather than an emotional response to Chocano's actual poetry. What the avant-garde most admired about

Chocano was his ability to position himself—as poet—in the market-place and in the corridors of power.

THE POET AND THE PUBLIC

The generation that followed that of Chocano and Prada featured a number of writers determined to push literature away from celebration toward oppositionality, through prose and public posturing rather than lyric poetry.[21] Foremost among them was Abraham Valdelomar, Peru's first outspoken avant-garde figure, who by striking various dandylike poses on the streets and in his writings for newspapers of the capital, determinedly insisted that modernity had arrived in Lima. If Chocano represented a swollen voice, Valdelomar made himself almost entirely body, taking it as his mission to spread modernity—understood as both aesthetic and political—physically through the country on a lecture tour of the provinces in the late 1910s. Valdelomar is in many senses the emblematic figure of this new generation. Having arrived in Lima from the provinces, to which he returned on two looping lecture tours, he was one of Peru's first professional writers (Arroyo Reyes; Bernabé). While earning his living from journalism, he unveiled and recast the relation between writer and public or market in a manner that recalls Baudelaire's activities and postures in nineteenth-century Paris:

> Mis compañeros de hoy en la literatura, y sobre todo, mis sucesores de mañana, no acabarán nunca de agradecerme el servicio que les he prestado ni podrán medir mi sacrificio. Antes de mí jamás se ocupó el público con mayor vehemencia, ni se discutió tanto ni se atacó y defendió tanto a escritor alguno. Así, los escritores carecían del estímulo que procura la popularidad y cuando editaban un libro—*rara avis*—nadie se tomaba la molestia de comprarlo, de donde el mejor libro resultaba ineficaz y estéril. Yo comprendí a tiempo que un escritor necesita, ante todo, una gran popularidad, un gran público que se interese por él, un mercado para sus obras. (Quoted in Zubizarreta 62)

> *My current companions in literature, and in particular, my successors tomorrow, will never be able to thank me enough for the service I rendered them, nor will they manage to measure my sacrifice. Before me, the public never paid such vehement attention to any writer, nor was anyone attacked or defended so strenuously. Writers therefore lacked the stimulus which comes from popularity, and whenever they published a book—rara avis— nobody took the trouble to buy it, with the result that even the best book had no effect. I understand in the nick of time that a writer needs, first and foremost, great popularity, a public who will pay attention to him, a market for his works.*

Valdelomar's determination to incarnate and disseminate literary modernity found a printed outlet in his editorship of the short-lived avant-garde journal *Colónida* (1916). *Colónida*'s somewhat mythical four issues blasted open a place for the avant-garde, through its existence and self-presentation more than its actual contents. Its most important gesture was to recuperate a number of underappreciated writers from Peru's present and recent past: the *colonidistas*' sponsor Prada but also, significantly, their contemporary José María Eguren, who kept himself outside Lima in the seaside resort of Barranco, working on quasi-medieval and Gothic little poems that had no precedent anywhere in Latin America and left little perceptible trace in their wake.[22] *Colónida* also made a weak attempt in its first issue to recuperate the eccentric and neglected Nicanor Della Rocca de Vergalo, a Peruvian poet who had fought in the 1865–66 war against Spain before settling in Paris, where he only barely eked out a living as journalist and private tutor—an uncanny antecedent for Vallejo.[23]

If *Colónida*'s declarations and gestures were consciously avant-garde, its own aesthetics were surprisingly anachronistic. As one of its most combative contributors, Alfredo González Prada (son of Manuel), later acknowledged:

> El colonidismo fue un estado espiritual de una generación: el eco, en la mocedad de 1916, de ciertas actitudes intelectuales y artísticas de Europa. De una Europa que ya no existía; pero que, como luz de una estrella, nos llegaba rezagada en el tiempo. (214)

> *Colonidismo was the spiritual state of a generation: the echo, among the youth of 1916, of certain intellectual and aesthetic attitudes which came to us from Europe. From a Europe which no longer existed; but which, like the light of a star, reached us with a time lag.*

This may be a fairer description of the poetry it included (e.g., Baudelaire's "L'Albatros," a poem significantly focused on the fact that the poet is now out of place) than of its occasionally belligerent critical positions. But it is surprisingly true to the collection of poetry that emerged as a sideline of *Colonida*'s critical project: the anthology *Las voces múltiples* (The Multiple Voices) (also 1916), which brought together poems by eight of the journal's collaborators, virtually all of them subscribing to a by now outdated *modernista* rendition of French symbolist poetry. The only exceptions are found in Alfredo González Prada's contribution, which included a sequence of explicitly erotic poems; tellingly, its inclusion was the subject of heated debate among the other contributors, who worried that it would shock the expected female readership. The sequence was ultimately left in as a provocative gesture, along with his long poem "La hora de la sangre (polirritmo bárbaro)" (The Hour of Blood [Barbarous Polyrhythm])—the only piece in the collection to touch directly on recognizably contemporary issues, in this case World War I.

The most marked divergence between a contemporary critical stance and an anachronistic aesthetic is found in Valdelomar's poetry. All belligerence disappears in his delicate, intimate poems on romantic and domestic themes, as does any concern with local representation such as is found in his prose. From 1913 onward Valdelomar had been producing short stories set in the port town of Pisco, inaugurating the genre of provincial—and specifically coastal—*cuentos criollos*.[24] In 1916 he began work on a new project, *Los hijos del sol* (Children of the Sun), a sequence of stories imagining life under the Inca empire, which significantly present poetry as the central genre of the pre-Columbian. Themselves intensely lyrical, they project a quintessentially lyric nostalgia onto a period that they attempt to resuscitate.[25] Thus if Valdelomar's public activism and prose writings were driven by the need to stretch the temporal and spatial coordinates of the nation—portraying both the provinces and a suppressed past—his own theory and practice of poetry affiliated it with anachronism, willfully outmoded and out of place.

This contradiction points to a divergence between poetry and prose in the period: a sense that poetry was not yet capable of freighting itself with contemporary concerns. When Alfredo Gonzalez Prada was invited to look back over the anthology three decades later, he noted the poetry's failure to grapple even minimally with local representation (214). Seeing everywhere signs of an alarming "desperuanización" (deperuvianization), he remarks repeatedly, "Vivíamos de espaldas a la realidad peruana, a los temas nacionales, al criollismo, al indigenismo" (We lived with our backs to Peruvian reality, to national themes, to creolism, to indigenism), signaling that the only reference to Peru is placed by Valdelomar in the mouth of a local drunk who cries out "¡Viva el Perú!" before collapsing in a stupor. The colonidistas had in their prose inaugurated a new and critical moment in Peruvian letters that their own lyric poetry failed to articulate.

CONTEMPORARY SCENES

What Valdelomar's ventures did point to, however, were incipient groupings of young oppositional writers undertaking collective projects of recasting Peru's cultural parameters. And while Peru's urban cafés and newsrooms were turning into spaces for ideological rebellion and literary subversion aimed at attacking dominant notions of the national, a similar gathering was taking place in Europe which would have a transformative effect on culture in the West. Because the target of the latter was the war-torn international scene rather than narrowly local politics, its assault on the aesthetic was more aggressively radical, putting art in a state of absolute crisis.[26]

In February 1916 a motley assortment of refugees from various war-torn countries gathered in Zurich's Cabaret Voltaire to mount their counterattack on an establishment culture whose civilization had revealed itself as bankrupt. Nightly shows offered an assortment of languages, artistic displays, and cultural barbarisms that threw aside the reigning culture's focus on polished artistic products in favor of intensely dynamic, self-critical, and ephemeral performances. The cacophony of those cabarets ironically mirrored the sounds of war, while hammering out new forms of transcultural and translinguistic communication, in evenings that sometimes featured single national traditions, but more frequently involved performances that collapsed hierarchies by sounding all languages at once. Harnessing the potential of a multiplicity of voices, Dada performances set them not in harmony but in overlaid polyphonies, leading to raucous din or to productive interplays.[27]

Dada quickly began to circulate as an unsettling rumor, an unexplained and ill-understood aesthetic that seemed committed to corroding art from within. Peru's cultural establishment almost immediately began to brandish the term *dadaísmo* against the productions of local poets, which, they argued, would have no staying power; their hysterical reaction to Dada's dangerous influence hints at an anxiety over literature's potential ephemerality, conflicting with the desire to produce lasting modes of representation. Surprisingly, one of the earliest sympathetic readings of Vallejo's poetry—by Juan José Lora—links him to the European movement in its very title, "El dadaísmo y sus representantes en el Perú" (Dadaism and Its Representatives in Peru) (1921).[28] Lora symptomatically misunderstands the very point and practices of Dada, reading it as a new Romanticism whose end-point is only the loosening-up of measured verse. The article presents Vallejo as continuing

Darío's mission of breaking Spanish-language poetry out of the "cár-cel" (prison) that the "palacio del arte poético" (palace of poetic art) had become; in Lora's timid account, the prison doors are not blasted apart but simply swing open, after a period of appallingly creaking hinges—a tone-deaf description of the liberating cacophonies of Dada. More revealing still is the organicist metaphor he offers for poetry's evolution from symbolism to the avant-garde; Lora suggests that the present moment shows the flowering of an aesthetic whose seeds were planted thirty years earlier by the *modernista* Darío. We might compare this with Walter Benjamin's comment, in his 1929 essay on surrealism, that "between 1865 and 1875 a number of great anarchists, without knowing of one another, each worked on their infernal machine. . . . [T]he astonishing thing is that independently of one another they set its clock at exactly the same hour, and forty years later in Western Europe the writings of Dostoevsky, Rimbaud, and Lautréamont exploded at the same time" (214). The Peruvian avant-garde, by contrast, is pre-sented not as explosion but as blossoming, not as radical rupture but as natural growth, which inscribes even the most critically thinking poets' activity in a continuity governed by taste and established conventions.[29]

As it happens, this is a relatively accurate description of the envi-ronment in which Vallejo composed his first collection of poetry, *Los heraldos negros,* which partly explains the bafflement the collection produced. A visitor to Trujillo in 1916—the scene of its production—depicted an "apacible y amable bohemia de provincias" (a gentle and likable provincial bohemia) (quoted in Orrego, *Mi encuentro* 178), con-sisting of Vallejo and several other poets, artists, and critics, busy de-vouring all they could find in local bookstores: French symbolists, Span-ish decadentists, Latin American *modernistas,* and Whitman. Despite the mildness of their aesthetics, the group was routinely subjected to rhetorical and sometimes physical attack by the cultural establishments of Trujillo and Lima. Vallejo moved to the capital in late 1917, where he won over several of his former detractors; nonetheless, his first col-lection, when it eventually appeared, met only with light mockery and silence. As Orrego would later note, the book made little impression in official circles but was quickly taken up as a model by the university generation, who seized on its nuanced updating of *modernismo* and symbolism as first steps on a path toward a new aesthetic.

But the reasons for its rejection also have to do with the broader pan-orama of cultural politics and aesthetic developments in the interplay between Latin America and Europe. Vallejo's first collection—discussed in more detail in the next chapter—was effectively caught in an uncomfortable middle position: between anachronistic local conceptions of poetry and radical reconceptualizations entering from Europe. These latter consisted not only of Dada, but, even more important, Futurism, whose aggressive understanding of artistic temporality involved both the declaration of a tabula rasa and the selective rescuing of certain prior historical experiments. Crucially, both movements worked this new sense of temporality into artworks themselves.[30] If the practices of Dada compressed time to an instant, producing disposable artifacts and performances, Futurism emphasized the speed of perception, production, and circulation; both aesthetics incorporated the critical moment into the creative performance, and neither one quite left behind a product for analysis, although they laid themselves out as models for future production.[31] Futurism in particular raced around the western hemisphere with a speed befitting its own aesthetics (Puchner). In fact, the unprecedented speed of circulation of the Futurist manifesto, after its publication in French on the front page of the newspaper *Le Figaro* in February 1909, was just as evident through much of Latin America as in other parts of the globe, which suggests that the continental cultural arbiters of the early 1910s were well attuned to the reinvigorating potential of new imports from Europe (Schwarz). Futurism's entrance was not unanimously celebrated anywhere (Kahn; Perloff)—it quickly turned into an easy insult brandished by the old guard against the new—and it might not have found fertile ground in Latin America, given the continent's far more uneven experience of technology.[32] Yet the mounting responses to it in Latin America over the following two decades allow us to track the local evolution of both avant-garde production and criticism, as poets began to turn into critics in response to what seemed the unstoppable spread of a new modern aesthetic.

Modernismo's progenitor, the Nicaraguan poet Rubén Darío, penned a condescending critique of Futurism just two months after the manifesto's appearance (Schwartz 373–79). His April 1909 article for *La Nación* in Buenos Aires attacked Marinetti's claim of radical originality on two fronts: first, by pointing out that the movement's name had already been used by the Catalan poet Gabriel Alomar in 1904 (although attached to a different aesthetic); second, by arguing that Futurism's rhetorical gestures—the praise of sport and speed—were already to be found in Homer and Pindar. Predictable paternalism aside, Darío's real unease at an aesthetic that not only sings of machines but also anticipates its own technical reproducibility through the laying out of new lyric modes, buttresses his own earlier caution to new poets to imitate no one.[33] But it also modernizes that warning, marking Darío's recognition of a contemporary shift in modes of lyric production that would make imitation not a question of unthinking repetition but of dehumanized automatism.[34]

This reading of Futurism had tremendous currency among establishment critics throughout the continent over the following decade, brandished against a generation of emergent avant-garde writers who were becoming intoxicated with strident tones and a machine imaginary. In 1916, for example, the "Pope of Peruvian letters," Clemente Palma, mocked a collection of poems sent to him by the young Alberto Hidalgo—*Panoplia lírica* (Lyric Panoply)—as the typically juvenile posturings of an immature poet not yet confident in his own aesthetic. Hidalgo's collection contained the long pro-war poem "Arenga lírica al emperador de Alemania" (Lyric Diatribe to the German Emperor), which coincides in vehement tone and theme, if not in rhetorical procedure, with Futurist postulates. Meant as a parody of Darío's trenchantly anticolonialist "Oda a Roosevelt" (Ode to Roosevelt), the "Arenga lírica" takes that poem's first four lines as an epigraph, which it clumsily reworks to send a "saludo de confraternidad" (fraternal greeting) to Kaiser Wilhelm II "desde una triste aldea del mundo americano" (from a sad little town in the Latin American world). Not in the aggressive aesthetics it promises, however, but in self-confessed "ditirambos en rimas de crystal" (dithyrambs in crystalline rhymes), which reground themselves in aesthetically refined *modernista* rhetoric even as they attempt to demolish it through their content.[35]

Machines are ceaselessly celebrated in the poems of Vallejo's most strident contemporaries, but as the example of Hidalgo suggests—and as Vallejo himself would pillory in essays from 1926 and 1927 (*ACC* I: 300–301, 421–25)—they tend to appear on the level of content rather than form, or in purely formal imitations of European models that mistranslated the experience of intermittent modernity in Latin America. Marinetti himself had insisted that new forms be grounded in a self-conscious experience of modernity, arguing in the 1913 manifesto "Words-in-Freedom" that in the new age, "lyricism is the exquisite faculty of intoxicating oneself with life, of filling life with the inebriation of oneself"; to communicate this excitement, the contemporary poet needed to destroy both syntax and the notion of nuanced literary language, working instead through a welter of visual, auditory, and olfactory sensations, playing up the shapes and sounds of words on and off the page (Apollonio 95–106).³⁶ What this tended to produce in Latin America, however, were imitations either of Futurist form or of Futurist content, rarely managing to marry one to the other in a textured rendition of the experience of uneven local modernity.

Vallejo's second collection, *Trilce*—discussed in more detail in the next two chapters—is one of the few books of the Latin American avant-gardes that makes barely any mention of machines, and which features only sporadic overt typographical play, both of which might suggest its author's lack of interest in Futurism. Yet the collection does contain one subtle play on Futurist models which takes the form of a negative critical engagement, thereby foregrounding the aporia of producing recognizably modern poetry in a stagnant setting.

TRILCE II

    Tiempo tiempo.

  Mediodía estancado entre relentes.
Bomba aburrida del cuartel achica
tiempo tiempo tiempo tiempo.

    Era Era.

  Gallos cancionan escarbando en vano.
Boca del claro día que conjuga
era era era era.

    Mañana Mañana.

  El reposo caliente aún de ser.
Piensa el presente guárdame para
mañana mañana mañana mañana.

    Nombre Nombre.

  ¿Qué se llama cuanto heriza nos?
Se llama Lomismo que padece
nombre nombre nombre nombrE.

The poem sandwiches repeated temporal nouns between its stanzas *(tiempo, era, mañana),* making them function virtually as Futurist "lighthouse" nouns. Casting their thumping monotony over the sounds and silences around them, they corrode the poem with a sense of immobility, setting up a deliberate clash with the dynamism central to Futurist conceptions of poetry and modernity. The barrenness of the poem derives from its absolute dependence on the aural (tied to temporality) and its proscription of the visual (and hence of space). What results is a sense of negative dynamism, in which the movement between parts of the poem serves only to underscore an immobility that is at once aesthetic, anecdotal, and existential; the passing of time in this context is felt but cannot be turned into experience. The direct referent here is Vallejo's three-month prison sentence—on the basis of his alleged instigation of a riot in his hometown—marked by a sensory deprivation that is felt through much of *Trilce*. But this also sounds like a comment on the lack of stimuli in the local environment, a reference to the dead time in which both *Los heraldos negros* and *Trilce* were composed.

This dead time, in Vallejo's perception, was that of the aesthetic and, more narrowly, of the lyric, which seemed deaf to the upheavals taking place in other realms. Political fractiousness was in fact the order of the day in both the capital and the provinces. The university reform movement was catching fire throughout the continent, finding a particular resonance in Peru under Victor Raúl Haya de la Torre's militancy; in 1918 Mariátegui and César Falcón founded the explicitly partisan journal *La Razón;* the Argentinean socialist leader Alfredo Palacios arrived in Lima with an infectious message of dissent; workers' revolts were fermenting; and a new regime was about to be instated under Augusto B. Leguía. But poetry itself showed little trace of revolt—until the explosive appearance of *Trilce*.

Vallejo's second collection, in keeping with Renato Poggioli's characterization of the avant-garde (93), immediately split the public. Reactions ran from acclamations by his firm supporters, who hailed the emergence of a radically new and defiant lyric voice, through somewhat bewildered responses by critics, who recognized its verbal power but were at a loss to understand its meaning, to a disdainful silence by establishment critics, who refused even to engage with the collection (evident in the fact that there are remarkably few printed reviews of *Trilce*). As Vallejo registered in an agonizing letter to Orrego, "El libro ha caído en el mayor vacío" (The book has fallen into an utter abyss) (quoted in *Mi encuentro* 115). But at the same time this lack of response confirmed his belief in the need for the modern lyric to operate according to its own dictates, grappling with the new directions imposed upon poetry by modernity and preparing itself for rejection. In his 1915 thesis Vallejo had prepared for his own early push toward a theoretical lyric liberty; appealing to the Romantic gesture of stylistic freedom as a way to fuse politics and culture with form, his terms recall Mallarmé's 1895 lecture "Crise de vers":

> Los principios de libertad literaria [de las reglas románticas], eran, después
> · de todo, genuinas manifestaciones, de la libre, confusa y compleja agitación

social y política de la época. Pues el lema de los adelantados caudillos del Romanticismo era la renovación del estilo y de la métrica en moldes de espontaneidad más libre, a fin de encerrar en ellos las nuevas actividades del siglo. (*ACC* Appendix, 33)

The [Romantic] principles of literary freedom were, after all, genuine manifestations of the free, entangled, and complex social and political agitation of the age. For the slogan of the forward-thinking leaders of Romanticism was the renovation of style and meter in forms of the greatest spontaneity, in order to enclose within them the new activities of the century.

But to find his own style, Vallejo would have to work with and through the competing options offered to him by literary history and by his changing contemporary environment. The next two chapters chart his struggles in *Los heraldos negros* and *Trilce* to hammer out a new language adequate to the contorted bodies and minds of modernity.

CHAPTER 2

Invasion of the Lyric

>   . . . nos darían
> su estímulo fragante de boñiga,
>   para sacarnos
> al aire nene que no conoce aún las letras,
> a pelearles los hilos.
>
>   *. . . they'd*
> *pungently incite us with cow dung,*
>   *to draw us out*
> *into the baby air that doesn't know its letters yet,*
> *to struggle over the strings.*
> —Vallejo, *Trilce* LII

BREAKING POETRY

This chapter explores the transformation of lyric language in Vallejo's first two poetry collections, *Los heraldos negros* (1919) and *Trilce* (1922). But does it even make sense to discuss these two collections in the same breath? If the first often sounds like a hackneyed recycling of earlier poetic discourses and their clichés—Romanticism, symbolism, *modernismo*—the second offers an intimate and intransigent performance of a new lyric voice, feeding off a broad range of the discourses of modernity to produce its own unsettling tones, senses, and meanings. *Los heraldos negros* is a long inhalation of literary influences; *Trilce* consists of short sharp exhalations of new forms. Voices in *Trilce* are dragged in and pushed out by the skin of their teeth, and in turn they get under the reader's skin, usually in uncomfortable ways. But the freshness and provocations of the second collection would not have been possible without the grinding-down of discourses in the first. We need to begin, then, by tracking the move from first to second by mapping Vallejo's shift from composition to decomposition, preparing for the tentative recomposition of the poet's language, body, and affects in the context of a newly modernizing lyric and social scene.

In the previous chapter I traced the various pressures being placed on the lyric in Peru, in the broader context of Latin America, and in the still-broader panorama of the international avant-gardes in the early decades of the twentieth century. Vallejo was clearly sensitive to these pressures, and the difficulty he faced in his two Peruvian collections was the challenge of writing about local spaces—whether indigenous towns or modernizing cities—using contemporary lyric discourses that failed to fit either one. This lack of fit would only become fully clear to him through his own attempts in *Los heraldos negros* to filter both spaces through superimposed or juxtaposed lenses: symbolist/*modernista,* mythological, biblical, and indigenous. What results is a series of un-easy collisions between discourses, a repeated clash between the poet's language and imagery and the spaces on which he turns his eye.[1]

Los heraldos negros insistently offers the image of a poet rejected by the places he visits or inhabits, in a failure that is not just personal or professional, but conjunctural: a referendum on contemporary poetry's inability to grapple with a changing environment. In the "Nostalgias imperiales" (Imperial Nostalgias) sequence at the center of the collection, forms of poetry are insistently coupled with the term *"derrota"* (failure)—whether in the form of "melenudos / trovadores incaicos en derrota" (routed / shaggy Incan troubadours) or of a horse track that "parece el alma exhausta de un poeta, / arredrada en un gesto de derrota" (resembles the exhausted soul of a poet, / withdrawn in an expression of defeat). But at the same time, as we saw in "Idilio muerto," the modern city—Lima or Trujillo—is just as unproductive a site for writing poetry. What this suggests is that neither the Andean space nor the modernized coast in their contemporary state lent themselves to poetry in its current conventions. Or rather, that contemporary poetry's refuge in anachronism and nostalgia blocked it from full engagement with the present.

Vallejo's growing awareness of this misfit has a twofold effect in *Los heraldos negros.* On the one hand, it provokes his gradual with-drawal from public spaces into private memories and experiences (the family household, scenes with a lover); on the other, it prompts his increasing retreat from the conventional modes of *modernismo*—sculpted language and intricate rhythms patterned after Parnassianism, precious cultural references and sensorial appeals modeled on symbolism—into a more idiosyncratic lyric language and viewpoint. His eventual rejection of the refined discourses of *modernismo* brings poetry closer to the modes of common speech and of everyday experience. Yet this theoretically more accessible aesthetic would ironically be rejected, in turn, by his readers as a degradation or vulgarization of poetry, thought to be less "readable" than the conventional forms of a learned *modernismo*.

This process is most legible in those poems for which we have two distinct versions. At times Vallejo's rewriting of poems follows a *posmodernista* strategy of replacing hyper-aestheticized imagery with more humdrum domestic symbols: "Los heraldos negros," for example, which opens the collection, notoriously replaces the modernista image of a golden cushion exploding in the sun with the bathetic disappointment of a burned loaf of bread.[2] But in still more interesting moments, modernista refinement is overwritten by graphic images that bring in bodily processes, putting a double image of putrefaction and fertility in the place of the exquisite and pristine images of symbolist-derived *modernismo*. A prime example is the revision of the third "Terceto autóctono" (Autochthonous Tercet), which recounts a festival and its aftermath in Vallejo's Andean hometown, Santiago de Chuco. The original version continued the attempt of the first two "Tercetos" to present a modernista transfiguration of the humble local scene:

> Entra la noche al pueblo, como una onda
> de negra envidia, crepitando estrellas . . .
> Mil farolitos chinos de áureas huellas
> dan a la fiesta su caricia blonda.

> *Night enters the town, like a wave*
> *of black envy, crackling the stars . . .*
> *A thousand Chinese lanterns leave golden traces*
> *giving the festival a blonde caress.* (My trans.)

But the final version of the poem replaces this with the debasement of the day after:

> Madrugada. La chicha al fin revienta
> en sollozos, lujurias, pugilatos;
> entre olores de urea y de pimienta
> traza un ebrio al andar mil garabatos.

Daybreak. The chicha *finally explodes*
into sobs, lust, fistfights;
amid the odors of urine and pepper
a wandering drunk traces a thousand scrawls.

As a local drunk stumbles onto the scene in place of the poet, Vallejo adds his own version of a scrawl on the screen of *modernismo:* scrubbing out the initial *a* of "áurea" (golden) to leave a pungent trace of *urea* (urine), he shifts attention from the sky (carved up by orchestrated patterns of fireworks) to the ground (mapped out in sodden staggerings). This is not just a cancellation of an ethereal lyric option, but its replacement with a startling aesthetic of the robustly material and directly sensorial. This undoing of elegance brings in the body and its waste products—as I discuss in more detail in the next chapter—but it is also enmeshed in a rethinking of modes of inscription, tied to an alternative concept of lyric composition; poetry here becomes a vehicle for the grotesque, the unmannered, the awkward, or, more simply, the contemporary. We could not be further here from conventional modernist dreams of lyric purification, nor, indeed, from a celebratory or decorative indigenism.

Modernismo's definitive decay is mapped out in the poem "Oración del camino" (Prayer for the Road). Finding himself rejected in an Andean town as a citified foreigner unable to reengage with a local scene, the poet becomes aware of the death rattle of his *modernista* muse, which is blotted out synaesthetically by a lingering pungent smell:

¡Queda un olor de tiempo abonado de versos,
para brotes de mármoles consagrados que hereden
la aurífera canción
de la alondra que se pudre en mi corazón!

An odor of time lingers fertilized by verses,
for the shoots of consecrated marble that would inherit
the auriferous song
of the lark rotting in my heart!

Vallejo's reimagining of poetry here combines both putrefaction and potentiality. It insists on the need to return to a degree zero of language, by literally breathing in and out the fertile local air—what is decomposing within it but also what is potentially germinating in the midst of decay (oxymoronically organic monuments, "shoots of marble"). This redolent inspiration—which reappears in *Trilce,* as cited in the epigraph to this chapter—suggests that the subjects for a new poetry are airborne, picked up by the nose, the ear, and the mouth, which recycles them outward; but they also carry traces of the ground or matter that makes up their context, their substance, and their history.[3]

By shifting attention from what is *seen* to what is more directly and physiologically *felt* (smells, tastes, and noises), Vallejo rejects the quintessentially modern attempt to seize hold of a scene through vision, thereby diverging from the practices of most of his contemporaries in Europe and Latin America.[4] Whereas their experiments tend to be anchored in visuality—such as the billboards that appear in the Peruvian Carlos Oquendo de Amat's *Cinco metros de poemas* (Five Meters of Poems) (1927), or the sketches that accompany the intensely scopic poems of the Argentinean Oliverio Girondo's *Veinte poemas para ser leídos en un tranvía* (Twenty Poems to Be Read on a Tram) (1922)— Vallejo's grounding is in sound.[5] The sounds he incorporates into his poetry are his own, as well as those learned from earlier literary options, but also the whispers, murmurs, conversations, and silences that make up his poetry's contemporary contexts. And as he learns to listen to and channel all these voices, he becomes increasingly self-conscious about his own modes of speaking and hearing.

In "Idilio muerto," as we saw in the previous chapter, Vallejo associates a spontaneous orality with the lost idyll of the sierra; the poet's former interlocutor, "mi andina y dulce Rita," continues to speak in the absence of the poet, who conversely languishes silently in an unproductive urban bohemia. But this does not restrict conversation to the utopian setting of the sierra in a kind of facile ruralism; facing his new situation head-on, the poet also turns to the new kinds of communication that can and must be generated in the space of the city. The poem "Ágape" places the lyric subject in his doorway, on the threshold of his presumably empty home, turned toward the street, hoping (without calling) for communication:

> [. . .] En esta tarde todos, todos pasan
> sin preguntarme ni pedirme nada.
>
> Y yo no sé qué se olvidan y se queda
> mal en mis manos, como cosa ajena.
>
> He salido a la puerta,
> y me da ganas de gritar a todos:
> ¡Si echan de menos algo, aquí se queda!

This purely hypothetical hawking of the subject's capacity for conversation suggests that, for Vallejo, both social and poetic communication are grounded in responsiveness rather than aggressive self-promotion or lyric monologues; without an interpellating voice or an interlocutor, it is not just the social subject but the lyric subject who is left speechless. What might look here like poetic modesty is also an insistence (*pace* Bakhtin) that the lyric impulse is not monologic but dialogic—that it is enmeshed with the world, often painfully so.

This appeal to an outside is further developed in *Trilce*, as the lyric subject struggles to hear and work the impersonal sounds of the street into his own experience. Once again, his engagement with his surroundings is not visual but auditory, as with the "serpentínica u del bizcochero / enjirafada al tímpano" (serpenteenic e of the sweet-roll vendor / engyrafted to the eardrum) (XXXII), which climbs up to the poet in a room positioned above the sounds of the street. This particular poem was initially mapped out in alternating hendecasyllables and heptasyllables; its radically new content, in other words, initially appeared in conventional form (Ortega, *Trilce* 164). Its revised form presents *Trilce*'s closest coincidence with a recognizably avant-garde aesthetic, featuring typographical play, fragmented lines, and the jolting mimesis of disconnected street sounds. In its foregrounding of onomatopoeia and orality, it connects to contemporary Caribbean experiments by Nicolás Guillén and Luis Palés Matos, while its cacophonous street cries, screeching streetcars, and fragmented utterances link it to Mexican *estridentismo* and to Argentinean *martinfierrismo,* not to mention Italian Futurism. But whereas these last three experiments focus on the signs of writing in the modern city—primarily in advertisements, rendered graphically within poems—Vallejo substitutes orality for billboards, hearing for seeing, as the sounds of the city (sales and transport) climb up to the speaker's window. In this overheated context, his pen and voice give out at the same time:[6]

> Si al menos el calor (-Mejor
>   no digo nada.
> Y hasta la misma pluma
> con que escribo por último se troncha.

> *If at least the heat (-Better*
>   *I say nothing.*
> *And even the very pen*
> *with which I write finally cracks up.*

This breakdown in communication takes place in solitary confinement, unlike the many other poems in *Trilce* that deliberately address themselves to listeners, objects, and other aesthetics; the voice in this poem silences itself in part because it has no one to speak to, floundering amid the city's competing voices. The breaking of the relationship between the poet, his learned language, and his environment, to be forged anew in a more radical imagining of communication, will be the crux of the passage from *Los heraldos negros* to *Trilce*.

"WHO'S MAKING ALL THAT RACKET?"

Both *Los heraldos negros* and *Trilce* open with poems that present an invasion of the lyric space by the outside world. They imagine the resulting clash in significantly different ways: paralyzing in the first case, catalytic in the second. The first poem of *Los heraldos negros* (which shares the collection's name) opens with a generalized statement of fact ("Hay golpes en la vida, tan fuertes . . . "; There are blows in life, so hard . . .), which disintegrates into silent ellipses, only to resuscitate in the weakly despairing (although affectively resonant) "¡Yo no sé!" (I don't know!). This faltering first declaration will reappear as the closing line of the poem, bracketing the whole expressive enterprise within a framework of ignorance and incapacity that is at once existential, linguistic, and literary. "Yo no sé" here deliberately replaces the auratic modernista "no sé qué" (a mimicking of the French *je ne sais quoi*), which feigned ignorance only to signal its opposite: a cultured ability to recognize the ineffable, and the possession of the shorthand to name it. By contrast, Vallejo's poem grapples despairingly with the attempt to give voice to life's sufferings, to find an image for them when direct language fails.

The poem therefore pulls the reader through a series of symbolist possibilities—similes ("like God's hatred") and metaphors (the deep falls of the soul's savior, a burned loaf of bread), which belong alternately to *modernismo, posmodernismo,* and a bathetic realism—marking both the expansion and the foreclosure of a multitude of lyric options. This parading of different voices is suddenly interrupted by the outside world in the last stanza of the poem: an interruption imagined metaphorically as a tap on the shoulder, which prompts the subject to wheel around in startled response. This interpellation—not vocal but physical—leads not to a recognition of the other but to an overwhelming awareness of the subject's own guilt:

> Y el hombre . . . ¡Pobre . . . pobre! Vuelve los ojos, como
> cuando por sobre el hombro nos llama una palmada;

vuelve los ojos locos, y todo lo vivido
se empoza, como charco de culpa, en la mirada.

And man . . . Poor . . . poor [man]! turns his eyes, as
when a slap on the shoulder summons us;
turns his crazed eyes, and everything lived
wells up, like a pool of guilt, in his gaze.

The performance of poetry is here cut short by the rough fact of life; language gets stuck at the level of paralyzed physical response, a sudden accumulation of experiences welling up in the subject's eyes, presented for shameful inspection. The work of both language and the body is cut off by experience and, significantly, by guilt before another; the lyric speaker's attempt to channel the voices and confident posturing of earlier poets crumbles before the world's abrupt brutality and his responsibility to it, which strikes him dumb.

Trilce starts out with an analogous scene but in altogether more cantankerous mode: a testy voice grumbles to itself about a voice from outside the poem which interrupts its own work. And that interruption actually precedes the poem. In *Trilce*'s very first line, in other words, the poetic voice asserts not only itself, but the presence of a second voice, which precedes and rivals its speech, threatening to cut it off—yet whose very threat produces the poetic utterance, as a response *to* it and *alongside* it:

Quien hace tanta bulla y ni deja
testar las islas que van quedando.

Who's making all that racket, and not even letting
the islands that go on remaining make a will. (Trans. modified)

This roundabout self-articulation is both an acknowledgment of and a competition with what Mladen Dolar—after Michel Chion—calls the "acousmatic voice" (60–61): a voice that can be heard but not seen, that both addresses and does not address the subject, yet which the subject feels compelled to respond to, whether to complain about it or to harness it for its own utterance. Throughout Vallejo's poetry we will hear echoes of this kind of language from outside, which relentlessly reminds us of the lyric's inscription in a knotty system of discourses: of literary tradition, of popular voices, and of social structures—domestic, legal, social scientific, and punitive.

Vallejo's lyric voice constantly reveals that it does not operate in or emerge from a vacuum; like any utterance, it is a part of a complex chain of utterances (Bakhtin, *Speech Genres* 136). *Trilce* presents it-self from the outset as caught up in a frictional dialogue with other voices against which it must assert itself, and which it must learn to accommodate and incorporate into its own speech without taming or silencing them. This goes against the grain of our tendency to think of poetry as monologic: as the utterance of a single speaker engaged in subjective reflections, whose coherent musings are, in John Stuart Mill's famous formulation, "overheard." *Trilce*'s poems reach insis-tently toward an addressee, at the same time laying bare the ways in which those utterances are structured by other discourses, and they shift position depending upon the perceived success or failure of their statements, emphasizing that their utterances are always in process.[7] This is an acutely nervous poetry, engaged in constant realignment as it reaches out to its objects and interlocutors, and this very ner-vousness demands that we remain inordinately attentive to its shifting tones in our readings.

On a more internal level, the voices of *Trilce* do not play into one an-other harmonically; instead, they interrupt one another constantly, and their friction is what motivates the poetry's movement. Overthrowing the *modernista* commitment to harmony, to mimicking "the music of the spheres," *Trilce* instead offers "bulla" (racket), "los más soberbios bemoles" (the most grandiose B-flats), a disharmony of monotonous notes and cacophonous cries that more accurately capture the sounds and senses of modern experience. It thereby coincides with an avant-garde interest in noise—eloquently theorized by the Italian Futurist Lu-igi Russolo in 1913, but found in many poems from the same period that orchestrate the outbursts of clashing voices and discourses which refuse to play harmoniously together. *Trilce* makes music just one of its many voices, taking off from the putatively central discourse in inde-terminate, indefinitely productive ways, as at the beginning of *Trilce* V:

[. . .] oberturan
desde él petreles, propensiones de trinidad,
finales que comienzan, ohs de ayes,
creyérase avaloriados de heterogeneidad!

[. . .] from it petrels
overture, propensities for trinity,
finales that begin, ohs of ayes
believed to be rhinestoned with heterogeneity!

We both see and hear an attempted taming of disruptive voices in *Trilce*'s opening poem—or rather, their successful invasion of the lyric. The poem's background noise, categorized as a "bulla," is separated by critical convention from our understanding of the lyric as harmonious; nonetheless, it is not only the catalyst for the lyric utterance, but also manages to insert itself typographically and thematically near the end of the poem:

DE LOS MAS SOBERBIOS BEMOLES

OF THE MOST GRANDIOSE B-FLATS

There are plenty of instances in *Trilce,* as hostile early criticism noted, that bring its poetry close to cacophony. But it is crucial to note that the clashing of languages and voices, which is so evident in the later collection, had already been introduced formally in *Los heraldos negros.* Even if the first collection had its grounding in the finessed articulations of *modernismo,* those articulations were shuffled together with parts of other discourses—symbolism, decadence, biblical forms and referents—as the poet listened to and gave voice to multiple discordant lyric options all at once. Tracking this practice allows us to see the extent to which Vallejo's entire poetic output casts lyric production not as an outpouring of subjectivity but as a response to a call that emanates from outside both poetry and the self, and that results in radically jumbled and fragmentary utterances. That call, as we will see in a moment, often emanates from literary history—the prior modes that speak themselves through the modern poet—but it is sometimes the claim of the absolutely contemporary, whose most radical, disorganized, and unsettling form is that of colloquial orality.

LYRIC COLLISIONS

Los heraldos negros presents several instances of an everyday language that should have no place in the refined lyric, modernista or otherwise. These surprising irruptions of orality or of colloquialism mark the beginning of a politics of the voice in Vallejo's poetry. This practice—as Antonio Cornejo Polar and José Antonio Mazzotti both argue—opens a path for the incorporation of marginalized sounds and voices into the lyric, especially when they work in markers of an Andean sensibility, such as the *poto de chicha* that so grated on the ear of Vallejo's contemporary José María Eguren.[8] But this question goes beyond indigenism; it also foregrounds the irruption of the vulgar present into hyper-aestheticized and putatively timeless discourses, hinting at an intersection between poetry and everyday life.

In *Los heraldos negros,* the incorporation of orality and colloquialisms alongside the formal written modes of lyric and biblical discourses multiplies poetry's options and cultural connections, but it just as importantly marks a shifting relation to intelligibility and to context, presenting a situation intelligible only in the intimate context of the poem itself. In several remarkable instances, the individual voices that pipe up are torn out of any explanatory context; anticipating the aesthetic of *Trilce,* they present us with snatches of conversation, in the form of one-sided dialogues that mimic lovers' quarrels, such as the strangely titled "¿ . . . ," which mixes *modernista* asides ("Bajo la alameda vesperal / se quiebra un fragor de rosa"; under the vesperal poplar grove / a blare of roses breaks) with elliptical outbursts of colloquial dialogue ("Estás enfermo . . . Vete . . . Tengo sueño!"; You're sick . . . Go away . . . I need to sleep!). In a more radical vein, "El palco estrecho" (The Narrow Theater Box) quotes unidentified speakers squeezed together in a theater audience, coming close to the practice of Apollinaire in his 1912 poem "Lundi rue Christine," which constructs its disconnected lyric on the basis of snippets of conversation overheard in a café.[9]

These overlapping, half-heard voices also appear in the form of clashing lyric discourses throughout *Los heraldos negros,* and they provide an image of Vallejo's poetic autobiography. To arrive at the experiments of *Trilce,* he had to run through the entire gamut of lyric options in Spanish—which also included the translations circulating among his generation, whether of French symbolists, Poe, or Whitman. In 1914 Vallejo had shown a sheaf of poems to Antenor Orrego that consisted of pastiches of Spanish Golden Age poets (*Mi encuentro* 44); he destroyed them at Orrego's urging, and his next project—a thesis on Spanish lyric romanticism, finished in 1915—marked a further progression through the history of poetry. By the time he began to write *Los heraldos negros,* his aesthetic affiliations had become more contemporary, and the collection seems intensely concerned with displaying its debts to various structuring discourses. Foremost among them are *modernismo* in its Darío- and Chocano-esque variants, and the French models on which both drew; the domesticity-tinged *posmodernismo* of the Uruguayan Julio Herrera y Reissig and the Peruvian Abraham Valdelomar; and biblical readings from Vallejo's home environment. As it works together these three discourses, stitching them together in often illogical ways, *Los heraldos negros* still appeals to the familiarity of its reading public with the cultural forms it invokes. Even the avant-garde thrust of the epigraph "Qui potest capere capiat" is itself biblical (Matthew 19:12), and it trusts that it will be recognized by its readers. Vallejo's gesture here both recalls and dilutes the notorious dedication to Baudelaire's *Les Fleurs du mal,* which not only addressed the reader as "Mon hypocrite lecteur, mon frère, mon semblable" but also, as Benjamin notes, "envisaged readers to whom the reading of lyric poetry would present difficulties" (*Writer* 170). Vallejo's address, by contrast, appeals only weakly to an imagined elite who might be capable of recognizing his lyric gestures.

Los heraldos negros raised hackles among the cultural establishment at the time of its publication, more for its occasionally blasphemous or vulgar content than for its forms, although it strikes us now as a timid attack on previous models. And faced with the relatively clichéd nature of the collection's various aesthetics, a majority of critics have focused attention on the advances it represents insofar as it moves beyond these models—in other words, in the degree to which it is *not modernista.* Nonetheless, the interweaving—often jarring or incoherent—of various discourses constitutes one of the collection's most radical facets; anticipating a more trenchant version of the discursive polyphony that fractures *Trilce, Los heraldos negros* begins to move in the direction of the avant-garde. A play with lyric personae was already a constant of the previous generation in both Europe and Latin America: the poetry of T. S. Eliot, to take a well-known example, drew upon the self-parodic discourses of Jules Laforgue and Tristan Corbiere (Nicholls 180). But the procedure in *Los heraldos negros* is more radical in its covert undoing of lyric subjectivity, for Vallejo presents a subject rushing through a series of discursive masks within *individual* poems. This leaves the reader with an impression not of a stable subject masquerading behind different voices or images but of a speaker making himself up out of multiple styles, producing an unsettling collage effect in which none of his voices are quite his own, and all are at odds with one another.[10]

In a majority of poems in *Los heraldos negros,* the structuring possibilities of images from various aesthetic languages break down in their clashing and/or unmotivated juxtapositions. And as these languages begin to corrode one another in their interplay, they mark out the limits of Vallejo's poetic imagination at the time of writing.[11] *Los heraldos negros* operates according to a principle of concatenation, poetic dissatisfaction. As I will demonstrate in a moment, the lines that unfurl in individual poems frequently write over what has already been said, offering new possibilities not linked logically or phonically to what precedes them, multiplying expressive possibilities with no regard for coherence. We think we can read the collection more quickly than we should because of its air of cliché; yet when we analyze individual poems, it becomes clear that we cannot predict the tracks they will follow, even if in retrospect we can organize their meaning.

What we witness in *Los heraldos negros* is a poet's process of learning not just one but several languages simultaneously, and putting all of them into practice at once. This kind of aesthetic polylingualism parallels Dada practices, not its nonsense poetry but its "simultaneous poems," such as "L'Amiral Cherche une Maison à Louer" (The Admiral Is Looking for a House to Rent), which sets interlocking voices (speaking German, English, and French simultaneously) against a backdrop of noise consisting of instrumental and vocal shrieks.[12] A similarly agonic enmeshment of the voice with the world in *Los heraldos negros* accounts for the often hysterical nature of Vallejo's voices, which shout their way through exclamations, break down through ellipses, and run through a dilating series of expressive possibilities in which the notion of correctness is overthrown in favor of essaying various poetic options all at once. The opening poem provides a key example of this, but more revelatory still are some of those poems that have been written off or understudied as excessively *modernista,* such as "Comunión":

¡Linda Regia! ¡Tus venas son fermentos
de mi noser antiguo y del champaña
negro de mi vivir!

Tu cabello es la ignota raicilla
del árbol de mi vid.
¡Tu cabello es la hilacha de una mitra
de ensueño que perdí!

Tu cuerpo es la espumante escaramuza
de un rosado Jordán;
¡y ondea, como un látigo beatífico
que humillara a la víbora del mal!

Tus brazos dan la sed de lo infinito,
con sus castas hespérides de luz,
cual dos blancos caminos redentores,
dos arranques murientes de una cruz.
¡Y están plasmados en la sangre invicta
de mi imposible azul!

¡Tus pies son dos heráldicas alondras

que eternamente llegan de mi ayer!
¡Linda Regia! ¡Tus pies son las dos lágrimas
que al bajar del Espíritu ahogué,
un Domingo de Ramos que entré al Mundo,
ya lejos para siempre de Belén!

The poem seems at first sight to be a straightforward "blasón," rendering parts of a woman's body in terms of images from a different sphere; it updates Golden Age metaphors by mapping her body parts not onto nature or precious metals but onto clichés of modernity or decadence. But fractures begin to appear in the sheer number of discourses invoked, which either complement or contradict one another in a multifaceted collage: ennui-filled bohemia; nature; anecdotal memories of domestic religiosity (Vallejo's childhood dream of becoming a bishop); biblical references that open up the geographical space of the poem (Jordan); and signposted *modernismo* ("my impossible blue," "two heraldic larks").[13]

The procedure here is more radical than it might initially seem, because Vallejo offers clashing discursive metaphors not just for different body parts, but often for the same one. The poem, in other words, multiplies not just expressive options, but the body parts they invoke. Signs used to refer to individual body parts mutate into different forms with no warning, their visual shapes transforming into utterly new images. There seems an utter lack of logic behind this, until we notice its coincidence with early animation, in which graphic signs morph into new signs, from Emile Cohl through Felix the Cat and even anticipating the Dalí-Disney experiment, *Destino*. In Vallejo's poem, the beloved's hair grows into the roots of the lover's vine, which in turn mutates into the impossibly unraveling thread of a bishop's miter; her arms are described as "chaste Hesperides of light,"[14] only to be immediately overwritten in the new simile "like two white redeeming roads," which in turn transforms into "two dying wrenchings of a cross." What at first sight seems a straightforward rendering of a paradox—"communion" as at once sacred and sexual—unfolds into a new orchestration of lyric connections that dispense with motivation, developing instead as an animated fugue through images belonging to different discourses. This "communion" is less an invocation of an experience at once sacred and blasphemous than a display of new combinatory modes; what is at work in the poem's metamorphic languages and images, on formal but also thematic levels, is a lyric performance of transubstantiation, whose lost mystical intensity is recaptured in poetic technique. Transformation, in other words, is revealed to lie no longer in the power of a symbol but in the inventiveness of an animated poetic performance, constantly on the move.

BABEL AND BABBLING

The formal practice of cutting and collage in these poems is mirrored on a thematic level in recurrent images of violence, broken love affairs, fantasies of self-immolation and societal disconnection. Yet this crack-up of language, situation, and meaning is coupled with a paradoxical heightening of affect, which is nowhere clearer than in the strange little poem "Babel." This poem directs itself to a specific context but erases the markers that would make it intelligible, offering a minimal dramatization of the lyric:

> Dulce hogar sin estilo, fabricado
> de un solo golpe y de una sola pieza
> de cera tornasol. Y en el hogar
> ella daña y arregla; a veces dice:
> "El hospicio es bonito; ¡aquí no más!"
> ¡Y otras veces se pone a llorar!

Unlike the more derivative poems of the collection, "Babel" seems to allegorically declare its sloughing off of an established style, casting its own construction as at once unitary and prismatic, involving both violence and tenderness. Its mini-narrative depicts an unpredictable and inexplicable polarity of behaviors and affects, of places and people and their functions. This home is also a place of temporary lodging; its occupant-host, Penelope-like, both destroys and restores, opens herself outward and collapses in upon herself, alternating between hope and despondency. As we are denied anything but elliptical access to the unidentified protagonist's world, we are forced to fall back on her own quoted utterance to construct an atmosphere or narrative; but that utterance itself sounds like a saleswoman's pitch to lure visitors into her lair, and thus cannot quite be trusted, particularly as it seems to fall apart in the more intimate moment of her weeping.[15] Under the sign of Babel, this poem performs the collapse of language in its reaching toward a referent, whether sacred or secular, at the same time that it insists on its quest for an audience. In its perplexingly simple language, its elliptical sketching of a context, its indeterminate tone and bewildering shifts between affects, "Babel" almost offers a transition to *Trilce*.

We may therefore be surprised to learn that the poem first appeared in 1917 in the schoolchildren's magazine *La cultura infantil,* for which Vallejo contributed several other poems of markedly pedagogic intent. To present to children a poem on Babelic languages and their implied collapse squares uneasily with pedagogical thoughts on teaching or learning a language; rather, it underlines the poet's own need to *unlearn* a language, to return to the state of infancy—of being prior to language—which is precisely what marks the passage from *Los heraldos negros* to *Trilce*.

What makes possible the move from one collection to the other is a performance of the exhaustion of lyric languages. The passage through the clashing aesthetics of *Los heraldos negros* brings the subject back to a zero degree of language, not by rejecting, but by grinding down previous discourses, in order to start over anew, stammering and stumbling and revealing an open and ongoing responsiveness to the world.[16] In Vallejo's own rare statements, and in the comments of his best early readers, this is gathered around the trope of infancy—which Agamben describes as "an *experimentum linguae . . .* in which the limits of language are to be found not outside language, in the direction of its referent, but in an experience of language as such, in its pure self-reference" (*Infancy* 6). Self-reference here signifies a turning away from the stability of prior poetic discourses and from the referent, moving into an experiment in babbling, which is what Vallejo's most perceptive critics have taken as the starting point of *Trilce* and which links his experiments to the contemporary avant-gardes (e.g. Ortega, "Prologue" 15). A similar quest for a primal language underlies both the Russian Cubo-Futurist "revolution of the word" and the sound poetry of Hugo Ball or Kurt Schwitters, amounting in all three cases to a rejection of representation in favor of linguistic abstraction.

Vallejo's earliest commentators, however, presented his experiments as, somewhat counterintuitively, the basis for a new practice of local representation. They argued that *Trilce* met with incomprehension not because it was inherently difficult but because Latin American ears were unable or unwilling to register either a radical break with tradition or the voice of a new identity (Orrego, *Mi encuentro* 116). The poet's slips and stumbles may have coincided with the international avant-gardes' commitment to risk and experiment, but they also entwined poetry with postcolonial politics: in Vallejo's poetry, Orrego insisted, a new poet was guiding a new continent toward its own new speech (219–20).[17]

Trilce itself, however, sidesteps any project of direct representation, presenting instead a double breakdown: of the poet's capacity to communicate with an audience and of his attempts to behave in accordance with linguistic and bodily norms. Vallejo made this explicit in a letter to Orrego shortly after the publication of *Trilce,* which once again takes up the image of the child, but from a curious position of embarrassment:

> Los vagidos y ansias vitales de la criatura en el trance de su alumbramiento han rebotado en la costra vegetal, en la piel de reseca yerba de la sensibilidad literaria de Lima. . . . Sólo algunos escritores jóvenes aún desconocidos y muchos estudiantes universitarios se han estremecido con su mensaje. Por lo demás, el libro ha caído en el mayor vacío. Me siento colmado de ridículo, sumergido a fondo en ese carcajeo burlesco de la estupidez circundante, como un niño que se llevara torpemente la cuchara por las narices. . . . ¡Y cuántas veces me he sorprendido en espantoso ridículo, lacrado y boquiabierto, con no sé qué aire de niño que se lleva la cuchara por las narices! (CC 46)

> *The whimpering and vital anguish of the baby being born have bounced off the vegetable scab, the parched-grass skin of Lima's literary sensibility. . . . Only a few unknown young writers and many university students have been shaken by its message. Aside from that, the book has fallen into an utter void. I feel showered with ridicule, swamped in the mocking laughter of the surrounding stupidity, like a child who embarrassingly lifts his spoon to his nose. . . . And how many times have I caught myself in a shockingly ridiculous gesture, stuck there with my mouth open, almost like a child lifting his spoon to his nose!*

Trilce's frontal assault on established lyric discourses and conventions is here recast as the awkward behavior of a child who not only fails to communicate his message, but, more embarrassing still, loses control of his bodily gestures. Lifting a spoon to his nose rather than to his mouth—an image repeated hysterically in the letter—not only stops the child from eating but also fills him with a shame that is at once private and public. But Vallejo turns this shame into the ground for new discoveries in bodily and linguistic possibilities. His exploitation of infancy both coincides with dada's playful infantilism—its creative destruction of received modes of production and the rearticulation of utterances from the level of the letter on up—and turns it into the basis for a new articulation of the body and of language.

The Peruvian context was itself rife with invocations of infancy in the 1910s and 1920s. Conservative critics attacked the childish gestures of a local avant-garde bent on imitating European frivolity, while progressive writers and theorists posited the need of a new beginning for the nation—whether in the recovery of a repressed pre-Columbian past or in a tabula rasa that would cancel out the colonial period. It also occasionally appeared in statements connecting the avant-garde and indigenismo as a way to posit Peru's advances beyond European models. Emilio Armaza seized hold of the avant-garde from a Latin American perspective by claiming that "el vanguardismo en Europa fue un feto; aquí es un rollizo especimen de raza" (the avant-garde in Europe was just a foetus; here it is a bouncing specimen of race) (quoted in Vich 57). Gamaliel Churata's article "Indoamericanismo" (*Boletín Titikaka* 22:1, May 1928) declared that "entre disensiones que duran varios siglos y tras de haber hartamente medrado del calostro materno, los pueblos de Indoamérica dan muestras de plenitud varonil" (after labor pains that lasted various centuries, and after a long period of development in the maternal cot, the peoples of Indoamerica are beginning to give signs of their virile plenitude). In both the avant-garde and indigenism, the figure of the infant points to a moment where poetry starts to become contemporary by beginning all over again, risking new forms of expression rather than remaining within an established and by now anachronistic aesthetic of good taste.

Not everyone, however, was positing a tabula rasa. Individual writers of Vallejo's generation were also looking back to a foundational Romantic moment that celebrated the pristine simplicity of the child's vision, albeit sometimes to show its fractures. The former perspective is enshrined in Valdelomar's lyrical prose stories, set in his childhood village of Pisco, which presented a hermetically sealed small-town vision through the similarly limited viewpoint of a child moving into adolescence, gradually becoming aware of lurking future losses. Eguren's poetry and photographs crack open this narrative of innocence on the cusp of perversion by introducing the uncanny into scenes of child's play, presenting the more unsettling and sinister aspects of the relation between dolls and their malevolent masters; his poems, and particularly certain contact prints, zoom in on those dolls in a manner that anticipates Hans Bellmer's monsters.

These latter examples coincide with the broader avant-gardes' foregrounding of visuality, but Vallejo's image of infancy involves a recollection that is physiological—sounds and physical affects—and even more important, linguistic. What Vallejo highlights in his evocations of childhood are the conversations between children, the ways in which they learn to mimic their elders and the mistakes that they make in speaking. This question of error or incorrect speech—closely related to vulgarity—is crucial to his poetry, as he revealed in a published interview with Manuel González Prada in 1918.[18] Vallejo's discussion with Prada centered on poetry in Peru and directions for the future; the defining moment comes in an exchange on language:

> —Sí, pues—me contesta—, hay que ir contra la traba, contra lo académico. . . . En literatura los defectos de técnica, las incongruencias en la manera, no tienen importancia.
> —Y las incorrecciones gramaticales—le pregunto—, evidentemente. ¿Y las audacias de expresión?
> Sonríe de mi ingenuidad; y labrando un ademán de tolerancia patriarcal, me responde:
> —Esas incorrecciones se pasan por alto. Y las audacias precisamente me gustan.

> *"Indeed," he responds. "One needs to go against the grain, against the academic. . . . In literature, technical defects or stylistic clashes are of no importance." "What about grammatical mistakes?" I ask him, "and bold forms of expression?" He laughs at my naïveté; with a flourish of patriarchal tolerance, he responds, "We turn a blind eye to mistakes. And it is boldness that most impresses me."*[19]

As Prada's reply hints, propriety of language was the center of debate in the 1910s and 1920s: the focal point of a clash between generations and ideological positions over the question of national representation. When in 1914 Valdelomar found himself briefly imprisoned for his connections with the recently deposed president Guillermo Billinghurst, he defended himself by saying that "por ahora, no conspiro sino contra la inviolabilidad de la gramática" (for the moment I only conspire against the inviolability of *grammar* [my emphasis]). Two years later, in a canny inversion of the cliché of avant-garde immoderation, Mariátegui launched a merciless attack on the historian José de la Riva Agüero for the latter's grammatical errors in a university lecture—errors deemed unforgivable in an opponent of the linguistic innovation being carried out by the avant-garde. The avant-garde, by contrast, claimed to have utter control of the faculties of decorous speech and writing; their *conscious* onslaught on correctness was calculated to reveal the deeper fault lines—stretching far beyond grammar—in the structure of Peruvian society.

Of course this was not just a Peruvian question. The avant-gardes throughout Latin America—from the *estridentistas* in Mexico to the experiments of Nicolas Guillén and Luis Palés Matos in the Caribbean, from the Martín Fierro group in Argentina to the Brazilian modernistas—cast their linguistic contortions as a provocative rethinking of cultural politics; as Vicky Unruh demonstrates, they combined their imaginings of a new cultural space with experiments in linguistic impurity (207–62). But unlike his contemporaries, Vallejo provided remarkably few indicators as to his own procedure. The reader must therefore approach *Trilce*'s language from the inside, experiencing it as a radically new lyric language being forged in the present tense.

"THE CREATIVE VOICE REBELS"

An early reviewer's conclusion that "Vallejo ha escrito uno de aquellos libros frente al cual la crítica fracasa" (Vallejo has written the kind of book before which criticism fails) may still resonate with readers today; this notoriously difficult collection both resists reading and demands it, playing an irresistible game of push and pull with its reader. *Trilce*'s difficulty lingers, but so does its haunting appeal. In spite of the challenges it poses, there is something manifestly engaging about the collection—something that makes the reader feel like its addressee, or even its interlocutor.[20] We love to try to make sense of it, wring meanings out of it, or simply listen to its language, feeling—as we inevitably do—that it is somehow talking to us. While startling us with its lyric shocks, it also prompts us to wrestle with its meanings, or as Ortega puts it, "nos conmueve, aunque no todo nos sea siempre claro" (it moves us, even when not everything is clear to us) ("Prologue" 11).

It is easy to see why *Trilce* would have presented such a shock in 1922. While mutilating *modernismo* and ripping rhetoric to pieces, *Trilce* also allowed for the emergence of a disconcertingly human, poetically incorrect lyric voice that is audacious and vulnerable at the same time. This voice is no longer the centered and often celebratory *yo* of romantic poetry but instead belongs to a subject who complains, stutters, and frequently fails to keep hold of his own discourse, who makes spelling mistakes and invents words, who refuses to separate scientific and literary language, who sometimes eschews language altogether in favor of numbers, who reveals himself in moments of the basest physicality—yet who also, paradoxically, soars lyrically. Stringing together series of disordered and lyrically unusual terms, *Trilce* often gives the strange sense that the poet is speaking with his mouth full, and not without some embarrassment.

The first level of difficulty in *Trilce* has to do with the rampant presence of often unfamiliar scientific terms, vulgar references, numbers, and neologisms, sending the reader immediately in search of a dictionary. But *Trilce*'s second level of difficulty is more endemic and problematic in the collection as a whole: the combination of too many clashing discourses, from the colloquial through the technical to the neologistic and archaic, which tangle the reader up in a net that seems to unravel—or as poem V puts it, "la creada voz rebélase, y no quiere / ser malla, ni amor" (the created voice rebels and doesn't want / to be a mesh, nor love). Those strands of discourse, as in *Trilce* IX, involve languages of the aesthetic, the domestic, the scientific, the technological—overlapping the natural with the artificial. The reader has to be able to recognize, sort, supplement, and respond to the heterogeneous interwoven discourses he or she encounters. As Saúl Yurkiévich put it, *Trilce* "ha sido concebido para inquietar al lector" (was conceived to unsettle the reader) ("En torno" 254).[21]

A further part of the reader's work consists in trying to decipher *Trilce*'s proliferating syntactical enigmas, which are often compounded by typographical play (as in XLIX's "no hay, no Hay nadie"; there is not, there Is nobody), resulting in a variety of possible interpretations—several of which can often be justified at once by reference to other parts of the poem. A notorious example is found in the poem XLIV. In the two editions of *Trilce* that were published in Vallejo's lifetime—in Lima in 1922 and in Madrid in 1930—the poem contained the line "lentas asias amarillas de vivir" (slow asias yellow with living); several later editions, however—beginning with Ferrari—have treated this as an original error repeated in the Madrid version and therefore substitute "ansias" (anxieties) for "asias." The problem is that both options find support elsewhere in the poem. "Ansias" connects to the larger consideration of suffering in the poem, but "asias" also connects to the charged racial connotation of "amarillas"; and both terms are associated with the Lima bohemia, referring either to its focus on suffering or to the opium dens of the *barrio chino* that it liked to frequent.

Even when we *can* clear up these kinds of questions, *Trilce* offers a further, and more idiosyncratic, difficulty: in individual poems it is frequently impossible to determine the lyric subject's context and, concomitantly, his relationship to an implied or invoked addressee. The ultimate effect is to render not merely the referent but the speaker, his situation, and his tone indecipherable. And yet we tend to feel that this poetry is talking to us (even in those moments when it appears to be talking to itself), because the dominant mechanism of *Trilce* is conversation. In however fragmentary a fashion, *Trilce* repeatedly foregrounds the activity of a lyric subject in the process of speaking or listening to someone else within a palpable environment, and we need to attempt to sketch out a situation if we are to approach the poems. I therefore want to borrow a procedure from Ricardo Piglia, who approaches another resistant or refractory text (Joyce's *Finnegans Wake*) and asks, "What would be the imaginary context in which the *Wake* could function? . . . Literary criticism should try to imagine the implied, fictional context of works of literature" (144). In other words, we need to ask ourselves: how and in what conditions does *Trilce* hear itself making sense?

THOUGHT IS MADE IN THE MOUTH

Whereas *Los heraldos negros* presents a poet channeling prior lyric voices, what we encounter in *Trilce* is a voice self-consciously listening to itself speaking multiple languages, making itself strange—and with it, our expectations of the lyric.[22] As these poems speak to us and to their often explicit interlocutors—"Esperaos. Ya os voy a narrar / todo" (Wait, all of you. Now I'm going to tell you / everything) (XLII)—they bear witness to an event in fragmentary language, wracked with stops, starts, abrupt shifts. Objects, memories, and interlocutors decide the direction of each poem; they appear in apostrophes, deictics, fragmentary and unconnected statements, all of which point us toward something going on in and around the spaces of the work; the poems offer not just their own voices, but the voices that populate their environment, presenting the inside *and* the outside of poetry.[23]

The poems themselves are divided between three general situations: an attempted lyric recuperation of a moment from an affective past, tied to scenes with family members or with a lover; a present-tense psychological narrative which tends toward extreme fragmentation; and the quasi-scientific observation of objects. All these modes share a common procedure or situation. *Trilce*'s poems are driven by the speaker's urge to capture something in language—a material object, an objectified memory, thought processes, or sensory experience—in order to transmit it effectively both to himself and to an implied interlocutor, who is often internal to the poem. The effort required produces a welter of discourses, abrupt shifts, interruptions, and contradictions in an ongoing dialogue with the self or with another, as the speaker both suggests and responds, accepting or rejecting his own formulations, admiring them or demanding their revision. And this excitable speaker often works approval or dissatisfaction or doubt into his own poetry: the self-congratulatory "Ea! Buen primero!" (Hey! A good start!) which concludes XVI is echoed in the following poem's "Buena! Buena!" (Good! Good!), only to be undercut by XIX's final "Se ha puesto el gallo incierto, hombre" (The cock has become uncertain, man).

These dialogues within the self, implicitly or explicitly directed toward an addressee, produce a destabilized subjectivity, emerging plurally through different voices—or better, a quintessentially modern speaker, seizing hold of the various truth-making discourses of modernity.[24] What the speaker is attuned to as he shapes his utterances is not only the insufficiency of his various discourses, but the need to convince his implied interlocutor. And what sometimes accounts for the shifts in his language is a curious lyric moodiness, as the subject struggles to keep hold of his objects, which tend to be every bit as mobile, shapeshifting, and Protean as the speaker himself. An example is *Trilce* V:

> Grupo dicotiledón. Oberturan
> desde él petreles, propensiones de trinidad,
> finales que comienzan, ohs de ayes
> creyérase avaloriados de heterogeneidad.
> ¡Grupo de los dos cotiledones!
>
> A ver. Aquello sea sin ser más.
> A ver. No trascienda hacia afuera,
> y piense en són de no ser escuchado,
> y crome y no sea visto.
> Y no glise en el gran colapso.
>
> La creada voz rebélase y no quiere
> ser malla, ni amor.
> Los novios sean novios en eternidad.
> Pues no deis 1, que resonará al infinito.
> Y no deis o, que callará tánto,
> hasta despertar y poner de pie al 1.
>
> Ah grupo bicardiaco.

In a meandering discourse that brings into play both science and art— two modes of experiment and evaluation—the lyric subject derives and arrives at conclusions, only to interrupt himself and move on abruptly at each stage of the process, as though never quite satisfied with his results. The speaker employs a variety of different discourses—which belong by turns to biology, music, zoology, poetry, conversation, teaching, experiment, creation, metaphysics, composition, art, dance, and mathematics—in a strange overlapping of instruction and entertainment, observation and exhortation. He appears in dialogue with himself, with an interlocutor, with the object itself, and with an implicit higher addressee who will be capable of tracking and recognizing not only the various discourses but also the sense that the speaker is attempting (and failing) to convey (or to establish for himself). Meanwhile, his object of study is itself in constant motion, as this poem exemplifies. Treating that object as an entity unfolding through time and space—its various parts developing in relation to one another but also autonomously—Vallejo here puts into practice a mode of "seeing historically," as John Shotter glosses the theories of Vygotsky and Goethe: the lyric subject puts himself in motion around his object, examining its present forms but also its future potential; his procedure is "perceptual" rather than "cognitive-theoretical" (236). Hence the careful choice here of a dicotyledonous plant, which is not only still embryonic but moreover has two distinct branches for development—and ultimately, two hearts.

At the same time, in these kinds of cases—rife throughout *Trilce*—the lyric subject's relation to *things,* and to his occasional interlocutors, reveals a great deal about the speaker himself. The poems offer us a portrait of unpredictably shifting and sometimes decidedly unpoetic moods, which contrast deliberately with the quasi-scientific observations or experiments taking place in the course of the poems. These moods point to passions, however momentary, and those passions put both the speaker's body and his language in movement. In the rare instances when an object itself is not in motion within the poem, the language used to describe it never stops shuttling from one register (e.g., scientific) to another (personal and petulant), zigzagging backward, forward, and sideways in a discourse that lunges at its referent obliquely. *Trilce* thus brings discourse back to its etymological basis, which, as Roland Barthes notes, is physical: "*dis-cursus*—originally the action of running here and there, comings and goings." This means that figures can be literal as well as figurative, can refer to bodies as much as to language; and the "lover at grips with his figures . . . spends himself, like an athlete; he 'phrases,' like an orator; he is caught, stuffed into a role, like a statue" (*Lover* 3–4). The lover's discourse moves around language and other bodies like a body itself, shuttling back and forth and gasping for breath. This language, in two senses, moves.

This constant movement points to the radical contingency at the root of *Trilce*'s poetics, which not only catches objects at stages of their ceaseless movement but also presents its lyric subject in shifting modes and moods, attempting to bring all of his "cuerdas vocales" (vocal chords) (LXXVII) into play. The poems announce themselves as unfinished, insisting that they are addressing themselves to a particular and contingent moment—and this gives a new twist to the role of orality in the poetry. In *Los heraldos negros,* the sounds and signs of spoken language tended to bubble up at specific moments, parodically taking the place of culturally prized *mots rares* in the poetry. In *Trilce,* however, orality shifts from the level of content to that of form—no longer just a part of the poetry's texture, but of its very structure, as the lyric speaker composes his poem in a radical present tense, modifying his approach as he speaks.[25]

It is illuminating to contrast Vallejo's procedure here with a comment by Borges, who in 1921 attacked the incorporation of "everyday language" into poetry not from an elitist or aestheticist perspective but rather because of its essential disorganization: "Sabido es que en la conversación hilvanamos de cualquier modo los vocablos y distribuimos los guarismos verbales con generosa vaguedad" (It is well known that in conversation we string words together any old way, spreading out our verbal signs with generous vagueness) (quoted in Schwarz 104). Borges mounts this attack during the period of his affiliation with *ultraísmo,* which—like Vicente Huidobro's *creacionismo*—built its poetics on the image, declaring its commitment to visuality.[26] Vallejo, by contrast, delves into the messiness of conversation and indulges in lyric concatenation because of his abiding insistence on sound over sight, on flux over fixity.

We can map this investment in sound onto *Trilce*'s preference for metonymy over the quasi-symbolist metaphoricity of *Los heraldos negros.* In *Trilce,* discourses are not pasted on top of one another—as we saw in "Comunión"—but are rather strung together, shuffling the reader without warning from one mode, one figure, to another, trying to keep up with the poet's racing mind and tongue. This signals an attack on the notion of the poem as a pre-thought whole, an object "fabricado de un solo golpe" (built in a single blow) as "Babel" put it, offering instead a meandering voice that wanders in and around and through the space it is supposed to occupy, paralleling Tristan Tzara's observation that "thought is made in the mouth."[27] *Trilce*'s poetic discourses often give the impression of being formed on the run and in an intimate conversation, proceeding through a concatenation of phrases and senses, linked in a succession which is as much that of affective association (getting carried away by a love of language) as of logic.[28]

This use of oral phrasing in *Trilce* also points to a tension between a kind of language that ought to be immediately intelligible and its positioning within the lyric, which denies the reader access to a context that might allow those statements to make sense. Part of the problem in reading *Trilce* is that it speaks to us directly, but from a position we do not share. It is striking that the clearest instances of orality appear in conversations rendered with loved ones, in particular, with a lover. In these instances *Trilce* offers what Barthes calls a "portrait—but not a psychological portrait; instead, a structural one which offers the reader a discursive site: the site of someone speaking within himself, *amorously*, confronting the other (the loved object), who does not speak" (*Lover* 3; emphasis in original). The intimacy that grounds the relationship obviates the need to explain what is being said, so that these conversations leave the reader casting about for clues as to the situation being evoked, forced to fall back on tone:[29]

> Mentira. Si lo hacía de engaños,
> y nada más. Ya está. De otro modo,
> también tú vas a ver
> cuánto va a dolerme el haber sido así.
>
> Mentira. Calla.
> Ya está bien.
> Como otras veces tú me haces esto mismo,
> por eso yo también he sido así.
>
> A mí, que había tánto atisbado si de veras
> llorabas,
> ya que otras veces sólo te quedaste
> en tus dulces pucheros,
> a mí, que ni soñé que los creyeses,
> me ganaron tus lágrimas.
> Ya está.
>
> Mas ya lo sabes: todo fue mentira.
> Y si sigues llorando, bueno, pues!
> Otra vez ni he de verte cuando juegues.[30]

This curious poem, LI, presents a situation of communication, but it only gives us one side of the conversation—fitting for what appears to be an argument, in which the speaker is interested in presenting his own version.[31] Yet the interlocutor's responses are in fact minimally recoverable, or can at least be intuited: the opening and categorical "Mentira" (It's a lie) cannot refer to what is following in the poem—that is, the poem presumably does not announce itself as a lie—but rather responds to an accusation being leveled at the speaker by an addressee who will be revealed in her "dulces pucheros" (sweet poutings) as a lover. The shifters that run throughout the poem ("el haber sido así"; to have been like that) hide the situation or referent of the discourse from us, making it a poem about the workings of language itself. This is in keeping with the genre of the lovers' argument, which unfolds at the level of form rather than content. Barthes contends that the lover's vexed statements do not have a significant substance but rather function as syntactical arias of annoyance; they "remain suspended: they utter the affect, then break off, their role is filled. The words are never crazed but the syntax is" (*Lover* 6).

When we try to read the more slippery poems of oral performance—XLII, for example—we find ourselves on shaky ground:

> Esperaos. Ya os voy a narrar
> todo. Esperaos sossiegue
> este dolor de cabeza. Esperaos.
>
> ¿Dónde os habéis dejado vosotros
> que no hacéis falta jamás?
>
> ¡Nadie hace falta! Muy bien.
>
> Rosa, entra del último piso.
> Estoy niño. Y otra vez rosa:
> ni sabes a dónde voy.
>
> ¿Aspa la estrella de la muerte?
> O son extrañas máquinas cosedoras
> dentro del costado izquierdo.
> Esperaos otro momento.
>
> No nos ha visto nadie. Pura
> búscate el talle.
> ¡A dónde se han saltado tus ojos!
>
> Penetra reencarnada en los salones
> de ponentino cristal. Suena
> música exacta casi lástima.
>
> Me siento mejor. Sin fiebre, y ferviente.
> Primavera. Perú. Abro los ojos.
> Ave! No salgas. Dios, como si sospechase
> algún flujo sin reflujo ay.
>
> Paletada facial, resbala el telón
> cabe las conchas.
>
> Acrisis. Tilia, acuéstate.[32]

This micro-story of pain not only comments on its own inaccessibility (as the speaker winkingly states, "ni sabes adónde voy"; you don't even know where I'm going) but, stranger still, it invokes or deploys various different literary genres. The opening line substitutes storytelling ("narrar") for the lyric; it announces what follows as a rather prosaic event; and the penultimate stanza gestures toward theater: "resbala el telón / cabe las conchas" (the curtain sweeps / nigh to the prompt-boxes). Deriving a narrative or a drama from what we hear or see unfolding in the poem is closer to child's play than we might think: literally closer. It sounds as if the activity alluded to is that of putting on a play: the speaker—dressed up as director—orders his friends around and pushes them into positions ("Rosa, entra del ultimo piso"; Rose, [come in] from the top floor), cajoles them for their uselessness ("donde os habéis dejado vosotros"; where have you left yourselves) and petulantly declares them unnecessary ("Nadie hace falta! Muy bien"; No one's needed! Very good). He reconsiders what he is doing in the moment of composition ("esperaos otro momento"; [just wait] a moment more), plays with different, quasi-symbolist possibilities for the staging ("Aspa la estrella de la muerte? O son extrañas máquinas cosedoras . . . "; Is the death star reeling? Or [is it] strange sewing machines . . .), overcomes some mild implausibilities in the plot ("penetra reencarnada"; [penetrate] reincarnated), brings in the orchestra ("suena / música exacta"; exact / music plays), admonishes his actors and audience to stay put ("No salgas"; Don't leave), and finally declares the play over and done with, packing everyone off to bed.

But the same fractured scenario can also be refracted quite differently; as happens with disconcerting frequency in *Trilce,* it changes radically depending on the angle from which it is viewed or heard. There may be no one there except the speaking subject—an adolescent misbehaving with his girlfriend ("No nos ha visto nadie. Pura / búscate el talle"; No one has seen us. Pure / search for your waist)—and he in any case alternates almost indiscriminately between his adult and infantile selves, playing various roles, as Vallejo does in *Trilce* itself ("estoy niño. Y otra vez rosa"; [I'm] a child. And once again [rose]), using different languages with clashing registers ("A dónde se han saltado tus ojos! / Penetra reencarnada en los salones / de ponentino cristal" (Where have your eyes popped [to!] / [Penetrate reincarnated in] the parlors / of western crystal). Or he may simply be storytelling, as he claims from the outset, telling a bedtime story to listeners before lights-out. But what if we take him at his word, and wait for him to make sense? "Ya os voy a narrar" (I'm about to tell you). Tell us what? Not a story, but "todo" (everything). And what is this "todo"? Nothing but parts of a narrative that refuses to resolve itself.

"I FEEL LIKE SHOUTING OUT TO EVERYONE"

As the hysterical interjections and repetitions of this poem suggest, the voices of *Trilce* are not just talking to themselves, but are determined to make themselves heard. They make this explicit through the figure of apostrophe—which, as Jonathan Culler notes, insists to such a degree on the process of voicing (making sounds more than making sense) that critics tend to pass over it with some embarrassment (*Pursuit* 135–54). *Trilce* abounds in apostrophes. The subject addresses interlocutors who cannot possibly respond to him—calling out to real or metaphorical ghosts (the mother, siblings, a lost lover), even occasionally turning his present interlocutors into corpses ("Estáis muertos"; You're all dead) (LXXV). He goes so far as to apostrophize inanimate objects in his environment, and at times he even addresses that environment itself—perhaps the clearest indication of Vallejo's insistence on working context into the lyric by other means than mere evocation. In all these instances, the poet turns what might be deadened description into an occasion for conversation, however one-sided: "Día que has sido puro, inútil . . . " (Day, you who've been pure, a child, a good-for-nothing) (LX); "Qué nos buscas, oh mar, con tus volúmenes / docentes" (What do you seek in us, oh sea, with your docent / volumes) (LXIX); "¡hablo con vosotras, mitades, bases, cúspides!" (I'm speaking to you, middles, bases, cusps!) and "Oh valle sin altura madre [. . .] Oh voces y ciudades" (Oh valley without mother height [. . .] Oh voices and cities) (LXIV).

 Trilce also addresses itself obliquely to an entire tradition of the lyric. It activates and incorporates preceding discourses in order to enter into dialogue with them, and transforms those discourses, that tradition, in the process. *Trilce* undertakes this maneuver to a radical degree, referring to previous formulations by negation (often literally so, as Paoli argues in reference to its phases of composition; *Mapas* 49–50). In the poetry this operates on a formal as well as an epistemological or representational level. Ortega perceives and summarizes this process best: reading *Trilce* as a "poética de la tachadura" (poetics of erasure) ("Prologue" 13), he argues that Vallejo "no busca [. . .] decir mejor sino decir por primera vez, y su meta no es la estética de decir sino la de desdecir" (is not seeking . . . to say better but to say for the first time; his is not an aesthetics of saying but of unsaying) (15); and "si el poeta optó por borrar las conexiones es porque se exigió otras, no hacia atrás sino hacia adelante" (if the poet chose to erase connections, that is because he demanded new ones, looking not backwards but forwards) (12–13). In Ortega's pithy formulation, "el poema es la escena de un vivir en balbuceo" (the poem is the scene of a living in stammering) (13), a way to write a different kind of autobiography.[33] The lyric subject learns to speak and actualizes diverse versions of the self by mixing discourses, offering a self-portrait constituted by written and oral inheritances, "según refieren cronicones y pliegos / de labios familiares historiados / en segunda gracia" (according to the brief chronicles and papers / of family lips historicized / in second grace) (XLVII), where "pliegos" are at once folds of paper and pursed lips.

There are remarkably few mentions of other poets in Vallejo's writings, and it is striking that *modernismo*'s progenitor, Rubén Darío, should be the only poet mentioned in *Los heraldos negros*. He appears there in the poem "Retablo," which condemns the "arciprestes vagos del corazón" (vague priests of the heart) and "brujos azules" (blue wizards) who were at the time perverting Darío's legacy, reducing it to worn-out rituals or "oficios." An earlier version of that poem, "Simbolista," contained a half-line later excised, which named the European symbolists (Francis) Jammes, (Albert) Samain, and (Maurice) Maeterlinck; the definitive version banishes them to the oblivion of literary history, leaving only Darío as a possible precursor. *Trilce* reincorporates one of those excised poets, Samain, through re-creative citation in LV, but only in order to declare the differential nature of Vallejo's own lyric language:[34]

Samain diría el aire es quieto y de una contenida tristeza.
Vallejo dice hoy la Muerte está soldando cada lindero a cada hebra de cabello perdido, desde la cubeta de un frontal, donde hay algas, toronjiles que cantan divinos almácigos en guardia, y versos antisépticos sin dueño.

Samain would say the air is calm and of a contained sadness.
Vallejo says today Death is soldering each limit to each strand of lost hair, from the bucket of a frontal, where there are algae, lemon balms that sing of divine seedbeds on the alert, and antiseptic verses with no owner.

Those ownerless verses declare that language belongs to no one, is up for grabs; but the subject who uses language invests it with his own tone, deploying it in a strident present tense ("Vallejo dice hoy") accompanied by grotesquely realistic detail that overwrites the precious euphemisms of a predictable lyric style ("Samain diría"). Verses that exist outside the realm of property are appropriated and distorted by a lyric subject who refuses to recognize propriety, who proclaims himself a "nuevo impar de orfandad" (new odd number potent with orphanhood) with immensely vulnerable arrogance.

This declaration of orphanhood is a pure avant-garde gesture, a sloughing off of affiliations in order to posit the self-as-origin (Krauss 157), but *Trilce* does obliquely acknowledge its debts to *modernista* forefathers, particularly Darío. In XXXVI, for example, Vallejo recuperates the figure of the Venus de Milo, toward whose "abrazo imposible" (impossible embrace) Darío's lyric subject had strained. Where Darío's 1896 poem "Yo persigo una forma" (I Am Chasing a Form) presented looping (or lassoing, to use Vallejo's term) images of harmony and circularity, Vallejo focuses upon dissymmetry, disharmony, fragmentation. He does not so much reach toward the mutilated Venus de Milo (who, as Darío noted, is physically incapable of embracing the poet) as apostrophize and incorporate her within the poem, making her (and her missing parts) just one part among many others in its material environment. Venus is here apostrophized with notable irreverence ("Por ahí estás, Venus de Milo?"; Are you out there, Venus de Milo?), almost as though she were eavesdropping on the poet's work, which no longer entirely needs her. But she also appears as an avatar of the poet, a mutilated figure elbowing her way through matter, a stutterer learning to speak—like Demosthenes—by filling her mouth with pebbles. This stuttering effect both corrodes and expands the poem's language, which "todaviíza" (stills, or neverthelessez) while its newborn parts crawl about the landscape ("aunes que gatean recién"; evens which have just begun to crawl), on the cusp of self-realization ("vísperas inmortales"; immortal eves). In place of Darío's impossibilities, Vallejo posits "inminencias" (imminences). He thus hints at his project of reanimating the potential of Darío's legacy, raising his voice to answer Darío's "desde la orilla opuesta" (from the opposite shore, as he puts it in a Paris chronicle [ACC I 298])—an "orilla" which is also that of the closing poem, which uses imperatives, hypotheticals, and conditionals to call for both a body of water and the vocal chords needed to greet it.

But poetry is not the lyric speaker's only context. As Tamara Kamenszain notes, *Trilce* presents a subject embedded in (if also severed from) a family and a domestic space, learning to speak both to and through parents, siblings, lovers, and friends. These conversations are sometimes evoked in a radical present tense, but they are more often an affective engagement with loss, as the lyric subject tries to channel the presence of a lost lover, interlocutor, or family member through their remembered voices. In III, for example, which presents a group of children waiting for parents who may never return, the poem not only oscillates between the subject's infantile and adult selves in the attempt to reanimate a familiar past; it also casts the speaker as a child trying to replicate adult tones ("sin pelearnos, como debe de ser"; without fighting, as it should be) to comfort his siblings, until he morphs into an adult aware of their own more recent disappearance. In other poems, absent the lover, the lyric voice is reduced to shouting in an attempt to conjure her presence, or to working her language into his own—now explicitly ("aquel su infortunado 'tú no vas a volver!'"; that unfortunate "You're not coming back!" of hers) (XXXVII), now implicitly ("la cerveza lírica y nerviosa [. . .] que no se debe tomar mucho!"; the lyric and nervous beer [. . .] of which you shouldn't drink so much!) (XXXV).

All of these voices create a fundamental environment for the lyric subject, who learns to speak by mimicking their language or reproducing their conversations. As Mladen Dolar jokes (66), the mother of all acousmatic voices is that of the mother, whose voice is a constant whisper in the ear; but the mother in *Trilce* is not just a guiding voice, but herself an ear, cast—as Reisz notes ("Entre" 359–60)—as a kind of Bakhtinian super-addressee, inherently capable of processing and making sense of her son's anxious babbling. Vallejo's mother died before the composition of *Trilce,* and her death informs a large part of the collection; this kind of communication is therefore doomed to failure, and XXIII closes on a moment of almost unbearable silence, following upon the speaker's plea: "di, mamá?" (well, Mum? [my trans.])[35] Those poems where the mother is recalled present a new level of difficulty, more deep-rooted than that of those poems which pose linguistic, syntactical, or symbolic challenges; here it is a question not of the irrecuperability of the referent in terms of expression but of its irretrievability in lived terms. In a very real sense, memory fails the poet. Remembrance of the mother produces not the longed-for maternal presence but rather her absence, which everywhere asserts itself, cutting away at the sense toward which the poetry so desperately strives. We can glimpse the referent, but we cannot touch it: "Y no vivo entonces ausencia, / ni al tacto" (And I do not then live absence, / not even to the touch [my trans.]) (IX).[36] The mother's loss marks the demise of a personal affect that had guaranteed meaning, grounded in a bodily connection; faced with the absolute lack of this referent, *Trilce*'s lyric subject is reduced to raising his voice, trying to supplement loss with loud noise, shouting out the word MADRE (MOTHER) at a table lacking a maternal host: "donde no asoma ni madre a los labios" (where not even mother appears at my lips) (XXVIII).

The silence of the mother finds compensatory echoes in the other plays of sound and silence that resonate throughout *Trilce*. The poems seem full of voices that are not always heard, that exist in the space of and around the poems ("Murmúrase algo por allí. Callan. / Alguien silba valor de lado"; Something is murmured over there. They [go] quiet. / Someone whistles courage from the side) (XLI), which the speaker tries to restitute by incorporating them or by allowing them to persist in their silence. While the final poem calls for the actualization of all the speaker's "increíbles cuerdas vocales" (incredible vocal chords), the penultimate poem addresses the question of speech, conversation, and ethical responsibility on quite another level. LXXVI's speaker announces: "de la noche a la mañana voy / sacando lengua a las más mudas equis" (all night long I keep / sticking out my tongue at the most mute Xes [my trans.]). As Julio Ramos argues (3–21), "sacar lengua" can be a mocking gesture, sticking one's tongue out, asserting the subaltern resistance of a subject who can only subvert discourse by sidestepping it, by using the organ of speech to make a defiant gesture; *Trilce*'s lyric subject thus gets his own back on those objects (or letters, or even Roman numerals: "equis") that refuse to speak. But as Ramos also notes, "sacar lengua" may further mean *giving* a voice, encouraging a mute other to say something, as a response or an overture to conversation. The poem states this second possibility still more emphatically: it speaks, it says, "en nombre della que no tuvo voz / ni voto" (in the name o'her who had no voice / nor vote), speaking for a subject that cannot actualize itself. *Trilce* thus announces that its poetry is grounded in an ethical relation, speaking of, to, and for others; ethics, to paraphrase Angel Loureiro (30), steps in between rhetoric and reference.

BODIES OF POETRY

That lyric tongue begins to move us in a direction that I explore in the next chapter, the reinstallation of the body in the lyric; for *Trilce*'s language, reaching toward interlocutors and objects, is also reaching toward bodies. The speaker's body often inserts itself into the poetry in moments of pain or suffering, as we saw in the headache of XLII; bodily awareness irrupts into language, both getting in the way of articulation and forcing voices to acknowledge their physical grounding. As Elaine Scarry writes, "What is quite literally at stake in the body in pain is the making and the unmaking of the world" (23). *Los heraldos negros* opens with a statement of pain that resists capture or effective externalization through language, although it cannot stop the speaker from making the attempt. This awareness of the aporia between experience and expression is extended in *Trilce,* where pain becomes a more frequent presence, bringing the subject back to himself, so that a personal log of suffering—detached from causes or contexts—is at times the only reality available for expression: "Mas sufro. Aquende sufro. Allende sufro" (But I suffer. Hither I suffer. Thither I suffer) (XX). As this suggests, suffering radically isolates the body. Yet it can also open up a potential conduit for solidarity.[37]

The insistent foregrounding of pain in this poetry as a solitary experience needing to be shared opens up a matrix for intimate encounters. The multiple collisions that structure the poetry—of bodily experience with malfunctioning body parts, of bodies with other bodies, and of bodies with the language that struggles to express them—move toward formulating an ethics of intimacy. In many senses this is a question of love, an intimacy related to one's own or another's private parts. The connection may be purely affectionate, residing in loving language, but it is also developed in sexual encounters in the poetry, where language reflects on what happens to itself when two bodies come together, when pain becomes enmeshed with pleasure, and both begin to corrode the conventions of lyric language. In its commitment to rendering an erotic relationship *Trilce* pushes beyond the descriptive or emotional tendencies of *modernismo;* it also goes against the grain of courtly love poetry, which declared its object inaccessible, deferring erotic gratification in favor of verbal pleasure (Agamben, *Stanzas*). Instead, *Trilce* strives to render the sexual experience in a poetic present tense: installing excitement in language, which frequently buckles under the pressure. *Trilce* XIII directly engages the relation between body, thought, and lyric language:

> Pienso en tu sexo.
> Simplificado el corazón, pienso en tu sexo,
> ante el hijar maduro del día.
> Palpo el botón de dicha, está en sazón.
> Y muere un sentimiento antiguo
> degenerado en seso.
>
> Pienso en tu sexo, surco más prolífico

y armonioso que el vientre de la Sombra,
aunque la Muerte concibe y pare
de Dios mismo.
Oh Conciencia,
pienso, sí, en el bruto libre
que goza donde quiere, donde puede.

　　Oh, escándalo de miel de los crepúsculos.
Oh estruendo mudo.

　　¡Odumodneurtse!

In its opening line, the poem announces that it is enacting a movement from thought to the body. But rather than realize this through a direct and facile displacement from intellection to experience, the language tracks a series of shifts that lead inexorably and experientially from one to the other, while at the same time throwing an entire lyric tradition of love poetry into question. It begins with a mental proposition ("pienso en tu sexo"; I think about your sex) but doubles back on itself to insist that thought follows after the body—or its constituent parts—has settled into place; or to put it slightly differently, that reason is grounded in emotion, but also in emotional control ("simplificado el corazón"; my heart simplified). To think about the body ("tu sexo"), emotion must be packed away, or at least pacified. But this is not quite the order of thought in this poem. That "simplified heart" is tucked between the repeated statement "Pienso en tu sexo," which has the air of a mantra; and in this logic, it is the attempt to think of the lover's unsentimentally depicted genitals that contaminates the speaker himself with affect, leaving him thinking lovingly rather than simply graphically.

When the mental proposition reappears, it is in a landscape now alive with physical possibilities, "ante el hijar maduro del día" (before the ripe daughterloin of day), where the misspelled "hijar" suggests at once a loin—projected onto as well as into the time of the sexually charged thought—and the procreative potential of the imagined organs. This is followed by a further shift from thought to body, as "pienso" is replaced by "palpo," intellection by touch. Within the logic of the poem, this makes the lover's body present, where before it had simply been mentally envisioned. And yet that body itself cannot help disappearing immediately once again, this time into natural metaphor, appearing displaced as a euphemistic "botón de dicha . . . en sazón" (bud of joy . . . in season). In this simultaneous movement of touching and rendering, an entire lyric tradition is both alluded to and overturned: "y muere un sentimiento antiguo / degenerado en seso" (and an ancient sentiment dies / degenerated into brains), an oblique comment on the kind of poetry that duplicitously submerges both desire and delight in a high-minded appreciation, an anachronistic "sentimiento antiguo" (ancient sentiment).

Nonetheless, the encounter patently cannot do without thought; a body cannot simply undergo an experience; and the lyric, perhaps, cannot do without metaphor. The mental proposition returns, this time accompanied by a further series of displacements from the purely physical into the natural ("surco más prolífico / y armonioso"; furrow more prolific / and harmonious) and then an impossibly anthropomorphized metaphysical realm ("aunque la Muerte concibe y pare / de Dios mismo"; even if Death were to conceive and bear child / from God himself [my trans.]). The poem sets up an ironic contrast between the abstract process of intellection and the physical drives of an untrammeled animal ("Oh Conciencia, / pienso, sí, en el bruto libre, / que goza donde quiere, donde puede"; Oh Conscience, / I am thinking, yes, about the free beast / who takes pleasure where he wants, where he can), as the speaker recognizes the gap between an animal freedom to enjoy thoughtlessly, without restrictions, and his own need to figure mentally and metaphorically an experience that otherwise cannot come to fruition. The experience cannot be thought, let alone fully had, without the lyric constraints of the poem; or to put it in more positive terms, it is not fully realized without at once realizing and negating the expressive capabilities of language. This will take three contradictory sequential forms. First, a conventional metaphorical description of an orgasmic flow, using a traditional setting and linguistic embellishment ("oh escándalo de miel de los crepúsculos"; oh scandal of honey of the twilights); thereafter, an oxymoron that paradoxically negates the sonic presence of the phenomenon at the same time that it relies on language for its rendering ("oh estruendo mudo"; oh mute thunder); and finally, a word that cannot be pronounced, that literally reverses the previous lyric exclamation, filling the mouth with silence or a mimetic mumble, articulating the impossibility of its own articulation ("odumodneurtse!"; rednuhthetum!).

The connection between body and thought turns here on the minuscule phonic difference between "sexo" and "seso": the mind of the speaker reaches after the body of the beloved and finds their conjunction in a sensibilized signifier, fusing mind and matter in muted metaphor. What is not clear, however, is who experiences the closing pleasure; or we might cast it differently, and say that this pleasure is precisely unrestricted. *Trilce* offers the body as a locus of communication with others, a way of experiencing (and sharing experience) more or less directly, shaping by crumbling language.

In a much-discussed poem, *Trilce* IX, Vallejo renders this contact in language even further derailed by the senses, focusing emphatically on touch and its end result.

> Vusco volvvver de golpe el golpe.
> Sus dos hojas anchas, su válvula
> que se abre en suculenta recepción
> de multiplicando a multiplicador,
> su condición excelente para el placer,
> todo avía verdad.
>
> Busco volvver de golpe el golpe.
> A su halago, enveto bolivarianas fragosidades
> a treintidós cables y sus múltiples, ·
> se arrequintan pelo por pelo
> soberanos belfos, los dos tomos de la Obra,
> y no vivo entonces ausencia,
>   ni al tacto.
>
> Fallo bolver de golpe el golpe.
> No ensillaremos jamás el toroso Vaveo
> de egoísmo y de aquel ludir mortal
> de sábana,
> desque la mujer esta
>   ¡cuánto pesa de general!
>
> Y hembra es el alma de la ausente.
> Y hembra es el alma mía.

As in XIII, the sexual encounter is still prone to or grounded in a series of metaphorical displacements, although the images are decidedly no longer those of the established lyric tradition. The referent explicitly remains the lover's genitalia, and the chosen metaphors not only deploy conventional natural images ("hojas"; leaves) but also draw upon geographical and scientific soundings of nature ("enveto bolivarianas fragosidades / a treintidós cables y sus múltiples"; I transasfixiate Bolivarian asperities / at thirty-two cables and their multiples). Other images yoked surprisingly together and to the referent relate to books ("hojas" as pages; "los dos tomos de la Obra"; the two tomes of the Work), technology ("válvula / que se abre"; valve / opening), and animals ("soberanos belfos," "el toroso Vaveo"; majestic thick lips, the torose Trool). The attempted connection with the other's body is represented first as leafing through a densely material book, then as mining, production, and ranching—but it is also drawn back into what it more nakedly is, a "ludir mortal / de sábana" (mortal chafe / of the bedsheet), an exercise in mutually exclusive "egoísmos." And this has nothing to do with lightness but rather is relentlessly grounded in matter, whose weight is disconcertingly stressed on several occasions (the thick materiality of the language—a "vaveo" slobbered through bestial lips; the dense interweaving of a variety of incompatible images; gravity's insistent pull), and which explicitly has potential material consequences (the to-and-fro here is between a "multiplicando" and a "multiplicador"). This poem's excitable speech, which semantically and sonically sets up blows against blows, even has matter built into it—vulva in "válvula," falo (phallus) in "fallo"—and the repeated but shifting misspellings are determinedly grounded in the body, which both gets in the way of and enables experience and expression.

The movement here is downward: from idealization to disconcert (in the choice of metaphors; in references to gravity and mining; in the frustration of speaker and reader alike), from the lover's lips to her genitalia, from the human to the animal. These movements, which are similarly mapped out in chapter 8 of Joyce's *Ulysses,* are germane to Bakhtin's scheme of the material lower bodily stratum:

> Down, inside out, vice versa, upside-down, such is the direction of all these movements. All of them thrust down, turn over, push headfirst, transfer top to bottom, and bottom to top, both in the literal sense of space, and in the metaphorical meaning of the image. (*Rabelais,* 370)

A further overturning takes place in the poem's explicit reflection on its own relation to the referent. On the one hand, the physical encounter is conceived of as pure presence—matter distorting the letter in the full throes of contact—and we are privy to a variety of observations that flesh out the situation in the present tense: an assessment of potential ("su condición excelente para el placer"; her condition excellent for pleasure), an assertion of past and continuing familiarity ("todo avía verdad," all readies truth, which suggests both "todo había," all had, and "todavía," still), and of course linguistic and physical expression which we hear straining over the course of the poem, seeming to share the time and space of the event. And yet the poem ends not with plenitude, dissatisfaction, sadness, or any of the other outcomes we might expect from the genre but rather with a change in tone, a further displacement, and an ambiguous image of absence: "Y hembra es el alma de la ausente. / Y hembra es el alma mía" (and female is the soul of the absent-she. / And female is my soul). This is disconcerting on a number of levels. The gendered relation here seems to counter the relation previously depicted ("de multiplicando a multiplicador"); what is given as gendered is in any case not the body but the soul; and that soul is placed in appositional relation with another soul, one that is determinedly absent, apparently contrasted with the woman hitherto depicted.

Of course this is not our first encounter with absence in this poem. In the midst of connection, in an apparent affirmation, a doubt had already crept in: "y no vivo entonces ausencia, / ni al tacto" (and I do not then live absence / even to the touch [my trans.]). Absence, here, is simultaneously posited and negated, negatively rendered in the typographic space that precedes "ni." But what does it mean to live, or not to live, absence? What does it mean not to live absence through touch? That touch cannot touch absence, or that it should do yet fails to? And is absence here positive or negative? Does the absence of absence point to a presence? And does that presence positively outweigh absence? Touch, tangential communication, might be the locus of knowledge, of plenitude or perfection, but it might also be the opposite, an illusory relation. Thus the body, *Trilce* seems to be telling us, can be the site of either understanding or ignorance, willed or otherwise.

As, indeed, can language: a consistent concern throughout *Los heraldos negros* and *Trilce* is the aporia that results from the attempt to represent either presence or absence. Paradoxically, it is as the poetry's language becomes ever more materialized that we become ever more distanced from its referents, even while it insistently appeals to us to follow its senses. But this is how the affective charge of *Trilce* works: staking everything on the struggle to represent an always-receding experience or referent, sidestepping the temptation toward facile rendering of presence, it irresistibly folds the reader into its agonistic engagement with language, with matters, with emotions. *Trilce*'s language, however much it might protest the opposite, is an enfolding "malla" (mesh), is "amor" (love).

CHAPTER 3

Lyric Matters

BIRDS OF A FEATHER

This chapter begins with an ostrich. In fact with several ostriches, which appear under different names and in various guises in Vallejo's first two poetry collections. An ostrich might seem an unlikely bird for the lyric—large, lumbering, flightless, with its only qualities being its speed and its valuable skin. Nor does it fit our image of a lovebird, and it hardly seems to stand for the local. Recent years may have seen a boom in the cultivation of ostriches in southern Peru for domestic consumption and export, but in the early part of the century their national profile was minimal at best, and they made no appearances in poetry or prose aiming to serve up regional flavor. By contrast, there are plenty of distinctly Peruvian birds that do surface in writings by Vallejo's contemporaries: Chocano's condors and Valdelomar's vultures provide panoramic views of incipient modernity and its discontents in the Andes and Lima, while the *coraquenque* that appears in a ballad by Prada was the source of feathers for the Incan ruler's headdress, stitching the present to the country's pre-Columbian history.

Coraquenque and *condor* both make a brief appearance in Vallejo's first collection—alongside equally locatable *llamas* and *pumas*—in the poem "Huaco," which presents an uncharacteristically direct lyric self-identification with a transhistorical regional symbol ("Yo soy el coraquenque ciego"; I am the blind *coraquenque*). Other birds that fly or wander into view in both *Los heraldos negros* and *Trilce* are plausible parts of everyday life in the Andes (cocks and hens in the family yard) or along the coast (petrels and pelicans). And those birds not justified by local tradition are instead underwritten by the lyric: the skylark who sings, flies, decomposes, or dies in four poems in the first collection—alongside the occasional nightingale—derives from Darío and, behind him, from a long line of songbirds.

But there are no typically *modernista* swans in sight in Vallejo's poetry, and I would suggest that the swan is being deliberately displaced by the ostrich, which makes four quite significant appearances in his first two collections. If the ostrich refers to the swan by negation, it functions as a more fitting homage to the swan's original meaning in Baudelaire's "Le Cygne"—an iconic sign for being out of context or out of place.[1] Throughout the *modernista* period the symbol of the swan had undergone so much repetition and lyric domestication that in 1911 the Mexican poet Enrique González Martínez was moved to call for a literal moratorium (via a wringing of its neck) on its use.[2] Vallejo's incorporation of the ostrich—foreign to poetry and foreign to Peru—is thus a formal recycling of an image's meaning, once the image itself has been used up, in what I will present as a characteristic maneuver of his postsymbolist poetics.

The poem in which the ostrich first appears in *Los heraldos negros* bears its name. But which name? Not the indigenous ñandú—the species found on the plains of northern Argentina and Bolivia—but *avestruz*, the Latinate term for the African species, whose name derives from the Greek for "camel bird." Here is "Avestruz":

> Melancolía, saca tu dulce pico ya;
> no cebes tus ayunos en mis trigos de luz.
> Melancolía, ¡basta! ¡Cuál beben tus puñales
> la sangre que extrajera mi sanguijuela azul!
>
> No acabes el maná de mujer que ha bajado;
> yo quiero que de él nazca mañana alguna cruz,
> mañana que no tenga yo a quien volver los ojos,
> cuando abra su gran O de burla el ataúd.
>
> Mi corazón es tiesto regado de amargura;
> hay otros viejos pájaros que pastan dentro de él . . .
> Melancolía, deja de secarme la vida,
> ¡y desnuda tu labio de mujer . . . !

The choice of the more exotic name cannot be fully explained by the assertive formal pattern of the poem: the acutely stressed *u* that governs the alternating rhymes of the first two stanzas is after all found at the end of both names for the ostrich. Preference here for the Latinate over the local term may underline a subscription to symbolist-decadentist rather than indigenist aesthetics, and this is borne out in the poem's clichéd invocation of a vampiric lover harvesting the speaker's inner organs. Stranger still is the referential gulf between the poem's title and its content. In place of any reference to the characteristics of an ostrich, the poem presents a series of biblically derived images of wheat fields, manna, and crosses, all of which sprout from or fall onto the lyric subject's body; the only reference to a bird comes in the form of a beak which pecks insistently at that body—not at its classically Promethean liver, but at its more loosely romantic heart and blood—and which is later recast as a dagger and finally as a woman's mouth. And the object or opponent invoked in the poem is not the avestruz itself but melancholy, which is oddly cast devouring the speaker not from within but from outside.

Once we look past the poetic clichés, however, it suddenly becomes clear that the poem is surreptitiously inverting its figurative and literal poles: melancholy becomes a figure for the ostrich rather than vice versa; landscape becomes a figure for the body. Meanwhile humors are projected out of the body into a parasitical adversary which then tries to burrow its way back into that body. The body, in other words, is the beginning and end-point of a circulatory system of images and affects, which map themselves outward onto the landscape only to be reabsorbed; this poem, like the "gran O de burla" of the grave, swallows its contents, ghoulishly positing a perfect fit between the space and its subjects. But the invocation of the grave as end-point is unsettling for more than thematic reasons. How are we to read that "O"? As an exclamation (a sound)? As a graphic depiction (the gaping mouth of the grave)? Or even: as a number? An early critic, Juan Larrea, took the inspired step of scanning the poem's meter and concluded that it needed to be read as "cero" (zero). And this has consequences that go far beyond prosody. If we read this "O" as proliferating in all three directions at once, and most suggestively, as presenting a zero quantity that nonetheless needs to be substantively vocalized, we get a first glimpse of Vallejo's peculiar materialistic poetics—which, as I will argue in this chapter, insistently conjoins presence and absence, experience and loss, value and waste.

The loss that appears in *Los heraldos negros* is largely underwritten by an aesthetic of Romantic melancholy. It tends to involve masochistic projections of the lyric subject's own bodily immolation or desecration, or of his physical rejection by a landscape that he nonetheless fertilizes with nostalgia. The collection's love poems, despite their intention to shock by conjoining the sacred and the sexual, hardly go more than skin-deep. They offer a litany of body parts derived from romantic cliché (hearts, eyes, lips, etc.) that quite easily offer themselves up as metonyms for a whole experience, and as the previous chapter noted, their actual materiality is rarely felt in the language. The indigenist poems of *Los heraldos negros,* in turn, put forward a more complicated relation between body and landscape than we might expect; instead of complementarity, they posit a surprising lack of fit between the two, repeatedly figuring the expulsion of the observing lyric subject from the Andean home or experience to which he attempts to return. If he cannot reinsert himself bodily into a now alien culture, his own urbanized body is itself fragmented; two striking poems ("Aldeana" and "Nostalgias imperiales III") cast him observing the shadow play of archetypal silhouettes from the edge of town, fixated on his own isolated body parts (e.g., "de codos yo en el muro"; my elbows on the wall).

A bad faith over the poet's failure to body forth Andean culture seems to linger, and in *Trilce* XXIV, the avestruz reappears momentarily as an indigenous ñandú. In a barely rendered scene, bracketed by a movement toward and away from another grave, the ostrich is glimpsed in memory, a "desplumado ñandú del recuerdo" (deplumed nandú of memory); the syntax, however, is refractory enough to leave us wondering whether we are looking at a remembered ostrich or at memory cast as a fleeing ostrich. Here as elsewhere, the literal and figurative poles dance around one another. This ostrich gives up its last feather to Saint Peter's celestial bureaucracy (mirroring the coraquenque's provision of feathers for the Incan ruler's headdress); it inscribes itself in the lyric—or inscribes its own history—by instrumentalizing part of its own body, generating and fixing memory with the materials to hand, however antiquated they might seem.[3]

The second fleeting appearance of the ostrich in *Trilce* XXI accompanies an icon of modernity, a motorcar. The car's occupant, a once-dandyish December now reduced to rags, is nostalgically remembered in his previous glory, alongside an ambiguously rendered "tender ostrich," a substitute for either the lyric subject or his lost lover. A similarly loving ostrich races through the hermetic *Trilce* XXVI, although this particular ostrich is inexplicably limping, and its physical mutilation is paralleled in an unidentified dismantled body which is laid out carefully in the second stanza of the poem, without any explanatory motivation or context:

> El verano echa nudo a tres años
> que, encintados de cárdenas cintas, a todo
>   sollozo,
> aurigan orinientos índices
> de moribundas alejandrías,
> de cuzcos moribundos.
>
>   Nudo alvino deshecho, una pierna por allí,
> más allá todavía la otra,
>   desgajadas,
>   péndulas.
> Deshecho nudo de lácteas glándulas
> de la sinamayera,
> bueno para alpacas brillantes,
> para abrigo de pluma inservible
> ¡más piernas los brazos que brazos!
>
>   Así envérase el fin, como todo,
> como polluelo adormido saltón
> de la hendida cáscara,
> a luz eternamente polla.
> Y así, desde el óvalo, con cuatros al hombro,
>   ya para qué tristura.
>
>   Las uñas aquellas dolían
> retesando los propios dedos hospicios.
> De entonces crecen ellas para adentro,
>   mueren para afuera,
>   y al medio ni van ni vienen,
>   ni van ni vienen.
>
>   Las unas. Apeona ardiente avestruz coja,
> desde perdidos sures,
> flecha hasta el estrecho ciego
>   de senos aunados.
>
>   Al calor de una punta
> de pobre sesgo ESFORZADO,
> la griega sota de oros tórnase
> morena sota de islas,
> cobriza sota de lagos
> en frente a moribunda alejandría,
> a cuzco moribundo.

Coming upon a mutilated body in the second stanza, the lyric voice incongruously sets about weighing up its usefulness. This calculated rethinking of what is ultimately a product fit for disposal seems to set the lyric on an unfeeling path of material practicality. But as often happens in a *Trilce* poem, the repressed knowledge of mutilation and pain resurfaces obliquely, through formal mirroring and thematic displacements. The poem's stanzas are themselves disarticulated, unconnected among themselves, disarranged on the page. And after some detours and imagistic meanderings, the speaker's thoughts are without warning brought back to a body—or to a body part, which is both in pain and inflicting pain: the nails, whose living section digs back into the fingers that bear them, exposing only their dead elements to the world.

But what is that world, and what does this have to do with representation? *Trilce* frequently presents an enclosed world of circuits or circulation, where the only possible movement is between fixed points of time or space, and that world is named with uncharacteristic specificity in this poem. The geographical positions that anchor its movement are given in the opening and closing stanzas—plural at first, later singular: "moribundas alejandrías" and "cuzcos moribundos." With one stroke Vallejo equates the centers of learning of two civilizations, the classical Western (Alexandria: first Egyptian, later Greek and finally Roman) and the pre-Columbian Incan (Cuzco); with another, he consigns both civilizations to eclipse, going to ground in a chariot that is rusting ("oriniento") and hardly a match for the previous poem's modern automobile, like the now-hobbled ostrich. In front of both, a strange declension of race is performed (from Greek to swarthy to coppery—although this is also literally a card trick), which seems to inscribe Latin America within a Spenglerian narrative of decline.

Nonetheless, this is not all simply ground-level movement of terrestrial bodies. "Auriga" is the term for a chariot but also the name of a constellation, the Charioteer, often taken as having the form of a shepherd with a goat flung over his shoulder; its original referent, the charioteer Auriga, was the accidental offspring of the crippled master craftsman Hephaestus and Mother Earth. Is it possible, then, that we are witnessing not a disarticulated reading of a dying global (or Western) landscape but an unlocatable reading of the night sky through the conventional matrices of astrology?[4] Once we notice this—and the peculiar shape of the poem, whose indents anticipate the constellated forms of concrete poetry—we begin to suspect that the ostrich is only lame by proximity to Hephaestus and that the "lacteal glands" are milky because they share space with the Milky Way. In other words, objects are beginning to pick up their neighbor's meanings, not making sense on their own. This kind of migration of meanings between distinct signs, or contamination by contiguity, is intrinsic to *Trilce*'s referential difficulty.

None of this interpretive work is made any easier by the fact that the poet, here as in other poems, suggests that he is laying literal or figurative threads for us to follow—threads that frequently turn into traps, but which sometimes allow us to stitch together a meaning. Threads in this poem turn from harnesses or leashes into ribbons and blood ties, but their knots are slashed, and they devolve only into the image of a broken body. The possibility of tying that body back together by sewing its material into a coat once again rescues the idea of threading, in an image that equates meaning-making with sewing—and which, as I will argue, is central to *Trilce*'s conception of female labor.

Yet certain suggestions and connections are beginning to come to the fore: the dying light of stars, the traces of dead civilizations, the dead nails that go on living inward. If we shift our perspective—recognizing that the poem is precisely concerned with shifting perspectives—we can start to think of those nails not as unexplained but as *explanatory,* not part of the poem's content but part of its internal technique, a body part worked into the poem's figurative surface in a way that recalls Picasso and Braque's early collages—or their analytic cubist paintings, which often included trompe l'oeil wall nails, in a trick going back to Baroque illusionism. Viewed from this position, the speaker seems to be using his index finger to trace the lines of the constellation, drawing connections between their dead points of light. And in explaining the contours of the constellation, it is not so much his skepticism about its usefulness as a figure that gets in the way but rather his own body: his attention falls back on his own fingers, with their aching nails.[5]

The figurative is here being elbowed aside by the literal, the metaphorical by the immediately material. Like Rilke's Horseman poem in the *Sonnets to Orpheus* (also published in 1922 and focused on a similar-looking constellation), Vallejo questions the satisfactoriness of a pattern imposed on the night sky; but unlike Rilke, he is less interested in demystifying the interpretive matrixes we impose on natural elements than in materializing events and our approach to them.[6] The act of reading presented in this poem, rather than seeing through signs, gets stuck at the horizons of the body. That body's intransigent materiality becomes at once the vehicle for reading and meaning and an obstacle to both; a trap for speaker and reader, but also an opening onto other worlds. Figurations, this poetry insists, are always caught in a loop from body to body.

I would suggest that Vallejo is here foregrounding the lyric propensity to map human and animal figures and affects onto external objects, but also the more basic tendency of our own bodies to block understanding—not simply by generating those metaphors, but literally by getting in the way. The body that appears in these poems—which is often caught in the act of producing the poems—is relentlessly material, with physical demands and desires. Its attention—its ability to keep its mind on the lyric—gets interrupted by hunger, mood swings, pain, and pleasure, which sometimes suspend the ability to produce poetry and sometimes radically expand its scope. The poetry of *Trilce* never lets us forget that someone is making it, that it is the product of labor and strain, which is not just poetic or cerebral but also physical—and the image projected is far less sanitized than we might expect; it reinstalls the body in the lyric, when the body, according to Barthes, is usually "what is lost in transcription" (*Grain* 5). That productive body's running commentary on its own activities, frustrations, and successes, stops the machine of production, freezing the speaking body and voice in a significant gesture. This procedure resonates with Benjamin's comments on the use of gesture in Brecht's theater ("Author" 768–82):

> The interruption of the action, which inspired Brecht to call his theatre "epic," constantly goes against the public's theatrical illusion. . . . The discovery of situations is accomplished by means of the interruption of the action. . . . In the midst of the action, it brings it to a stop, and thus obliges the spectator to take a position toward the action, obliges the actor to adopt an attitude toward his role.

Vallejo's self-interruptions have a threefold function. Their jolting between levels stops the reader from seamless reception of the poetry, pulling her up short and forcing her to focus on the very production of this poetry, and on her own role (physical, intellectual) in sense-making. They also ironize the poet's relation to his work, incorporating his running commentary and corrections. Finally, they insistently reveal the body behind the poetry's production, engaged in carousing, playing, conducting experiments, eating, drinking, defecating, and making love, but not explicitly starting to sing until the final poem. They thus continually direct our attention to the labor behind that poetry, to its physical costs and gains. Unlike Rilke, who notoriously and willfully subordinates life's work to art (whether in his poems or in his numerous confessional statements), Vallejo in *Trilce* insistently brings life to the foreground, folding art into its many activities. Everything in this poetry is figured as being at work, if not always working; there are numerous instances of attempts and failures in the collection, which again forms a contrast to Rilke's satisfaction with art's compensatory gestures, its ability to create convincing images. But the interests of the two poets significantly converge around the figure of sculpture, which for Rilke gave an example of how to work (through his contact with Rodin before composing his "thing-poems") and which for Vallejo serves as a way to articulate the connections and struggles between bodies and what surrounds them—whether it be the material that must be sloughed off for a sculptural body to take shape, as in Richard Poirier's reading of Michelangelo's process, or the emptiness into which it emerges.[7] Vallejo recasts sculpture as a site for thinking through relations between matter and lack, metaphor and metonym, but also for reconsidering the forms of labor—poetic and otherwise—that go into its making.

This is most explicit in *Trilce* XXXVI, which rewrites Darío's 1896 "Yo persigo una forma . . . " (I am chasing a form . . .); both poems take as their object the Venus de Milo. In Darío's *modernista* rendering, the statue's lack of arms plays into the continual postponement of meaning, making possible the high-minded symbolist erasure of the material body (as the statue inevitably resists the poet's embrace). In Vallejo's poem, on the other hand, the lyric speaker does his best to make Venus's lack the image of a new plenitude, but he cannot avoid his own body's attempt to supplement her missing parts—while realizing that her mutilated form points to the imperfect perfection of his own:

> Tal siento ahora al meñique
> demás en la siniestra. Lo veo y creo
> no debe serme, o por lo menos que está
> en sitio donde no debe.

> *So now I feel my little finger*
> *[too much] on the left. I see it and think*
> *it shouldn't be me, or at least that it's*
> *in a place where it shouldn't.*

While recasting his own body as excessive, Vallejo focuses on the ways in which one of the statue's missing arms tries to elbow itself into existence alongside the world's moving material facts ("verdeantes guijarros gagos"; greening stuttering pebbles). But Venus de Milo's fragmentation, more crucially, engenders a new relationship between body and world: instead of either excessive bodily integrity or a facile complementarity between figure and environment, what the poem posits is a productive asymmetry, where things—objects, bodies, experiences—no longer balance one another in apposition or cut themselves off from each other but rather bleed together, continue and extend one another, even—or especially—if their interaction is based on a kind of lack. "Hembra se continúa el macho, a raíz de probables senos, y a raíz / de cuanto no florece!" (Female is continued the male, on the basis / of probable breasts, and precisely / on the [root] of how much does not flower!).[8] If we initially suspect that this logic is based on an ideological gendering of bodies, the poem not only ironizes the procedure through the jutting-out of that little finger, but effectively overturns it by reducing gendered bodies to their missing parts, left prospective: breasts that are probable, flowers that stay in their roots, bodies that refuse to develop as expected. Moreover, this poem critically problematizes the notion of gendered labor that crops up repeatedly through the collection: female associations with sewing; male connections to maritime and agricultural forms of work. Venus de Milo, instead, is androgynously cast as a "laceadora de inminencias," lassoing and tying meaning together, in an image that conjoins stereotyped men's and women's labor.

Poetic images in *Trilce,* as these examples suggest, are composed of both absolutely concrete bodies and their metaphorical projections; they are made up of their own material but also of what they are not, of the spaces or objects or histories that surround them. In carrying the traces of other bodies, other images, and of their own evacuated by-products, they flicker between presence and absence, incorporation and evacuation. This point will persist through Vallejo's Paris chronicles: looking at Leonardo's painting of John the Baptist, for example, he comments (*ACC* 303–4):

> Mirad el brazo izquierdo. Cómo se esconde tras del otro y cómo se obstina en disolverse en el tórax y tan sutil y aladamente, hasta el punto de no hacerse echar de menos. Dentro de la impresión que da el conjunto del cuerpo, ese brazo del corazón está como si no estuviese. . . . [S]e oculta y se niega y defiende su viva desnudez. En tanto el brazo diestro, dueño de todo el cuerpo, desafía cara a cara al deseo, he aquí que el izquierdo huye, se escuda, resiste, repele el supremo contacto.

> *Look at the left arm. See how it hides behind the other, how determined it is to dissolve into the thorax, but so subtly and fleetingly that it is barely missed. Within the impression of wholeness that this body gives, that heart-sided arm is there as though it weren't. . . . It hides itself, denies itself, defends its vivid nakedness. While the right arm, master of the whole body, stares down desire, the left escapes, shields itself, resists and repels the supreme contact.*

Presence is here recast as a provocative absence. We might draw a connection with Rilke's "Archaic Torso of Apollo," in which an excess of
figuration conceals and reveals what is missing, the sculpture's head;
this head is, paradoxically, the most direct and effective part, exhorting
the observer to "change your life." But in Vallejo's reading, the figure is
what resists touch; that part of the body which should touch withholds
itself. And that seems to be precisely what touches us.

THE BODY IN PIECES

The fragmentation of the human body that we will see throughout
Trilce can be interpreted more broadly as an attempt to dismantle facile
images of matter and bodies, resisting their packaging for circulation
and consumption. In the local context, Vallejo's target may have been
the temptation to supplement political and economic inequities and im-
balances with a compensatory cultural image of wholeness, in an implicit dialogue with Romantic models. In his 1916 university thesis, "El
romanticismo en la poesía castellana," Vallejo had laid the ground for
thinking through the question of the lyric's relationship to place and history, concluding—in an evident debt to Taine and the positivist modes
of thinking dominant in early-twentieth-century Latin America—that
the poet's productions were entirely conditioned by race, milieu, and
moment.[9] Yet even in his earliest pedagogical poems, as I noted in chapter 1, Vallejo focused on demystifying Romanticism's aesthetic mirroring between bodies and landscapes by exposing the scientific bases of
natural (animal, vegetable, and mineral) behavior.

By the time he arrives at Trilce, the Romantic ideal of vocative and
physical fusion between lyric subject and landscape—central to the Latin
American avant-garde's aesthetic of representation, as Vicky Unruh has
argued (27)—is overthrown by the manic and seemingly arbitrary collision and fusion of bodies and their environments in his poetry. Contrary
to Latin American fantasies of mimetic lyric speech, from Andrés Bello's
nineteenth-century neoclassicism to Pablo Neruda's twentieth-century
neo-Romanticism, Trilce's voices neither fully articulate a location nor
incarnate an identity but rather propose a temporalized, partial, and contingent relationship to place and the lyric speaker's position within it. In
other words, they shed light on the ways in which bodies, landscapes,
objects, memories, and desires momentarily bear on and transform one
another, resulting in a poetry that focuses on malleability, mobility, and
mutation rather than static mimesis or stable articulation.[10]

Vallejo's procedure here also carries a clear debt to the Baroque poetry he had devoured—and occasionally imitated—as a university student, with its extreme violence done to the human form. His particular debt is to the seventeenth-century Spanish poet Francisco de Quevedo, although *Trilce* drags Quevedo's conceptual, metaphysical violence back into the realm of the unremittingly physical, insisting on the concrete nature of experience, on its processing by a body that often misses its meaning. All of the referents in *Trilce* that can be broken up into constituent parts (bodies, landscapes, time, objects, memories, voices) *are* broken up into those parts. And when put back together in the space of the poem, they tend to get jumbled up with the parts of their neighboring objects, with the result that bodies are mixed with landscapes, time and space take on human attributes, and limbs are grafted onto natural elements.[11]

This commitment to fragmentation evidently resonates with contemporaneous experiments by the European avant-gardes, and like those experiments, it presents numerous barriers to interpretation. As Benjamin, Bürger, Nochlin, Perloff, and others have argued, the fragment becomes the off-center centerpiece of avant-garde art, a part that resists easy integration with the parts that surround it to compose a totality, and this poses a problem for any—however residual—New Critical model of reading poetry as the sum of its parts. As Bürger puts it:

> The [classicist] organic work intends the impression of wholeness; its individual elements have significance only as they relate to the whole, and they always point to the work as a whole as they are perceived individually. In the avant-gardiste work, the individual elements have a much higher degree of autonomy and can therefore also be read and interpreted individually or in groups without its being necessary to grasp the work as a whole. (72)

Yet the oddness of Vallejo's procedure in *Trilce* is not simply the isolation of parts, but their unusual entanglement with other elements around them—as in the case of the Charioteer poem—where objects, through a kind of friction, take on their neighbor's attributes. Part of the problem with dissecting *Trilce* in general is that as soon as we isolate a fragment—such as a body part—and try to pull it out of its context, it brings any number of other fragments along with it; and within the poems, no sooner does something come into view than it disappears or transforms into something else. With this in mind, we should insert a caution by another body-oriented writer:

> I began writing this book by trying to consider the materiality of the body

only to find that the thought of materiality invariably moved me into other domains. I tried to discipline myself to stay on the subject, but found that I could not fix bodies as simple objects of thought. Not only did bodies tend to indicate a world beyond themselves, but this movement beyond their own boundaries, a movement of boundary itself, appeared to be quite central to what bodies "are." I kept losing track of the subject, I proved resistant to discipline. Inevitably, I began to consider that perhaps this resistance to fixing the subject was essential to the matter at hand. (Butler ix)

But we can still begin by separating things out somewhat. The poems of *Trilce* practically draw an anatomy of the human: they catalog hair, temples, eyelids, eyes, ears, noses, cheeks, dimples, lips, teeth, jaws, necks, napes, breasts, genitalia, flanks, hips, thighs, knees, shoulders, arms, elbows, wrists, fists, hands, feet, nails, fingers, toes. They also bring out into the open unseen body parts: skeletons, bones ("hasta el hueso!"; even the bone!) (XLIX), vertebrae, ribs, hearts, arteries, ovaries, tear ducts, alveoli, glands, membranes, tympanums, vocal chords. These body parts appear not as metaphors but as metonymies, and they are quickly tangled up in contiguities, caught up in intimate relations with one another ("la confluencia del soplo y del hueso", the confluence of breath and bone [LXII]; "dedos pancreáticos", pancreatic fingers [XXXV]), with the parts of another body ("puntas que se disputan / en la más torionda de las justas"; tips that contend / in the most rutty of jousts) (XXXVI), and with a myriad collection of other objects or spatiotemporal contexts rendered in fragmentary form ("el corazón un huevo en su momento, que se obstruye"; my heart / an egg at its moment, that gets blocked) (LXI). Connections between them may be metaphorical, as in this last example, or based entirely on relations of linguistic contiguity, for example "Calor. Ovario" (Heat. Ovary), two metonymies that seem to hide a symbolic third term "Calvario" (Calvary) in IV. These fragments bear upon one another or touch one another in different ways: they trace one another's outlines ("tus manos y mis manos, recíprocas se tienden / polos en guardia, practicando depresiones, / y sienes y costados"; reciprocal your hands and mine stretch forth / poles on guard, practicing depressions, / and temples and sides) (LXXI), they find themselves inevitably interlaced ("desde dónde los míos no son los tuyos"; from what point are mine not yours [my trans.]) (LXVIII), or they fail to connect with one another ("caras no saben de la cara, ni de la marcha a los encuentros"; faces do not know of the face, nor of the / walk to the rendezvous) (XVII). As they project themselves onto environments ("los dobles arcos de tu sangre"; under the double arches of your blood) (LXV) and give shape to its objects ("ciliado arrecife donde nací"; ciliate reef where I was born) (XLVII), they make metonymic metaphors, mapping themselves inside and outside and onto other things.[12]

And these bodies, appearing in pieces, do not appear out of context; alongside anatomy, *Trilce* is punctuated in places by place itself. This poetry is ineradicably situated, even if the context is frequently irretrievable, given in discrete parts that do not add up to much; the indeterminacy of this context points to a yielding resistance, a locatedness that usually marks not a determinative origin (as indigenist critics have tended to argue) but a tangential or tactile relation to place. Many different kinds of places are alluded to: prisons, hospitals, urban streets, the village home, often reduced to their constituent parts (a sickbed, a doorway, a table) with which the lyric subject has a physical relationship, knocking up against them when unable to use them comfortably.

These places are recognizable spaces in a poetic autobiography, remembered affectionately (those of family ritual, of clandestine meetings with a lover) or hailed disconsolately (the four walls of the cell), but they also extend beyond the speaker's immediate environment, situating him more radically in a landscape in which he has grown up and which he is now forced to grow out of. The Andes may be "inhumanable" (LIX), the valley of home may now be "sin altura madre, donde todo duerme horrible mediatinta, sin ríos frescos, sin entradas de amor" (without mother height, where everything sleeps a horrible halftone, without refreshing rivers, without beginnings of love) (LXIV), the hyperbolic "amazonas de lloro" (amazons of crying) (LXXI) may be a despairingly placed metaphor, but the Pacific remains "preñado de todos los posibles" (pregnant with all possibles) (LIX). The sea—as we see in the opening and closing poems—is still rife with potentiality, offering not just a locus of enunciation but also one of education: "Qué nos buscas, oh mar, con tus volúmenes / docentes!" (What do you seek in us, oh sea, with your docent / volumes!) (LXIX).[13] The sea is a space in which the lyric voice learns to express itself, from which it takes its objects, at the same time that it constitutes its very ground, even if seismically shaky. The relations that emerge between bodies and landscapes, based on the contact of parts rather than full immersion, point not to determinism or fusion but to friction and momentary contiguities; these relations, for this reason, tend to be grounded in the material senses of touch, smell, and taste much more than in the visuality that underwrites the European and Latin American avant-gardes alike.

This reading goes against the grain of more usual critical approaches to Vallejo, which stem from the earliest readings by Mariátegui and Orrego, who not only treated Vallejo's writing as the voice of a particular location, but presupposed a one-directional movement: from location to raced body to voice to poem. Vallejo's relation to both his body and his place of origin, as I am suggesting here, is much more fragmentary and volatile than this suggests; what he presents in the interplay between body and world is circulation, treatment, transformation. In other words, a two-directional, even three-step movement: the reception of the world by the body, its processing and reproduction back into the world. In this poetry, everything moves through the body. Naturally, what is produced in the process is some waste. But not all waste is waste; by-products, as Raymond Williams reminds us ("Ideas" 83), are themselves products, and may have their own distinct value.

LYRIC ACCOUNTS

What I am suggesting here is that, in the passage from *Los heraldos negros* to *Trilce*, Vallejo transforms the possibilities of lyric representation in the early period of the Latin American avant-gardes by bringing circulating symbols back to their material bases. But to raise the question of representation at all in the case of *Trilce* might seem like a dubious proposition: the assumption underlying most critical approaches is that this poetry refers to everything and nothing, undoing its own discourse while opening itself outward to an uncontrollable proliferation of meanings. Nonetheless, I will argue here that significant matters are repeatedly perceptible throughout the collection, be they bodies, landscapes, affectively charged objects, or places that populate the seventy-seven mini-narratives to which the lyric speaker is subjected. *Trilce,* in its insistent reference to visible and palpable parts of a body, of a landscape, of daily life at the crossroads of traditional structures and incipient modernization, seems to be undergirded by an aesthetics of referentiality or materiality. But at the same time, as I began to suggest in the previous chapter, both the matters of the poems and the languages that envelop them are subjected to extraordinary processes of fragmentation and transformation, which change both how the lyric means and why that might matter.

Trilce's dismantling and recasting of representation follows three distinct yet interwoven threads that I have been using to follow ostriches. The first involves an onslaught on symbolist modes of representation, rejecting conventional practices of metaphorical transubstantiation in favor of a metonymic poetics of contiguity, in which the figurative is frequently displaced by the literal. The second parries the demand that Latin American poetry yield up its local referents in an easily usable form, presenting instead a transformed poetics of the oblique, the mixed, and the fragmentary. The third undertakes the incorporation of waste, of absence, of nonvalue and negativity, into a lyrical rethinking of presence and potentiality. All three approaches involve techniques of fragmentation, of circulation and of transformation, and all three resist the temptation to mimic economic practices of producing raw materials for consumption abroad. Unruh has underlined the extent to which local articulations of postsymbolist poetics in the 1920s cleave much closer to straightforward representation than do contemporary experiments in Europe, which do not face the same imperative of self-figuration. Vallejo's poetry, however, responds in provocative and oblique ways to this imperative, sidestepping the direct presentation of local matter, insisting that matter only matters insofar as it is mediated.

We can begin to trace these questions by looking at the strange evolution of *Trilce*'s title. The neologism "Trilce" has been endlessly discussed, turned inside out, disassembled into its possible constituent parts, but it was in fact only the final term in a series of different proposed titles: *Féretros* (Coffins), *Scherzando* (a musical term for playfulness), *Solo de Aceros* (Soloing Steels). The collection actually went to press under the name *Cráneos de bronce* (Bronze Skulls), which marks the overthrow of a straightforward symbolist aesthetic in the first three titles—now lugubrious, now playful, now combative—in favor of a more directly representational mode. This momentary title marks the poems from the outset as anatomical, figuring them as the part of the body that houses thought, pointing to a symbolic interchange between representation and reflection, or incorporation and articulation. It also foregrounds the question of race: most immediately, with a benign reference to the highly developed pre-Columbian practice of trepanation, drilling into the skull for medical purposes.[14] But it more insidiously raises the specter of phrenology, used as a marker of racial determination—for example, in S. G. Morton's mid-nineteenth-century work on "crania americana," which included among its evidentiary objects a Peruvian skull. This is reinforced by the addition here of an adjectival phrase that explicitly points to race: "de bronce" (bronze).[15] Vallejo's initial intention was thus not just mimetic but Chocano-esque cultural or political representation. Imitating the author Anatole France, who had been awarded the Nobel Prize during *Trilce*'s composition, Vallejo signed the volume with the pseudonym "César Perú," underlining his "aspiration to be the national voice" (Franco, *Dialectics* 54). He surrendered this pseudonym and title only at the urging of friends, and it would literally cost him in terms of reprinting, making the final title— *Trilce,* purportedly deriving from "tres soles," the cost of that reprinting—an ironic comment, perhaps, on the sale of the heritage. This new title also foregrounds the cost *to* rather than compensation *of* the poet for his labor: it announces not what the book costs to consume but rather to produce—or in this case, *re*produce.

In his choice of this eventual title, Vallejo replaces loaded terms with a term that may ultimately signify nothing. At the same time, the rejection of symbolist multiplicity in the move to this singularly abstract title does not cancel out an implied plurality; the poems carry not titles but Roman numerals, suggesting that what is being presented is not a bounded set of indigenous archetypes (bronze skulls) but an open series of experiments whose end-point is arbitrary. The poems seem to follow no particular order; we can trace occasional continuities of tone, style, or theme from poem to poem, but these continuities are the exception, and they almost seem designed to give us a sense of false security.[16] And the collection itself rejects the impression that it possesses boundaries, is self-contained. The opening poem posits a preexisting noise, while the closing poem opens itself outward by prospecting for future poetry, calling for more use of its own vocal chords. As Ortega notes, the final poem, "en tanto poética, revierte todo el proceso de *Trilce* y lo muestra como un inicio, como una exploración previa" (as a statement of poetics, undoes the entire process of Trilce by showing it to be only a beginning, a prior exploration) (*Teoría* 70). Moreover, the inexplicable revisiting of the collection—or at least its title—in the 1923 poem "Trilce" suggests a regret at having stopped at seventy-seven poems, however mystically significant that number—if we are to believe certain critics—might be.[17]

In a forthcoming article on economic functions in *Trilce,* Justin Read argues that we need to stop interpreting those numbers mystically and begin to approach them materially, focusing on the rhetorical but also the real play—set up in poems such as XLVIII, "Tengo ahora 70 soles peruanos" (I now have 70 soles)—between Peruvian coins, the shifting metal standards to which they were set, and larger questions of circulation and exchange within imperial and mercantile systems—not to mention the poet's own awkward positioning vis-à-vis systems of producing meaning and wealth. This question can profitably be brought back to metaphor, to Vallejo's onslaught on symbolist modes of meaning. We can begin with Derrida's observation (after Mallarmé and Nietzsche) that metaphors not only pass into common circulation through the erasure of the original image that motivates them, but that coins themselves offer an insidious example of the way in which exchange value is passed off as use value—through the erasure of the image on their surface, and of the cost entailed in their production ("White Mythology" 216–19).[18] As Vallejo intimates, the only way to reanimate a figure honestly and productively is by making it once again concrete, literal. For this reason, metaphor is largely elbowed aside in *Trilce* by other techniques. When the body appears in *Trilce,* it does so resolutely as itself, and more often than not, as one of its constituent parts, such as the obstinate, out-of-place little finger of XXXVI.

This might suggest that what is at work in *Trilce* is not metaphor but metonymy, or at least synecdoche; but, as is common in much of the poetry of the period, parts here do not lead to wholes, do not reconstitute themselves in seamless ways. Instead, when bits of the body jut into the language of *Trilce* they do so alongside other fragments from a variety of different spheres, which also refuse to act as symbols; the sense is almost of an assembly of heterogeneous objects trying to resolve themselves into something but not ultimately adding up to anything. Take XVI with its "ceros a la izquierda" (zeros on the left). A zero's only hope of reference or density is to attach itself to a figure on the left, not through addition, subtraction, or multiplication, but through juxtaposition: a 1 and a 0 will always add up to 1, a 1 multiplied by 0 leads implacably to 0, but put them next to one another in the right order, and each is measurably increased, turning into something else (like metaphor) while still retaining their own materiality. But a zero on the left is a failed zero; or perhaps a successful one. A zero on the left is a presence that counts for nothing, but also an absence that obstinately affirms itself.

Trilce thus recurs to the most unpoetic of languages (mathematics) and what its practical application (economics) normatively excludes (negative quantities); its aim is to reorient a prior discourse whose symbols had been guaranteed by an economy based on exchange value (such as Darío's swan, or the proliferating jewels of *modernismo,* which can be traced back to the baubles brought in by Columbus).[19] A complex negotiation takes place in *Trilce* between numbers (written out in full or given as digits), letters (the Roman numerals that form the only titles of these poems), and the symbols that each designate—or fail to designate, whether because their meaning has been worn out, their supplies have been exhausted, or they are inscribed within an illegible system.[20] The worker (or poet, in this instance) is utterly separated from the source of wealth, yet he strives toward a connection with it by playing with its material icons (coins), even as he recognizes their abstractness (and his own lack of them).[21] Faced with his material poverty, his financial nonproductivity, and the uselessness of the images he can offer, the lyric speaker frequently projects numerical values onto economically nonproductive acts, rendering them as differently productive—for example, sex, involving a "multiplicando" and a "multiplicador"; or the dicotyledonous organism of *Trilce* V, with its "propensiones de trinidad" (propensities toward trinity). At certain moments the speaker resolves to gain control over numbers, to make them, for example, produce a third term (which we might of course find in the collection's very title, generated—as André Coyné suggested—from "triste" [sad] and "dulce" [sweet]).

Meanwhile, almost anything that can be calculated in the collection (times, coins, temperature, body parts, poems themselves) *is* calculated. But accounting is ultimately an activity not well suited to poetry, not working in favor of the subject: "haga la cuenta de mi vida / o haga la cuenta de no haber aún nacido, / no alcanzaré a librarme" (if I make the account of my life / or make the account of not having yet been born, / I will not manage to free myself; my trans.) (XXXIII). This gesture seems on the one hand to offer a sarcastic commentary on poetry's lack of substantive value, the unlikelihood that it will amount to anything. On the other, it spells out a different kind of poetics, one that will not be constrained by conventional lyric symbols, and which points to both the historical derivation of images and the cleaning up or wiping out of their original referents. *Trilce* will attempt to turn a negative into a positive without facilely canceling out histories of disuse or abuse.

The poems of *Trilce* offer a number of different modes of reconceptualizing value, extracting meaning from dispossession and loss. As the speaker of XLV proclaims, "si así diéramos las narices / en el absurdo, / nos cubriremos con el oro de no tener nada" (and if in this way we bang head-on / into the absurd, / we'll cover ourselves with the gold of having nothing). The nothingness frequently alluded to in the poetry is made into a positive quantity through typographical and syntactical sleights of hand. If in XLIX the lyric subject discovers that "en los bastidores donde nos vestimos / no hay, no Hay nadie" (offstage where we dress,

/ there's, there Is nobody), the capitalization of "Hay" breaks up the syntax to suggest that nobody in fact *is there,* that "Hay nadie"; while LVII's "nada alcanzó a ser libre" (nothing managed to be free) allows "nada" its realization.[22] And if this is a poetry corroded by absence and lack, it constantly proclaims various kinds of presence, as we can hear if we italicize the verbs in the following:

> Veis lo que *es* sin poder ser negado,
> veis lo que *tenemos* que aguantar,
> mal que nos pese. (LIII)

> *You see what there* is *which cannot be denied.*
> *You see what we* have *to put up with,*
> *however it weighs on us.* (My trans.)

Nonetheless, as the speaker acknowledges, these are still the equivalent of card tricks with symbols, syntax, and language (like bouncing coins off one another to create the illusion that they are multiplying); the poetry, in its recuperation of negativity, still needs to move beyond the magic tricks of metaphor. It does so first of all in its foregrounding of real instances of dispossession, loss, and pain—which cut away the referent that should generate symbolic correspondences—and by seeing what, if anything, can be generated from the negative.

In many respects, *Trilce* looks like a poetics of pain: an opening of the wound of or to experience and expression. Pain, in this poetry, is a referent that stops, resists, but also sometimes provokes expression; it can both cut the subject off from community (catapulted back to a paralyzing awareness of his own body) and open him up to one (through a wound but also through empathy).[23] Vallejo's own writing, in his own words, is concerned not with a Proustian "recherche . . . del tiempo perdido" but with the absolutely material quest for "el pan nuestro de cada día" (our daily bread) (CC 105), and this insistently bodily need is just one of the myriad forms that pain takes in his poetry, as Paoli notes (*Mapas* 11). Subjects and objects in *Trilce* are wracked by pain, subjected to all sorts of violence built upon on the "golpes en la vida" (blows in life) that opened Vallejo's first collection. Here the speaker not only struggles and sweats but also suffers from fierce headaches and earaches cast in relentlessly physical terms, going into the very ducts of the body: "rechinan dos carretas / contra los martillos / hasta los lagrimales trifurcas" (two carts grind against the hammers / down to the trifurca lachrymals). Pain marks moments of existence with blows (a "cabezazo brutal" [brutal headbutt] that comes out of nowhere in LIII), and it bubbles up in agitated language, sometimes appearing as a shout at the very surface of expression—in the "gritos" that occasionally punctuate the poetry—or in more subdued form, paradoxically bordering even on masochistic pleasure, as in the "ohs de ayes" of *Trilce* V.

There is a particularly concrete instance of suffering that wracks certain poems in *Trilce:* Vallejo's three-month prison term in 1920–21, an experience felt most strongly as the denial of "material, animal freedom." *Trilce* notoriously opens with a plea for "un poco más de consideración" (a little more consideration) while defecating in the prison yard—resonating clearly with Foucault's writings on prisons, which emphasize the example made of the prisoner's body, the absolute opening up of the insides ("abriéndonos cerrándonos los esternones"; opening / closing our breastbones) (L) in an utter excoriation of even the most incontrovertible physical privacy. And pain here is not only experienced internally, but is projected onto the surroundings against which the prisoner repeatedly comes up short. This fleshes out Foucault's insistence not merely on "the materiality of the body of the prisoner" but also on "the materiality of the body of the prison" (Butler 34); in XVIII, Vallejo rails against "los cuatro paredes de la celda . . . / que sin remedio dan al mismo número" (the four walls of the cell . . . / which inevitably add up to the same number), although he also makes the startlingly empathetic gesture of including the architecture of the prison in the misery undergone by its inmates: "En la celda, en lo sólido, también / se acurrucan los rincones" (In the cell, in what's solid, the / corners are huddling too) (LVIII). The prison offers no room for playful games with mathematics; no counting, no progression is possible in this space both outside and inside time, compounded by the warden's malevolent exploitation of regulated time: "Por un sistema de relojería, juega / el Viejo inminente, pitagórico! / a lo ancho de las aortas" (Through a clockwork system, the imminent, / Pythagorean! old man plays / widthwise in our aortas) (L).[24] Even outside the prison, suffering in *Trilce* runs like clockwork: it takes the banal shape of a "tedio enfrascado" (bottled tedium) buzzing "bajo el momento improducido y caña" (under the moment unproduced and cane) (XXIX); a "martes cenagoso" (swampy Tuesday) gets caught in tear ducts for six days so that a week cannot pass; and those weeks that do come to an end are brutally beheaded (LXVIII). The speaker is sufficiently conscious of misery's regularity to comment calmly, "Ha triunfado otro ay. La verdad está allí" (Another ay has triumphed. The truth is there) (LXXIII); but once our ears have been sensitized to the blows and cries that break through, it is impossible not to hear that "allí" as another "ay," welling up now to fill both space and time.

But pain, absence, loss, in more defiantly declarative moments, are turned into the ground for a new productivity: this dispossessed lyric subject, unburdening himself of lyric conventions, strives to accord himself and his activities a new value, pronouncing himself a "nuevo impar / potente de orfandad!" (new odd number / potent with orphanhood!) (XXXVI); the appeal "dame, aire manco, dame ir / galoneándome de ceros a la izquierda" (give me, armless air, give me leave / to galloon myself with zeros on the left) (XVI) mirrors the autonomous object of XXXVIII that "márchase ahora a formar las izquierdas, / los nuevos Menos" (now goes off to form lefts, / the new Minuses). This declaration of orphanhood is clearly tied to a poetics of the avant-garde, the gesture that declares the self as historical origin; as Rosalind Krauss writes, "More than a rejection or dissolution of the past, avant-garde originality is conceived as a literal origin, a beginning from ground zero, a birth" (157). Yet rather than beginning from zero, Vallejo positively incorporates the negative gesture of erasure, or rescues what is conventionally discounted, positioning himself on the wrong side of numerical accounting to offer an incalculably rich new beginning for the Latin American lyric.

LOCAL MATTERS

Vallejo's contemporary commentators insistently proclaimed that *Trilce* offered a new set of origins for both lyric and political discourse in Peru. But what is particularly curious about *Trilce*'s investment in fertile origins is that it tends to pull its power not from the given but from what is lost or rejected, deriving presence and promise from absence and degradation, placing waste at the center of a reflection on value, and shifting aesthetics away from considerations of both beauty and utility to focus on what it normally and normatively excludes. That waste is located both inside and outside bodies and landscapes, comprising both their substance and their context, and the significance it is accorded in this poetry shifts the discourse on both local politics and lyric matters as each one enters a new phase of modernization. Value here is time and again extracted from depleted or degenerated stocks (guano, worn-out language, an exhausted lyric tradition), as well as from what is conventionally cast as negative or valueless (by-products, popular language, difficult poetry), orienting them toward productivity in the very midst of exhaustion. *Trilce* thus proposes a peculiar poetics of matter that condenses a new kind of lyric investment in history, as well as an insistent inscription of history in the lyric.[25]

But to begin to account for *Trilce*'s formal mediation between poetry and history, we need to revisit the intensely charged issue of reference in 1920s Latin America. At the time of *Trilce*'s emergence, a chain of political and aesthetic discourses on the question of representation ran the length and breadth of the continent, and what is striking about many of these discourses is their concern with figuring the voice within a landscape, with articulating a region by reference to its constituent features—features that, moreover, are often given in strictly physical, often anthropomorphized terms. This practice itself had a history: Renaissance metropolitan cartography had a proclivity for corporeal mapping, inserting figures of a monarch, for example, into maps of Europe, or tracing the as yet incompletely anatomized Latin American continent as a monstrous giant resting its head on the Antarctic.[26] In the modern period, however, this figure came to be aggressively articulated by Latin American writers themselves; as Unruh notes, "calls for American cultural unity were often expressed through metaphors of an anatomically explicit body-continent with a spinal column and vascular system traversing the Andes and a speaking voice embodied in the new American intellectual or artist" (131). And calls for some such representation or referentiality echoed throughout the continent during the postindependence period. In Puerto Rico, Tomás Batista and Vicente Palés Matos issued a resoundingly synthetic call to Latin American poetic arms in their *Segundo manifiesto euforista* (Second Euphorist Manifesto) of 1923, insisting on a continental beauty conceived as *both* aesthetic and useful, natural and industrialized:

Levantemos poetas, levantemos sobre la grande ruina del pasado la inmensa mole de una nueva literatura cantadora de la belleza útil y exaltadora de nuestra América. . . . Pongamos nuestras estrofas en armonía con las cataratas del Niágara y que se abra la emoción como la boca del Orinoco. Pase el escalofrío de la cordillera andina en nuestros poemas, canten las locomotoras locas de vértigo que cruzan como relámpagos sobre las montañas y las lagunas, truenen las trucks, y salte, crudo y fuerte, el salitre de nuestras costas en las estrofas masculinas. . . . ¡Conquistemos la América! (Schwartz, 157)

Poets, let's raise up on the great ruins of the past the enormous mass of a new literature which will sing of useful beauty and will celebrate our America. . . . Let's put our stanzas in harmony with the cataracts of Niagara, and let their emotion open up like the mouth of the Orinoco. Let the shudder of the Andean range pass through our poems, let the madly vertiginous trains

sing as they cross our mountains and lakes like lightning, let the trucks thun-
der, and let the saltpeter of our coasts leap raw and strong in our masculine
stanzas. . . . Let's conquer America!

In Peru, the cultural and political touchstone for Vallejo's generation
was Manuel González Prada, who, in a 1886 talk in Lima's Athenaeum,
had called for the assumption or creation of a Latin Americanist discourse, with an important caveat:

> I no tomemos por americanismo la prolija enumeración de nuestra fauna i de
> nuestra flora o la minuciosa pintura de nuestros fenómenos meteorolójicos,
> en lenguaje saturado de provincialismos ociosos i rebuscados. La naciona-
> lidad del escritor se funda, no tanto en la copia fotográfica del escenario
> (casi el mismo en todas partes), como en la sincera espresión del yó i en la
> exacta figuración del medio social. Valmiki i Homero no valen porque hayan
> descrito amaneceres en el Ganjes o noches de luna en el Pireo, sino porque
> evocan dos civilizaciones muertas. (32)

> *And let's not accept as an Americanism the lengthy enumeration of our flora*
> *and fauna, or the meticulous description of our meteorological phenomena,*
> *in a language saturated with gratuitous and recherché provincialisms. The*
> *nationality of the writer is based not so much on a photographic copy of the*
> *landscape (almost the same everywhere) as on the sincere expression of the*
> *self and in the precise presentation of the social environment. Valmiki and*
> *Homer are valued not because they describe sunrise over on the Ganges or*
> *moonlit nights in Piraeus, but because they bring to life two dead civiliza-*
> *tions. (Free 25)*

In a bold gesture, Prada cuts through the reigning trope of Latin America's material specificity—presumed by others to be easily rendered or
exported in poetry, after the model set forth in Bello's 1826 *Silva a la*
agricultura de la zona tórrida—and calls for a different relationship
to matter, a more complex mimetic practice resting not so much on
representation as on transformative evocation. The matter of poetry, in
these terms, is the given but also the lost: as Prada intimates at a critical
juncture in Peruvian history—the immediate aftermath of defeat in the
War of the Pacific—national matter is shot through with both presence
and absence, and the process of articulation is charged with giving voice
not only to what *is* there but also and just as importantly to what is *no*
longer there, what subsists in ruins.

In this context, we can posit that *Trilce,* for all its referential in-
tractability, follows upon and opens itself up to the ongoing economic,
political, and artistic debate condensed in the following questions: what
constituted the significant matter of Latin America, and what was the

appropriate signifying mode of Latin American writing? On the one hand, as numerous postindependence theorists and writers argued, in economic terms Latin America figured as the locus and source of raw materials, extracted and exported to Europe with no visible benefit to the local economy; on the other hand, in cultural, political, and economic terms, the continent was forced to rely on imports from the metropolis.[27] Taking this a step further, the foreign exploitation of Latin American raw materials—the dependence on foreign markets that determined what materials were cultivated and prized, which has a cultural counterpart in the primitivist phase of the metropolitan avant-gardes—effectively invalidated that matter itself as locally valuable.[28] Vallejo himself points chiasmically to this aporia in cultural and political reality in chronicles from 1927 and 1933 respectively. The first bears witness to a concern with local raw materials themselves and the need for their exploitation:

> En cuanto a la materia prima, al tono intangible y sutil, que no reside en perspectivas ni teorías del espíritu creador, éste no existe en América. En América todas esas disciplinas, a causa justamente de ser importadas y practicadas por remedo, no logran ayudar a los escritores a revelarse y realizarse, pues ellas no responden a necesidades peculiares [de nuestra psicología y ambiente], ni han sido concebidas por impulso genuino y terráqueo de quienes las cultivan. (*ACC* I: 422–23)

> *As for the raw material, the intangible and subtle tone, which does not reside in the creative spirit's perspectives or theories—this does not exist in America. In America all these disciplines, being imported and practiced secondhand, do not help writers to reveal and realize themselves, because they do not respond to the particular needs [of our psychology and environment], nor have they been conceived by the genuine and terraqueous impulse of those who cultivate them.*

Six years later, Vallejo signals the obverse side of this process, acknowledging the exploitation of those local materials, but by foreign companies rather than local industry:

> La vida económica peruana descansa enteramente en la agricultura y en la minería. No existen por decirlo así, industrias de transformación y menos aún, por supuesto, industrias pesadas. Casi todas estas explotaciones pertenecen a empresas extranjeras cuya única actividad en el país, en cuanto fuente de trabajo y de riqueza, consiste en la pura y simple extracción del mineral y en su exportación en bruto al extranjero. (*ACC* II: 915)

> *Peru's economic life rests entirely on agriculture and mining. There are no transformational industries to speak of, and even less heavy industry. Al-*

most all explorations are carried out by foreign firms whose only activity in the country, as a source of work and wealth, consists in the pure and simple extraction of minerals and their bulk exportation overseas.

What was needed, then, was a homegrown language, technique, and method that could make use of a specific local material reality, and effectively make it matter. But this process evidently risked replicating the fate of Latin America's own raw materials: to simply give account of or render that matter threatened to turn it into a commodity (again, the lingering threat of the primitivist avant-gardes).

Vallejo's poetry therefore makes every effort to deny the kind of reading that would simply seek out the referent—that would assign Latin American poetry a meagerly referential role.[29] It does not attempt to produce new objects for circulation in the way that Huidobro does in his 1916 "Arte poética"—approaching the problem of original production virtually as a question of patent, and casting language as a singularly unproblematic vehicle for it:

Por qué cantáis la rosa, oh Poetas!
Hacedla florecer en el poema.

Why do you sing the rose, oh Poets!
Make it flower in the poem.

Nor does it share the transatlantic *ultraísta* movement's faith in tropes, placing metaphor at the center of the poetic enterprise for its Poundian power to "make it new," to create through unexpected juxtapositions, ranging from Baroque conceits to quasi-surrealist chance encounters. Vallejo was no stranger to the power of metaphor, having excelled at imitations of Spanish Golden Age poets in his youth; but figuration works very differently in *Trilce*. To take a limit case, we might point to the dearth of similes in this poetry, which is extremely significant if the simile is, as Derrida reminds us, a figure in order to signify figuration ("White Mythology" 210), and which installs itself resolutely as a productive avant-garde poetic principle in the opening line of Pablo Neruda's *Residencia en la tierra*: "Como cenizas, como mares poblándose" (Like ashes, like seas populating themselves). Instead Vallejo plays a game of hide-and-seek with the referent, often by hiding it in full view, or cramming it into a collection of other referents, so that the reader is not sure where to look, to begin to unpack each poem. What the poet offers instead are a welter of metonymies, of body parts and bits of life, which cannot be reassembled without doing violence to economies of experience and expression, but which can nonetheless be traced.

EVERYDAY AUTOBIOGRAPHY

It is surprising to discover that, for all its syntactical and referential fragmentations, its temporal, spatial, and tonal shifts, *Trilce* actually maps out a poetic autobiography, one composed of insistently material instances. The collection is strung together on a nonchronological thread of experiences, which run a gamut from the speaker's birth ("ciliado arrecife donde nací"; ciliate reef where I was born) (XLVII) to early childhood ("en pañales"; in diapers) (X) through games with brothers, sisters, cousins, and friends and adolescent/adult sexual encounters with a lover or alone; the speaker moves from the country to the city and enters the workplace ("Pero he venido de Trujillo a Lima. / Pero gano un sueldo de cinco soles"; But I have come from Trujillo to Lima. / But I earn a wage of five soles) (XIV), passes through sickness ("este dolor de cabeza"; this headache) (XLII) and health ("Me siento mejor. Sin fiebre, y ferviente"; I feel better. Without fever, and fervent) (XLII), spends some time in prison, loses a lover and a mother, and is everywhere accosted by death and desire.

Through all these moments, Vallejo points to the generative possibilities of the mundane, the opportunities it affords for knowledge, even when the very experience of living in a material present tense threatens to block access to meaningfulness—when bodily experience seemingly refuses to yield a higher meaning, or even any meaning at all. *Trilce* anchors even the most opaque moments in the everyday and the human. One of the areas in which this is mostly clearly manifested is the representation of the most humdrum or repetitive of experiences—eating, drinking, defecating, sex—which here are invested with extraordinary affect, with the potential to give sense to experience itself. Vallejo insists on those primary needs or elemental activities that tend to be left out of or disguised in poetry; in *Trilce,* they are made the cornerstone of poetic composition. What is more, they tie the speaker not merely to the production of poetry but also to social relations, to varying kinds of past, present, and prospective intimacy.

Eating, for example, becomes not just a figure for the ingestion of experience, but a ground for experience itself, and it allows for the treatment of a variety of forms of sociability (or solitude, in extreme cases); in its foregrounding of this basic bodily activity and its ramifications for the social, the poetry performs the same meditations that underwrite Derrida's insistence on "eating well" (*Points* 282). In *Trilce*, eating often takes place within a domestic setting that asserts both sustenance and community, as well as the comforts of habit or custom. It significantly reaches back to infancy: the subject's memory of childhood is first and foremost a memory of eating, which is sometimes cast as an artistically productive "almuerzo musical" (musical lunch) (LII) with brothers and sisters, or appears in games, as the children prepare "barcos [. . .] fletados de dulces para mañana" (boats [. . .] loaded with candy for tomorrow) (III). In infancy and maturity alike it is tied to the ethical question of community: the adult relives guilt over stealing another child's lunch food in the schoolyard (LVIII), which he answers by assuming responsibility for his cellmate's food, administered with his own spoon. Attempts to forge relations by sharing food are sometimes frustrated ("Se tomaría menos, siempre menos, / de lo que me tocase erogar"; One would take less, always less, than what I have to give [my trans.]) (LVIII), in an echo of the earlier poem "Ágape," where the speaker bewailed his unwilling isolation in similar terms: "En esta tarde todos, todos pasan / sin preguntarme ni pedirme nada" (On this afternoon everybody, everybody passes by / without inquiring or asking me for anything).

In the dystopian space of the prison the subject is monitored by the warden, who remains "a la pista de lo que hablo, / lo que como, lo que sueño" (on the trail of what I say, / what I eat, what I dream) (L), asserting vigilance over all levels of activity. And a different kind of vigilance is embodied in the figure of the mother, whose physical presence (or absence) permeates so many of these poems, and whose memory is a memory of provision and dinner-table sociability. Faced with her loss, the speaker is left unable to either speak or swallow, in a distraught lyric performance of Freud's observation that while digestion is a crucial stage in mourning, severe forms of melancholia are characterized by a refusal of nourishment, in an unconscious recognition that the object is no longer available to be devoured (*General* 171).

The poetry insistently traces a second elementary loss: that of the lover, who is also a figure for eating (although as a dinner-table companion more than as a maternal provider). Rather than being mournfully devoured, however, she can be catapulted back out in a different form, as a recovered memory which—because she (unlike the mother) is repeatable—turns a past loss into a possible future repetition. In XXXV the lover not only caters to memory, preparing "el plato que nos gustara ayer [. . .] pero con un poquito más de mostaza" (the dish that we liked yesterday [. . .] but with a bit more mustard), but offers her own body up as a more adult meal. Encounters with another body recur time and again in culinary terms—most playfully, as a "merienda suculenta de unidad" (succulent snack of unity) (LXXI)—in an ironic restatement of the blasphemous poems of *Los heraldos negros,* where the beloved's body stands in for Christ's. Herself consuming the lyric subject "en suculenta recepción" (in succulent reception) (IX), the lover supplements the missing mother, replacing breast milk with beer, but repeating the maternal imperative: "la cerveza lírica y nerviosa a la que celan sus dos pezones sin lúpulo, y que no se debe tomar mucho!" (the lyric and nervous beer / watched over by her two nipples without hops, / of which you shouldn't drink so much!) (XXXV). And it is not only characters who demand feeding in this poetry: numerous objects in *Trilce* are driven by a lack that is physiological, like the "tierno automóvil" (tender car) that races along driven by thirst, "móvil de sed" (XXX). Even the muse is cast as chewing ("a hablarme llegas masticando hielo"; to speak to me you arrive chewing ice) (XIX); the poet responds with a collective imperative calling for fierier sustenance: "mastiquemos brasas" (let's chew embers).[30]

We can link this to the broader Latin American avant-gardes, for whom eating is a figure for a relationship to an entire poetic tradition, in particular, that of the metropolis.[31] Where Darío had primarily been concerned with overcoming the stylistic imitation of Europe by creating an autochthonous poetic product, Vallejo's contemporaries adopted a more aggressive stance, using the figure of eating to posit an active aesthetics of consumption and production. The Argentinean Oliverio Girondo, for instance, inserted globally digestive metaphors in the letter-epigraph to his *Veinte poemas para ser leídos en el tranvía* (Twenty Poems to Be Read on a Tram, also 1922), proclaiming that

> en nuestra calidad de latinoamericanos, poseemos el mejor estómago del mundo, un estómago ecléctico, libérrimo, capaz de digerir, y de digerir bien, tanto unos arenques septentrionales o un kouskous oriental, como una becasina cocinada en la llama o uno de esos chorizos épicos de Castilla. (6)

> *We Latin Americans have the best stomach in the world: eclectic, free-willed, ready to digest anything (and digest it well), be it Northern herrings or an Eastern couscous, a flame-cooked snipe or one of those epic Castilian chorizos.*

The Brazilian *antropófagos* gleefully seized upon cannibalism as a cultural program, willfully resemanticizing the stereotype in order to seize power: the power to eat whatever one wanted, and thereafter to produce at whim and will. Closer to home, Orrego hailed the advances made by another Peruvian poet in practically identical terms:

> En Chocano el trópico se encuentra únicamente como alegoría, como enunciación verbal y epidérmica. En Alcides Spelucín se halla transfundido y simbolizado. Se diría, para emplear un símil fisiológico, que está 'digerido'. Es preciso insistir, sobre todo, en el significado de esta última palabra, porque es la que revela el efectivo y sutil americanismo del poeta. ("Palabras prologales" 28)

> *In Chocano the tropics appear only as allegory, a skin-deep verbal statement. In Alcides Spelucín they are transformed into symbol. We might say, to use a physiological term, that they have been "digested." We need to emphasize the meaning of this last word, because it points to the poet's effective and subtle Americanism.*

But all of these formulations stop at the moment of ingestion, not caring to examine what follows; the usually unsqueamish Batista and Palés Matos, for example, declared, "El poeta debe ser para la humanidad un tónico y no un laxante" (The poet should serve humanity as a tonic, not a laxative) ("Manifiesto euforista" [1922]; Schwartz 155). Vallejo's lyric speaker, in contrast, like his strict contemporary Leopold Bloom, delves deliberately into both ingestion and excretion ("has contado qué poros dan salida solamente, y cuáles dan entrada?"; Have you counted which pores solely allow exit, / and which ones allow entrance?) (XLIII) and demands a revaluation of the changed product: what has passed through the body and comes out differently, with a new value.

> Este cristal ha pasado de animal,
> y márchase ahora a formar las izquierdas,
> los nuevos Menos. (XXXVIII)

> *This crystal has passed from animal,*
> *and it's off now to form [the] lefts,*
> *the new Minuses.*

The body in *Trilce* demands to be treated in all its physical messiness and ingloriousness, but it also functions as a figure for a relation to both poetry and history; the collection willfully presents a variety of those elements that tend to get expelled—from the body, from the lyric, from history—out of a sense of decorum or a practice of sublimatory erasure. Just as he reveals absence within presence, Vallejo rescues loss, waste, what is generally not only ascribed no value but also assiduously hidden away; he confronts the regulation of the closed body (embodied in the figure of the prison warden who "quiere ya no haya adentros" [doesn't want any inwardness]) (L) by opening it outward, portraying not just what goes into the body but also what comes out of it. In the boldest of terms, *Trilce* overflows with bodily excretions, with blood, sweat, urine, semen, excrement. Sometimes the products of pain, they are more often released in the throes of pleasure, as in the case of the "hombre guillermosecundario" who "suda felicidad a chorros" (william-the-secondary man [who] sweats happiness in streams; my trans.) (XX), or the sun that "se derrama cauteloso en tu curiosidad" (spills out cautious in your curiosity; my trans.) (LXXI). These excretions, produced at the most unexpected moments, strike postures, respond defiantly to nonsense: "Absurdo, este exceso sólo ante ti se / suda de dorado placer" (Absurdity, only facing you does this ex- / cess sweat golden pleasure) (LXXIII). They are sometimes made coterminous with the production of the poem, for instance through a metaphor that points as much to autoeroticism and to the labor of giving birth (or midwifery) as to writing (XII):

Carilla en nudo, fabrida
cinco espinas por un lado
y cinco por el otro: Chit! Ya sale.

The knotted page, factures
five thorns on one side
and five on the other: Ssh! Here it comes.

In the face of other losses, what the speaker *has* to a certain degree comes out of his own body. At the same time, as he is constantly aware, that excreted matter has its own agency, its own natural power and laws, which means that he can never be fully in control of it, that "la creada voz" always "rebélase" (the created voice rebels) (V)—which we also hear as the opposite movement: "revélase" (reveals itself).

These poems, in short, insistently foreground the process by which things come out of the body and take on their own form and value. *Trilce* takes those elements that are produced by man as detritus and overturns their value, rewriting beauty in terms of what is conventionally proscribed. As Dominique Laporte notes:

The poet proposes himself as the ploughman of language, the cultivator who prunes language and transmutes it from "a savage place to a domesticated one", ridding it of waste, saving it from rot, giving it its weight in gold. . . . If "our language, once so scabrous and impolite," is to be "made elegant," cautions du Bellay, not only must it rid itself of muck and mud; its grammarians and writers must transform waste into a novel form of beauty." (9–10)

In *Trilce,* this rescuing of by-products is frequently accomplished through gestures of affection, a care for the other that is also a care for the self. A fellow inmate's daughter, for example, uses her misspelled "saliba" to both clean and dirty her shoe, either to prolong her father's labor or to extend an act of affection, and in so doing embarks on her own learning process; she wets her finger on a tongue "que empieza a deletrear / los enredos de enredos de los enredos" (which starts spelling / the tangles of the tangles of the tangles) (XX), physically trying to untangle knots of reason. Even the saliva that comes out of the subject accidentally in the same poem, in place of or alongside speech—"se me cae la baba" (My drool drips out; my trans.)—is not excised from the lyric arena as a grotesque by-product but is offered as evidence that "soy / una bella persona" (I am / a beautiful person), one who makes slips and slobbers and suffers from all manner of indignities that yet make up the subject. As Vallejo will later argue:

> Todo cuanto existe, digno es de entrar en la obra de arte, porque todo goza de la inmanente dignidad de la existencia. El arte no distingue cosa sucia o inferior. . . . Son muy ilustrativos, a este respecto, el arte y la literatura soviéticos. . . . En un cuadro de pintura, figura un obrero en actitud de defecar, sentado en un confortable *water-clos.* . . . No hay que confundir la naturalidad humana, libre y racional de la vida, con su desnaturalización infra-animal. (*ERC* 399–400)

> *Everything that exists is worthy of entering into the artwork, because everything enjoys the immanent dignity of existence. Art does not set aside what is dirty or base. . . . In this respect, Soviet art and literature are illuminating. . . . A certain painting shows a worker in the act of defecating, sitting in a comfortable water-closet. . . . There is no need to confuse human naturalness, free and rational, with its sub-animal denaturalization.*

Vallejo is of course in good company here. James Joyce's *Ulysses* (also 1922) placed Leopold Bloom squarely on the toilet, using excerpts from prize-winning stories in newspapers—that is, what is accorded official value—to wipe himself, while in *Finnegans Wake* (1939), the writer Shem makes "synthetic ink and sensitive paper for his own end out of his wit's waste," producing "from his unheavenly body a no uncertain quantity of obscene matter not protected by copriright in the United Stars of Ourania," with which he writes "over every square inch of the only foolscap available, his own body" (*FW* 185). The shift from modernismo to the avant-garde in Vallejo's writing looks like an actualization of Flaubert's embattled pronouncement: "I have always tried to live in an ivory tower, but a tide of shit is beating at its walls to undermine it" (200).

Instead of feeling besieged, Vallejo throws his arms open to what comes in from outside, or to what comes out from inside; in so doing, he echoes the ecstatic revolutionary sentiments of another Frenchman, this time a resolutely "excremental philosopher," as Breton put it.[32] In a series of texts from the 1920s and 1930s, Georges Bataille placed base matter at the center of his poetic-philosophic system, calling for an overturning of values through a focus on what gets hidden while helping beauty along:

> Risen from the stench of the manure pile—even though it seemed to have escaped it in a flight of angelic and lyrical purity—the flower seems to relapse abruptly into its original squalor: the most ideal is reduced to a wisp of aerial manure. . . . While the visible parts are nobly elevated, the ignoble and sticky roots wallow in the ground, loving rottenness just as leaves love light. (12)

Bataille's explicit focus is upon processes of metaphorical displacement, whereby "the sign of love is displaced from the pistil and stamens to the surrounding petals . . . because the human mind is accustomed to making such a displacement with regard to people" (11), which recalls Derrida's observations on metaphor and the cancellation on which it depends; but just as central to this process is what we might call metonymic erasure. Parts deemed unworthy of representation, in other words, tend to be excised: from poems, from the discourse of love, the "language of flowers." One of these parts, in Bataille's account, is the big toe, ignored despite its usefulness in helping man stand erect (22).

Critics have for the most part sidestepped various actual physical presences and tropes in Vallejo's poetry, almost entirely ignoring the enmeshment of matter—bodies, landscapes, and other natural and man-made objects—with the languages that saturate it and vice versa. One of the strangest examples of this is found in Antonio Cornejo Polar's *Escribir en el aire* (Writing in the Air), which delves into the political import of Vallejo's growing concern with orality from the 1919 *Los heraldos negros* onward. Discussing in detail the third poem from Vallejo's final collection, *España, aparta de mí este cáliz* (1938), which inscribes a misspelled message from a fallen soldier within the lettered space of the poem ("Viban los compañeros . . . Viban con esta b de buitre en las entrañas"; "Long lib my comrades . . . May they lib with this bumbling b in their insides" [my trans.]), Cornejo Polar convincingly makes this instance of oralized writing the cornerstone of Vallejo's poetics and politics (215–24). Nonetheless, there are two points to be made about this maneuver. First, this play with phonetics, which is already rampant in *Trilce,* is insistently linked with physicality, pointing to the inextricability of bodies and their awkward attempts at articulation: "buenos con b de baldío, / que insisten en salirle al pobre / por la culata de la v / dentilabial que vela en él" ("Buenos" with the b of barrens, / that keep backfiring for the poor guy, / through the dentilabial / v that keeps vigil in him) (LII). Second, by privileging orality, Cornejo Polar quite explicitly erases the place of the body in Vallejo's poetry. Where the cited poem contains the line "solía escribir con el dedo grande en el aire" (he used to write with his big finger/toe in the air), the title of the critical work is condensed to remove all reference to that indicative digit (whether a long finger or a Bataille-like big toe), presenting us instead with a disembodied "[escritura] en el aire" (writing in the air).

The erasure is especially ironic in light of a later anecdote recounted by the poet, hinging on the need (expressed as political) to name repressed matters explicitly:

El chico que dijo, señalando el sexo de su madre: mamá tienes pelo aquí. La madre le dio un manazo: ¡chut! Mozo liso. El chico vio, sin embargo, una cosa existente y su conocimiento fue roto y controvertido por su propia madre, cuya palabra le merecía toda fe. Aquí está la raíz de la farsa social y de los fracasos de la historia y de las luchas entre los hombres. (*Ensayos* 532)

A boy said, pointing to his mother's sex: mummy you have hair there. The mother gave him a slap: Shush! Bad boy. The boy, however, had seen something which existed, and his knowledge was broken and countered by his own mother, in whose word he had utter faith. This is the root of the social farce, and of the failures of history and of struggles between men.

To this end Vallejo repeatedly undertakes to reveal the repressed of poetry: the "guano" with which the collection opens, or the syncretic conceit of the closing poem, which connects composition not to inspiration or idealization but to foraging in muck or manure. The poems themselves, this suggests, may be pearls, but they are collected in (if not by) "el hocico mismo / de cada tempestad" (the very snout / of every storm) (LXXVII), and the beloved's teeth—the usual poetic referent behind the symbol of pearls—is replaced by the tusks of a pig: a very different sense of casting pearls before swine.[33]

Of course to bring degraded body parts, or base matter and the organs that produce it, into the light of literature was no easy matter;

even if, as Barthes wrote, "when written, shit does not have an odor" (*Sade* 137), for many of Vallejo's contemporaries, *Trilce* stank to high heaven. Even today, these elements of the poetry are often suppressed, along with many incredible moments of the body's excitement, where language begins to buzz. The bits of the body that Vallejo depicts evacuating, ejaculating, excreting, and enjoying come forward and outward humbly, asking politely and ardently to be recognized and touched while almost modestly withdrawing themselves. And they are treated with caution and care in the poetry; excrement is lovingly tended, guarded, evaluated, a "peso bruto" (brute weight) that asks to be handled gently so that its true value, its usefulness, might be revealed. *Trilce* practically puts a positive spin on Yeats's cry: "Love has pitched his mansion in the place of excrement" ("Crazy Jane Talks with the Bishop," 310).

Where European symbolists and Latin American modernistas had cast the poet as a sometimes besmirched, sometimes pristine swan, *Trilce* offers a startling new avian portrait of the artist: as the awkward ostrich that we met at the beginning of this chapter, but also as an "alcatraz" (of the pelican family). Unlike the ostrich, the alcatraz is valued not for its own body but for its by-product guano, kept in a state of maximum value by the conditions of the local environment (the state of near-constant drizzle off the Peruvian coast), before extraction for use at home and abroad. Vallejo lingers on this humble substance at two key moments in *Trilce,* making it stand as a figure for revalorization, for the extraction of the positive from what is conventionally cast as negative; in *Trilce,* both language and the body with its by-products are together resemanticized within a shifting national landscape. But guano is not only a present remnant; in the mid-nineteenth century, it was briefly the linchpin of the Peruvian economy, and it therefore marks a key moment in its social, cultural, and political history (Gootenberg; Skaggs; Cadava). So before a final burst of poetry, a little history.

GUANO ISLANDS

Alexander von Humboldt in 1806 was the first to report on a commodity with extraordinary fertilizing properties discovered on his Latin American travels, consisting of the dried excrement of seabirds, piled up on islands off the coast of southern Peru. Equally interested in its potential and in its history, Humboldt uncovered references to guano's pre-Columbian use in the Inca Garcilaso's writings, which confirmed his suppositions about its regenerative mineral content.[34] Nonetheless, he failed to interest scientists in Europe in its potential, and it was not until 1838—when two Peruvian businessmen sent samples to Liverpool—that its potential began to be seriously evaluated worldwide. Guano entered international markets at a roaring pace based largely on its promotion in agricultural journals, which set about evaluating the product scientifically in order to account for its beneficent powers; primers attested that guano's fertilizing properties resided in its mixture of nitrogen (to promote growth), phosphates (to stimulate the roots), and potassium (to guide to maturation). By the early 1880s, however, supplies were nearing exhaustion, and North American sellers began to offer synthetic fertilizers at a lower rate, which would gradually overwhelm the market. The heyday of the guano industry was over, but not before it had in some senses changed the face of Peru: laborers were ferried in from the Pacific Islands, China, and Hong Kong to work under conditions that few Peruvians—aside from conscripted prisoners—were willing or able to stomach. Workers (frequently captured into slavery) were paid appallingly low wages, made to subsist in nightmarish conditions: badly fed, trapped on offshore islands among unbearable odors exacerbated by heat, they developed severe respiratory and gastrointestinal conditions, often dying from injury or by suicide. It was over their dead bodies that the modern nation was built, and also lost.

Ironically, the brief boom in worldwide demand for such a base raw material had not managed to put the country on the global map as anything more than a trading label. As the German scholar E. W. Middendorff would acerbically comment, the raw material may have been found in Peru, but it was always understood that guano was a European discovery; that is, it only became valuable after being introduced into world markets by those Liverpool businessmen, ironically replicating the terms of the original "conquest" of Latin America (166). Nor were foreigners entirely to blame for this. The Peruvian government chose to option off selling rights to European and North American buyers in order to cover its foreign debts, which meant that the entirety of the guano revenues over a period of four decades flowed out of the country along with the product. Rather than being put into projects of national modernization, the revenue that remained in Peru stayed in the hands of its oligarchy, resulting in the formation of a capitalist bureaucracy with unbroken lines of continuity from the preceding feudal aristocracy. Moreover, the grounding of Peru's new wealth and (relative) global visibility in a waste product rather than in precious matter was an irony not lost on contemporary commentators. As Mariátegui noted, Peru's entrance into capitalist modernity involved a somewhat embarrassing inversion: whereas Spanish interest had been oriented toward her supplies of silver and gold, the countries with which Peru opened trade in the mid- to late nineteenth century were more interested in an animal by-product (*Siete ensayos* 22).

Vallejo's poetry is not the first instance of a cultural reclamation of this base raw material. In 1918, shortly after he had begun work on *Trilce,* and in the context of fraught nationwide elections, a debate re-ignited in the pages of one of Lima's main newspapers, *El Tiempo,* over the mishandled history of guano. The columnist Manuel Romero Ramírez chose to raise the specter of Peru's mismanaged guano deposits in order to attack the avant-garde writer Abraham Valdelomar (who was running for deputy of Ica), charging that an ancestor of the historian José de la Riva Agüero—for whom Valdelomar was at the time working directly—had shared blame for squandering the guano revenues (Sánchez, *Valdelomar* 391–92). Valdelomar would counter this blow obliquely in his 1919 campaign speech, proclaiming that "por mis labios habla una patria que se anuncia" (through my mouth a country is announcing itself), opposing the alleged loss with his own potential to regenerate the country. But this was not the first time he had chosen to equate himself with this formerly valuable national commodity. In September 1916—shortly after Vallejo's arrival in Lima—Valdelomar had used a review of José Antonio Lavalle y García's dry economic tract, *Las necesidades del guano en la agricultura nacional* (The Need for Guano in National Agriculture), to make some exorbitant claims on behalf of the newest literary generation, for which he was both spokesman and appointed leader. In Valdelomar's account, Manuel González Prada had in a private conversation hailed that new generation as "la más fuerte, fecunda, y valiosa de cuantas generaciones literarias haya tenido este pueblo" (the most potent, fertile, and valuable literary generation that this country has yet seen) (Sánchez 233)—in other words, as a new avatar of guano. National agriculture, that is, may have been forced to rely upon depleted and neglected supplies, but Peruvian literature could be reanimated by a generation aligning itself with a once invaluable national resource. What had been exhausted in reality—not to mention squandered in the service of foreign debt—could and would be figuratively recuperated in the realm of culture.

The appearance of guano in *Trilce* condenses a particular kind of investment in history and reveals a commitment to the question of representation, to the reinstallation of materialism and the recovery of repressed origins.[35] Guano can be read here as both completely material and completely metaphorical, as something that is both resolutely itself and potentially other, encouraging the production of other elements, sprouting from the soil in which it is invested. What is more, it is matter given over to a future, a prospective element that looks forward to realization, yet carries the traces of a decomposed past within its own materiality. It is also intimately bound up with the question of value, and connects with the trope of the body and its outpourings in *Trilce:* a country's economy is made dependent upon by-products, and its squandering of its resources is tantamount to a failure to capitalize on waste. Finally, *Trilce*'s foregrounding of guano dovetails with early-twentieth-century attempts to rationalize the body and maximize its productivity—attempts mapped onto materially rich landscapes in an era of increasingly industrialized agriculture and mining. As Tim Armstrong notes, "Waste-production is the point where the man-machine metaphor fails: where the body declares its irreducible presence, and linear time is replaced by the cyclic time of the body" (65). *Trilce* protests against the demand that bodies and landscapes render themselves in an efficient and timely fashion, and it reveals instead their excessive and wasteful by-products; it thereby resists the notion that poetry too easily yield up its meaning or referent, letting it surprise us with its productions.

I will close this chapter by looking at the ways in which guano appears in two poems in *Trilce,* suggesting that the peculiar difficulty of these poems points to a formal mediation between poetry and history, art and labor, matter and discourses, bodies and landscapes. Here is the first poem in which guano appears, which happens to be the opening poem of the collection:

Quién hace tanta bulla y ni deja
testar las islas que van quedando.

Un poco más de consideración
en cuanto será tarde, temprano,
y se aquilatará mejor
el guano, la simple calabrina tesórea
que brinda sin querer,
en el insular corazón,
salobre alcatraz, a cada hialóidea
 grupada.

Un poco más de consideración
y el mantillo líquido, seis de la tarde

DE LOS MÁS SOBERBIOS BEMOLES

Y la península párase
por la espalda, abozaleada, impertérrita
en la línea mortal del equilibrio.[36]

From its very opening lines, *Trilce* thrusts us into a double dynamic of production and evaluation.[37] The production is itself double: on the one hand, islands, which must be evaluated or perhaps evaluate themselves, bearing witness to their presence and their own value; on the other, a noise that cannot be precisely quantified, that is categorized as a din, and that seems to be getting in the way of the crucial evaluative process going on in the mini-narrative of the poem. These opening lines, then, offer up a commodity that will be put to use once its value has been articulated; but they set it against a socially useless noise which hinders that very articulation.

Who is producing or evaluating these various products in the first place? The rhetorical status of the opening question throws into crisis any attempt to posit the identity of the noise-maker, and those islands have a curious way of emerging: "van quedando" (lit., "they go staying"), shuttling back and forth between presence and absence, staying and leaving. The tension between the indeterminate identities of the producers is echoed in the tension between the products, revealed as dependent on one another in both helpful and hindering ways. The "bulla" (sonic and artificial) may get in the way of both the evaluation (social and intellectual) and the formation of those "islas" (material and natural), but these items or activities will begin to trespass into one another's territories. By the third stanza the noise will take on densely material form (DE LOS MÁS SOBERBIOS BEMOLES), while the poem insistently emphasizes that organic matter relies upon thought and reflection to acquire social as well as poetic value. The raw materials of sound and substance, in other words, need to be mediated.

We may be able to pronounce with some confidence that *Trilce* I is concerned with balance, with weighing and measuring, with extracting value from raw materials and from waste; nonetheless, its very language undercuts the process of evaluation, seeming to point in a variety of directions at once. We can look closely, for example, at the opening of the second stanza (repeated mantra-like at the beginning of the third): "un poco más de consideración." What kind of consideration is being called for, and by whom? Active, intellectual reflection on the part of the evaluating agent, devoted to the task of ascertaining value? Or passive, courteous inaction by the noise-maker, keeping quiet to allow work to be done? The focal point of all this consideration—guano—behaves in similarly ambiguous ways, mimicking those earlier islands, which were in some ways a metaphor for guano (not wanting to name the substance) and for which it serves as a metonym (being part of those islands). Vallejo's characteristic use of the indeterminately reflexive or pronominal "se" (i.e., either "it will be assayed" or "it will assay itself") further begs the question: will the guano evaluate itself, or does it require the work of an outside agent, one who knows something about these things and can keep his mind on the job? Moreover, the florid description of bird droppings as "la simple calabrina tesórea" installs bipolarity in the heart of the object: the guano is foul-smelling—paradoxically conveyed through a rather elegant archaic term ("calabrina")—but also invaluable, "tesórea." Both terms also contain elements that point in yet another direction: "calabrina" suggests corpses, underlining that guano is made up of dead matter that will be used to reanimate the soil; "tesórea" is built upon a suffix that recalls *estercórea* (excrement). The poem thus insists upon the presence of negativity, of waste, of decomposition, in a substance that is highly valued, that recycles by-products, and that is fundamental to composition as well as to present and future development.

Despite all these indeterminacies, the dynamic at work in the poem is quite clear, and is developed with increasing concentration over the course of the first three stanzas. Each one posits a three-way activity: between production, evaluation, and matter. The opening stanza casts all three in a symbiotic relationship, with some tension between them. The second stanza is divided between evaluation (lines 3–5) and production (lines 7–10), in an inverted mirroring of the dynamic of the opening, with guano (the object being both produced and evaluated) at their midpoint. When guano appears in line 6, it is immediately evaluated by apposition as "the simple fecapital ponk"; but rather than organize discourse, it produces a series of syntactic ruptures continuing into the next stanza, breaking down all the elements of the process (consideration, substance, noise)—almost as if the poem were digesting its contents.[38] Events or objects (consideration, guano, noise) are now not so much linked together as standing in apposition to one another, existing—like time, "seis de la tarde"—in pure substantiality.

In the final stanza, the carefully referential and historically significant content disappears into an untenable image, "the peninsula stands up / on the back" (my trans.), which welds together body and environment in an impossible position, in a precarious space. Yet there may in fact be a specific historical and geographical source for the image of islands turning into a peninsula, bodies blending into landscape. There are two islands directly off the coast of Lima near the port of Callao: Isla San Lorenzo, an important nineteenth-century source for guano, and its neighboring Isla el Fronton—popularly thought to resemble a recumbent man—on which a prison was opened in 1917; prisoners were free to roam the island from 6:00 A.M. to 6:00 P.M. In 1912 President Guillermo Billinghurst had explored plans for building a bridge to connect Isla San Lorenzo with Callao (*Caretas* 368, February 1968)—which would have turned the island into a peninsula, behind the other island's back.

Whether or not it builds on a specific historical reference, this closing figure—as in many of the poems of *Trilce*—seems to both depart from and capitalize upon the consideration and exposition of the foregoing lines. Where the dominant temporal mood of the poem had oscillated between a repetitive present (of production) and a prospective future (of evaluation) within a defined place, this final stanza turns that space itself into a subject, existing substantively, facing into an uncertain future. What is more, that subject has swallowed up the opposition: matter has not so much harnessed the noise as consumed it, and it now remains willfully mute.[39]

The elements in this poem behave like so many others in *Trilce*, being dynamic, transformative, referentially volatile: "bulla" is echoed by or turns into "BEMOLES"; islands are made up of or contain guano, which later becomes or is overlaid with a "mantillo líquido." The noise that earlier came from nowhere (or from an unspecified body) now seems to be coming from the peninsula, which acquires a muzzle and becomes mute, rendering the very question, perhaps, moot. Even frames of reference bleed into one another, such that the body and the landscape in which it is situated, and within which it produces and evaluates, blend together: first in the relatively unproblematic metaphor of the "insular corazón" (in which it is nonetheless unclear which term is literal, which figurative: the heart of the islands, or an isolated heart), then in the challenging image of the final stanza, "y la peninsula párase / por la espalda, impertérrita, abozaleada."[40] And yet they all inhabit a determined space, are all caught up in sound, and all inhabit a particular body, through which they circulate.

The latter term, of course, is not innocent: *Trilce*'s opening poem proposes a certain circulation or cycle of objects and activities, organized around parts of the body which depend upon one another in order for the whole organism to keep functioning. The "consideración" of the second stanza takes as its object something produced "en el insular corazón"; just as the natural and social are brought together, so too are heart and head, affect and intellect. But where does guano itself come from? The poem still has enough tact not to probe this explicitly, but the rectum here is not entirely hidden.[41] Guano may here be displaced to the bird's mouth (which "offers" it in a toast), but a knowledge of the actual process of its production brings us ineluctably back to a Bakhtinian material lower bodily stratum. Reason and emotion alike, these poems insistently remind us, are inextricably bound up with ingestion, digestion, and excretion.

Where the opening poem significantly gives guano as its explicit referent, organizing its images (for the most part) around the attributes of both guano and "bulla," *Trilce* XXV has an unsettlingly vanishing center, replaced with a sticky surface to which a variety of images and associations attach themselves.

> Alfan alfiles a adherirse
> a las junturas, al fondo, a los testuces,
> al sobrelecho de los numeradores a pie.
> Alfiles y cadillos de lupinas parvas.
>
> Al rebufar el socaire de cada carabela
> deshilada sin americanizar,
> ceden las estevas en espasmo de infortunio,
> con pulso párvulo mal habituado
> a sonarse en el dorso de la muñeca.
> Y la más aguda tiplisonancia
> se tonsura y apeálase, y largamente
> se ennazala hacia carámbanos
> de lástima infinita.
>
> Soberbios lomos resoplan
> al portar, pendientes de mustios petrales
> las escarapelas con sus siete colores
> bajo cero, desde las islas guaneras
> hasta las islas guaneras.
> Tal los escarzos a la intemperie de pobre
> fe.
> Tal el tiempo de las rondas. Tal el del rodeo
> para los planos futuros,
> cuando innánima grifalda relata sólo
> fallidas callandas cruzadas.
>
> Vienen entonces alfiles a adherirse
> hasta en las puertas falsas y en los borradores.

XXV's expository logic resembles that of the opening poem: it begins with an observed activity, then proceeds into a series of claims of causality or consequentiality, and concludes with a new situation ("vienen entonces"), which in this case does not differ markedly from the opening proposition. In other words, this poem does not quite get anywhere. This is evident not just in certain terms that crop up in the poem ("rondas," "rodeo"), but in its very reference to guano, once again filtered through the image of its site of production: "desde las islas guaneras hasta las islas guaneras." The poem's movement is between these two spaces, which appear to be identical, suggesting that Peruvian history and poetry in the postindependence period are stuck between those guano islands.[42]

This poem, rather than keeping its eye on its valuable matters, seems to be getting carried away by language: a proliferation of "alf" sounds loudly proclaims itself from the very beginning, related to the very notion of a beginning by reference to the first letter, "alpha."[43] And this is especially surprising and frustrating, as José Cerna Bazán notes, given the fact that it organizes itself around a clearly discernible historical referent: guano, its extraction and circulation (193–94). Yet the poem is so materially overcharged, so semantically overloaded, that it becomes difficult to see the referent, to discern the story it appears to be telling. In place of separate strands of meaning that might be translated (or at least disentangled) according to a symbolic pattern or code, what this poem offers us are knots of sense—"innumerables nudos / latientes de encrucijada" (innumerable knots / throbbing with crossroads), as LXVI puts it—tying up a whole welter of inherent or adherent meanings that knit together various lines of historical and contemporary reference. Nonetheless, as I hope will by now be clear, those threads are the same ones I have been chasing through this chapter: reflections on different kinds of work (maritime and agricultural labor, numerical accounting, storytelling); awkward and embarrassing physical habits; body parts, bits of space, their conjoined histories.[44]

With recourse to a dictionary—the first thing *Trilce*'s reader reaches for—a number of those specific conjunctions begin to become at least minimally intelligible. A primary nucleus introduces us to a new animal, one specifically brought to Latin America by Spanish colonizers: a horse.[45] We can find other animals and their parts or attributes here as well, either encrypted or openly named: a nape; dirty honeycombs; a falcon *(grifalda)*. There are also a number of references to country life: parts of plows *(estevas)*, practices of furrowing, even a word for small meal portions consumed in the course of agricultural work *(parvas)*. But the poem's landscape is also maritime, seen in the "caravelas" and their "socaires," and of course the "islas guaneras." Alongside all this taxing manual labor, there are numerous (more recondite) references to sewing: "cadillo" may also mean a cloth's outer threads; "deshilada" can suggest an unraveling that is either accidentally destructive or deliberate—letting tassels hang at the end of a cloth, or fraying the edges, leaving loose threads. This string of connotations is also military: "escarapelas," or insignias, are fastened to the saddle; "deshilada" can imply a procession, which loops back to and actualizes the military resonance of several terms already mentioned (e.g., *grifalda*'s close homonym, *grifalto,* meaning a culverin or medieval cannon). But what we seem to be witnessing in movement are not disciplined bodies; the bodies or bodily behaviors—usually embarrassing habits or wasteful activities—that keep obtruding into the space of the poem make its objects cartoonish as well as buffoonish. If we disentangle this suggestive series of metaphors—all involving labor, movement, evaluation, and power, often in the same moment—the poem's fabric appears at once densely interwoven, highly adorned, and also to be coming apart somewhat at the seams, not unlike Peru's economic, political, and cultural history.

Speaking of seams, it is significant that in a poem featuring frictional registers there should be a number of terms that relate directly to joints, to sutures, to dividing lines: those uncanny "alfiles" get in cracks, stick to "junturas" and even to the line (the "sobrelecho," or underside) dividing the numerator and denominator in a fraction. Other elements in the poem bear forcefully upon one another (the "escarapelas" rub against the horse that wears them on its saddle; the ship's sails puff up to harness the force of the oncoming wind); and sometimes the limit between things is actually a circuit that encloses emptiness, like the line that demarcates an empty mathematical set: "desde las islas guaneras hasta las islas guaneras," "rondas," "rodeo." In this labor of delimiting, the poem (or the agent apparently at work in it, commenting on events and surroundings) is concerned with outlining objects, activities, and values while also pointing to their merging, their trespassing into one another's areas. The ships are clearly going somewhere, and the term "carabelas" would seem to point to colonial ships, on a later-alluded-to crusade; guano is the beginning and end-point of the journey, which suggests that it is being harvested in an interminable historical enterprise. Agents are doing rounds, taking notes in "borradores," which, we must surmise, contain not sketches for poems or fictions but rather fractions: in other words, counting things up, ascertaining what is there, assessing its value. Perhaps those outmoded artillery pieces or guiding falcons are designed to help them in their activities, whether asserting force or mapping a route, and this mapping also involves storytelling, however muted: "innánima grifalda relata sólo fallidas callandas cruzadas." The undertaking, it would seem, is doomed from the start; "planes futuros" devolve into crusades that fail, that are not to be recounted but rather hushed up, rubbed out (in the Latinate form *callandas*). Nonetheless, even those failed missions and economic relations are recuperated by this poetry, are captured and rendered in their complicated movements. And in affording us glimpses of national and international socioeconomic activity in such a dense poem, Vallejo, I would suggest, is insisting on the need to take account of history, to work against its erasure: to reanimate it in self-consciously difficult poetry, which points to the inextricable imbrication of any number of activities, concerns, and objects that map out the coordinates of Peruvian history and literature in the postindependence period.

By referencing guano in an avant-garde collection often read as hermetically sealed, Vallejo formally works history into the lyric, exploiting poetry's relatively untapped potential for mining socioeconomic matter while refusing the possibility of facilely reflective writing. By intertwining the natural (guano) with the social (evaluation) in *Trilce*, Vallejo signals that natural products have as strong a historical charge as do man-made creations (e.g., poetry), and that the two can only be considered or evaluated in their entanglements. And while considering value, he further presses the question of historical residue, of a presence that bears the traces of a (mutilated) past. What is more, *Trilce* raises the issue of potential, of a present—even in the form of guano's absent presence—that still holds out some promise for a future. As Vallejo obliquely suggests in these often indeterminate poems, guano and its avatars can and must be resuscitated, evaluated, used to bring forth new potential, turning absence into presence, negatives into positives, and deriving a future (poetic, national, continental) from a fertile past and a fallow present. At stake is the possibility of reading and writing the modern nation.

CHAPTER 4

Lyric Technique, Aesthetic Politics

El fin del arte es elevar la vida, *acentuando* su naturaleza de eterno borrador. El arte descubre caminos, nunca metas. Encuentro aquí, en esta esencia horizontante del arte, toda una tienda de dilucidaciones estéticas que son *mías en mí*, según dijo Rubén Darío, y que algún día he de plantear en pocas pizarras, como explicación—si esto es posible—de mi obra poética en castellano.

—Vallejo, "Salon del otoño" (1924)

The aim of art is to elevate life, accentuating its character of eternal sketchpad. Art discovers paths, not goals. I find here, in this horizontalizing essence of art, a whole store of aesthetic dilucidations which are mine alone, as Rubén Darío once said, and which I will someday lay out on a few blackboards, as an explanation—if this is at all possible—of my poetic work in Spanish.[1]

The critic who might best have responded to Vallejo's provocations in *Los heraldos negros* and *Trilce*—José Carlos Mariátegui—missed the moment of their publication. Mariátegui spent the years 1919 through 1923 in de facto exile in Europe, where his acquaintance with the international avant-gardes set him thinking seriously about their import for Latin American cultural production. Being based in Italy, his closest encounters were with Futurism; what he appreciated in the movement—despite its unfortunate political alignment—was its attempt to jettison the classicism that had diverted attention from Italy's contemporary situation (*Artista* 56–59). The movement's name and artistic principles, in other words, hinted at ways to overcome the backward glance of nationalism, offering a direct contrast with the "pasadismo" reigning in his contemporary Peru, which kept the country mired in an attachment to its colonial past.[2] After his return from Europe in 1923, Mariátegui repeatedly insisted on the need to approach the question of tradition dialectically rather than conservatively, arguing that cultural and political traditions alike needed to submit themselves to constant self-modification. Mariátegui's onslaught on Peruvian traditionalism is woven into a broader attack on the propensity of all nations to rest on the laurels of their past rather than turn a clear eye on their present; his invocations of a contemporary indigenism, grounded in solidarity with the present-day population, throw out any lyrical nostalgia for the pre-Columbian moment, and they equally circumvent the temptation to negate the interim history of colonization.[3] By taking stock of the contemporary state of Peru, Mariátegui would strive to make it contemporaneous with the rest of the world, casting the entire Western panorama as undergoing a process of self-correction.[4]

But Mariátegui's reading of the European avant-gardes was aesthetic as well as political, and his focus turned repeatedly to the *form* of new works in a period cast as a transition. For a revolutionary period to produce finished works, Mariátegui suggested, was an ideological misstep; the most suggestive new modes—such as Dada—consisted of momentary outbursts which expressed an unfolding history in relatively unmediated form. Futurism as a model not only purged the present of any parasitical reliance on the past; its dramas or *sintesi* further resisted constructing a facile narrative of a process, offering instead a richer, rawer image of the present instant (*Artista* 187). Mariátegui's own arguments mimicked this form, in a series of rapidly successive essays in weekly newspaper columns. Those articles in turn enshrined the lyric as the genre best fitted to capture the contemporary; poetry, he suggested, would most effectively express the immediate instant, once it learned how to make its lyrical outbursts a revolutionary expression of the contemporary moment. In overlapping essays by Mariátegui and his interlocutors in 1920s debates over the avant-garde, what rises to the surface is the possibility of a poetic writing that would engage reflectively, critically, but also lyrically with the present. This is a remarkable attempt to elevate experimental poetry to the status of a critical nationalism.

But how could poetry express the present in a manner that would go beyond lyric solipsism? And how could it do so in a culture that was beginning to take its own representational mission so seriously? On his return to Peru from Europe in 1923—three months before Vallejo's departure for Paris, and apparently not crossing paths with him— Mariátegui found few echoes of the experimentation he had detected abroad; despite the burgeoning numbers of young poets beginning to publish in newly proliferating newspapers and cultural supplements, too few of them, he argued, were taking the risks necessary to bring the lyric up to date with contemporary reality both at home and in the European avant-gardes. And this, he suggested, was in large measure due to the solemn stance of the local cultural opposition. If experiments in Europe were committed to corrosive playfulness, the Peruvian avant-gardes had fallen into the trap of playing the game according to the rules laid down by the establishment, insisting on lines of continuity with the past rather than throwing themselves wholeheartedly into a quest for the new. Conservatives and revolutionaries alike, as Prada had noted a generation earlier, were luxuriating in national nostalgia rather than gambling on the future. As Mariátegui declared polemically when judging a poetry competition in which he found few points of combustion, "No nos faltan nuevos poetas. Nos falta, más bien, nueva poesía" (We do not lack new poets. What we need, however, is new poetry) (*Peruanicemos* 16).

A further anxiety, however, resided in the fact that poetry was still seen as an unproductive activity, a pastime, opposed to the metaphorically muscular activism of the new journalistic prose. Mariátegui himself seemed to abandon his own directly literary activities in the 1920s as he concentrated on various critical and political projects, which included the establishment of journals and activist groups and the production of a literary history of Peru. In 1927, however, he revealed that he had been working "en mis horas de recreo" (in my leisure hours) on a theory of three modes of contemporary poetry: "épica revolucionaria, disparate absoluto, lirismo puro" (revolutionary epic, absolute nonsense, pure lyricism), epitomized in the Russian Sergei Essenin, the Peruvian Martín Adán, and the German Rainer Maria Rilke (*Artista* 123–25). The death of Rilke, for Mariátegui, marked the demise of the pure lyric, clearing a path for the emergence of a new Romanticism in which modern landscapes were urban, not bucolic, and which abandoned the cult of the self and opened itself to registering the new. The poet was no longer the vessel in which beauty slowly sediments; in the new contemporary context,

> el poeta sumo no es sólo el que, quintaesenciados, guarda sus recuerdos, convierte lo individual en universal. Es también, y ante todo, el que recoge

un minuto, por un golpe milagroso de intuición, la experiencia o la emoción del mundo. En los periodos tempestuosos, es la antena en la que se condensa toda la electricidad de una atmósfera henchida. (125)

the supreme poet is no longer solely the one who preserves his memories in quintessential form, who turns the individual into the universal. He is also, and above all, the person who seizes in a single moment, through a miraculous stroke of intuition, the experience or emotion of the world. In stormy periods, he is the antenna that channels all the electricity of a swollen atmosphere.

One of the immediate results of Mariátegui's call was the emergence of a generation of indigenist avant-garde poets, who in their most inspired moments harnessed the energies of a projected technological modernity for meditations on local reality.[5]

INDIGENISM, THE AVANT-GARDE, AND POLITICS

It is somewhat ironic, then, given his critical subtlety and his familiarity with the European avant-gardes, that Mariátegui should have been most responsible for a blinkered indigenist reading of Vallejo.[6] To explain this, we need to take a short biographical detour through both writers' trajectories in the 1920s, ending in a moment that sees Vallejo caught between indigenism and Marxism: a juncture that has structured bifurcating readings of Vallejo's poetry to date, which nonetheless tend to bypass their entanglements and his hesitancies and shifts with regard to either one.

Vallejo's first two collections of poetry, *Los heraldos negros* and *Trilce* had sunk almost without trace in Peru, after prompting some viciously mocking commentary. Partly to leave this bitter disappointment behind him and partly to elude a lingering arrest warrant that had already seen him serve jail time, Vallejo set off for Europe in 1923, practically passing Mariátegui on the high seas on the latter's return. Over the next two years Mariátegui would begin to disseminate his thoughts on the political and aesthetic dimensions of the European avant-gardes in newspaper articles in *Variedades* (collected in his 1925 *La escena contemporánea* [The Contemporary Scene]); at the same time, he set about bringing himself up to date on recent developments in Peru, taking over the column "Peruanicemos el Perú" (Let's Peruvianize Peru) in *Mundial*. Vallejo, meanwhile, was struggling to find a source of income in Europe; he continued to publish the occasional poem in magazines in Spain and in Peru, but no real option was left to him other than the journalism he had resisted in Lima. He wrote initially for *El Norte* in Trujillo, but eventually found a commission as Paris correspondent for the Lima-based *Mundial* and *Variedades,* and by mid-1926—when polemics over the avant-garde and indigenism were beginning to ignite at home—most Peruvian writers and intellectuals were referring to him as a foreign-based journalist rather than as their prized local poet. Vallejo and Mariátegui thus coincided in the pages of Peru's two most important newspapers in the mid-1920s: one of them having moved away from Peru and into international culture, the other bringing his knowledge of the international scene to bear on his readings of the local. Both of them, from distinct geographical positions, were keeping one eye on world culture and the other on Peru.

After producing several early articles on Peruvian writers and on Latin American cultural mediators in Paris, Vallejo increasingly trained his attention on the local French scene and the broader European avant-gardes. But in 1926 he turned back to writing directly about Latin America, with a screed against the paltry support for the local avant-gardes in his two-issue pamphlet *Favorables Paris Poema.* Accompanying it was his quickly notorious article "Poesía nueva" (*ACC* I: 300–301)—an attack on the poetry appearing in both Europe and Latin America which predicated its modernity solely on its incorporation of the semiotics of contemporary science and industry ("cinema, motor, caballos de fuerza, avión, radio, jazz-band, telegrafía sin hilos"; cinema, motor, horsepower, airplane, radio, jazz band, wireless telegraphy). Mariátegui was sufficiently impressed by the article to reprint it in the third issue of his journal *Amauta* in November 1926, adding his own piece, "Arte, revolución y decadencia" (Art, Revolution, and Decadence), as an appreciative response.

This was not Mariátegui's first response to Vallejo's writing. In a late 1925 article praising the Argentinean Oliverio Girondo for finding his way home via a cosmopolitan detour, Mariátegui hinted that a similar engagement with the international might teach other Latin Americans to appreciate their local writers; the local, in other words, became most fully visible through the lens of the global (*Peruanicemos* 78). And Mariátegui pressed further still: a postcolonial country, he suggested, reaches the stage of national articulation less through a reconnection with its past than through a critical engagement with the world, an opening to the outside which enlarges the frame in which a country can view itself and its culture. The stages of progression, in other words, ran from colonialism through cosmopolitanism to nationalism (72–79).

Mariátegui's example of a writer whom he had learned to read after and through his European readings was Vallejo—not, however, for the latter's parallels with the European avant-garde, but for the indigenous substratum of his poetry:

> Lo que más nos atrae, lo que más nos emociona tal vez en el poeta César Vallejo es la trama indígena, el fondo autóctono de su arte. Vallejo es muy nuestro, es muy indio. El hecho de que lo estimemos y lo comprendamos no es un producto del azar. No es tampoco una consecuencia exclusiva de su genio. Es más bien una prueba de que, por estos caminos cosmopolitas y ecuménicos, que tanto se nos reprochan, nos vamos acercando cada vez más a nosotros mismos. (79)

> *What most attracts us—what most moves us, perhaps—in the poet César Vallejo is the indigenous thread, the autochthonous grounding of his art. Vallejo is very much ours, very Indian. The fact that we appreciate him and understand him is not the result of chance. Nor is it simply a product of his genius. Rather, it is proof that, along these cosmopolitan and ecumenical routes for which we are so roundly criticized, we are coming ever closer to ourselves.*

Where Mariátegui celebrates other writers' cosmopolitanism as a momentary virtue and a route home, he presents the reader with a lacquered version of Vallejo's localism, which largely seals the direction of future readings. In part this was an attempt to pull Vallejo back from the too narrowly international path he seemed to be following while also raising his profile back in Lima.[7] Mariátegui's subsequent attempts to draw Vallejo into the 1927 indigenism polemic at home, however, met only with silence.[8] Vallejo's own articles from the period place him determinedly in the camp of the international avant-garde, showing more interest in Huidobro's 1925 disagreements with surrealism, in the 1926 French debate over pure poetry, and in a strangely one-sided dialogue with Jean Cocteau than in engaging seriously with experiments and emergent formations at home.

In 1926 Mariátegui set about formalizing his thoughts on Peruvian writing into a literary history, laid out in a series of twenty-one articles in *Mundial* on writers from postindependence to the present.[9] The culmination came in the form of two articles on Vallejo, whom he presented as Peru's most contemporary poet but also as its most *representative* writer. These articles place the accent firmly on Vallejo's incarnation of an autochthonous sensibility; the opening salvo declares, "Vallejo es el poeta de una estirpe, de una raza. En Vallejo se encuentra, por primera vez en nuestra literatura, sentimiento indígena virginalmente expresado" (Vallejo is the poet of a bloodline, of a race. In Vallejo we find, for the first time in our literature, the virginal expression of indigenous sentiment) (*Siete* 280). Mariátegui reads Vallejo's symbolism as an autochthonous reworking of European modes, casting the nostalgia he traces in both collections as a quintessentially *indigenous* mind-set, which filters elements of recent and contemporary European writing (from symbolism through expressionism and Dada to surrealism) (281). While he quotes several *Trilce* poems as evidence of this ubiquitous nostalgia, it is clearly *Los heraldos negros*—and then only in parts—which fits his indigenist premise. Indeed Mariátegui's interest lies so squarely in the first collection that he not only declares it "el orto de una nueva poesía en el Perú" (the dawn of a new poetry in Peru), but tellingly claims that "*Los heraldos negros* podía haber sido su obra única" (*The Black Heralds* might well have been his only work) (280). Significantly, the substratum of Vallejo's writing is taken as visible to his readers rather than to the poet himself: "Su autoctonismo no es deliberado. . . . Su poesía y su lenguaje emanan de su carne y su ánima. . . . El sentimiento indígena obra en su arte quizá sin que él lo sepa ni lo quiera" (His autochthonism is not deliberate. . . . His poetry and his language emanate from his body and his soul. . . . Indigenous sentiment is at work in his art even despite his knowledge or desire) (282).

The articles reached Vallejo—who sent a courteous response—in Paris, where he was himself pondering the question of unconscious production, most likely in response to the surrealist manifestos but now also with Mariátegui's reading of his own work on his mind. From 1926 to 1928 he published three separate yet formally similar articles circling around the topic: one focused on the avant-gardes ("Poesía nueva," 1926; *ACC* I: 300–301); the second focused on indigenism, composed a few months after reading Mariátegui's articles ("Los escollos de siempre," 1927; *ACC* I: 495–96); and the third, on socialism ("Ejecutoria del arte socialista," 1928; *ACC* II: 652–53). In each one, Vallejo makes an unconscious processing of knowledge and experience into the mainstay of writing—not in alignment with the surrealist model, however, nor with a deterministic version of indigenism which cast the poet as medium, but as a materially inflected mode of articulating history or historicity, filtered through bodily experience. Ethnicity, politics, and art, these articles suggest, involve an organic irradiation from a central core of sensibility which is nonetheless continually modified by changing experiences: the writer possesses a porous historical body, always open to change. Vallejo thus subtly reinflects Mariátegui's reading to connect his own work to broader panoramas and cultural questions of modernity and to allow for a necessary flexibility in self-positioning.[10]

LYRIC TECHNIQUE

Of the three topics, socialism posed the greatest challenge to the lyric, because it questioned its very reason for being, its excessive focus on individual subjectivity. As I discuss in the next two chapters, Vallejo stopped publishing poetry while in Paris, although he never ceased to write it, and it is tempting to assume that his encounter with Marxism prompted him—as it did so many others, including Marx, if we can allow the pleonasm—to abandon poetry in favor of direct political action and analytical prose writings. Yet Vallejo's engagement with Marxism paradoxically offered him a new way to conceptualize his work as a poet, and this reorientation, as we will see, takes place *through* rather than *in spite of* a critical disconnect between lyric poetry and politics.

When Vallejo arrived in Europe in 1923, he was leaving behind him the memory of the ridicule the collection had met with in Peru. His publication of the poem "Trilce" in Spain that same year—an opaque gloss on the collection—was perhaps a way to advertise the collection beyond the unappreciative bounds of his homeland, and to reiterate its value.[11] But a lingering doubt over the collection's merits flashes up at certain points in his later writings, in flippant comments about lines from his Peruvian poems finally finding a meaning in European reality. For example, "Escribí un verso en el cual crecía hierba. Unos años más tarde, en París, vi en una piedra del cementerio Montparnasse un adjetivo con hierba. Profecía de la poesía" (I wrote a line in which grass was growing. Several years later, in Paris, I saw on a stone in Montparnasse cemetery an adjective with grass in it. The prophecy of poetry) (*ERC* 529). Far from guaranteeing poetry's prophetic powers, this somewhat glib comment reduces the lyric to the level of parlor games or aesthetic trickery, with no real purchase on the present, no real way to shape the future, and, most important, no self-control.

This was an acute concern for Vallejo in the late 1920s. While sharpening his writing in newspaper articles in Paris, he managed to find a way to orient his prose in the direction of social critique, but he had not yet succeeded in hammering out either an aesthetic or a political statement on the modes of his own poetry. Flickering through various fragmentary comments from the 1920s is Vallejo's anxiety over being seen as an avant-garde writer erring on the side of aesthetics rather than politics. This anxiety was to some degree inflated: as Jean Franco notes, his failure to publish poetry while in Paris meant that he was known to most of his associates there as a political activist *(Crisis)*; even his widow confessed to some surprise on discovering how many poems he had been filing away in drawers through those years. But his profile in Peru—and Vallejo was acutely conscious of his reception on both sides of the Atlantic—was quite different, settling around the lingering discomfort over what were seen as the provocations of *Trilce*. In the mid-1920s Vallejo found himself, all of a sudden, being reclaimed and critiqued by two different camps at home, who were beginning to read his poetry in the context of overlapping debates on indigenism (the proper forms of local representation) and the avant-garde (negotiating between political and aesthetic commitment). The indigenists, represented most articulately by Mariátegui, tended to rescue his poetry (in particular, *Los heraldos negros*) as an emergent voice for a silent ethnic majority; the politicized avant-garde, by contrast, either attacked him as an anachronistic and Europeanizing dilettante, or accepted the revolutionary nature of his writing while underlining the linguistic excess that arguably undermined it (emblematized in *Trilce*).[12] Caught in the crossfire of these simultaneous polemics back in Peru, Vallejo began to reconsider his own writing, in the immediate context of intense debates in Europe over the convergences and disjunctions of aesthetics and politics.

The publication of the second edition of *Trilce* in Madrid in 1930 was therefore a mixed blessing. Although it promised to raise Vallejo's profile as a poet in Europe, it also erased the nine-year period since *Trilce*'s composition, which included what Vallejo saw as his political reeducation. This discomfort seems apparent in an interview he gave in Madrid in early 1931, which shows him determined to shrug off his connection to the modes of the earlier volume, to deny it any kind of seriousness. Asked by his interviewer for an explanation of the title, he dismissively replies, "*Trilce* no quiere decir nada. No se encontraba en mi afán ninguna palabra con dignidad de título y entonces la inventé: *Trilce. ¿No es una palabra hermosa?*" (*Trilce* doesn't mean anything. I couldn't find a single word worthy of the title so I made one up: *Trilce*. Isn't it a lovely word?) (*ACC* II: 884). His faint praise here for the beauty of an invented word has to be set against his statement elsewhere in the interview that his current obsession is "precision," the elimination of any extraneous words, "ya que no se puede renunciar a las palabras" (given that one cannot renounce words themselves). What Vallejo is renouncing here, I would suggest, is not lyric language *per se* but the "excessive" language of *Trilce*.[13]

From the mid-1920s onward, Vallejo would repeatedly announce his wish to move beyond style—to abandon his commitment to the *mot rare* in favor of a search for the *mot juste*, a word that would not simply be appropriate, but would be inscripted in the fight for social justice. But the republication of *Trilce* forcibly reattached him to the volume, and it must have prompted his sudden decision to try to salvage the earlier poetry by reading it through a Marxist lens.[14] He found a ready-made lens where we might least expect it: in Mariátegui's 1926 essay. What he retrieves from Mariátegui's reading of his poetry—significantly sidestepping that reading's indigenist thrust—is the assertion that "su técnica está en continua elaboración" (his technique is under constant elaboration) (*ERC* 467). Although the dialectical thrust of this is important, it is the question of conscious technique—which Vallejo pinpoints as a nexus between Marxism and the lyric—which will become a touchstone of his thought on poetry from this moment onward.[15] In this same piece, he fleshes out Mariátegui's comment with the addendum "como la técnica industrial y la racionalización de Ford" (as in industrial technique and Fordist rationalization), understood not in their North American but their Soviet applications, which seemed to offer both a metaphor and a mode for suturing intellectual to manual labor.[16] It is no accident that, in the 1931 interview, he gave the title *Instituto Central de Trabajo* (Central Institute of Labor) for a volume of poetry he claimed to have in preparation.

Vallejo's new commitment to technique, understood in Leninist terms as the need for the worker—or writer—to be conscious of what and how he was producing, clearly inflects his agitated readings of several contemporary writers in the heated atmosphere of 1930. His particular targets in this respect are the surrealists, whom he pillories for their notions of lyric inspiration and practices of automatic writing—setting poets apart from the populace while abdicating any control over what they produced—and whom he criticizes for the anarchist bent of their socialism.[17] Yet this accent on technique runs strikingly counter to Vallejo's own firmly defended beliefs up to this juncture. Vallejo's journalism, as I discuss in chapter 5, repeatedly insists on the value of the amateur viewpoint, reserving its highest praise for those who act without being certain of the outcome, or even of their own motivation. In a series of chronicles from 1926 and 1927 he takes special issue with extremist positions on either the left or the right, staunchly defending the autonomy of art against the propagandizing programs of Haya de la Torre, Diego Rivera, and others. And Vallejo's 1928 articles, while drawing upon his new readings in Marxist theory, still reserve room for critiquing those he classifies as communism's "grammaticians"; moreover, these articles repeatedly align themselves with Trotsky against the more "bureaucratic" inclinations of Stalin.[18]

After his second trip to Russia in late 1929, however, Vallejo's writings begin to toe the party line to a remarkable degree. The language of his chronicles shifts from the lyrical-humanistic toward the rigorous terminology and logic of Marxist doctrine, and from this point on, we largely lose any trace in the prose of Vallejo's idiosyncratic voice and viewpoints. His claim, in his "reportage" on Russia, that he travels and writes as a free agent is hard to square with the doctrinaire tones and opinions expressed in his articles.[19] We should not underestimate the excruciating nature of this reorientation in Vallejo's writing, which follows significantly different paths in his poetry and prose. In a late 1925 chronicle—apparently written in response to the Chilean poet Vicente Huidobro's polemic with the surrealists, which critiqued Breton's 1924 emphasis on intuition over intelligence, Vallejo had made a definitive declaration:

> Ah, mi querido Vicente Huidobro, no he de transigir nunca con usted en la excesiva importancia que usted da a la inteligencia en la vida. Mis votos son siempre por la sensibilidad . . . como función más que psíquica, fisiológica. (*ACC* I: 180–83)

> *Ah, my dear Vicente Huidobro, I will never reconcile myself to the excessive importance you give to intelligence in life. My vote is always for sensibility . . . as a physiological more than a psychic function.*

This introduced a third term into the reason-unconscious binary: namely, sensibility, presented not as innate but as open to modification and training by external influences and experiences. A letter from late December 1928, written just before Vallejo signed the first statement of the Parisian cell of the Peruvian Socialist Party (founded by Mariátegui), reconciles this emphasis on sensibility with his new political leanings: "Voy sintiéndome revolucionario y revolucionario por experiencia vivida, más que por ideas aprendidas" (I am beginning to develop a revolutionary feeling, through my lived experience more than through any learned ideas) (*CC* 316). What Vallejo now begins to demand of himself and other poets in the exercise of the lyric is a full concordance between personal sensibility, poetic technique, and revolutionary commitment.

This alignment, however, was virtually impossible to achieve for those writers who had come of age before the revolution, as Vallejo suggested in his notorious 1930 diatribe against Vladimir Mayakovsky, written shortly after the latter's suicide (ACC II: 851–55). Vallejo attacks Mayakovsky not as an antirevolutionary but as an *insincere* revolutionary; what troubles him in Mayakovsky's writing is not any lingering trace of Futurist modes but the utter sacrifice of his personal sensibility in his submission to communism. Mayakovsky, in Vallejo's reading, was temporally out of step with the revolution, having formed his sensibility in the prerevolutionary moment of the artistic avant-gardes; he was therefore incapable of reshaping his base sentiments—if not his political beliefs—to coincide sincerely with the revolution. There are of course glaring contradictions here—Vallejo elsewhere insists that sensibility undergoes constant dialectical modifications through contact with external influences—and the reason for this is most likely narrowly biographical. Mayakovsky was only a year younger than Vallejo, and therefore his exact contemporary in historical terms. His perceived agony in submerging his lyric voice into a political program might have earned more sympathetic comments from Vallejo in earlier or later years; in 1930, however, at the height of Vallejo's own commitment to Soviet socialism, his writings drown out any dissenting voices—in part, we might surmise, as a way to quiet his misgivings about his own writing. Yet those voices do find a curious way to reassert themselves: in his own reading of Mayakovsky, for example, which we might take as a covert self-analysis as he considers ways to align his own poetry with his newly politicized sensibility.[20]

To properly grapple with this question, which is at once personal, theoretical, and historical, we need to pull our lens back one more time to see what the panorama for poetry looked like in the late 1920s. It was one thing to consider poetry from the standpoint of the revolution: Mariátegui, for instance, initially hailed poetry as the genre best suited to the revolutionary moment, because of its immediate production, relative ease of circulation and consumption, and short duration. But it was something else entirely to think about the revolution from the standpoint of poetry. The implicit conflict that presents itself here between subjectivity and collectivity—and the poet's responsibility to both—is never fully articulated by Vallejo, but it comes into clear relief when we set certain of his prose writings alongside one another. The early 1930s notebook *El arte y la revolución,* for example, contains two companion pieces: *Ejecutoria del arte bolchevique* (*ERC* 380) and *Ejecutoria del arte socialista* (*ERC* 380–81) (where *ejecutoria* signals both a final judgment and a patent of nobility). The first makes Bolshevik art utterly coterminous with propaganda, and in the process sidelines the poet, whose role and temperament, Vallejo claims—without further explanation—are unsuited to this task. The second, however, focuses entirely on the poet, making poetry one of many activities radiating outward from a central core of sensibility. Poetry in this argument is not prophetic or didactic but reflective and reflexive, grounded in the present tense of contemporary history and of the lyric utterance, and only indeterminably oriented toward the future; separated from directly serving the exigencies of practical politics, it fixes instead on finding its own sincere mode of expression. Understood thus, poetry can be socialist—as, Vallejo emphasizes, can any activity—but never propagandistic, because of the incalculability of its effects.

It is noteworthy, then, that while Vallejo submits his prose writing to the terms and logic of Marxist doctrine, he sets his poetry apart, unrestricted by anything that might look like a theory. This discrepancy might explain the disappointment of many readers on encountering his prose writings on Russia, which speak only words that are not their author's own, and are trapped in their historical moment, of which Vallejo was not an especially perceptive prose analyst.[21] But it also explains Vallejo's failure to produce any statement on his own poetic technique, despite the stringent demands he placed on his contemporaries to do just that. It is this theoretical failure to articulate his technique that must have lain behind his reluctance to *publish* his poetry. Vallejo's only statements on his own technique appear in the form of elliptical notes in *Contra el secreto profesional,* where he groups poetry by himself and Neruda under the unexplained rubric *verdadismo* (truthism) (*ERC* 515), referring elsewhere to his own poetry as an exemplar of dialectical technique (following Mariátegui's reading), or listing Goethe, Whitman, Valery, and Poe as examples of writers possessing a "scientific" knowledge of their own art (516). Artists, he claims in this notebook, should not submit themselves to theory but should understand their own procedure; his examples, as I discuss further in chapter 6, are Chaplin and Eisenstein (518).[22] Yet he never manages to produce a clear statement of his own technique—and without that statement, it was impossible for him to put his poetry into the public arena.

NEW MEDIA

Vallejo was not alone in his misgivings about poetry's capacity to grapple consciously and critically with politics, to make itself a voice of or for history. Mariátegui's consecration of the lyric as an effective counterpart to both prose and politics was significantly only momentary. By the end of the decade, as the revolutionary moment settled into a period of reconstruction, he would complain of a "superproducción poética" (overproduction of poetry), emphasizing the need for reflective prose to take its place (*Correspondencia* 472). And the interest of both writers was increasingly gravitating toward the medium of film, fixed on for its capacity to *travel*—which potentially gave it far greater reach than poetry, as Vallejo emphasized in an excruciating article from 1929.[23] By writing about film and by modeling their own journalistic writings on its montage forms, Vallejo and Mariátegui both hoped to find a new way to frame Latin American writing for both local and foreign audiences.

What both Vallejo and Mariátegui offer in their newspaper articles from the mid-1920s is a "pantalla inteligente" (intelligent screen), as Vallejo puts it in a 1925 article (*ACC* I: 88), an active and activist membrane facing in two directions at once. Vallejo produces chronicles about Latin America for European audiences and vice versa; Mariátegui in those same years—and indeed in the same venues, the Lima periodicals *Mundial and Variedades*—writes interlocking columns on Europe and Latin America.[24] In a number of articles from 1925, Mariátegui presented film as a method to be emulated in journalism, as a vehicle for thinking about the local and the national in the context of the international; "cinematic" journalism, he argued, could offer a new image of the contemporary, a present tense made up of discrete moments, not run together to create a narrative, but juxtaposed to give account of different temporalities and spaces that make up the present moment.[25] Vallejo similarly wrote admiringly of certain directors and their practices, most notably montage (e.g., *ERC* 147–56), which—as in Mariátegui's argument—offered new possibilities for putting discrete times and places into dialogue.

These questions were relatively abstract, and toward the end of the 1920s both Mariátegui and Vallejo began to look for something that could capture the imagination and the attention of the public: in other words, a body. Both of them found it in the mobile slapstick figure of Chaplin, who in the late 1920s was being dismantled and reassembled by a growing number of European and North American writers and theorists. For Mariátegui, Chaplin's antics and human comedy breached the gap not only between different regional audiences but also between high and popular culture, entertaining "bookworms and boxers" alike; he could, moreover, address a universal audience from a resolutely local position, as the Frankfurt school analysts would also foreground.[26] For Vallejo, Chaplin first and foremost provides the hinge for an articulation of aesthetics and politics: literally through his body, which continually unhinges and disarticulates itself in order to transform itself from one thing into another; the tramp's disarticulated body performs an effective incorporation of the marginalized into popular culture.

But Vallejo's fixation on the figure of Chaplin also looks like an attempt to screen off viewings of his *own* body, which was at the time being insistently localized and indigenized by his admirers, among them Mariátegui. Replacing an uncomfortable emphasis on his own localization with a figure universally acclaimed as, precisely, universal, Vallejo substitutes a thoroughly mediatized and mobile modern figure for the notion of the poet as medium, absolving himself of the responsibility to speak directly for a collective, for a nation, or for a particular ethnic identity.

As I suggested in chapter 1, the concept of the poet-as-medium was the central thrust not only of Mariátegui's reading of Vallejo but also of Antenor Orrego's comments on his poetic performances at the pre-Columbian ruins of Chan-Chan, center of the Chimu empire. Orrego's readings elsewhere of Vallejo, however, are more nuanced than this, and somewhat surprisingly—given Orrego's less explicit subscription to Marxism—more dialectical. While Mariátegui argues that *Los heraldos negros* articulates a preexisting indigenous identity with closer ties to the precolonial past than to the present, Orrego suggests that *Trilce* ("el grito de la raza que se articula"; the shout of a self-articulating race [113]) gives voice to a nation yet-to-come, an emergent collectivity that would be generated from the friction of two prior and previously irreconcilable forms: indigenous on the one hand, Hispanic on the other (128–29). In this light, Vallejo becomes the herald of a new identity, a "Colón que descubre a su propia raza, que la hace hablar con su propia lengua y que la inflama con el pentecostés de su espíritu" (Columbus discovering his own race, making it speak with his own tongue and inflaming it with the Pentecost of his spirit), as Orrego syncretically put it (113).

In the mid-1930s Vallejo finally turned his attention to Perú, in a series of articles written for European newspapers; their method is deliberately dialectical and historical-materialist.[27] Rather than facilely declaring poetry capable of reawakening the past, he calls for serious scholarly investigation of history, to provide a ground on which to build for the future:

> Habría consecuentemente que crear un método nuevo de investigación que, aplicándose al estudio científico de la materia histórica—hombre, paisaje y ruinas—, fuese apto para elaborar un enunciado social acorde con las posibilidades y características en potencia de esa materia. (*ACC* II: 939)

> *One would need, therefore, to create a new method of investigation which, applying itself to the scientific study of historical material—man, landscape, and ruins—would be prepared to elaborate a social statement in tune with the possibilities and potential characteristics of that material.*

There were, nonetheless, serious obstacles to be overcome. On the one hand, Vallejo charged that the Peruvian state itself had insufficiently capitalized on a history of material wealth and potential, having abandoned for centuries the exploration of the nation's archaeological sites and leaving the most recent process of "discovery" to foreign researchers (e.g., Hiram Bingham, who stumbled upon Machu Picchu in 1911). On the other hand, he recognized that that history itself had a subsequent history, which posed problems for any attempt to reanimate former potential:

> La colonia primero y, de modo más acentuado todavía la república, han tratado al indígena como un extranjero en su propia tierra. . . . Tal acción paralizadora ha acarreado, a la larga, un gran atrofiamiento de la raza. No queda de ella . . . sino escombros. . . . ¿Cómo pretender identificar o explicar un proceso histórico de tan inmenso valor, como el del pasado sudamericano, con la sombra o cadáver de las poderosas razas que lo crearon? (*ACC* II: 939)

> *First the colonial powers, and then in even more accentuated ways, the republic, have treated the indigenous citizen as a stranger in his own land. . . . This paralyzing action has ultimately led to a full-scale atrophying of the race. All that is left of it . . . is debris. . . . How are we to identify or explain a historical process of such immense value as was that of the Latin American past with the shadow or corpse of the powerful races which created it?*

His problematic theoretical route around this impasse at times involves positing present-day indigenous communities as occupying the same—literal and metaphorical—place in the landscape as ruins. But in more clear-sighted moments, Vallejo argues that the present-day *indígena* should neither be deified nor taken as degenerated; he insists that the indigenous question involves subjects who are alive and kicking against their current state of oppression and whose satisfaction is intimately embroiled with that of the global proletariat, "el problema mundial del momento" (the worldwide problem of the present) (*ACC* II: 940). On these grounds, he calls less for folkloric or archaeological excavations of Peruvian history than for an anthropological or sociological study of past lives—treating these, in other words, as living organisms rather than as defunct documents. Archaeology, to paraphrase Nietzsche, could only produce "conceptual mummies"; a fully engaged historical reading, by contrast, which remained alert to the past, the present, and the possible futures of objects, turned those objects into vital lessons. Or as Vallejo put it elsewhere, "La historia no se narra ni se mira ni se escucha ni se toca. La historia se vive y se siente vivir" (History is not narrated nor looked at nor listened to nor touched. History is lived and is felt to be living) (*ERC* 482).

A poetry alive to these questions could only be in the present tense, depicting figures in constant agonic or ludic engagement with the natural and cultural environments in which they were embedded, in conditions inherited from the past but now struggling toward modernization. This is the procedure that underpins all of Vallejo's poetry, from beginning to end—or rather, through successive new beginnings, such as those called for in the closing poem of *Trilce,* which announces itself—as Ortega succinctly noted—as an open or *imperfect* book, in the sense of incompletion, reaching beyond itself toward ever-renewing horizons of poetry and historical circumstance (*Teoría* 70). Vallejo did possess a technique, although he lacked the theoretical tools to articulate it: an exploratory spontaneity, in the sense of a continual expressive and physical adaptation to the changing circumstances of modernity. As we have already seen, and as I map out further in chapter 6, Vallejo's poetry is relentlessly written in and embroiled with a contemporary moment that presses upon the lyric voice and body, mapping out the restrictions imposed upon both as they chafe their way toward new possibilities of articulation, both individual and collective. His poetry is therefore best described as—in his own words—a "horizontalizing" aesthetic, on the same wavelength as contemporary experiments throughout the West, depicting "hombre, paisaje y ruinas" (man, landscape, and ruins (*ACC* II: 939) on the threshold of modernity. But this is achieved only through a full immersion in modernity itself, mapped out in the contortions of his Parisian journalism, to which we now turn.

CHAPTER 5

Literature Under Pressure

To be an adult means, precisely, having reached the point of
understanding that it is not in one's native land that one has
been born, but in a larger, more neutral place, neither friend
nor enemy, unknown, which no one could call his own and
which does not give rise to affection, but rather, to strangeness.

—Juan José Saer, *The Investigation*

On June 17, 1923, Vallejo sailed away from Lima, on the run from
an arrest warrant whose status remained ambiguous. He would never
again set foot in Peru, despite intermittent attempts to do so over the
next fifteen years—stymied in part by economic worries, in part by
concern over his legal status, and, increasingly, by his sense of abandonment by the Peruvian establishment. But his distanced relationship
to Peru was offset by his newly immediate exposure to contemporary
international culture, which would result in a different form of writing: roughly three hundred newspaper articles for a variety of Peruvian,
Latin American, and European newspapers from 1923 until 1930 and
sporadically thereafter until 1938, in which Vallejo processes metropolitan modernity for both local and foreign audiences.[1] These Paris
chronicles marked Vallejo's tentative entry into the marketplace, producing writing on demand for a specific public, and opened a space
for him to engage directly with the structuring discourses of interwar
modernity—playfully, parodically, corrosively.

As far as his Peruvian readers could discern, Vallejo's newfound role
as journalist displaced his poetic activities, getting in the way of both
composition and publication.[2] Perhaps out of nostalgia for that poetry-
which-might-have-been, and certainly because of the generic difficulties
posed by chronicles both as a genre and in Vallejo's practice, few critics
have delved into his numerous newspaper articles in any depth.[3] Despite

the incontrovertible fact that so many modernist writers supported their properly literary writings with journalistic work, there is still a general reluctance to connect "literature under pressure"—as Susana Rotker (43) describes the chronicle genre—with a poetry whose putative autonomy lifts it above history. Nonetheless, as I argue here, Vallejo's chronicles form a crucial hinge between his early and late poetry and are indispensable for understanding his parallel aesthetic and political development. In his chronicles, Vallejo commits himself to what Rotker suggestively dubs an "archaeology of the present" (47), putting his own body and language at the service of cultural translation and information. In the process, he unveils the breakdown of physical and linguistic communication across classes, races, cultures, and nations within a rapidly transforming geopolitical scene. As his articles on culture and society in interwar Paris play out against a backdrop of failing peace conferences, ominous economic reconfigurations, and increasing disconnections between geographical areas, political ideologies, and social strata, they display the contortions that bodies and languages were forced to undergo in a period of hyper-modernization and burgeoning political and economic crises.

Vallejo's chronicles also provide a revelatory counterpoint to utopian narratives of Paris as cultural capital in the interwar years. Memoirs of Paris in the 1920s by successful French and foreign (usually Anglophone) writers are by now very familiar, from Hemingway's *A Moveable Feast,* Stein's *Paris France,* and Cowley's *Exile's Return* through Ellmann's and Kenner's accounts of the figures clustered around Joyce and Pound to retrospective analyses by Roger Shattuck and Jerrold Siegel. Recent years have also seen immense recovery projects for pan-African groups in Paris (Stovall; Fabre; Edwards, *Diaspora*), while narratives of the sizable Latin American community have just begun to emerge (Marcy Schwartz; Weiss), alongside treatments of individual writers in their Parisian context (Henighan; Birkenmaier). These studies tend to offer glimpses of communities in formation outside the bounds of their home countries, and of writers in contact with larger groups associated with the international avant-garde. Vallejo's experience in Paris, however, was one of radical isolation, of disconnection from Peru and from more established Latin Americans in Paris, as well as from the central circuits of cosmopolitan culture.

This sense of marginalization at the center, I will suggest, pushes Vallejo to align himself with the common *transeúnte,* or passerby, a figure marked by class more than by ethnic identity.[4] His short, timely pieces insistently set a marginal experience of Parisian culture against official accounts and circuits, shadowing and undercutting the activities of established artists and commentators in the space of cosmopolitan modernity. Finding himself excluded from the Parisian feast, Vallejo determinedly unveils the material bases of cultural and political praxis which denied a variety of potential participants access to cosmopolitan modernity, dreaming—as William Rowe puts it—of a *modernidad completamente horizontal* (completely horizontal modernity) ("César Vallejo" 178). His chronicles thus give an ethical shading to readings of Paris as a filter for international culture in the period of the avant-gardes, demanding that we consider the city's submerged layers alongside its surface flourishes. The shadowy figures who swarm in Vallejo's chronicles around the more recognizable names of international art and politics are subaltern in class and culture; those unexamined figures will eventually populate his late poems, providing a contrapuntal "no-yo" (non-I) to their retreating lyric subject, who—as Vallejo puts it in the shattering poem "Un hombre pasa con un pan al hombro" (A Man Walks by with a Loaf of Bread on His Shoulder)—can no longer speak of the other without screaming.

Finally, these chronicles—and the unpublished poems composed alongside them—form a hauntingly resonant counterpart to the kind of works that Paul Saint-Amour gathers under the rubric "encyclopedic modernism": novels such as Joyce's *Ulysses,* composed as virtual time capsules in the face of potential catastrophe, from which a civilization threatened with disappearance might be rescued and reconstructed.[5] Vallejo's chronicles, by contrast, operate—like his poems—according to a principle of dispersal. Pointing to the imminence of a second world war and of economic and social catastrophes for its civilians, but refusing—unlike contemporary journalism—to give the impression that they can make the interwar period coherent in its unfolding, their Cassandra-like voice can only be fully heard through a retrospective reading that traces their analyses and their warnings. And by reading these chronicles, which unveil the experience of a modernity unraveling across a broad swath of areas and social classes, we glean a new understanding of the entanglements of national cultures and international politics in the interwar years as they bore down upon artists, workers, the unemployed.

PROSE OF THE PASSERBY

Vallejo's first chronicle from Paris, published on the front page of Trujillo's *El Norte* in October 1923, paints a precarious picture of a Spanish speaker's entrance into metropolitan cultural life (*ACC* I: 25–27). It
begins by satirizing its author's own pretensions: fresh off the boat and
cruising along the Champs-Elysées, Vallejo imagines himself blending
seamlessly into the crowd, until he is pulled roughly out of his reverie by a stranger who recognizes him—not for his poetry, but for his
type: "Usted viene de América. Ya lo había notado" (You're from Latin
America. I could tell).[6] His odd interpellator, a Spaniard from Andalu-
sia, pulls him into a zigzagging conversation and *dérive* through Paris,
speaking sometimes in Spanish, sometimes in poor French; Vallejo, unsettled but enthralled, lets himself be carried from site to site, topic to
topic, before finally bundling into a taxi to Montmartre to escape the
hordes who pack the cafés of the right bank. His strange Virgil, he
quickly discovers, has nothing but contempt for contemporary Paris,
but he reserves just as much mockery for the Latin Americans who
visit it in search of enlightenment. Vallejo, however, takes pains to cor-
rect any false impression by declaring himself "un obrero del Perú" (a
worker from Peru), come to discover the old continent but also, naturally, "to work." That work, as he embarked on his new career as
a journalist, was observation; what he crucially observes in this first
wandering through Paris is not civilization but barbarism—a belated
barbarism to boot.

En route to a dive in Montmartre, the two foreigners encounter a
carnival scene that turns stereotypes about European culture and Latin
American primitivism literally on their head.[7] Bodies fused into a single
monstrous form—a girl dancing with a "cloven-footed mammal," in-
distinctly human or animal—offer up a nightmarish cabaret act which
is worlds away from expected displays of European refinement.[8] Their
performance recalls the bodily contortions that Vallejo himself had presented in *Trilce,* but these seem completely out of place in the cradle of
old world culture; equally unsettling is the spectacle's pacifying effect on
its audience, whom it leaves "transportadas de goce, como niños" (beside
themselves with delight, like children). Vallejo's Andalusian friend, suddenly more Iago than Virgil, whispers suggestively in his ear that this is
the new figure for European civilization: a monstrous mammal with un-
natural protrusions, who needs to be elbowed aside by "otras anatomías"
(other anatomies), by a Latin American race ready to flex its muscles.[9]

What Vallejo himself seems most concerned with, however, is not the opening of a space for Latin America but the closure of an eccentric European promise. It quickly becomes apparent that what Vallejo was initially looking for in Paris was neither the future nor the most up-to-date scenes of modernity but the past. On arriving in Europe, his first planned port of call was a romanticized bohemia, the "real thing" after the imitative and anachronistic bohemias of Trujillo and Lima. However, no trace of the bohemia of Murger and Verlaine remains in Montmartre, where marginality has turned to kitsch and where audiences are kept in a state of passive contentment by freak shows and the farcical repetition of the past.[10]

Grotesque connections and disconnections are not restricted to bodies here; when Vallejo and his Andalusian friend leave the cabaret to continue their conversation in the restaurant, strange pieces of information and snatches of language begin to bubble up to the surface. Not only does Vallejo's guide claim to know each one of the strange characters arrayed around them, but he further insinuates that they are all something other than they seem. This is not a world of benign shape-shifting: if everyone is known to everyone else in different guises, this is because everyone is a professional conspirator, plotting with and against each other in a world in which languages are at once passwords and signs of exclusion, where a minority language is both a stigma of marginality and a badge of protection.[11] "Hablemos en castellano," Vallejo's companion hisses at him, "nos están oyendo" (Let's speak Spanish; we're being listened to). Filled with shame and confusion, Vallejo ends the chronicle by freezing his gesture, albeit with a Spengler-tinged suggestion of Latin American promise and defiance: "Yo me quedo, con el tenedor a medio levantar bajo los labios, mirando las ventanas. Todavía el poniente está azulando" (I stop with my fork half-lifted to my lips, looking out the window. In the west it is still dawning).

This carefully staged opening statement on Paris thus closes in a state of linguistic and positional suspension, with its author feeling both out of time and out of place—but by the same token, we suspect, perfectly immersed in his new culture. For the experience of bohemia is the feeling of occupying a different place, striking attitudes opposed to the dominant culture whether by will or by necessity, the anti-bourgeois gesture here given an anti-European twist. But if Vallejo's initial romanticized conception of bohemia mistakes its nineteenth-century version for a conscious choice made by artists, his experiences in Paris will reveal to him the miserable extent to which a "bohemia inquerida," or

unwanted bohemia, is grounded in real material difficulty for those occupying a different stratum, whether inside or outside the center.[12] In
Vallejo's case, this is compounded by his speaking a minority language,
communicating only via newspaper articles with a Peruvian audience
that never responds to his reports about a culture in which he cannot
afford to fully participate.

This account may seem to resonate with Raymond Williams's description (in *Politics of Modernism*) of the formation of a minority
artistic culture in Paris in the interwar years, where the alienation of
the artist was turned into a badge of distinction and the basis for cultural revolution.[13] But if Williams's argument potentially holds true for
groups of French-, German-, and English-speaking writers, Vallejo's experience of radical isolation in Paris offers a less triumphalist account
of cultural life in the cosmopolis. For unattached foreigners speaking
minority languages, Paris in the twenties was a site of conflicted cosmopolitanism, dominated by paranoia, code switching, and the need
to occupy multiple and covert roles, often grotesquely shadowing the
position of foreign correspondent or diplomat held by their upper-class
compatriots.

Vallejo does not, however, catapult himself to the opposite end of the
social spectrum, into the underworld momentarily inhabited by Orwell
and Brassaï. As Brassaï noted, "There are many similarities between
what we call the 'underworld' and the 'fashionable world.' Entry into
both these exclusive societies, made up primarily of the idle, is not easy.
Each has its regulations, its customs and usages, its moral code, its affairs of honor. . . . Even the languages are similar, both tainted with
snobbery" (n.p.). Lacking Orwell's French skills and Brassaï's camera
(a different kind of passkey), Vallejo was excluded even from this sec-
tor. Yet while other writers and artists found in Paris a foothold for an
oppositional culture grounded in artistic praxis, Vallejo's inability to
find a place for himself in that space leads him to a different conception
of the need for social justice—one that emerges from his own material
experience of poverty rather than from an avant-garde practice ham-
mered out among fellow artists. His exile in the center of avant-garde
culture effectively undercuts his own avant-garde leanings, moving him
in the direction of an insistence on the need for communication, critique, empathy, and protest. His experience thus exposes the underbelly
of what we tend retrospectively to imagine as the apotheosis of transnational culture in interwar Paris.

As I demonstrate in what follows, Vallejo's exclusion from the cultural center leads him to an ever-increasing focus on bodies rather than on language in his writing, replacing momentary dreams of polyglot artistic utopias with an emphasis on social justice and effective international cooperation. On the one hand, Vallejo writes on cosmopolitan scenes and multicultural encounters in the fashionable cafés of Paris and resorts on the coast, setting them in an acutely ironic contrast with postwar peace conferences ("Deauville contra Ginebra" [1927]; ACC I: 485–87), pointing to a growing and unavoidable disillusionment with the mechanisms of cross-cultural communication. On the other hand, he becomes increasingly sensitive to the fact that those spaces are closed off not just to non-French-speaking intellectuals, but to poor French and foreign subjects alike, which gradually prompts a shift in his focus from culture to class. This sensitivity to class hierarchies and human indignities significantly predates his immersion in Marxism (beginning in 1927), and it is his material experience in Paris that must be seen as laying the ground for his later theoretical engagements rather than vice versa; as he puts it in a December 27, 1928, letter to Pablo Abril, "voy sintiéndome revolucionario y revolucionario por experiencia vivida, más que por ideas aprendidas" (I am beginning to develop revolutionary feelings, through lived experience more than through any learned ideas) (CC 316). As he loses his initial faith in the capacity of languages and bodies to communicate with one another, he begins to hammer out a new conception of the shapes and modes of linguistic and bodily experience, a conception that will irrupt into the lyric forms of the *Poemas humanos*. But to forge that understanding, Vallejo first had to put his writing and imagination at the service of describing those spaces that material constraints prevented him from entering into bodily.

Throughout the twenties, Vallejo effectively inhabits Paris as a kind of antiflâneur, lacking not just the money to enter into fashionable spaces, but more basically, the shoe-leather. Rather than following his contemporary surrealists in pacing the streets and gazing into shop-windows (as mythologized in Aragon's *Paris Peasant,* Breton's *Nadja,* and Soupault's *Last Nights of Paris*), he tries to restrict his movements so as to make his footwear last as long as possible; rather than traveling by metro, like Breton's Nadja, he descends into stations to find a place to sleep for the night. The minutiae of his maneuvers, as Bazán recounts, add up to an excruciating regimen of bodily restrictions:

> Para que las suelas de los zapatos no se le gasten, no baja nunca de los vehículos—tranvías o coches del subterráneo—en marcha; lo hace delicadamente, sin frotar los pies, cuando están completamente detenidos; para

que los fundillos del pantalón no se pongan brillosos y se rompan, evita el roce y permanece de pie, lo más que puede, en todas partes; para que las solapas del saco se mantengan exentas de manchas, cuando va de vez en vez al restaurante, se envuelve el busto, imitando a algunos ancianos franceses con la servilleta a manera de babero para niño. En estas últimas circunstancias de burla de sí mismo, sonríe dulcemente y recuerda a Charles Chaplin porque ha observado que nadie como él saber reunir en un hilo de angustia lo trágico y lo cómico. (59)

So as not to wear out the soles of his shoes, he never alights from a vehicle— a tram or a subway car—while it's in motion; he does so delicately, without brushing his shoes against the ground, when the vehicle has come to a full stop. To prevent the seat of his pants from growing shiny or threadbare, he avoids all friction and remains on his feet as much as possible, wherever he might be. To protect the lapels of his jacket from stains, on the rare occasions he goes to a restaurant, he covers his chest, imitating those old Frenchmen who wear their napkins like children's bibs. In such circumstances, laughing at himself, he smiles sweetly and alludes to Charles Chaplin, knowing that no one has been more successful in threading together the tragic and the comic.

Although Vallejo's chronicles recount scenes from the cultural cosmopolis for a presumably avid Peruvian audience, most of these must have been the product of his imagination or of his readings in Parisian newspapers. After the first year or so, he rarely evokes himself in these chronicles, in part because in real terms he is barely there, and the authorial subject of his writings dissolves into a style that parodies modern discursive modes from within. And instead of moving—as in Williams's account of the avant-gardes—in the direction of an ever-greater linguistic intransigence, he becomes increasingly aware of the need to communicate with the common man or *transeúnte*, whose travails— like Chaplin—he begins to experience in his body and foreground in his writings, to culminate in the intense socialist humanism of the *Poemas humanos*.

Vallejo therefore speaks in his chronicles not as a professional but as an amateur; meandering through the spaces of marginal culture (cafés and music halls), he observes official circuits from afar. Vallejo effectively shadows that official culture from his first moments in Paris: he witnesses the induction of new members into the Académie Française, attends official Latin American gatherings, comments on war memorials, and assiduously visits art exhibitions, all the while attempting to develop his own mode of relating to these unfamiliar events in a new critical prose, which often includes covert self-readings.[14] He quickly familiarizes himself with the modes of French criticism—of art, theater, politics, and science—although he insistently sets his own sensorial re-action against what he presents as the anesthetized intellectual modes of established criticism.[15] By presenting himself as a figure who asks rather than answers questions, he parodies both the forms of official discourse—surveys, statistics, professional proclamations—and the mo-tions of established artists. The two modes were epitomized, for Vallejo, in Jean Cocteau's 1924 *Le secret professionel,* which he excoriated (in the title of his 1927 article "Contra el secreto profesional" [*ACC* I: 421–25] and in the body of other chronicles) for its fetishization of the professional secret; instead, Vallejo insists on putting things out in the open, exposing the hidden mechanisms and exclusionary systems of culture and politics. In the process, his discourse undergoes a rapid and radical modernization: from romantic to hyperbolic to sarcastic to ideologically committed. His chronicles therefore shed a different light on the changing possibilities of language on the banks of interwar Paris, set against a backdrop of the changing forms and rationales of the body and of art, moving toward a social and artistic vision with a resilient grounding in material fact.

A PERUVIAN IN PARIS

In his first year in Paris, Vallejo experienced both the euphoria of arriv-ing in the cultural capital of the world and a defiant recognition of his exclusion from full participation in it. He arrived on July 13, 1923, and a letter dated the following day to his brother Néstor checked off all the sights he had already seen: the Eiffel Tower, Les Invalides, the Arc du Triomphe, the Champs-Élysées, even Versailles (*CC* 57). That day was of course Bastille Day, and Vallejo celebrated it in a ceremony at the Peruvian Consulate, where he was toasted by the ambassador; the lan-guage of his letter is unsurprisingly giddy, as he waxes lyrical not only about the wonders of Paris but also about his rapturous reception by his compatriots abroad.[16] A mere two weeks later, however, he was begin-ning to realize the extent of the misery that awaited a writer without a fixed position; his new friendship with a fellow Peruvian, the musician Alfonso de Silva—who gave him tips on how to save his shoe leather, overcome hunger, and find places to sleep and eat—brought home to him the physical reality of a precarious existence in Paris.

Nonetheless, Vallejo was determined to put his body at the service of cultural mediation as effectively as possible, and he insistently places more faith in his own sensorial reactions than in the intellectual responses of Parisian critics. In a review of a performance of Maeterlinck's *Bluebird,* he complains of the play's excessive assault on the spectator's nerves, taking it as evidence of a decay in sensibility—of neurasthenia tipping over into aesthetic anesthesia—in the metropolis (*ACC* I: 29). He attended the Salon d'Automne the same month (October 1923); the language of his chronicle comes close to the phrasings of his earlier poetry, still hewing to a search for the *mot rare:*

> Largas horas he permanecido en el Salón de Otoño, al amor de los plafones opulentos, apurando un banquete de emociones, saboreando dulcentas inefables. Durante largas horas en el Salón de Otoño he comido, he bebido harto y bueno, de piedra, de lienzo, de carne, de corazón. (*ACC* I: 44)

> *I have spent long hours at the Salon d'Automne, under the loving warmth of its opulent ceilings, finishing off its banquet of emotions, savoring ineffable cider apples. During long hours in the Salon d'Automne I have eaten and drunk my fill of stone, of canvas, of flesh, of heart.*

Vallejo avoids intellectual meditation on the newest productions in art, insisting instead on a bodily response to them; he presents himself greedily gobbling up a banquet laid out for the visitor (in part to compensate for his own real hunger), which he will digest and process for his Peruvian audience. In the exhibition itself he is most drawn to bodies, especially sculptures by the French Leon Leyritz and the Belgian Arsène Matton, which he admires (and unusually relates to his own literary practice) for their unfinished quality, their depiction of bodies in motion within the stone that should constrain them, performing an aesthetic that he describes as an "esencia horizontante del arte" (horizontalizing essence of art) (*ACC* I: 46). The body—both sculptural and authorial—that appears in this chronicle is in movement within a material landscape, scanning the horizon for possibilities, digesting what it finds in order to turn it into a new product.[17]

Vallejo initially contemplates his own new horizon as a Columbus-in-reverse: as a New World citizen come to experience the Old World in order to report back on forms and practices at the center of modern culture while planning—like so many other Latin Americans in the twenties—to return home as soon as possible.[18] But unlike his co-continentals, Paris for Vallejo remains the space of *information* rather than *formation,* since he is reduced to reporting on it for a Peruvian public rather than participating in it.[19] His approach to Paris, as Podestá notes (7), amounts to a savage ethnography, parodying the modes of official discourse from a position of peripheral marginality; as he carries out his fieldwork in the capital of cosmopolitan culture, he reads from the outside as a resolutely Peruvian or Latin American subject.[20] Defiantly embracing his exclusion from the center, Vallejo sends home sarcastic reports on the stagnation of the French theatrical scene, on the commercialization of Cubism, on the European lack of interest in anything but the most folkloric or exoticist expressions of Latin American culture.

Yet at the same time, Vallejo's writings display a staunch belief in the imminent possibility of real interhemispheric dialogue and in journalism as its most promising vehicle. Many of his first chronicles, when not gazing into the kaleidoscope of cosmopolitan culture in Paris, fix on the figures of Latin American mediators in Europe and their attempts to build bridges between the two continents through periodicals, translations, catalogs, and guides. In 1924 he interviewed a variety of mediating figures: the García Calderón brothers—standard-bearers of the previous generation in Peru—who were working to introduce their compatriots to a European audience; the Guatemalan Enrique Gómez Carrillo, one of Latin America's foremost *modernista* travel writers, friend of Wilde and Maeterlinck; the Bolivian Alcides Arguedas, eminent indigenist abroad; the Ecuadorian writer and diplomat Gonzalo Zaldumbide; and the Uruguayan Hugo Barbagelata, director of the magazine *L'Amérique latine (ACC* I: 55–74). When later that year Vallejo found a public relations position in a new enterprise of interhemispheric, *Les Grands Journaux Ibéro-Américains*—proposed by the Argentinean Alejandro Sux as a vast project of mutual illumination in the areas of finance, politics, art, and science—he saw it as a sign of Latin America's soon-to-be-realized full arrival on the European scene (*ACC* I: 85–88). Sux's much-vaunted newspaper never materialized, and Vallejo instead found himself in the ignominious position of tutor to the children of visiting diplomats, barely managing to get a press card through Maurice Waleffe—of *Paris-Midi* and *Le Journal*—that would grant him access to some of the events he needed to cover for his Peruvian journalistic commissions.[21]

Throughout this early period Vallejo continued to write chronicles for Orrego's Trujillo-based weekly *El Norte,* and in 1925 he was named Paris correspondent for the Lima weekly *Mundial,* supplemented the next year by a commission for Lima's biweekly *Variedades*. He contributed to both on a semiregular basis until 1929, when he began to publish exclusively in Lima's *El Comercio,* until political pressures forced his ouster the following year.[22] Between 1923 and 1930, then, Vallejo spoke regularly as Paris correspondent to a Peruvian public, following in the journalistic footsteps of a previous generation of Latin American poets such as José Martí (writing in New York for Spanish-language newspapers or for periodicals in Buenos Aires and Mexico) and Rubén Darío (writing from various locales for the Argentinean *La Nación*). Two of his Latin American contemporaries—the Guatemalan Miguel Ángel Asturias and the Cuban Alejo Carpentier—also served as Paris correspondents during these years. Asturias, as Stephen Henighan argues, used his chronicles to keep up a dialogue with his home country on local issues, while Carpentier—as Anke Birkenmaier analyzes—focused on transmitting news of European modernity to Cuba. Vallejo's position, however, was far more precarious than either of theirs. Although on the payroll of four periodicals, he rarely received payments from three of them; more crucially—given his acute concern with an audience—he was unsettlingly unsure of actually being read, since he received hardly any correspondence from home. Vallejo thus had little sense of communication with an interested public and received little compensation for his efforts, all the while hampered by his shrinking knowledge of the changing state of Peru.[23]

At the same time, this disconnection was partly a product of his determination to open up a dialogue with international rather than narrowly local culture. As I noted in the previous chapter, Vallejo declined to enter into the 1926–27 indigenism polemic in Peru, and—as critics have been careful not to notice—his early chronicles tend to align Latin America with a Latin or more narrowly Spanish heritage rather than with indigenous history. A 1926 article offers an unusually direct personal affirmation: "De mí sé decir que mi creencia es firme en que nuestra evolución irá acercándose más y más a la latinidad y que si América llega a ser el centro de la civilización futura, ello se hará a base de nuestro contacto con el pasado, por medio de la raza latina" (As for myself, I firmly believe that our evolution will move ever more in the direction of the Latin, and that if [Latin] America ends up at the center of a future civilization, it will be on the basis of our contact with the past, through the Latin race) (ACC I: 188–92).[24] Moreover, his few chronicles on Peruvian writers in the early to mid-1920s—aggressively attacking the local avant-garde's imitation of European practices but also the preceding generation's lack of guidance—aroused only irritation among Peru-based writers who were hammering out their own positions on political and aesthetic vanguardism (Lauer, *Polémica*).

But Vallejo's isolation also derived from a growing sense of abandonment by both Peruvian officials and his friends and family at home. After a serious illness in late 1924, he began to request funds for a ticket to Lima but was ignored by the Peruvian government; his repeated appeals through the late 1920s went similarly unanswered, and his anxiety over a possible return was compounded in 1926 by the temporary reactivation of his arrest warrant.[25] By late 1928, as he began to undergo a political reorientation toward Marxism, Vallejo was still complaining bitterly about his severance from Peru, wondering why "este pobre indígena" (this poor indigenous man) (CC 285), alone among his compatriots abroad, was ignored by Leguía's government. Notably, the letter in which he voices this complaint also contains his first reference to his readings in Marxism—the writings of Max Eastman—alongside a suspicion that his sidelining by the Peruvian government has as much to do with class as it does with race. Vallejo's commitment to internationalist left-wing politics must therefore be seen as at least in part a consequence of his involuntary disengagement from Peru, which paradoxically prompted his new embrace of a raced identity, inflected by his developing sense of class inequities.

Vallejo's wounded sense of abandonment by official Peru occasionally sent him in search of analogies among other ignored Peruvian artists: the nineteenth-century painter Ignacio Merino, whom he studied in the Bibliothèque Nationale (ACC I: 441–43); his still-unsuccessful contemporary, Macedonio de la Torre (ACC II: 746); or Paul Gauguin, whom he attempted to reclaim for Peru as part of a broader debate within the avant-gardes over the ethnic identity of this important primitivist predecessor (ACC I: 356–57). He did, however, strike up a different kind of relationship to Peru through its growing community of expatriates in Paris—from artists, musicians, and writers such as Alfonso de Silva, Felipe Cossío del Pomar, Carlos and Ernesto More to political dissidents such as Víctor Raúl Haya de la Torre and Eudocio Ravines (More 63)—who held parties in the Costa Rican sculptor Max Jiménez's former studio, singing not the ubiquitous tango but Peruvian songs *(marineros, yavaríes, huaynos)* among a small group of other Latin Americans, Spaniards, and Germans (More 29).[26] But Vallejo's connection with Peru abroad served to sever the original tie more than to reaffirm it; as he insisted in a 1926 chronicle (ACC I: 332–33), a traveler abroad—*really* crossing borders, as he puts it—becomes less rather than more patriotic, because of a dawning awareness of the need for and the critical potential of new and shifting attachments.

If Vallejo's stance as a Peruvian journalist in Paris was undercut by his severance from Peru on multiple fronts, he found it no easier to step into the role of Latin American correspondent or spokesperson, having had only minimal access to continental cultural developments while in Lima. As Mariátegui repeatedly underlines, in the 1920s there was little direct connection or exchange between countries within Latin America; those writers who moved from one point on the continent to another tended to do so to evade political persecution, retaining only the most precarious links to their countries of origin, while the movement of ideas was constantly beset by censorship and material constraints.[27] Connections between parts of Latin America were instead invariably triangulated through Paris: not as a reflection of a Eurocentric bias, but rather due to Paris's hospitality to cosmopolitan rather than narrowly French culture, which made it such a magnetic destination for writers from Latin America, Africa, North America, Eastern Europe, and Asia in the twenties, as again in the fifties and sixties (Weiss 2). When the Spanish-born writer and critic Guillermo de Torre proposed shifting emphasis from Paris to Madrid as the "intellectual meridian of Spanish America," he was greeted with derision and postcolonial outrage. This underlines the different ideological resonance of Paris for Spanish American intellectuals in particular: France was sufficiently Latin without being Spanish to constitute a viable alternative option for cultural alignment. And in practical terms, Paris was a space where writers and artists could rub shoulders with counterparts from various points of the globe but also have access to a cultural and material infrastructure that allowed them to make more effective connections with their own compatriots. It was therefore through the multicultural passageways of the cosmopolis that Vallejo—like many of his contemporaries—effectively and critically discovered Latin America.[28]

But cultural experience, as Vallejo insists throughout his chronicles and as is abundantly clear in his own Parisian experience, is also striated by class. Although he struck up an early acquaintance with the financially independent Chilean avant-garde poet Vicente Huidobro and the well-established García Calderón brothers, Vallejo's group of Latin American friends was composed of insolvent figures on the margins of Parisian cultural circuits: the Salvadoran caricaturist Toño Salazar, the Costa Rican artist Max Jiménez, and the journalist León Pacheco, a handful of Mexican writers and painters, and the Peruvian More brothers.[29] Vallejo was also notably resistant to promoting himself among better-known Latin American and Spanish mediators. When convinced by Alcides Arguedas to attend a gathering of Spanish-speaking intellectuals (sponsored by the League of Nations International Commission on Intellectual Cooperation), it only confirmed his suspicion that culture in Paris was divided between official and marginal groups—or between "dos hemisferios de artistas y escritores transatlánticos" (two hemispheres of transatlantic artists and writers), a comment that trenchantly maps a class division onto a geographical hierarchy. As he explained:

> La esfera oficial está formada por quienes vienen a París a brillar y triunfar y por quienes, debido a sus cargos diplomáticos, están obligados a una vida espectacular y cortesana, que muchas veces está lejos de agradarles. La esfera no oficial está formada por quienes vienen a París a vivir libre y honestamente, sin premuras de llegar, ni preocupaciones de relumbrón. La esfera oficial opera de smoking y, en todos los actos públicos, pasa lista y dice en el protocolo: ¡presente! La esfera no oficial opera en particular, tácitamente o, mejor dicho, no opera sino actúa, que es muy diferente. (*ACC* I: 396)

> *The official sphere is formed by those who come to Paris to shine and triumph, and by those who, due to their diplomatic positions, are obliged to live a spectacular courtly life, which in many cases is far from agreeable to them. The nonofficial sphere is formed by those who come to Paris to live freely and honestly, with no concern to "make it," no anxieties about shining. The official sphere wears dinner jackets and loudly declares its presence at all public events. The nonofficial sphere operates on its own account, tacitly—or rather, instead of operating, it acts, which is something else entirely.*

"Shining" examples of that official culture included the Chilean poet Gabriela Mistral, whose speech at the event—calling for European sponsorship of Latin American cultural production—so enraged Vallejo that he retracted his earlier espousal of Peru's Latinate heritage, insisting instead on the need to bring both pre-Columbian and present-day Indo-American culture into the light of day (*ACC* I: 398). This new commitment to indigenism, merged with his growing sensitivity to questions of class relations, also motivated Vallejo's avoidance of the Spanish philosopher Miguel de Unamuno during the latter's exile in Paris; although they both frequented the Café de la Rotonde in Montparnasse, Vallejo resisted making Unamuno's acquaintance because of his alleged disdain for Darío's indigenous heritage but also because of Unamuno's refusal to accept a cup of coffee from a stranger (Bazán 66).

La Rotonde offered, nonetheless, an irresistible cosmopolitan cultural scene, and one of Vallejo's earliest chronicles is devoted to capturing its whirl of polyglot activity, composed of the Spanish, Latin American, Senegalese, Swiss, Indian, English, Japanese, French, and

international Dada artists and writers who frequented the café, forming a less subversive version of the Cabaret Voltaire. The language of
Vallejo's early 1924 chronicle on La Rotonde (*ACC* I: 38–40) comes
close to the disorientating descriptions of *Trilce:* he hails the café as an
"hipogeo ambiguo, tablero iridiscente, ruidoso alvéolo de sarna cos-
mopolita: (ambiguous underground cavern, an iridescent chessboard, a
noisy alveolus of cosmopolitan mange) set amid the crisscrossing telegraphic wires and prowling walkers of the Boulevard Montparnasse,
and in which "hay uñas ocultas que nos rascan una íntima llaga in-
efable" (some unseen nails scratch our intimate ineffable wounds). As
in his description of the Salon d'Automne, Vallejo registers the way in
which various parts of his body are touched by the kaleidoscopic scene:
"el corazón se sienta aquí, en su lugar izquierdo; se agita a manera de
una caja de fósforos para ver si hay en ella cerillas, y toda la noche está
quema que quema sus palitos amarillos" (the heart sits down here, on
its left side; it shakes like a box of matches to see if it has any contents,
and the night strikes away one by one its little yellow sticks)—as he
settles into an intensely local debate with Latin American friends on the
lineages of Spanish-language poetry. La Rotonde is the gate through
which Vallejo's body and writing enter into the metropolitan chronicle
and its contents: structured by signs of the modern, by residues of old
hierarchies and bohemian gatherings, and by an emergent new cosmopolitan culture, it stands at the nexus of the official and the marginal,
whose overlappings and exclusions will form the tracks of Vallejo's meanderings through Paris.

PARIS IN THE ROUND

In an unusually rhapsodic chronicle from late 1926, "El crepúsculo
de las águilas" (The Twilight of the Eagles) (*ACC* I: 354–57), Vallejo
praises Paris as a cosmic rather than a cosmopolitan city. If the latter is
inhabited by a mix of foreigners who retain the customs of their place
of origin, the *ciudad cósmica,* he suggests, produces a new mode of *con-
vivencia,* in which foreigners become not French but Parisian, not conscripted into the national imaginary and practice but dwelling together
in an extranational capital city.[30] Paris, Vallejo insists, is not a space
through which one passes but a place in which one takes the time to
elaborate a new mode of living. Echoing the Andalusian guide from his
first chronicle, he excoriates those Latin Americans who treat Paris as a
stop on a grand tour (*ACC* I: 458–60), who expect it to offer itself up

for quick processing—like Baudelaire's museum-goers, checking off the paintings they have already previewed in lithographs (*Selected Writings* 390)—and who are inevitably disappointed by its sights, without realizing that the promise of Paris is its encouragement of an "exploración vital y humana, es decir generosa y acendrada" (exploration which is vital and human; in other words, generous and deep-rooted). As Vallejo resigns himself to settling in Europe, Paris begins to appear in his writings not as a space for rootless cosmopolitans but as an extranational city where one puts down cosmopolitan roots.

Paris, moreover, contained all other cities—sometimes literally so, as in the Art Deco exhibition that Vallejo visited in 1925. Paris's capaciousness went beyond miniatures or simulacra: all aspects of life in other cities, Vallejo contended, were found on its streets, in its music halls, its cafés, and its cinemas. And if Paris momentarily appeared as a microcosm of the modern, it was at the same time—and increasingly so in the 1920s, as Stovall notes—in competition with several other cities: New York and Moscow, above all, but also an array of satellite cities such as Buenos Aires, Madrid, London, and Rome. Paris, in this view, is not a condensed metaphor for the modern but a metonym, just one in a series of dots on a map of modernity shaded by divergent ideologies. In Madrid and Moscow, for example, Vallejo suggests that the machine is given a benign tint, even humanized, because it is seen as working for the population (*ACC* I: 185; II: 725). In New York, by contrast, human time has become machine time, as bodies are pressed through Taylorized systems of management and productivity, which inflects even leisure time; the North American man, as Vallejo envisions him, is forced to shuttle through an increasing number of automatic actions, gestures, even suits, according to the exigencies of each daily moment (*ACC* I: 291).[31] In Paris the dichotomy of the human and the machine takes the direct form of a struggle between pedestrians and drivers; passersby who are trampled by a developing traffic system begin to germinate seeds of revolt, forming a "General Society of Pedestrians" which aims—to little avail—to take back the streets (*ACC* I: 186). And even as they pace those streets, the bodies and minds of passersby are constantly infiltrated by machine technologies and modern imaginaries: just as cubism is co-opted by an advertising system that transmits and reproduces mass consumer desire,[32] the mass itself is increasingly chopped up by forms of calculation and journalistic or bureaucratic accounting that categorize, hierarchize, and process the bodies moving through the city's cartographic and discursive grids. While the city strains nerves to the point of exhaustion, it also channels those nervous systems in the direction of consumption and habit, replacing quality of experience with efficacy of response.[33] Art or culture becomes one more node in that trained consumer system, as bodies and minds are prompted to respond to all sorts of stimuli not instinctively but automatically—to the extent that when two viewers look at a picture, "la que más pronto se emociona, esa es la más moderna" (the one who is moved most quickly is the most modern) (*ACC* I: 174).

Modern journalism, as Vallejo describes it, aims to respond to these generalized anxieties about how best to experience and process modernity. It offers interlocking explanations derived from new forms of science (physical and social), but as he repeatedly complains, it tends to bypass economics, which determines who gets to experience what and under which conditions. Vallejo's chronicles themselves move seamlessly from art to science to politics to fashion, charting the telegraphic relays between all of these fields while insisting on bringing them back to their material bases. The chronicles present a dizzying array of different social topics—art, music, dance, theater, film, sport, science, politics, economics, technology, internationalism, a combination of which usually appear in each chronicle—arranged in accordance with the chaotic logic of frenzied modernity.[34] Rather than maintaining a separation between discourses—following the classificatory impulses of the "señores norteamericanos, especialistas por excelencia, que habéis dividido y subdividido la actividad humana en innumeras casillas" (North American sirs, specialists par excellence, who have divided and subdivided human activity into numerous pigeonholes) (*ACC* I: 160)—Vallejo is careful to point to real conversations between art and surrounding systems of modernity (science, politics, sociology, cultural criticism). His chronicles thus follow a principle of simultaneity, setting clashing discourses and experiences alongside one another to foreground their mutual undercutting or illumination. The discursive dialogism of Vallejo's earlier poetry is here placed in the service of social critique, pointing—often with a light sarcastic touch—to art's coexistence with other discourses, its embeddedness within social practices. Rowe ("César Vallejo" 183) argues that Vallejo's aim here is not to mimic but to critique the modern; I would suggest that his parodic performance puts both in play, producing a mimetico-critical mode, which simultaneously reflects and dissects urban modernity.

Vallejo's 1925 chronicle "Las fieras y las aves raras en Paris" (Rare Beasts and Birds in Paris) (*ACC* I: 160–65) offers a succinct illustration.

It begins by praising the dances of Isadora Duncan, Anna Pavlova, and Tórtola Valencia for the ways in which they suggestively overlap the human with the animal, only to chart a progressive degeneration as those dances are mimicked in the spheres of cultural and social fashion. The article tracks the transformation of a scandal in the leisure spaces of high society—a leopard's escape from the Bois de Boulogne zoo—into a popular dance in music halls and cabarets, calculated to appeal to "el exotismo y la mansedumbre de los buenazos clientes de ambos lados del globo" (the exoticism and meekness of their doting clients from both sides of the globe); thereafter it meanders into both political caricature (an endangered French leopard on a diplomatic visit to Washington) and fashion (a new vogue for leopard skin). The spread of the metaphor prompts Parisian *modistes* to up the ante by introducing a new animal skin (kangaroo), which in turn leads to the development of kangaroo-effect high-heeled shoes that force their wearers to hop. From this latest permutation, in Vallejo's imagination, it is only a hop, skip, and jump to a newly fashionable dance: the kangaroo-step. While seeming to praise modern agility, this chronicle subtly excoriates modish contagion, the training of the populace to incorporate news-as-information into their thoughts and gestural routines automatically and uncritically—without, to use a Vallejian term, digesting it. The result is that everything—politics, sport, artistic movements, religion—devolves into a spectacle of fashion that offers no food for thought. Fashion becomes a metaphor that maps itself metonymically onto all aspects of modern cosmopolitan culture, leaving no time for the experience and processing of traumatic and catalytic moments of growth and change.

Vallejo's focus on fashion's infiltration and structuring of society at all levels leads not only to a Baudelaire-like sketch of contemporary culture in transformation but also to an analysis of the different layers that make up that culture, including an uncommon focus on spheres of production inside and outside the spaces where objects are consumed. In a mid-1925 chronicle (*ACC* I: 100–107) he reports on a protest over the sweatshops of China which weave the warp of Parisian high society at great cost to laborers' bodies; the protest, led by Chinese students at the Sorbonne, counters both official culture and national policy by contradicting the statements issuing from the Chinese embassy. This nuanced differentiation among layers of an immigrant populace is set in acute contrast with a high-society fashion show at the Grand Palais, presided over—as is the whole of Paris—by a glowing ad for Citroën on the Eiffel Tower. Under the watchful, winking eye of advertising,

Vallejo lays bare the suggestibility and happy ignorance of an undifferentiating consumer public in an era in which all areas—from politics and economics through science and art—are flattened out to fit into the same frame, too easily illuminating and corroborating one another, their material bases erased.

Significantly, it is in this same article that Vallejo maps out the coordinates of the modern Parisian chronicle, drawing on an example from the popular *Paris-Midi*. The modern chronicle, Vallejo asserts, is "rápida, insinuante, cinemática" (rapid, suggestive, cinematic) (*ACC* I: 105), composed of questions that reflect the uncertainty of the contemporary scene, and structured by montage. This montage is symptomatic of the disconnections that make up contemporary experience, yet in establishment journalism of the interwar years, Vallejo suggests, it tends to be used to fold events together formally, to create the illusion of a deeper coherence. His own chronicles, conversely, heighten the formal jaggedness of montage, pressing it into the service of ironic contrast; his virtually filmic writings set clashing images from the modern scene alongside one another to reveal the divergent ways in which urban modernity is experienced by subjects from different classes and cultures, such as the shows attended by members of Parisian high society where barely a foreign or a working-class face is to be seen.

Vallejo's practice here also amounts to an expansion and a corrosion of the journalistic modes of the previous generation of Latin American writers. Noe Jitrik has argued that the *modernista* chronicle set about building a "semiotic machine" for processing and representing an incipient or projected modernity; Aníbal González points out that that machine—however paradoxically—was also geared toward the production of a personal style. Vallejo's Parisian chronicles, by contrast, perform a parodic dismantling of the machine, feeding into it an often hysterical concatenation of isolated events of the modern day-to-day. Personal style here appears only in ruins. Remarkably, there is rarely any vestige of a speaking (or writing) subject in these chronicles; they appear to offer us only a record of what is seen—and especially what is read—by any perceptive newspaper-reading inhabitant of the capital.[35] Their author, however, operates as an organizing intelligence that gathers together that information: not to provide a seamless montage of daily life in cosmopolitan modernity, but to play up its contradictions, its insidious interlockings, and its exclusions. To paraphrase Rowe (186), Vallejo's sidelong parodies of modern journalistic modes comment not on the meaning of life but on the meaning of meaning in modernity, especially as mediated by the media.

Vallejo's chronicles span an always unpredictable but carefully interwoven range of subjects: from gatherings of spinsters on St. Catherine's Day—an explicit parallel to his own "bohemia inquerida" (unwanted bohemia) (*ACC* I: 370)—to automobile and art exhibitions; from convergences of rich foreigners and French luminaries at fashionable coastal resorts to international economic postwar conferences. Within individual chronicles, Vallejo weaves together figures from a variety of different spheres—from politicians through writers and starlets to his own marginal friends—satirically mimicking the vogue for soliciting nonsensical or contradictory opinions from the celebrities of the day. His chronicles insistently parody modern journalistic practices of knowledge gathering and organization: they take particular aim at the opinion polls and surveys that proliferated through the period—on questions ranging from artistic interdisciplinarity and scientific advances to modern notions of happiness—and that referred to experts in various fields instead of consulting the masses. Central to Vallejo's conception of aesthetics and cultural praxis, by contrast, is the need to judge their effect on humans rather than on what he calls "technicians"; those who should be emitting opinions on film, he declares, are actual moviegoers rather than the usual lineup of Chaplin, Epstein, Delluc, and Jannings. Our Peruvian avant-garde poet thus reveals himself unexpectedly as an early proponent of cultural studies, but his analysis of modes of consumption also extends to modes of production. In other words, it is not just the consumer but the artist who must channel a human response to modernity—which does not, however, amount to the espousal of a naive or unmediated response:

> ¡Es muy difícil ser hombre, señores norteamericanos! Es muy difícil ser esto y aquello, artista y hombre, al mismo tiempo. Un hombre que es artista, ya no puede hacer ni decir nada que se relacione con el arte, sino como artista. . . . Los expertos se apalean entre los hilillos de los bastidores y se fracturan la sensibilidad, caídos por el lado flaco del sistema, del prejuicio o del interés profesional. . . . En general, sólo vale en esta cuestión el parecer del hombre rigurosamente profano que no sea, naturalmente, un inculto. (*ACC* I: 412)

> *It's very difficult to be a man, North American sirs! It's very difficult to be one thing and the other, artist and man, at the same time. The man who is an artist can no longer say or do anything related to art as anything but an artist. . . . The experts fight it out in the wings and in the process fracture their own sensibility, falling on the weak side of the system, toward prejudice or professional interest. . . . In general, the only opinion on this question which*

has any value is that of the rigorously profane man—as long, of course, as he possesses some rudiments of culture.

While contrasting his own skeptical, questioning style to the authoritative assertiveness of critics and journalists, Vallejo deploys techniques of fragmentation to undercut the cohesionary tendencies of cultural and sociological panoramas found in the modern newspaper; railing against totalizing and homogenizing vistas of modern culture and politics, he repeatedly calls for a focus on the individual within the collective, which will be a focus of his late poetry, as I argue in chapter 6. His goal is not, however, an espousal of individualism but rather an insistence on differentiated experiences of and responses to the modern ("personal y no individual," as he puts it in a chronicle from late 1928; *ACC* II: 653). Vallejo's chronicles therefore provide a kaleidoscope of viewpoints and a welter of tonally disparate observations on a bewildering range of topics, accompanied by carefully selected images—photographs or caricatures—to give a more three-dimensional view of modernity. His model, he occasionally suggests, is the circus—a model shared by Eisenstein and Chaplin—with its manically successive and unconnected sketches performed in the round.

INTERFACES

Two art forms in particular appear repeatedly in Vallejo's chronicles as a site for thinking through the body's place in urban modernity: sculpture and theater. The former offers an image of a body existing in an environment and interacting with it: now implicitly, in war memorials that gather both the nation's history and contemporary masses of citizens and tourists around themselves; now explicitly, in Cubist and Futurist attempts to work the surrounding space into the sculptural object. As we saw in *Trilce,* Vallejo's eye determinedly catches bodies in movement, and his chronicles on sculpture are no exception to this, insisting on the sculptor's use of touch alongside imagination, which brings stone to life while bringing art closer to manual labor. But the most direct staging of the relation between a body and its environment is found in theater, which shows—especially in the naturalist modes of Ibsen and Shaw, which had such a profound impact on Vallejo— the shaping of the human subject by outside pressures. This staging connects directly to Vallejo's ongoing concern with the production of thought and speech in a particular context, which points to a politics of placement and gesture in his work; as he writes in a mid-1929 chronicle on new theatrical scenography in France and Russia:

> El pensamiento o, más ampliamente, el espíritu de un personaje varía, y no puede dejar de variar, siguiendo consustancialmente el desenvolvimiento de sus gestos, el tinte de su rostro, los pliegues de su vestido y el lugar donde se halla. (ACC II: 756)

> *A character's thought or, more broadly, spirit varies—cannot help varying—in accordance with the unfolding of his gestures, the tint of his face, the folds of his costume and the place where he finds himself.*

Clothing and context, in contingent relation to the body, shape its possibilities of experience and expression at any moment. The resulting mutability of the body poses problems for any artistic attempt to capture a character in both its momentary appearance and its longer duration; this is clearly a concern of Cubists and Futurists alike, and Vallejo draws it out in comments on attempts by artist-friends to capture his face. When the Spanish-born sculptor José de Creeft produced a bust of Vallejo for the 1925 Art Deco Exhibition in Paris, the poet's failure to recognize himself in the final work led him to a meditation on new forms of portraiture (ACC I: 153), which is rounded out by the comments of another friend in Paris—the Salvadoran caricaturist Toño Salazar—who laughed at Vallejo's inability to present his face to an artist:

> "Usted no sabe, por lo visto, el código del gesto. Menester es que lea usted a Thooris, a Thumazean y a los modernos terapeutas ingleses, que tratan de la gimnasia facial. . . . Lea usted a estos sabios y no solamente sabrá posar para los artistas malos y para las mujeres bonitas, sino que podrá usted hasta llegar a ser un hombre verdaderamente hermoso." (ACC I: 378)

> *"Apparently you're not familiar with the code of gesture. You need to read Thooris, Thumazean, and the modern English therapists who write on facial gymnastics. . . . Read these learned men, and you'll not only learn how to pose for bad artists and beautiful women; you may even turn yourself into a truly handsome man."*

Salazar might also have suggested that Vallejo read Mina Loy's 1919 essay, "Auto-Facial-Construction," which examines "our inherent right not only to 'be ourselves' but to 'look like ourselves'" and which promises to teach "men and women who are intelligent—and for the briefest period, patient—to become masters of their facial destiny" (Loy 165).[36] Loy's essay looks like a parody of beauty advertisements and training manuals; but as the ubiquity of those genres attested, parody had become popular practice. Along the same lines, Vallejo views theater and its gestures as just an exaggerated form of daily performance; this same chronicle looks backstage at actresses preparing for their onstage roles by performing facial exercises, then cuts to a view of female audience members on their way to the theater, performing exactly the same exercises as they prepare to present themselves in public, albeit on the other side of the curtain (*ACC* I: 378).

This split-screen observation is folded into a broader study of the transformation of the body in modernity. In Vallejo's chronicles, the body becomes the nexus for thinking through a number of crucial topics: artistic versus manual labor, behavior in society and in the workplace, and the modern phenomenon of international competitions—all of which are organized around the question of the body's increasing rationalization and training. As we saw at the outset, Vallejo presented himself on his arrival in Paris as a worker rather than as an artist, and his comments in various chronicles point to the need to use all parts of the body in both end-driven production and aesthetic experiment. Echoing but also contorting Schiller's tirade against mankind's modern division through specialization, Vallejo calls for the division of labor to be reincorporated into the body itself—in other words, to accept that different parts of the body perform different functions. His preferred shorthand for this is the French expression "le violon d'Ingres," an allusion to the artist Jean-Auguste-Dominique Ingres's cultivation of a hobby—playing the violin—to balance out his professional dedication to painting. Just as a retouched Man Ray photo of 1924 tattooed a violin's f-holes onto both sides of Kiki de Montparnasse's body, Vallejo maps Ingres's violin directly onto the human physique by dividing the latter between left and right sides—although here, as in *Trilce,* he allows for imbalance.[37] To be a fully functioning artist, in Vallejo's account, is to use both sides of the body, tempering convention with rebellion, learning with unlearning, reason with sentiment, always remembering the needs and senses of the body, whether producing art or labor.

As we saw in Vallejo's early poetry, his body is constantly misbehaving (or merely behaving) by irrupting into poems, getting in the way of language; but in his developing experience in Paris—seen in his chronicles and later poetry—the movements and requirements of the body become inflected by economics. If his shame in producing *Trilce* was related to a feeling of his own immaturity in the face of the Peruvian literary establishment, in the 1920s and 1930s that shame becomes more directly and materially social; the body, in these later iterations, is never able to step out of its class positioning, however much it tries to resist the training and placement foisted upon it. This point loops around to the second function of the body in Vallejo's Paris writings: its inscription in and performance of modern techniques of behavior. The leisure practices of the interwar years, as his chronicles reveal, are structured by the twinned imperatives of fashion and sportsmanship, which determine how the body behaves in society, how one body triumphs socially or competitively over another.

Vallejo is unsurprisingly ambivalent about the question of fashion. While his material exclusion from high (or even midlevel) society motivates his critique of fashion's exclusivity, his concern with the body's relation to all that touches it calls forth a more nuanced reflection on the role of clothing. This ranges from a recurrent interest in costume designers' work for theater companies to more extended analyses of the shaping of bodies—in particular, female bodies—through the latest fashions. The figure of the female body comes insistently to the fore in Vallejo's chronicles on modernity, in repeated references to fashion, film stars, cabaret performers, international beauty contests, female athletic events, and feminist assemblies, not to mention ubiquitous war widows. Yet he insists on the impression of sterility gleaned from clothing on the boulevards; women's fashion, he complains, denaturalizes the body, alluding to and supplanting pregnancy through prosthetic bumps that shift the nineteenth-century bustle from back to front of the body. And it was not only bodies that were being constrained by fashion designers. So too were imaginations, and especially the imagination of the gullible tourist—who, Vallejo claims, was met at French ports by models sent to parade the latest fashions on trains to the capital, such that by the time potential buyers arrived in Paris they were already trained in the novelties they should desire (*ACC* I: 127).

As is so often the case in Vallejo's chronicles, what looks like a local or purely frivolous concern is carefully mapped onto international conflicts and political debates, then taken back to its economic bases. Thus the new vogue for ever-shorter skirts in Paris and New York (following Mona Palva's "indecent" dance on the Parthenon; *ACC* I: 176, 313–14) not only marks a competition between two capitals of consumer society, but is itself revealed to be a disguised response to rationing in France, covering up the fact that material is running short. As his chronicles progress and as his own clothes become more threadbare, Vallejo increasingly turns his attention to fashion's solidification of divisions along lines of class and culture, which becomes especially visible in "fashionable" settings and at borders: the rich tourist, he notes, is made aware that he is crossing a border by a series of bureaucratic requirements, whereas the impoverished traveler, who has nothing to declare but the tattered clothes on his back, passes through without noticing the break (*ACC* I: 332). Several of his chronicles focus on the clothing of the disenfranchised, directly echoing the emphases of Chaplin's films; but, like Chaplin, Vallejo can also be incredibly funny about the question of fashion, drawing zany connections or relays between nature and artificiality. Will the new vogue for slimness be followed by one of shortness, he wonders, and does nature itself go through its own fashion cycles? Are mushrooms caps an inspiration for the latest vogue in headwear, or a response to it? (*ACC* I: 275–78). Vallejo not only takes the wolf-in-sheep's-clothing as a sign of dandyism in nature, but extends the covert human fascination with animals and their skins to a meditation on science's animal experiments.

MONKEY GLANDS, MIMESIS, MODERN BODIES

One such experiment was Serge Voronoff's sale of monkey glands as the key to human rejuvenation and beautification, which was all the rage in interwar Europe. Vallejo's chronicles from 1926 offer a running commentary on Voronoff's experiments (*ACC* I: 178–79, 270–73, 307–8; see also Armstrong 143), which not only bear upon questions of beauty but also connect via their monkey base to larger questions of mimesis, which structures both fashion (socialization through imitation) and public culture (theater's code of gesture). This runs on multiple levels, as Vallejo gleefully exploits all aspects of the new vogue. The insertion of monkey glands into the human is treated metaphorically as a question of biological montage, creating hybrid human bodies fused not with machines but with animals, ironically moving them backward along the evolutionary chain. Popular theater, he claims, similarly thrives on the incorporation of foreign elements, making itself up out of preexisting forms, and bad theater—such as works by the wildly successful Cocteau, whom Vallejo attacks repeatedly and somewhat enviously throughout 1926—relies so heavily on histrionic gesture that it might easily be performed by monkeys (*ACC* I: 229). Finally, the wholesale human investment in the regenerating potential of animals is taken to absurd extremes: if humans realize that through their new machines they have managed to imitate birds in flight, Vallejo jokes, it is only a short step to expecting to be able to lay eggs—an outrageous mimesis that wanders from metaphor into metonymy (*ACC* I: 271). "Voronoffisme," like Borges's Tlön, has gradually infiltrated all spheres of modern life; the term may have been kept out of the dictionary (*ACC* I: 272), but it makes its way into popular and high culture through scientific and artistic imaginations, as a practice of hopeful, but also fundamentally inorganic, montage. It is tempting to think of the Voronoff vogue as inflecting Vallejo's essay on "Poesía nueva" (also 1926), which critiques the facile incorporation of technological terms into poetry before they are processed by the body.

Sport offers Vallejo another opportunity to discuss not only what is grafted onto the modern body but also the reformulation of that body in both its labor and leisure hours. As we have learned to expect from his chronicles, the question forks outward into divisions between professional and nonprofessional forms, trained and spontaneous movement, high-society spectacles and popular pursuits. In his dispatches the broken bodies of World War I are replaced not by George Grosz's prosthetic monsters but by "sportsmen" who have learned to live at the speed of modernity, whose mental and emotional responses are as swift as their physical reflexes. The epitome of the modern writer, for Vallejo, is Henri de Montherlant (*ACC* I: 514–16), with his interest in such performances of hypermasculinity as bullfighting and soccer; the zigzagging, lunging movements of his prose and public persona make him the equivalent of Chaplin, both of them deploying mental agility and montage-like movements in the service of surprise. Vallejo astutely links both Montherlant and Chaplin to Satie, whose *Gymnopédies* were themselves inspired by Greek sport and whose music—with its unpredictability, humor, and virtuosity—trained the audience to listen critically and actively (*ACC* I: 255 61).

Vallejo locates sport's greatest potential not in the end-directed or repetitive movements of games that train and strain muscles to the point of paralysis (his reading of tennis offers a veiled commentary on Taylorization; *ACC* I: 250–51) but in its capacity to break records, to reveal new possibilities of human achievement—sometimes with the aid of machines, as in the case of Charles Lindbergh, who flits through several of Vallejo's chronicles in the mid-1920s. Discoveries made by bodies in motion map out the horizon of the possible and lead to the quick popularization of bodily feats (*ACC* I: 452); thus the sudden masses of swimmers crossing the English Channel from 1926 onward (Gumbrecht 87–89) belie the difficulty faced by the first person to believe and prove it possible. Vallejo reserves his praise for those who—like Columbus—

put themselves in movement without being certain of the outcome, beginning from a moment of suspension that is incipiently political rather than simply aesthetic (*ACC* I: 207). It is in a chronicle from this period, imagining a dialogue about a cycle race that pits spectators against performers, that he lays out a preliminary prose version of the poem "En el momento en que el tenista . . ." (At the moment when the tennis player . . .); the poem's closing invocation, "Oh Marx! Oh Feuerbach!" coincides with the beginnings of Vallejo's formal engagement with Marxism, connecting the apparent dichotomy between thought and action to what he calls a purely animal moment of openness, which characterizes both the philosopher's wavering on the brink of a new thought and the tennis player's hopes before hitting the ball (*ACC* I: 488–90).[38] This kind of motion is neither repetitive nor trained but plays against and beyond its own limits; its sudden burst of achievement gives an aura of heroism to modern sport, a heroism filtered through Vallejo's developing readings in Marxism into an apotheosis of revolutionary action, to be tempered by a slowly emerging but longer-lasting heroism of thought. Here Vallejo distances himself from the Marxian concept of permanent revolution, issuing instead a virtual call to order at the end of what he posits as a transitional period; in a chronicle from late 1927, which explicitly states that "el comunismo y el sport son, desde el punto de vista moral, dos signos paralelos de la época" (communism and sport are, from a moral perspective, two parallel signs of the era), he insists that the grace of sporting events and revolutions alike resides in their necessarily short duration (*ACC* I: 502–3).

But how were untrained, nonprofessional bodies to perform in sport and revolution?[39] Although Vallejo increasingly foregrounds sport's potential to train mass bodies in the art and mentality of rebellion, his vision rejects the forms of the fascist mass spectacle, or any form of purely physical collective movement. Thus he criticizes equally the fashionable imitation of earlier sporting achievements—which hinders the imagining of new goals—and the unthinking movement of mass subjects alongside other unthinking bodies.[40] Sport, moreover, was palpably prey to co-optation by nationalist ideologies in the proliferating international competitions of the 1920s (tennis matches, boxing, beauty contests, the Olympic Games), which frequently affirmed the hegemony of rationalized American bodies over their weakening European rivals while reducing their audiences to passive masses. His chronicles insist instead on the need to practice sport as an individual rather than a collective or purely observational pursuit; they reserve their most trenchant critique for society's ethos of comparison and one-upmanship, which impedes what Vallejo sees as the paradoxically selfless development of the individual: "La vida como match es una desvitalización de la vida" (Life as a match devitalizes life) (*ACC* I: 476). Vallejo here makes one of his only explicit comments on his ethos prior to his full immersion in Marxism:

> Yo no vivo comparándome a nadie ni para vencer a nadie y ni siquiera para sobrepujar a nadie. Yo vivo solidarizándome y, a lo sumo, refiriéndome concéntricamente a los demás, pero no rivalizando con ellos. No busco batir ningún record. Yo busco en mí el triunfo libre y universal de la vida. (*ACC* I: 477)

> *I do not live comparing myself to anyone nor trying to beat anyone nor even to lord it over anyone. I live by putting myself in solidarity with others and, at the very most, by referring concentrically to them, but without competition. I am not trying to break any records. I seek in myself the free and universal triumph of life.*

In his chronicles of the late 1920s, Vallejo increasingly sets sporting events against stymied interwar peace conferences, intimating that the former provide more edifying and effective instances of international communication, which needed to take place through bodies rather than through clashing languages. If we set this alongside his Spanish-speaking exclusion from supposedly polyglot artistic gatherings and his developing sense of connection to anonymous suffering bodies on the Paris streets, we begin to glimpse the shift in his thought from the promise of linguistic communication to that of bodily empathy which will become so prominent in his late poetry. Under the pressure of material fact in the cosmopolis and in light of the failing ventures of the League of Nations, the conversational situations enshrined in his earlier poetry were being forced to cede to the experiences of the body, whose common materiality seemed to present the only possibility of cutting across lines of both culture and class. The body, moreover, offered a redemptive interface between technology and art, nowhere more palpably than in the *theremin* (invented in 1919 and sponsored for development by Lenin), an apparatus with two antennas that was manipulated by a performing body from a slight distance (*ACC* I: 522–27). If the Italian Futurist Luigi Russolo's *intonarumori* of the previous decade represented the first viable technological instrument to reproduce the sounds of the century, the theremin made the body itself a vehicle for the production of sound, removing the need to lay hands on the musical instrument, keeping the machine subservient to the human figure rather than rendering the latter obsolete (*ACC* II: 642). Vallejo's enthusiasm stems from the extension this implies of the body's capabilities: producing gestures as well as sounds, inspiring music rather than remaining subservient to it, and sculpting empty space.

Vallejo's concern, however, was not only with the body of the artist, but with the massed bodies of the audience for art, which were increasingly finding themselves excluded or hierarchized. If spectators were being kept at arm's length from artworks in museums—as Vallejo slyly comments of the attempt to protect paintings from the effects of visiting bodies, "el aliento del hombre mata a la historia" (man's breath kills history) (*ACC* II: 695)—they were also being pushed farther away from a proper theatrical experience, whether by ticket prices, growing swarms of tourists, disruptions by the surrealists or visiting politicians, or a stagnating French dramaturgy. Or, indeed, by their own cultural- and class-consciousness: Vallejo repeatedly complains about the fact that Spanish speakers are nowhere to be found in the foyers of Paris's grand theaters, preferring instead to cluster around popular entertainment and music halls (*ACC* I: 255). Yet the music hall also had a pronounced draw for Vallejo himself, and it coincides with his interest in black theater and music in Paris from the first irruption of the *Revue nègre* in 1925. Music halls not only opened their doors to a more diverse clientele but also allowed for experiments in "international style" (Edwards; Klein), weaving the French chanson together with tango, *son,* and rumba while turning their multicultural spectators into participatory bodies.[41] Furthermore, by drawing upon new technologies of scenography—such as the quick scene changes it was learning from cinema—the music hall revue, Vallejo maintained, heightened the experience of being in the world as well as in the theater; representing dazzling sequences of shifting cultural scenes that nonetheless foregrounded their own artificiality, they demanded of the spectator a critical reflection on the relation between art and life.

Black theater and revues were especially suggestive for Vallejo because of their performances of displacement: dislocated bodies and body parts dislocating culture.[42] As the composer George Antheil recalled, "Black music made us remember at least that we still had bodies which had not been exploded by shrapnel" (cited in Kahn, 66). These self-fragmenting bodies paradoxically portended a newly integrative, international culture—even while, as Vallejo ironically noted, the French were attempting to renationalize this distinctly African American form by claiming to have coined the term *"jasse"* (*ACC* I: 198). The jazz band itself, as even a quick scan of Latin American avant-garde poems from the 1920s can attest, quickly became the preeminent sign of global modern culture; the performer Louis Douglas appears alongside Tagore and Spengler in one of Vallejo's lists of the most influential figures of the modern era (ACC 210). But Vallejo also takes black theater as an unusually direct analogue to his own production, using it as an occasion for reflecting—however obliquely—on the relation between art and ethnicity. Commenting on the "conquista de París por el teatro negro" (the conquest of Paris by black theater) through its performances in Rolf de Maré's Théâtre des Champs-Élysées, Vallejo prefaces his remarks with the following statement:

> No voy a relacionar para nada mis elogios al arte negro con mi obra poética, ni vaya a verse en aquéllos explicación alguna de mi estética. Libre es el blanco de llamar a mi verso, verso negro, y el negro de llamarlo blanco o rojo. Yo no me meto en ello. (ACC I: 170)

> *I'm not going to draw any connection between my praise for black art and my own poetic work, nor should any explanation for my aesthetic be sought in the former. White readers are free to call my poetry black poetry, and black readers to call it white or red. I have nothing to say on the subject.*

The initial disclaimer is immediately arresting: despite Vallejo's insistence on decoupling art from the artist's raced body, the only way to respond to his unmotivated injunction *not* to connect black art and his poetry is precisely to connect them; the negative here seems a surreptitious positive. His reading of African American dance forms—insisting on their auditory more than their visual nature—loops back to his unusual interest in sound over sight, reasserting his investment in an artistic commitment to rhythm that prepares for the body's full entrance into both performance and reception.[43]

As Vallejo witnessed the anticommunist maneuvers of the Western powers and the covert replacement of international dialogue with multinational superbanks (ACC II: 845–47), his faith in the possibility of effective linguistic communication began to falter. At this critical geopolitical juncture, Vallejo turns his attention to the ways in which bodily gestures can overcome linguistic differences, focusing on those art forms that conjoined the two modes of communication: theater and film, especially in their respective deployments of bodies. The interwar period saw these two forms pitted against one another, modifying one another and themselves through their competition, against the backdrop of debates over the emergent form of sound film, which threatened to dismantle the carefully constructed theoretical armature of cinema in its silent opposition to theater. From the mid-1920s onward, Vallejo's chronicles offer an obsessive monitoring of this unsettled conflict, which forks through scenography, the languages and national bases of theatrical and filmic modes, the gestural syntaxes of theater and film, international circulation, and, finally, the possibilities that both forms offered for reflecting on art's relationship to life, to praxis, and to the world. In the process, he maps out a cultural and political panorama crisscrossed by linguistic disconnections and indifference to bodies, yet that also offers glimpses of a possible redemption through art in a state of crisis.

WORLD STAGES, WORLD SCREENS

From Vallejo's very earliest chronicles, theater marks a shifting point in a kaleidoscopic image of Parisian culture. Surveying the experiments of local theater and tracking the movements of foreign companies through the city, Vallejo studies the recalibration of the contemporary theatrical scene as it responds to developments in other artistic media and in different geographical areas. The theater offers a sometimes covert, sometimes open space in which politics is both analyzed onstage and conducted in the audience; as previously discussed, Vallejo directs his gaze simultaneously to the performers onstage and to the social performances taking place among the audience, which included clashes of and within classes and encounters between rival politicians and/or artists. And as with all facets of modern culture that appear in his chronicles, theater and its stars continually appear alongside figures from a variety of fields—science, politics, philosophy, high society—in a frictional interrelation between spheres of the social.[44]

Several figures from the theatrical world draw Vallejo's particular attention in these chronicles, and it is noteworthy that they tend not to be Paris-based. While he rails against the stagnation of French drama— reduced to a reliance on rhetoric rather than fully exploring the possibilities of gesture—he praises productions of plays by George Bernard Shaw and Luigi Pirandello, admiring the political humanism of the former and the philosophical investigations of the latter (ACC I: 171; II: 867).[45] Both Shaw the naturalist and Pirandello the vanguardist, in Vallejo's reading, were reconstellating connections between art and life, offering potent reelaborations of questions of social justice. This was especially significant now that audiences had been shut out of public trials, which had previously satisfied their desire for a glimpse behind the curtain of legal mechanisms—a situation that had in turn comprised a triple spectacle for the cultural critic, offering a simultaneous view of a narrative (the criminal case), an audience (the mass public), and a governing code (the justice system) (*ACC* I: 239–40).

Vallejo reserves some of his highest praise for the productions of the Cartel group—Charles Dullin, Georges Pitoëff, Gaston Baty, Louis Jouvet—who drew upon Russian experiments to revolutionize not just theatrical narratives or dialogues but also scenographic theories and practices (*ACC* II: 757). Vallejo's own theater reviews enact a progressive shift in focus from the actual text of a drama to its staging. This is in part a continuation of his commitment to exploring the body's relationship to its context but also an oblique reflection of his difficulties as a Spanish-speaking audience member catching only snatches of dialogue. This is not simply an anecdotal point. Vallejo insistently locates theater's fullest promise in its capacity to reach across cultures, through its physical enactment of a problem rather than a linguistic presentation of a theme; his chronicles meditate on and grapple with theater's capacity to overcome its own linguistic grounding by developing the possibilities of gestural communication, which, he suggests, is its only defense against the growing threat of sound film.

Theater, in Vallejo's chronicles, is both a closed system and a stage that opens onto the world. As with sport and fashion, he presents it as a direct and often ironic analogue to contemporary local and global politics; his most prescient articles on contemporary drama establish a sarcastic counterpoint with the floundering League of Nations, which was not only unable to halt a barely disguised arms race among the Western powers, but had reduced its stewardship of the international community to a focus on membership fees (*ACC* I: 356). By contrast, Vallejo comments approvingly on the efforts of Firmin Gémier, who had laid the basis for a popular theater to promote social change through artistic experiment and who in 1925 founded the Société Universelle du Théâtre to encourage connections between theater artists from a variety of countries (*ACC* I: 172; II: 643). Gémier's proposal seemed an ideal response to Vallejo's concern with the monolingualism of French theatrical culture; it promised to facilitate tours of foreign companies through Paris, which to this point had taken place largely—and too sporadically—through Rolf de Marié's Théâtre des Champs-Élysées, which presented the Ballets Suédois and the Ballets Russes, Futurist concerts and Ukrainian choirs, and, of course, the *Revue nègre*. A second example was offered by Granovsky's Moscow Jewish State Theater, whose performances in Yiddish nonetheless reached beyond a narrow linguistic community by drawing upon the scenographic and gestural resources of circus, music hall, dance, and film (*ACC* II: 641–42).[46]

Although these examples seemed to portend a withering away of nationalism in the theater, the late 1920s pointed to the increasing Americanization of stage and screen (*ACC* II: 643), which Vallejo saw paralleled in the growing Western anticommunist bloc represented by the League of Nations. As a counterpart and corrective, Vallejo heralds new developments in Russian theater and theory. This takes on a new urgency after his first two visits to the Soviet Union in 1928 and 1929 where he delighted—in spite or precisely because of the language barrier—in the representation of new scenes and scenarios, collective bodies, and machinery, all of which he would work into his own experiments in theater. He goes so far as to suggest that the "fábula materialista y viviente de la dictadura proletaria" (living and materialist fable of the proletarian dictatorship) constitutes an entirely new theatrical genre, the latest in a line running from Greek tragedy, medieval passion plays, and Wagner's mythology through to bourgeois symbolist drama (*ACC* II: 891–93).[47]

But these glimmers of hope for theater are set increasingly against the threat posed to it by film, on which Vallejo begins to reflect in 1926.[48] As he noted in the manifesto-like "Se prohíbe hablar al piloto" (Do Not Speak to the Driver) (*ACC* I: 348–49), film was by this point well on its way to invading all art forms—including poetry—due to its greater technical capacity for capturing the rapid shifts of modern life or "vida cinemática" (cinematic life) (*ACC* I: 344). If theater actors had previously dominated the scene of Vallejo's chronicles as the most representative figures of interwar life—possessing integrated and trained bodies that were so valuable they needed to be insured (*ACC* I: 119)—film rather worked with fragmentation, undercutting any need for bodily wholeness or presence. The figure of the film actor, as Benjamin ("Work of Art") noted, was entirely the creation of the medium and of its governing organism, the studio, which produced a whole image of the actor through montage and publicity; Siegfried Kracauer extended this line of thought to a reflection on the modern public, whose body was being carefully woven together in mass spectacles by fascist choreographers. For both of these theorists, the figure of the diva emblematized the divorce between worker and product in the age of technological reproducibility: even her bodily movements no longer belonged to her.

Vallejo's compatriot Mariátegui gave this gendered analysis of film a further twist, pitting the diva against the writer in a discussion of cultural circulation and geographical hierarchies: if the former, through her recorded screen performance, could travel easily, silently, and ethereally to reach a range of different publics, the writer was constrained by the slowness of his work, uncertain access to both audiences and celebrity, the need for agents and mediators, and linguistic constraints (*Artista* 195–96).

In Vallejo's chronicles, however, female bodies tend to be associated with theater, whereas film is the province of male bodies—and, in particular, the mobile slapstick body of Charlie Chaplin. Throughout 1927 and 1928, as Vallejo develops his readings in Marxism and begins to modify his conception of art's role and critical potential, Chaplin is the figure who comes most frequently to the fore; in fact the shift in Vallejo's sense of art's capacity to treat questions of social justice can be located in two chronicles that touch on *The Gold Rush* (1925). In the first, "Religiones de vanguardia," from 1927 (*ACC* I: 412–14), Vallejo noted that cinema was developing its own audience of devotees largely because of the immensely affective performances of Chaplin; ironically, the public's passionate attachment to the Tramp coincided with and was partly driven by the lurid spectacle of his divorce from Lita Grey, who put the most intimate details of Chaplin's private life on display. For Vallejo, this sordid affair becomes the occasion for a reflection on private versus public bodies, on the artist as both human being and representative of social types, stitching together a concern in his chronicles with interrelations between the elites and the anonymous masses. The crux of the debate around Chaplin, Vallejo notes, has come to settle on the material contradiction between Chaplin the millionaire and Charlie (Charlot/Carlitos) the tramp. Whereas most commentators revealed their discomfort with the sharply ironic contrast between the two, Vallejo praises Chaplin's ability to stage a touching encounter between social classes—not simply by producing films that reached the broadest possible variety of publics (across classes, cultures, and languages), but through the movements of his own body as well.

In the early 1928 chronicle, "La pasión de Charles Chaplin" (The Passion of Charlie Chaplin) (*ACC* II: 560–62), Vallejo asserts that in *The Gold Rush* "Chaplin, sumo poeta de la miseria humana, pasa por la película de espaldas a sus dólares" (Chaplin, supreme poet of human misery, walks through the film with his back to his dollars), investing his immense wealth in the creation of a figure of absolute poverty who nonetheless capitalizes on every unsuspected resource of human dignity. Chaplin the filmmaker and Charlie the tramp both possessed the capacity to transform the most insignificant, useless objects into the mainstays of a man trying to make do, giving waste products and throwaways a new value (another avatar of Chaplin/Charlie is of course Leopold Bloom). Most crucially, Chaplin uses his own well-known, well-to-do body to reach out directly and touchingly to the most dispossessed creatures; the film offers the potent political image of "Charles Chaplin, gentleman y multimillonario, rascándose las ingles de Charlot mendigo y comido de grandes piojos dignos" (Charles Chaplin, gentleman and multimillionaire, scratching the thighs of Charlot the tramp, being nibbled by great dignified fleas). Chaplin's body is therefore not simply a collage (made up of scraps of clothing), but a palimpsest, in which millionaire and mendicant illuminate and touch one another. From Vallejo's perspective, Chaplin's portrayal of the marginalized other is not a patronizing or easy source of entertainment but shows a determination to put himself in the very place of the other, experiencing the impoverished other's physical discomfort and representing it for an otherwise indifferent public; demanding an empathetic response, his painful but proud impersonation creates "nuevos y más humanos instintos políticos y sociales" (new and more human political and social instincts), grounded in bodily identification. *The Gold Rush* thus stands as "una sublime llamarada de inquietud política, una gran queja económica de la vida, un alegato desgarrador contra la injusticia social" (a sublime flaring-up of political concern, a great economic complaint about life, a heartrending argument against social injustice).

It deserves note that Chaplin served as a nexus between a quite startling array of discourses on modernity issuing from different parts of the globe in the late 1920s, from pan-European Cubists, Futurists, and surrealists through Frankfurt school theorists and Russian constructivists to Spanish and Latin American defenders of aesthetic and political avant-gardes.[49] Traveling quickly around the world and reaching across classes and cultures, his films nonetheless met with culturally specific responses, which revealed the national-ideological underpinnings of responses to culture in the interwar years. As Chaplin himself noted, while he was attacked in the United States for his private scandals he was celebrated in Russia as a realist revolutionary; acclaimed as an intellectual in Germany but received as a clown in England and a comedian in France (85). If Chaplin insisted instead that he was a tragedian, Vallejo reads him as a messianic figure (note the title of the chronicle) but one who secularizes the practice of Christian compassion. Chaplin's capacity to transcend cultural differences also made him a powerful metonym for silent cinema, the mode to which he clung. Chaplin famously resisted the full incorporation of sound into film until *The Great Dictator* (1940) which, as the title suggests, aimed to show the abuse of rhetoric (connecting to Vallejo's own misgivings about the efficacy of political language). In *Modern Times* (1936), the few voices heard are mediated by modern technology, alluded to in *The Great Dictator*'s excoriation of "machine men, with machine minds and machine hearts"; a momentary exception comes in the nonsense song performed by Chaplin's character, which has traces of Italian, English, Spanish, and French but which by garbling all languages restricts itself to none, and hence holds open its accessibility to all audiences.

This preservation of silence is central to Vallejo's growing interest in cinema as a critical counterweight to the hollow rhetoric of theater and international conferences alike. Cinema quickly displaces Vallejo's interest in theater, in large measure because it offered a sensorial respite from linguistic histrionics through its purely visual syntax. But his engagement with film coincides with the medium's own moment of crisis in the face of the imminent incorporation of sound—a crisis that paralleled the threat film posed to theater. The late 1927 chronicle, "Contribución al estudio del cinema" (Contribution to the Study of Cinema) (*ACC* I: 511–12), casts Vallejo and a friend taking refuge from the cacophony of the streets in a movie theater, only to find that the film, *Ben Hur,* is drowned out by its orchestral accompaniment.[50] The development of sound film was the focus of intense cultural debate at precisely the moment of Vallejo's chronicle, as the introduction of sound into film threatened to undermine what had been taken to be film's essence: quick scene changes, montage, close-ups and pans, framed bodies, a self-circumscription to the visual, all of which had marked cinema's difference from (and arguably its superiority over) drama. Vallejo coincides with the established film theorists of his day—whose debates he was evidently following closely—in noting that the intrusion of speech cuts off film's ability to circulate around the world but that it also rings the death knell of theater, marking the final appropriation of theater's modes by a cannibalistic new medium (*ACC* II: 643). Like both Chaplin and Sergei Eisenstein, Vallejo counterintuitively locates cinema's greatest possibility of survival in a return to theatrical strategies—not to theater's actual language, but to its ransacking of disappearing modes such as the circus and the music hall.

But Vallejo occasionally reveals a profound unease about film's facile representations of different historical spaces and periods, its too-easy recuperation of periods lost to history. Thus he criticizes a number of important silent films—such as *Ben Hur* and *Napoleon*—for relying on cinematic sleight of hand, which allowed for the detailed depiction and hence apparent rescuing of distant moments and places, and he rails against the notion that this amounts to a redemption of history (*ACC* I: 525). His discomfort rests in film's supposition of an unthinking viewer, passively consuming images that gave a specious and fleeting sense of familiarity with the necessarily unfamiliar, colluding in a generalized modern belief in the possibility of possession through vision (Gunning, "Whole World"). Film in this sense amounted to little more than cultural tourism, mimicking the activities of rich Latin Americans on grand tours of Europe in which experience played itself out on the retina, providing no real material for thought or development (*ACC* I: 460).[51] But most troubling to Vallejo was not film's easy connection of different spaces but its elision of the question of temporality and loss. Convincing representations of lost historical periods, or the presentation of other cultures as occupying a place outside history, stood in the way of serious ethnographic study or cross-cultural understanding; instead, they presented the viewer with images of the past or of distant places that required no real engagement with history or with other cultures. Finally, fantasies of technological reanimation, which underlay both Isadora Duncan's museum-based dances and the pageantlike historical films of the 1910s and 1920s, created the too-comforting impression that history itself was easily recuperable.[52]

Nonetheless, it was in film's processing of time that Vallejo also located its greatest capacity for reeducating the viewer, as long as its own devices were laid bare. Drawing on different art forms and working through montage, he suggested, film could reconnect different temporalities: not simply by offering more convincing reenactments of history, a quicker documentation of contemporary life, and wilder imaginings of the future than theater, but also by experimenting openly with different mediatic techniques of representation that revealed their artifice. Vallejo's chronicles sketch out two key examples of this, both of which open the discourse on cinema outward toward its engagement with and of the public. The first involves avant-garde movie houses in Paris, such as the legendary Studio des Ursulines, which offered triple bills of films from different periods—showing a film from the earliest days of cinema alongside a film offering a conventional narrative (whether historical or contemporary) and an example of avant-garde film, characterized by a different kind of technique that explicitly plays up montage and fragmentation over the construction of a narrative (*ACC* II: 608–11). The triple bill required viewers to deal with three different techniques and periods at once, making them conscious of the temporality of techniques themselves and inviting them to focus on the relation between different spaces on screen. Vallejo's second example takes up an idea from Alfonso Reyes's 1924 collection, *Calendario,* which lays out a fantasy for a living museum. Where Reyes's suggestion involves theatrical actors, however, Vallejo's reworking brings in film technology: screening images from the past alongside projections of present-day figures and actual visitors while also projecting images of the future (*ACC* I: 415–17). Rather than corralling the past and presenting it in easily digestible form, this reconfigured museum would open a space in which the past, present, and future could literally or virtually rub against one another, allowing for nonhierarchical encounters between cultures and classes. Museum and movie house could thus provide a virtual space for the "passerby" to witness other cultures while remaining conscious of the artificiality of the encounter: producing active viewers, preparing minds and bodies alike for encounters with other times and spaces, to develop a more mobile and conceptually dense experience of the contemporary, as well as a more critical awareness of modes of representation.

For Vallejo, cinema—like the theremin—also presented a potent interface between the body, technology, and the world. Its storage mechanisms captured the present for the future, assuring the survival of the contemporary and its potential for critical dialogue with whatever might follow. It also allowed for the elaboration of new codes of gesture that—like Chaplin's body—could travel across cultures. This was an acute question given Vallejo's faltering faith in the power of the word. In a 1926 chronicle on Esperanto (*ACC* I: 200–202) he had called for the elaboration of a universal language of understanding—especially necessary in an era of international conferences aiming to prevent future wars, such as the 1925 Treaty of Locarno, which he repeatedly presented as collapsing into a cacophony of different languages, beset by mistranslation of both words and intentions; as he succinctly puts it, "siempre queda para escoger, en idioma como en política, entre la Nación y la Internacional" (one must always choose, in language as in politics, between the Nation and the International) (*ACC* I: 202). But in one of the last signed chronicles he would write—a 1931 piece setting "capitalist" against "proletarian" literature—he disconsolately voiced his sense of a generalized breakdown in communication, grounded in a use of language whose emptiness was attributable to capitalism's promotion of the individual over the collective and which could also be read as an epiphenomenon of a recrudescent nationalism:

> El verbo está vacío. Sufre de una aguda e incurable consunción social. Nadie dice a nadie nada. La relación articulada del hombre con los hombres se halla interrumpida. El vocablo del individuo para la colectividad se ha quedado trunco y aplastado en la boca individual. . . . Tácitamente, en la cotidiana convivencia, todos sentimos y nos damos cuenta de este drama social de confusión. Nadie comprende a nadie. El interés de uno habla un lenguaje que el interés del otro ignora y no entiende. (ACC II: 895–96)

> *The word is empty. It suffers from an acute and incurable social exhaustion. No one says anything to anyone. Man's articulated relation to other men has been interrupted. The word of the individual to the collectivity has been cut off and crushed in individual mouths. . . . Tacitly, in daily life together, we all feel and notice this social drama of confusion. No one understands anyone. One person's interest speaks a language which the other's interest can neither recognize nor understand.*

Vallejo may have momentarily placed his faith in the capacity of "proletarian literature" (Sinclair, Gladkov, Pasternak, O'Flaherty, and others) to restore plenitude of meaning to language (ACC II: 898), but after this chronicle, his own writing would effectively disappear for more than six years behind his political activism. His subsequent letters make elliptical references to political contretemps, to mysterious maneuvers, to recurring bodily ailments, but none to composition. By 1936, as his already qualified enthusiasm for Soviet socialism begins definitively to fade, we find him wavering desperately in his letters between his few possible options for a livable life: in Peru, in New York, in Madrid, none of which he ultimately finds palatable or plausible. Vallejo's despondent tone in these few letters shows nothing but the winding down of his artistic pulse.

This sense of stagnation, of loss of faith in both language and activism, was suddenly and forcefully broken by the irruption of the Spanish Civil War; as a letter from October 1936 euphorically declared, "¡Nos tienes tan absorbidos en España, que toda el alma no nos basta!" (We are so absorbed in Spain that even our entire soul falls short!). In his support for the Republican militants, Vallejo found new avenues for working across borders with the avatars of official culture—Huidobro, Neruda, Picasso, José Bergamín, and others—in an activist artistic defense of the Republic. His last two years in Paris, until his death in April 1938, were spent in a feverish whirl of activity: organizing a magazine, convening an international writers' conference, and, eventually, producing two final and fiery explosions of poetry: the untitled *Poemas humanos* and *España, aparta de mí este cáliz*. The political cataclysm of the Spanish Civil War, and a faith in the Republic's capacity for resistance, suddenly presented a new possible nexus between ethics and aesthetics, an alternative organization of international bodies. But Vallejo's sense of the writer's role in the struggle was far from naive. In one of his final chronicles, from early 1937, he presents a nuanced defense of aesthetic politics:

No nos hagamos ilusiones. Escritores hay de izquierda que cerrando los ojos a la experiencia y a la realidad, superestiman la influencia política inmediata del intelectual, atribuyendo a sus menores actos públicos una repercusión que no tienen. Hoy más que nunca, la mecánica social fundada en el triunfo de la técnica industrial, funciona completamente de espaldas al consenso del espíritu, personificado por el artista, el escritor o el sabio. . . . Mas los fueros del pensamiento tienen su revancha. Si la protesta en comicio y de viva voz, si el ademán viviente, en carne viva, de combate, se estrellan, en realidad, contra los poderes económicos coaligados, la inflexión intemporal de la idea contenida en un discurso, en un artículo del día, en un mensaje o manifiesto, es petardo que se hunde en las entrañas profundas del pueblo, para estallar, en cosecha segura, incontrastable, el día menos pensado. (ACC II: 957–58)

Let's be under no illusions. Some left-wing writers choose to close their eyes to experience and reality, overestimating the intellectual's immediate political influence, attributing to their smallest public acts a repercussion which these do not possess. Today more than ever, social mechanics—grounded in the triumph of industrial technique—work completely behind the back of the spiritual consensus, as personified in the artist, the writer, or the sage. . . . But the prerogatives of thought have a way of reasserting themselves. Even if full-throated protests in assemblies and live gestures of struggle by living bodies may smash against the coalition of economic powers, the atemporal inflection of an idea contained in a speech, a daily article, a message or a manifesto, is a firecracker which buries itself in the deepest entrails of the people, only to burst into flame, on the least-suspected day, yielding a certain and incontrovertible harvest.

In this clear-eyed statement of the limits of the word, we nonetheless catch the glimmering of a new faith in the possibilities of poetry, ushering in a final frenzied burst of composition later that year, which would also rescue the poems Vallejo had stashed away in drawers during his years at a journalist. We will turn now to that poetry as a contrapuntal voice to the chronicles, a hidden meditation on the subjectivity of the poet and of the figures who surround him and on the lyric's capacity to reentangle itself with history.

CHAPTER 6

Making Poetry History

Me dirijo . . . a las individualidades colectivas, tanto como a
las colectividades individuales, y a los que, entre unas y otras,
yacen marchando al son de las fronteras o, simplemente,
marcan el paso inmóvil en el borde del mundo.

I address myself . . . to collective individualities, and to indi-
vidual collectivities, and to those who, between one and the
other, lie marching to the sound of the frontiers or, simply,
mark time without moving at the edge of the world.

—Vallejo, "Algo te identifica" (Something Identifies You)

TRYING TO BE GOOD

Vallejo's Paris sojourn was an experience of radical dispossession. Between 1923 and 1938 he lived isolated among a handful of Spanish
speakers in the capital of cultural modernity, losing contact with Peru
while finding no new audience in Europe, made miserable by his material circumstances and by recurring physical illness. In the background
were rising poverty and frenzied industrialism; class and ideological
tensions within and between countries; economic reconfigurations, military preparations, colonial depredations; policies of "nonintervention"
in the Spanish Civil War; and the unchecked rise of fascism in Italy
and Germany. In the face of all this, the lyric might well have been left
speechless.

Yet Vallejo produced some of his most powerful verse during these
years: poems that trace the ignominy and indignities suffered by the
working classes of the world, left unsupported or unemployed by local
socioeconomic systems, and kept barely alive by their needs, desires,
and basic possessions. Gathered for the sake of critical convenience under the title *Poemas humanos*, published in 1939, a year after his death,

these poems protest at criminal and civil justice systems while offering mini-portraits of the modern citizens subjected to them. Given this subject matter, we might expect the later poetry to be both unremittingly bleak and transparently political. This is the impression given by much criticism, which tends to focus on those figures who are most locatable in a specific historical panorama: Bolsheviks, miners, laborers, the unemployed. However, these figures actually appear in only a handful of poems and in situations of enormous tonal and syntactic complexity; we miss half the power of these poems if we pay attention only to their recognizable names and fragmentary invocations and if we reduce their tone and function to the descriptive. Although they are sometimes desperately bleak and sometimes contain virulent protests, these poems are also studded with wit and unsettling tonal shifts; in fact the politics of this poetry may inhere less in its contents than in its form and humor, the latter occasionally of the blackest kind.[1] Depicting their subjects from the inside out and back again, the *Poemas humanos* have the best of intentions but sometimes also the worst of intentions. And this complicated intentionality—of both the poet and his subjects—is the only way for this poetry to rescue subjectivity: as an excess that cannot be neatly co-opted by economics, politics, sociology, bureaucracy, or lyric poetry.

Despite the bareness of the language they use to evoke their subjects—"gray urban anthropoids," as Paoli (*Mapas* 28) memorably puts it—these poems resist offering sober, realist portraits along the lines of contemporaneous Farm Security Administration works, such as the photographs of Walker Evans. The multiple portraits that teem in Vallejo's poems in fact come closer to caricatures, sketched out in lines of piquant affection and occasional irascibility; they capture the diverse human subjects of modernity in their failures and tiny triumphs, their dignified and shameful needs, their great joys and sufferings, but also their petty gripes and pleasures. Zooming in and out on their clothing, their affects, their body parts, their minimal possessions, and their environment, the *Poemas humanos* aim to offer multiple and kaleidoscopic views of the world's *transeúntes* (passersby). This latter term, which recurs repeatedly in Vallejo's poetry and prose, insists that the human as categorical entity is both temporal and historical, a figure in constant motion, caught up in contingent relations with others, with objects, with affects, and with civil systems, on a baroquely foreshortened route from cradle to grave. As Franco notes, in these poems Vallejo often behaves like a seventeenth-century poet, "not shrink[ing] from playing with words at the threshold of the grave" (*Dialectics* 196); yet in his updated version of the Baroque, the material is allowed to elbow aside the metaphysical, because "a lo mejor, me digo, más allá no hay nada" (chances are, I say to myself, beyond there is nothing), as he puts it— hedging his bets a little—in the poem "A lo mejor, soy otro" (Chances Are, I'm Another). Vallejo also, and somewhat surprisingly, blends Baroque conceits with more modern techniques drawn from cinema—and in particular, from slapstick. As a result, these poems are exercises in movement, but not always in the ways we expect.

Vallejo showed great interest in Russian experiments with montage during the late 1920s, especially those of Sergei Eisenstein and Dziga Vertov (e.g., *ERC* 147–56). Their work with montage, for example, in *Battleship Potemkin* (1925) and *Man with a Movie Camera* (1929), offered a way to organize human subjects as well as camera shots, but their process—not coincidentally—tended to obscure views of the individuals who made up the masses. As Eisenstein would acknowledge in the 1934 essay, "From Theater to Cinema," "our enthusiasm produced a one-sided representation of the masses and the collective; one-sided because collectivism means the maximum development of the individual within the collective, a conception irreconcilably opposed to bourgeois individualism" (16). This is an important suggestion of the recuperability of subjectivity for mass politics, and it harmonizes with a chronicle from late 1928, in which Vallejo places a determined accent on the *personal,* as distinct from the notion of the bourgeois *individual* (*ACC* II: 653).[2]

In this respect, Vallejo's poems come close to the work of Abel Gance, whose films offered indelible portraits of the individual members of various large groups. In *Napoleon* (1927), for example, despite the film's ostensible focus on a magnetic central figure, what leap out at us are the teeming figures who participate in the fights in the military school, or who throng riotously in the halls of the National Convention—idiosyncratic and often irascible individuals forming momentary communities. Similarly, although Vallejo's sympathies are ultimately with the anonymous masses who populate his social and political panoramas, he never loses sight of the individuals who comprise them. And in depicting those individuals, rather than underlining basic human decency, the poet makes plenty of room for evocations of moodiness, selfishness, recalcitrance. In fact his poems do not just include character flaws in their jagged portraits, but actively try to catapult their characters into complexity; as the speaker of "Me viene, hay días, una gana ubérrima, política" (There Comes to Me, [Some Days], an Exuberant, Political Hunger) puts it, "quiero ayudar al bueno a ser su poquillo de malo" (I [want] to help the good one become a little bit bad). The poem's concluding statement, "Y quisiera yo ser bueno conmigo / en todo" (And I would desire to be good to myself / in everything), signals a program not for altruism but for self-interest, as the basis for any relation to the other but also as a stubborn residue in the lyric.[3]

Vallejo's immensely humane but also slightly roguish humor keeps these late poems closest to the modes of Chaplin—who makes an appearance in the poem just quoted when its speaker expresses a desire to kiss one of his neighbors "en su Dante, en su Chaplin, en sus hombros" (on his Dante, on his Chaplin, on his shoulders). Like Chaplin, Vallejo presents characters who are recognizable and organized human subjects of modernity, whose own immediate concern is not with their place in a collective but with holding themselves together with whatever comes to hand: body parts, minimal possessions, spontaneous adjustments to a situation, a capacity to transform common objects into unlikely props for survival. In their struggles, these figures are set against both their environments and their own misbehaving bodies—recast with Baroque ghoulishness as "el sarcófago en que nacen" (the sarcophagus in which they are born)—which sometimes fail them completely ("hay gentes tan desgraciadas, que ni siquiera / tienen cuerpo"; there are people so wretched, they don't even / have a body) ("Traspié entre dos estrellas"; Stumble between Two Stars). Their dispossessed situation makes them representative figures for a collective political crisis, but their instinct for self-preservation keeps their stubbornly personal needs and desires in the foreground. They therefore need to be seen, this poetry suggests, from inside and outside at once, on their own and in groups, persistently present if always slipping out of view.

What frequently obscures their view, paradoxically, is an intensely self-critical but also stubbornly self-interested portrait of the poet, who looms large and loud in these poems, reflecting on his own relations to the modern citizens around him, testifying to their impact on him, struggling to represent them, even if this often means taking their place. One of the unsettling oddities of these poems is that it is often deliberately unclear whether the speaker is presenting himself as a distinct individual or as an indistinct type, as a poet or as a member of the species. When the poem "Altura y pelos" (Height and Hair) raises a series of questions meant to foreground elements of a common humanity—such as the self-emptying "¿Quién no se llama Carlos o cualquier otra cosa?"

(Who isn't called Carlos or some other thing?)—the speaker's answer, repeated twice at the end of each stanza in different forms, is an ironic, hyperbolic statement of his own difference: "¡Ay, yo que sólo he nacido solamente!" (Ay! I who only was solely born). The pressure of this sense of distinct indistinction, which is that of the modern subject as much as of the poet, registers itself with sidelong humor in the speaker's speeches to himself: "y entre mí, digo" (And among myself, I say; my trans.), as he puts it in a poem whose title, "Epístola a los transeúntes" (Epistle to the Passersby), dreams of a much larger audience.

This sense of the lyric as being stuck in the mode of self-address also has an anecdotal basis. Vallejo published a grand total of five poems in the years between his arrival in Paris in 1923 and his death in 1938. All of these appeared during his first few years in Europe, before his proper engagement with Marxism in the late 1920s:

a. "Trilce," published in the Spanish avant-garde journal *Alfar* in 1923;

b. "Me estoy riendo" (I Am Laughing) and "He aquí que hoy saludo" (Behold That Today I Salute), published in each of the two issues of his coedited little magazine, *Favorables Paris Poema,* July and October 1926, respectively; and

c. "Altura y pelos"—later retitled "Actitud de excelencia" (Attitude of Excellence)—and "Lomo de las sagradas escrituras" (Spine of the Sacred Scriptures), both published in the Lima weekly *Mundial* in 1927.

He appears to have hidden his ongoing lyric production in the Paris years from even those closest to him. After his death, his (allegedly surprised) widow, Georgette, found a hundred or so poems hidden away, Dickinson-like, in drawers, which she published as a single volume in 1939; several more have come to light over the intervening decades. As a result, we currently have 114 metrical, free verse, and prose poems from Vallejo's European period.[4] But these poems were never gathered by Vallejo himself into a collection, and—aside from the Spanish Civil War cycle—they have no definitive overarching title.[5] Although he seems to have revised the early but largely undated Parisian poems (47 of them, from 1923 to around 1936) and left a notebook of typed-up versions of the later poems (67 in total, all from late 1937), we do not know how, or whether, he would have arranged and published them.[6]

Of these poems, only a handful—primarily the fifteen poems organized into a Spanish Civil War cycle, *España, aparta de mí este cáliz*—reflect on datable current events. A large number of the very last poems have the date of their composition (late 1937) appended, revealing that Vallejo was shuttling back and forth—sometimes on the same day—between poems related to the Spanish Civil War and less explicitly historical poems. Of these, the allegorical "Al revés de las aves del monte" (Contrary to the Mountain Birds) internally declares its historical commitment:

> Pues de lo que hablo no es
> sino de lo que pasa en esta época, y
> de lo que ocurre en China y en España, y en el mundo.

> *For what I'm talking about is just*
> *what's happening in our epoch, and*
> *what's happening in China and in Spain, and in the world.* (Trans. modified)

But Vallejo's poetry is nowhere else so explicit about its relation to contemporary events, nor is it ever so straightforward, and we have to look elsewhere for its relation to history—in its choice of subjects, certain marked words, discursive modes. As Michael Wood gnomically emphasized in a recent article on Yeats, "A poem can refer to history in more than one way, and to more than one history." History enters into Vallejo's poems less as a *grand récit* than in its minor narratives—the specific forms of suffering and need, but also of pleasure and desire, experienced by anonymous passersby and poets in the interwar years. This is more a question of historicity than of history; in Ortega's words ("Prologue" 6), "de lo que se trata, en *Poemas humanos,* es de hacer hablar a la historicidad moderna" (*Poemas humanos* aims to make modern historicity speak).

What is especially striking is that the tonal, formal, rhetorical, and imagistic modes of Vallejo's late poetry often come surprisingly close to those of *Trilce*. This assertion runs against the grain of most critical readings of both the *Poemas humanos* and *España, aparta de mí este cáliz,* which present these collections as a politicized rejection of Vallejo's earlier avant-garde experiments, a replacement of immature aesthetics with a mature and timely politics. These readings are part and parcel of a broader tendency to read artistic works from the 1930s as an overcoming of the less settled modes of the avant-gardes' earlier decades.[7] Yet as Tom Gunning argues in a suggestive recent article, the two modes—"shock" and "flow"—continue to coexist, even to interact dialectically, throughout this period, as in the piston of the gasoline motor, in which "a contained explosion is converted into consistent motion" ("Modernity" 310). I suggest in this chapter that it is through an ongoing struggle with avant-garde forms that Vallejo most compellingly grapples with questions of political representation and that to erase one in the name of the other is to deaden the machine of his late writing.

It has been relatively easy to sidestep the avant-garde residues of the Paris poetry due to a chronological accident. As the majority of these poems were not published in Vallejo's lifetime, they are effectively cut off from the context that gave rise to them; it therefore becomes both tempting and feasible to read them from the standpoint of their final moments (the context of the Spanish Civil War) rather than of their ongoing production (the interwar years in general). My aim here is to reconnect them to that context and to restore some sense of their unsettled, unsettling nature, showing the ways in which they attempt to offer an image of interwar modernity in its totality, at the same time that they undercut any notion of totality, including their own.[8] This late poetry, despite its greater explicitness with regard to social and political questions, is every bit as difficult as the earlier poetry; as I will suggest, the ways in which it wraps formal complexity around explicit content may constitute its most political gesture.

Vallejo's peculiar gambit is to make poetry a voice for the contemporary moment and for political commitment without falling into either a facilely reflective or a compensatory mode, stretching itself and its readers without allowing either one to settle into the comfort of full comprehension. Consequently, the demands that this late poetry places on its reader are unremitting. As Jean Franco insisted, "If his poetry means anything at all, it means the confrontation of difficulty and complexity, not their submersion in the reductionism of tactics" (255). There are four particular difficulties that I will tease out in this chapter. The first is the shifting position of the lyric subject, who speaks either as a poet or as an average civilian, a distinct individual or an indistinct modern type, in a self-critical probing of poetry's capacity to render the self, the other, or both at once. The second is the meaning of images, which seem to escape any overarching symbolic system and which are piled alongside one another with few discernible connections, standing ambivalently in paratactic, accumulative, or substitutive relation to one another. The third is the organization of the poems themselves, which tend to feature compelling rhetorical structures, seductive rhythmic patterns, and, occasionally, recognizable metrical forms, which are nonetheless undercut by the illogic of their own contents, giving the reader a sense of understanding on an emotional but not an intellectual level. Fourth and finally is the tone of these poems, which oscillates jarringly, unpredictably, and often indeterminately between sarcasm and sincerity, celebration and self-critique, humor and solemnity, playing up the contradictions of modernity and of the discourses that attempt to make sense of them—from the political to the economic, the sociological to the lyric. Given the interlocking nature of these various difficulties, I explore them all in a necessarily long chapter, divided into three distinct sections to consider three dominant concerns: the place of the poet in modernity, the formal organization of subjects in a politically sensitive modern poetry, and a lyric engagement with history.

SECTION ONE: PORTRAIT OF THE ARTIST

In his late poetry, as in his chronicles, Vallejo explicitly rejects the professionalization of the modern artist, which subjected production to the rhythms and demands of the market. He claimed that his models in this regard were Charles Baudelaire and Juan Gris, both of whom found themselves unable to produce poetry on commission, rather than Jean Cocteau, who had gone too far in the opposite direction, raising poetry's distinction from mass culture to the level of a "professional secret" (*ACC* II: 576). Positioning his own practice against Cocteau's, Vallejo reaches to connect his writing to the common *transeúnte*. This, however, was significantly easier to achieve in journalism (speaking directly to or for a public with a shared experience or interests) than in the lyric. A central focus of Vallejo's later poetry is therefore the question of how to say "I" without cutting the poet off from those to whom and for whom he wishes to speak, and whose misery he increasingly shares. In his final notebook jotting (from 1936/37), Vallejo asked himself whether it was preferable to position "yo" (I) or "el hombre" (man) as the lyric subject, and his answer surreptitiously conflates the two: "Desde luego, más profundo y poético, es decir 'yo'—tomado naturalmente como símbolo de todos" (Of course it is more profound and poetic to say "I"—taken naturally as a symbol of everyone). But his actual poetry does not get around the impasse so easily: a pivotal anxiety of his lyric experiments is the relation between the poet and the man on the street. The poetry insistently prods this relation in an attempt to undercut notions of lyric distinction and to lay bare the structures and strictures of social modernity but without—and this will be a crucial point—entirely canceling the category of the poet within it.

This question begins to raise itself even before Vallejo's immersion in Marxism—which dates roughly from late 1927—and intriguingly, it finds an initial form not in the lyric but in prose poetry.[9] Between 1924 and 1928 Vallejo composed a series of prose poems that reflect on questions of identity and memory while paradoxically working toward the erasure of the lyric subject. The early prose poem "La violencia de las horas" (The Violence of the Hours) provides a register of figures from his home in Peru—"de quien[es] me acuerdo cuando llueve y no hay nadie en mi experiencia" (who I remember when it rains and there is no one in my experience)—to jog the speaker's memory. The self-hollowing "Voy a hablar de la esperanza" (I Am Going to Speak of Hope) takes the breach between subject and experience as a provocative new ground:

> Yo no sufro este dolor como César Vallejo. Yo no me duelo ahora como ar-tista, como hombre, ni como simple ser vivo siquiera. Yo no sufro este dolor como católico, como mahometano ni como ateo. Hoy sufro solamente. [. . .]
>
> *I do not suffer this pain as César Vallejo. I do not ache now as an artist, as a man or even as a simple living being. I do not suffer this pain as a Catholic, as a [Muslim] or as an atheist. Today I simply suffer. [. . .]* (Trans. modified)

This fantasy of an uncategorizable voice, emanating from an undifferentiated body, cannot do without rhetoric, as is evident from the obsessive returns and careful structuring of this prose poem, whose four stanzas (two long, two shorter) make it look, if not sound, like a sonnet. This is the antithesis of surrealist automatic writing—its immediate historical analogue—even if the concerns of these prose poems often trace out explicitly psychoanalytic complexes (an Oedipal attachment to the mother and a virtual erasure of the father), which also detach them from their more explicit model in Baudelaire. What Vallejo's prose poems obsessively articulate is the quandary of a distinct personal voice trapped between two inescapable modes of subjective indistinction: on one hand, the unconscious; on the other, everyday modern discourse.

Prose poetry is in some senses the quintessentially modern genre, in spite of—but also by virtue of—its linguistic excess. As various critics have argued, it offers a critical site for commenting on the place of the poet in modernity and for ironizing the representational capacities of literature in its engagement with the social; in those moments when it seems most turned upon its own literariness, it thematizes its engagement with an outside world. Jonathan Monroe reads prose poetry as both "a critical, self-critical, utopian genre, a genre that tests the limits of genre" (16) and a "model for the apprehension of fundamental social as well as more narrowly 'aesthetic' conflicts" (19); Richard Terdiman points to its refusal to resolve social tensions in a harmonic whole, aiming instead to "radicalize contradiction in representation" (*Discourse* 270). It also, as Terdiman signals, crucially emerges in competition with the modern newspaper. If the job of writing newspaper articles gave the lyric poet a new function in modernity, prose poems foregrounded the irony of the poet's disappearance into prose journalism and the urban masses. And if journalism operated according to a principle of quasi-objectivity and condensation—emblematized in the sketch—the prose poem made room for expressive excess and outrageous viewpoints, which emptied out the pieties of bourgeois commonplaces and beliefs by pushing them to extremes, running them down on their rhetorical axes until they ground to a halt.[10]

Vallejo's prose poems, operating as a hinge between his chronicles and his poetry, often set his voice alongside those of the unidentified others who populate his environment, setting up a performative antagonism between his words and theirs. "Conflicto entre los ojos y la mirada" (The Conflict between the Eyes and the Gaze) enacts a parodically hysterical meditation on the loss of individuality or privileged subjectivity in the space of the modern city. It has none of the swagger of Baudelaire's prose poem "Les Foules" (The Mobs), which proclaimed the lyric poet's ability to insert himself at whim into the characters who surrounded him, without losing any trace of himself; the "painter of modern life's" expansive "*moi* insatiable du *non-moi*" had in the interim faced the serious threat of self-cancellation, crushed among his doubles or multiples in the swelling crowds of the modern city. In the 1903 essay, "The Metropolis and Mental Life," Simmel pointed to the tendency among city dwellers to exaggerate their personal traits in an effort to mark their difference from others; Vallejo's prose poem depicts the poet in similarly combative mode, challenging passersby on the street to a verbal duel, testing their performance in the most banal or phatic of conversations—a response to the weather—and despairing at their coincidence with his own viewpoints and linguistic contortions. The poet here is not only rendered culturally obsolete, but dissolves on a personal level into the masses of passersby; the one of the poet disappears into the many of the people. The paranoia of the lyric poet, faced with the loss of his value (or of his halo, as Baudelaire would say), sends him rushing from person to person in a useless effort to demarcate his difference; and to cover up his failures, the poem simply cuts off other voices, ending with the dictatorial pronouncement: "y nadie sentirá lo que yo siento. Y nadie ha de poder ya suplantarme" (And no one will feel what I feel. And no one will have the power now to supplant me).

This self-aggrandizement stands in ironic counterpoint to the central tenet of lyric poetry—that the poet communicate his personal feelings to a universal audience—but also to the utterances of the other voices in the poem. For the passersby quoted represent not the lowering of discourse but a rise in the general level of culture and creative thought.[11] The characters that the lyric subject quizzes during his wanderings out-speak him because they speak *like* him; his first interviewee, comment-ing on the "sol flavo y dulce" (sweet, fallow sun), sounds uncannily like the poet of *Trilce*. If the prose poem as a genre tends to structure itself around a clash of discourses, Vallejo's poem presents a moment when that clash has been overcome—and not for the professional good of the lyric poet.[12] The moment is treated parodically in "Conflicto," yet the parody underlines Vallejo's increasingly acute anxiety about the place of the poet in a world whose more pressing demands were political, economic, and social and which had little need of the lyric.

The same concern asserts itself in Vallejo's metrical poems, and sig-nificantly these often make the place of the poet a question of form, grounded in an ability to shape or contort common discourse. Very few of Vallejo's Paris poems are metrically regular, but the majority of them carry intimations of regularity, such as the many poems which draw upon the Golden Age mode of the *silva*—a metrical predecessor to free verse, featuring flexibly interlocking heptasyllables and hendecasyl-lables. Most offer a medley of lines of different extension, combined so unpredictably as to make recognizable patterns leap out at us, activat-ing our metrical muscles and thereby heightening—as Derek Attridge writes of poetic rhythm—our emotional receptivity, as is the case of the piercing "¿quién me preguntará por mi palabra?" (who is going to ask me for my word?) ("Entre el dolor y el placer . . . "; Between Pain and Pleasure . . .). These poems often contain metrical tours-de-force at the microlevel, showing off their capacity to encase both utterly col-loquial expressions and specialized knowledge. "Y no me digan nada" (And Don't Say Anything to Me), for example, manages to fit into per-fect hendecasyllables both the cut-off line "uno hace cuanto puede, no me digan . . . " (one does what one can, don't say another . . .) and the name-stuffed line "la de Heráclito injerta en la de Marx" (that of Heraclitus grafted on that of Marx), which relies upon counting correctly both the *esdrújula* of "Heráclito" and the acutely stressed, hence syllable-short "Marx." The poem "Pero antes que se acabe [esta dicha]" [But Before All This [Happiness] Ends), whose content focuses on measurement and slicing, is almost entirely composed of well-divided hendecasyllables and heptasyllables, with the exception of some significantly longer lines, when the poet is put into more expansive mode by his enthusiasm for a subject who exceeds all measure: the multitalented "soldado del tallo, filósofo del grano, mecánico del sueño" (soldier of the stalk, philosopher of the grain, mechanic of the dream).

Most interesting of all is "Calor, cansado voy con mi oro" (Heat, Tired I Go with My Gold), which is the second poem from Vallejo's late 1937 lyric explosion. The first, "Miré el cadaver" (I Looked at the Corpse), focused explicitly on the Spanish Civil War and would become number XI of that cycle; "Calor . . . ," however, sees Vallejo shuttling back into earlier modes, and into a meditation on his years in Paris, which not only appears in the content, but is adeptly thematized in its form. The poem consists of five quatrains, almost entirely composed of hendecasyllables; the final lines of the first four quatrains are repeated (with one minor change) in the last stanza—a Baroque procedure known as "lexical dissemination-recollection," which occasionally characterizes Vallejo's Paris poems, as Ferrari and Paoli (*Mapas*) have analyzed. But more striking still is that the third line of each of the first four quatrains features either phrases or entire lines in French, and this unusual bilingualism has a peculiar effect on their meter. The first and third examples, "C'est Septembre attiédi, por ti, Febrero!" (September is cooled by you, February!), and "C'est l'été, por ti, invierno de alta pleura! (It is summer, for you, winter of high pleura!),[13] in which seasonal dichotomies in the northern and southern hemispheres are played off against one another on each side of the caesura, fit the established hendecasyllabic pattern.[14] The third verse of the second and third quatrains, by contrast, falls short in terms of metrical accounting, and significantly, this varies depending on whether we follow French or Spanish prosody. "C'est Paris, reine du monde!" (It is Paris, queen of the world!) is a hexasyllable in Spanish, although the fact that it is end-stressed earns it an extra syllable; read through French prosody, it automatically sounds out as a heptasyllable, which in Spanish terms is an acceptable counterpoint to the prevailing hendecasyllabic structure. However, the third line of the fourth quatrain, "C'est la vie, mort de la

Mort!" (It is life, death of Death!) has seven syllables when counted in Spanish, and its stressed final syllable turns it into an effective octosyllable; it is only a hexasyllable in French.[15] Both options throw off the established pattern of the entire poem, but in different ways. Vallejo's metrical and translinguistic play here thus not only foregrounds the collision of two environments (felt at the level of the body) in his experience in Paris; it hints at a calculable difference in value between the two languages.

Strikingly, the most conventionally metrical poems of Vallejo's late period—which also feature careful rhyme patterns—are those in which he reflects most explicitly on his own situation in Paris: "Piedra negra sobre una piedra blanca" (Black Stone on a White Stone), "Sombrero, abrigo, guantes" (Hat, Coat, Gloves), and "París, octubre 1936" (Paris, October 1936). In the sonnet "Sombrero, abrigo, guantes" this is reduced to the coordinates of the Café de la Régence, where Vallejo composed many of his chronicles and letters. It was in the doorway of this café in 1926 that he met Henriette Maisse, who would become his companion for the next two years, which gives an anecdotal meaning to the clause "en el humo se ve / dos humos intensivos" (in the smoke can be seen / two intense fumes). And within this space Vallejo presents himself in confrontation with the Comédie Française across the street—identified in his chronicles as a site of cultural stagnation—and with the ghosts of writers past, given material shape in the "polvo inmóvil" (unmoving dust) that rises up to greet him as he enters. But there is another allusion here that marks the incipient politicization of Vallejo's writing space, and bears directly on his developing sense of poetry's possibilities. It was in the same café, in autumn 1844, that Friedrich Engels and Karl Marx began collaborating on *The Holy Family,* an attack on the immensely influential Young Hegelians, which marked the beginnings of a materialist theory of social organization. The Marx-Engels meeting seems to flicker in Vallejo's declaration that "importa que el otoño se injerte en los otoños, / importa que el otoño se integre de retoños" (it is important that autumn graft itself to autumns, / it is important that autumn integrate itself with sprouts), which suggests a desire to stretch politics into other forms.

The Marx-Engels polemic with the Young Hegelians may also have offered an analogue to Vallejo's discomfort with the surrealist reign in Paris. Vallejo read surrealism not in accordance with its own claims—as a rejuvenation of the individual subconscious meant to lead to a conscious, collective repudiation of capitalism and commodity culture—

but as a jettisoning of critical reason in an age that had most need of it ("Autopsia del surrealismo," 1930; *ACC* II: 828–33). If this poem's quatrains indicate that Vallejo increasingly saw the Parisian cultural scene as composed of dust and rust, the final tercet counters only with a series of paradoxes and oxymorons sidelined as the ravings of a madman: "importa oler a loco postulando, / ¡qué cálida es la nieve, qué fugaz la tortuga [. . .]!" (it is important to smell like a madman postulating / how warm the snow is, how fleeting the turtle [. . .]!) It is impossible to determine the tone here, which is characteristic of much of Vallejo's late poetry: we cannot ascribe either sarcasm or sincerity to the speaker with any certainty. Nonetheless, the invocation of surrealist madness, coupled with the intimation that Baroque paradoxes ("how warm the snow") constituted an unproductive withdrawal from immediate urgencies, suggests that the chances for poetry, in this historical context, looked minimal—that its importance was relative and restricted. A bad time for the lyric, as Brecht would later say.

The sense that poetry could not materially rectify anything, that it could only bear weak witness to brutality, seems to underwrite the poem "Piedra negra sobre una piedra blanca." One of the bleakest lyric statements from Vallejo's Paris years, it prophesies the death of its own author, making none of the kind of self-immortalizing claims that a tombstone poem might be expected to make:

> Me moriré en París con aguacero,
> un día del cual tengo ya el recuerdo.
> Me moriré en París -y no me corro-
> tal vez un jueves, como es hoy, de otoño.
>
> Jueves será, porque hoy, jueves,
> que proso estos versos, los húmeros me he puesto
> a la mala y, jamás como hoy, me he vuelto,
> con todo mi camino, a verme solo.
>
> César Vallejo ha muerto, le pegaban
> todos sin que él les haga nada;
> le daban duro con un palo y duro
>
> también con una soga; son testigos
> los días jueves y los huesos húmeros,
> la soledad, la lluvia, los caminos . . .

This poem offers no summation of Vallejo's achievements as poet, no linkage to an illustrious lineage of artists, no statement of philosophy; it moves rather in the direction of a self-cancellation, marking only the abdication of the poet's ability to speak under the repeated blows of some unnamed adversaries.[16] It shies away even from the charge of Brecht's early 1930s poem "I Need No Gravestone," which suggested as an ironic epitaph the bare lines "He made suggestions. We / carried them out." In fact Vallejo's poem betrays a peculiarly marked discomfort over its own status *as poem*. Although it follows the rigorous construction of a sonnet, it internally designates its own process of composition as prosaic—"proso estos versos" (I prose these verses)—and it relentlessly distances itself from any effort at lyric embellishment; its own language is so unremittingly sparse that we feel we are being beaten with its repeated nouns and clauses, which mimic the blows raining down on its speaker, who seems to question the usefulness of leaving a testament to anything in the impractical form of the lyric.

"Piedra negra sobre una piedra blanca" dates from the late 1920s, and it offers a revealing portrait of Vallejo's conception of poetry as he tries to shape his thoughts into tough-minded political consciousness. The poem's title was allegedly meant as a mocking gloss on a photograph taken of him at Fontainebleu, which shows the poet dressed in dark clothing resting self-consciously against a white wall, his Andean features outlined against the sky. The poem's content, however, shows him more concerned with sidestepping his image as *poet,* presenting himself as a rather prosaic writer who has the technical capacity to put a sonnet together but who cannot testify to lyric value.[17] In narrative terms the poem announces little more than its place and act of composition: a lonely, rainy Thursday in Paris, spent remembering past and present grievances. Sketching a life of monotonous misery made up of trivial circumstances, it reduces itself to summoning those contingencies as impossible witnesses for a futile posthumous defense. The poem's spare words are relentlessly repeated, denied any symbolic content, made simply literal (the Thursdays, the humerus bones, the solitude, the downpour, the pathways); they undergo no allegorical transfiguration, and they weakly peter out in an ellipsis. This reduces the poet's activity to cataloging what fills in the blanks of a bare existence, given illusory shape by the structure of a sonnet.

Vallejo's body, meanwhile, becomes its own tombstone, on which he writes not the poetry that will immortalize him but the marks of the beatings received. And that body itself is no longer a reliable ground for articulation: his humerus bones, which should write his epitaph, are not the last surviving remnant of the expressive human in him but something as external as clothing. In the poem "París, octubre 1936," that clothing will swallow him whole; possessions here not only supplement the subject, but threaten to supplant him. The poem's title states its time and place of composition, going on to present a fragmented version of the poet's life in Paris—condensed in the bench he sits on, broadened out to include the Champs-Élysées and the Rue de la Lune—only to leave it all behind: "De todo esto yo soy el único que parte" (From all this I am the only one who parts). The speaker here conceives himself as a part of a whole that he can abandon without the whole's batting an eyelid. As he bids farewell to Paris, he momentarily steps outside his own body to observe himself, alone in the crowd—"y, rodeada de gente, sola, suelta, / mi semejanza humana dase vuelta" (and, surrounded by people, alone, estranged, / my human resemblance turns around)—and finds that his subjectivity is in excess, as all that modernity needs of him is his external form:

> Y yo me alejo de todo, porque todo
> se queda para hacer la coartada:
> mi zapato, su ojal, también su lodo
> y hasta el doblez del codo
> de mi propia camisa abotonada.

> *And I move away from it all, since all*
> *stays behind to provide my alibi:*
> *my shoe, its eyelet, as well as its mud*
> *and even the elbow bend*
> *of my own shirt buttoned-up.*

As the modern subject's external objects provide an alibi for the disappearing body— suggesting that both intimacy and identity have become a crime—they also do away with that body; or as Simmel put it in 1903, in urban modernity, objective existence had come to obliterate the subjective. This threatened to throw the lyric's raison d'être into crisis. How was the modern subject to speak without being overwhelmed by objects? And on a related note, how could the poet speak to and for others without canceling himself out?

"I ADDRESS MYSELF"

It has to be living, to learn the speech of the time.
It has to face the men of the time and to meet
the women of the time. It has to think about war
and it has to find what will suffice.
—Wallace Stevens, "Of Modern Poetry"

The poem "A lo mejor, soy otro" (Chances Are, I'm Another), as the tonal ambivalence of its title suggests, takes a now-breezy, now-despondent tack on Rimbaud's slogan for modernity, *je est un autre.* This potential interchangeability of identities crops up repeatedly in Vallejo's late poetry, as the poet reflects on his relation to the innumerable men who make up his environment, whose material difficulties he shares but for whom he does not quite feel qualified or entirely willing to speak. The poet sometimes appears as one among many voices in these poems: "El momento más grave de la vida" (The Lowest Point in Life), for example, offers a list of statements by individual men, one of whom seems identified with Vallejo in his allusion to imprisonment in Peru.[18] But he seems to have recognized early that to simply include the words of others in poetry would be a facilely compensatory gesture. Unlike many of his modernist contemporaries, he resists the temptation of impersonation, opting instead for a performance of shared everyday language, which could naturally be achieved most effectively by speaking for himself. Throughout these poems Vallejo therefore offers his own voice as a stand-in for those around him, intimating that amid the leveling of modernity, and in a common experience of impotence and material lack, to speak of the self is to speak for the other.

This sense of either connection or indistinction, however, is grounded less often in an awareness of shared languages than in the fact of a common physical basis, which is sometimes evolutionary, as Franco has analyzed at length. When in the poem "Fue domingo en las claras orejas de mi burro" (It Was Sunday in the Clear Ears of My Jackass) the lyric subject refers to his "ciclo microbiano" (microbial cycle), we cannot be sure whether this characteristic is meant to set him apart from or to underline his biological similarity to his fellow humans. At the same time, this basic knowledge of physical resemblance grounds a feeling for and of others that is at once political and physiological. From this perspective, the body parts of the disenfranchised subjects around the poet, by virtue of their very familiarity, make up a literal body politic, connecting him to his co-suffering citizens of the world: in touching himself, he implicitly touches them. And this often takes place behind the back, so to speak, of the poet's verbal gestures, investing all of poetry's potential in a reconnection of subjects not through linguistic address but through the regrounding of each one in their own bodies.[19] The poem "Epístola a los transeúntes" styles itself in its title as a Pauline letter to a collective; yet rather than address itself to the masses, it speaks instead as a lyric murmur to the self, focused on the speaker's own body as he checks his constituent parts:[20]

Y, entre mí, digo:
ésta es mi inmensidad en bruto, a cántaros,
este mi grato peso, que me buscara abajo para pájaro;
éste es mi brazo,
que por su cuenta rehusó ser ala,·
éstas son mis sagradas escrituras,
éstos mi alarmados compañones.

And, within myself, I say:
this is my immensity in the raw, in jugfuls,
this my grateful weight, which sought me below as a pecker;
this is my arm,
which on its own account refused to be a wing,
these are my sacred scriptures, .
these my alarmed companionaballs. (Trans. modified)

Rejecting the metaphysical flights of its title, this poem brings the speaker back down to his own base matter, invoked directly and through a series of puns that both tether him to himself in solitude (*pájaro* alludes not only to a bird, but to masturbation) and link his body to those of others (*compañones* is a contemporary word for "testicles" but also, as Eshleman notes, an antiquated term for "companions"). This is a remarkably succinct statement of Vallejo's attempt to conjoin a focus on the subject—as both poet and man—with an attention to the subjectivities that surround him. It is condensed still further two stanzas later:

éste ha de ser mi cuerpo solidario
por el que vela el alma individual

this will be my solidary body
over which the individual soul keeps watch

The body here, through the permutation of a letter, is rematerialized, made solid, and moves from solitude to solidarity, without losing contact with individual subjectivity—a pun that exemplifies Vallejo's determination to retain the personal within the collective, achieved through both the intricacies of lyric language and a phonic play (a *d* replacing a *t*), which, as so often in his poetry, does not hierarchize speech and writing but maximizes the potential of their conjunction.[21]

At the same time, and in full recognition of the contradiction, Vallejo in his late poems frequently foregrounds the barrier that separates one body—and specifically, that of the thinking, talking poet—from another.[22] In the poem "Pero antes que se acabe [toda esta dicha] . . . ," this barrier takes the literal form of a material membrane—the eardrum of the unidentified other, which inspires the poet's attempt to make it reverberate:

> En tu oreja el cartílago está hermoso
> y te escribo por eso, te medito
>
> *In your ear the cartilage looks beautiful*
> *and so I write you, I meditate you*

This unlikely and disarming paean to the inner ear takes us back to the bodily materialism of *Trilce,* with the lyric reaching directly toward another body. But the second line pulls us up short with a syntactical quibble: is the poet here writing *to* or *about* the other? This is heightened by a still more radical indeterminacy in the following stanza, which interrupts the poet's apostrophe to his interlocutor with an unsettling parenthesis:

> (¿Me percibes, animal?
> ¿me dejo comparar como tamaño?
> No respondes y callado me miras
> a través de la edad de tu palabra.)
>
> *(Do you perceive me, animal?*
> *do I allow myself to be compared as a size?*
> *You do not respond and silently you look at me*
> *across the age of your word).* (Trans. modified)

Who is speaking here, who remaining silent? Our immediate impulse is to treat this as the poet's voice—lowering the tone and volume of his address to a mute interlocutor, approaching him more intimately—but we might also hear it as the response of the one who is being described: revolting against the condescension of the poet, refusing to be measured, and dismantling the poet's language in advance.

In recognition of the potential recalcitrance of his subjects, Vallejo therefore speaks frequently in his late poetry *as a poet,* whose voice requires a separation from that of others in order to retain any validity. The hovering anxiety of these poems is less the inability to speak fully for others than the potential cancellation of the poet's own voice, lost in the attempt to be responsible toward others. In the poem "Y no me digan nada" (And Don't Say Anything to Me), the speaker momentarily seizes hold of his own subjectivity ("asumo con éxito mi inmensidad llorada"; I assume successfully my wept immensity), only to find his own voice ebbing away among the multitudes who surround him ("me ahogo en la voz de mi vecino"; I drown in my neighbor's voice). Yet this is also one source of the poetry's disarming critical power: it continually insists that the poet, in struggling to find a voice for the bodies of others, is also openly preoccupied with securing his own position. Even in those many poems focused on presenting others, the poet makes an inevitable appearance, and this takes the form of a self-critical residue; Vallejo avoids the temptation to pretend that he can speak to the other as anything but a poet, even while signaling that the immediate power of poetry resides in a delusion. It is hard not to hear ironic notes creep into the poet's claim that he speaks "por el órgano oral de tu silencio" (through the oral organ of your silence) ("Los desgraciados"; The Wretched).

Vallejo's Paris poems insist that the lyric can never entirely move beyond subjectivity, yet they ceaselessly intimate that the flexion of its voice, whether reaching toward the other or withdrawing into itself, entangles it self-critically with the world.[23] This is often stated directly by the poet, who formalizes this to-and-fro movement in the *yo-tú* structure of the poems, but sometimes it is accidentally blurted out, revealing the deeper tensions of the poem or of poetic activity per se.[24] In "Otro poco de calma, camarada" (A Little More Calm, Comrade), the speaker spends seven stanzas analyzing what his addressee can accomplish and giving him advice on how to act ("anda no más; resuelve, / considera tu crisis, suma, sigue, / tájala, bájala, ájala"; go right ahead; decide, / ponder your crisis, add, carry, / hack it up, humble it, crumble it) in what sounds like a sketch for Vallejo's own fragmented modes. In the closing stanza, he launches into what looks like a final exhortation, but it contains a slip that shifts the poem onto a different track:

> Vamos a ver, hombre;
> cuéntame lo que me pasa,
> que yo, aunque grite, estoy siempre a tus órdenes.

> *Let's see, man,*
> *tell me what's happening to me,*
> *for, even when shouting, I'm always at your command.*

Rather than asking his addressee to "cuéntame lo que *te* pasa," the poet suddenly pulls attention back to himself, asking his addressee to read *him,* which sounds like a retreat into lyric narcissism; yet in this very turn away from the other, which hierarchizes their difference, he claims to be placing himself entirely at the other's service, apologizing in advance for his own linguistic and tonal excess. The excessiveness of the lyric is precisely what is at stake in these late poems. If Baudelaire, Darío, Rilke, Apollinaire, and a host of others had clung to the poet's distinction amid the leveling of modernity, Vallejo's concern is also with the ethical appropriateness of lyric language in a society that was becoming ever more striated. His response is to recuperate that excessiveness as a way to resist and parody the categorical simplicities of political, sociological, juridical, and even poetic discourse. Recognizing that subjectivity has become an excess quantity in both the politics and the poetics of modernity, Vallejo attempts to rescue it in fragmentary and self-critical forms, finding a reason and place for himself and his fellow subjects but also for poetry, in a tense historical moment which threatened to silence all of the above.

Vallejo's poetry is paradoxically most political in its emphasis that neither doctrinal politics nor the lyric were giving proper shape to their human subjects; the collectivism of the former and the individualism of the latter left no space for the articulation of the average man's subjectivity. In various prose statements from the late 1920s and early 1930s—the high point of his commitment to orthodox Marxism—Vallejo toed the party line by insisting that the central question of the time was economic; yet implicit throughout his late poetry is the nagging sense that by treating man solely as an economic creature, Marxist theory reduced the subject to the status of an object, leaving no room for the personal affects of the masses. By focusing exclusively on human needs, in other words, Marxism was erasing the importance of human desires ("Las lecciones del marxismo" [The Lessons of Marxism], 1929; ACC II: 684–86).[25] The late 1937 poem "Los desgraciados" (The Wretched) gestures toward this erasure. In what seems a parodic citation of political discourse, the speaker consoles the destitute masses by assuring them that their trembling is not personal but rather structural and collective, "el estado remoto de la frente / y la nación reciente del estómago" (the remote state of the forehead / and the recent nation of the stomach); he counsels them not to waste their time grieving, for "no es de pobres / la pena" (grief does not belong / to the poor). Happiness and pain, when not directly harnessable for revolutionary action, were being counted as an excess quantity—yet it is precisely their excessiveness that is rescued and foregrounded in this poetry.

What Vallejo's poetry therefore grapples with, beyond its own self-articulation, is a lyric responsibility not only to represent others by naming them (most strikingly in the poems "Traspié entre dos estrellas" and "Un hombre pasa . . . " [A Man Walks By . . .]) but also to force a recognition of the subjectivity of the average passerby, the one who is "sujeto a tenderse como objeto" (subject to laying himself down as an object) (from "Considerando en frío . . . "; Considering Coldly . . .). This subject-object dynamic alludes to the exploitation of the worker in capitalist modernity, but it also looks like an ironic comment on the poet's habitual self-authorization to speak for the other—turning the other into the illusory subject of a poem and corroborating a specious sense of poetry's ability to represent those denied self-representation.[26] Vallejo's poetry, by contrast, attempts something much more complex. It recognizes that it writes of and to the other who cannot read it ("para el analfabeto a quien escribo"; for the illiterate to whom I write) ("Himno a los voluntarios de la República"; Hymn to the Republican Volunteers), and it continually emphasizes the uncomfortable position of the lyric poet as he attempts to represent the other—as in the case of the Bolshevik worker of "Salutación angelica" (Angelic Salutation), before whom he finds himself "callado y medio tuerto" (silent and sort of one-eyed).[27] The anxiety is not only over how to be a poet, but how to be a responsible member of a collective: "Cómo ser y estar, sin darle cólera al vecino?" (How to be / and to be here, without angering one's neighbor?) ("Guitarra")

Vallejo's own experience of absolute material need in Paris actually brought him much closer to the average *transeúnte* than his position as an intellectual allowed him to acknowledge.[28] It is thus enormously significant that Vallejo's only direct impersonation of another character comes in "La rueda del hambriento" (The Hungry Man's Rack), which features a destitute protagonist who is at once an unidentified city dweller and the poet; their shared experience melds in the blankly devastating final line, "y ya no tengo nada, esto es horrendo" (and now I have nothing, this is horrendous; trans. modified). The poem announces itself as something that simply comes out from between the speaker's teeth—as ephemeral as smoke, a by-product of the body:

> De entre mis propios dientes salgo humeando,
> dando voces, pujando,
> bajándome los pantalones . . .

> *From between my own teeth I come out smoking,*
> *shouting, pushing,*
> *pulling down my trousers . . .*

Poetic speech is here just one more uncontrollable bodily function, reproducing itself in entreaties to passersby. The poem presents the barely subsisting human as made up, Chaplin-like, of his fraying clothing, his

needy body parts, and his minimal desires. It offers Vallejo's most direct
statement of destitution and its effect on both the body and the voice—
both of which, denied concrete sustenance, start devising fantastical
forms and mini-narratives for the most basic objects, such as a desperately craved piece of bread. The poem forms a pair with "Por último,
sin ese buen aroma sucesivo" (Finally, without That Good Continu-
ous Aroma), which builds to a direct condemnation of the "execrable
sistema" (abominable system) whose logic underwrites the paradox of
"la cantidad enorme de dinero que cuesta el ser pobre" (the enormous
amount of money it costs to be poor; my trans.). In both poems the lyric
subject directs his vehemence at the system that determines his material
poverty—not only as a poet, but also as a civilian. And Vallejo's beg-
gar here looks uncannily like the poet-figure who appears in his other
poems: both self-figurations reach out to the passerby, with little hope
of response. Poetic and physical need and desire, in other words, are at
the core of an attempt to entwine the lyric with political statement and
are placed on the same level, cast in the same image; both of them place
the desire for a response over the need for economic satisfaction.[29] By
going-into-character in "La rueda del hambriento," Vallejo mimics the
gestures of Chaplin the millionaire putting on the rags of the tramp—
with the difference that in this case, poet and pariah already inhabit the
same body.

"HOW TO SPEAK OF THE OTHER WITHOUT SCREAMING"

For poetry makes nothing happen: it survives
in the valley of its making where executives
would never want to tamper, flows on south
from ranches of isolation and the busy griefs,
raw towns that we believe and die in; it survives,
a way of happening, a mouth.

—W. H. Auden, "In Memory of W. B. Yeats"

In most immediate need of expression in capitalist modernity, as this
last example intimates, were not so much the voices of others as their
physical selves. If Vallejo's Peruvian poetry, as I suggested in chapter 2,
was invaded by the words of others, his later poetry is taken over by an
awareness of their bodies, being pushed through the formalized modes
of civil discourse (bureaucratic, religious, legal), which appeared to offer them a grid in which they made sense, yet which tended to exclude
their needs or desires. *Poemas humanos* lays bare in different ways the

easy structuring of the human in these various discourses, moving itself through a series of inordinately complex and self-critical renditions of the responsibility of the lyric poet toward the subject(s) of the poem.

The staggering poem "Un hombre pasa con un pan al hombro" (A Man Walks by with a Loaf of Bread on His Shoulder) maps this out in unusually direct terms, in thirteen couplets that counterbalance a real event with a hypothetical intellectual response.[30]

> Un hombre pasa con un pan al hombro
> ¿Voy a escribir, después, sobre mi doble?
>
> Otro se sienta, ráscase, extrae un piojo de su axila, mátalo
> ¿Con qué valor hablar del psicoanálisis?
>
> Otro ha entrado a mi pecho con un palo en la mano
> ¿Hablar luego de Sócrates al médico?
>
> Un cojo pasa dando el brazo a un niño
> ¿Voy, después, a leer a André Breton?
>
> Otro tiembla de frío, tose, escupe sangre
> ¿Cabrá aludir jamás al Yo profundo?
>
> Otro busca en el fango huesos, cáscaras
> ¿Cómo escribir, después, del infinito?
>
> Un albanil cae de un techo, muere y ya no almuerza
> ¿Innovar, luego, el tropo, la metáfora?
>
> Un comerciante roba un gramo en el peso a un cliente
> ¿Hablar, después, de cuarta dimensión?
>
> Un banquero falsea su balance
> ¿Con qué cara llorar en el teatro?
>
> Un paria duerme con el pie a la espalda
> ¿Hablar, después, a nadie de Picasso?
>
> Alguien va en un entierro sollozando
> ¿Cómo luego ingresar a la Academia?
>
> Alguien limpia un fusil en su cocina
> ¿Con qué valor hablar del más allá?
>
> Alguien pasa contando con sus dedos
> ¿Cómo hablar del no-yo sin dar un grito?

This poem immediately hits its mark in the reader. Not just for its content, which is shattering, but also for its formal procedure, which is self-evident, and perhaps even a touch disingenuous. If the first line in each couplet sketches scenes from a nonliterary life, the second line maps out the range of options available to an intellectual versed in the most up-to-date literary, artistic, and philosophical theories of metropolitan modernity. Each scene of eating, cleaning, suffering, scavenging, working, cheating, grieving, and calculating has a potential reductive complement in a contemporary method or literary theme: the double, psychoanalysis, philosophy, surrealism, theories of the self and the infinite, poetry, mathematics, theater, art, metaphysics. The poem implicitly critiques all of these modern modes for their failure to engage directly with the facts of material life in modernity—not so much by ignoring them as by abstracting them out. The central question of the poem is not what an artist does while ignorant of social reality but what an artist *can do* and *cannot do* once he becomes aware of the iniquities that surround him, even if the question of what he *must do* is left unsaid.

Although the poem's message looks like it can be condensed into a sarcastic punch line, its careful formal elaboration requires that we pay attention to its modes of coupling and grouping. There is sometimes no direct relation between the verses of each couplet; at other times it is implicit, sometimes explicitly ironic or sarcastic. There seems nothing especially problematic, for example, in taking the bread-toting man of the first couplet as the poet's actual double, while the person entering the Academy is unlikely to renounce his or her post out of sympathy for a mourner at a funeral. The latter example only takes on a more sinister shading when we remember that the members of the Académie Française were referred to as "immortals" and hence thought of as above the everyday business of mere men. More directly ironic is the suggestion that Picasso's cubism is a realistic copy of the contorted bodies of Paris's outcasts, or the juxtaposition of metaphysics and philosophy with the intensely material scratchings of those subjects who have nothing but their own fleas. Strangest of all is the line about weeping in the theater: this may refer to an actor adopting an insincere attitude, but it more likely refers to a theatergoer—not a producer of art, but a consumer of it. "Con qué cara?" not only signifies the idiomatic "what a cheek," but alludes to the theatrical masks of comedy and tragedy; more fundamentally, it suggests that the theatergoer is performing for fellow audience members—attending a play not to see it but to be seen, and in the process, missing the inequities being staged on the streets outside.

There is something else very odd at play in this poem, which tends to be obscured by our focus on the couplets as a developing litany of binaries whose point exhausts itself easily. And that is that the poem effectively consists of two separate poems: one composed of the first verse of each couplet and one of the second. The second is, importantly, the less interesting of the two. There seems to be little relation between the second verses of each couplet, and that lack of relation suggests a lack of critical, political, or aesthetic coherence linking the different artistic modes of the period. The first verses, by contrast, are very carefully structured. They begin in conventionally descriptive mode, with a stereotypical man on a Parisian street toting what is probably a baguette, then progress through a series of different figures who suffer in varying degrees and from different maladies. These figures are organized, above all, grammatically: a man, another, another; a cripple, another, another; a bricklayer, a merchant, a banker, an outcast; someone, someone, someone. This catalog of characters suggests an organization of social personae in modernity, most of whom suffer the material consequences of their abandonment by a political system; some of them are identified, but the majority are not. The first group of unnamed subjects ("otro"; another) includes those experiencing direct material lack, and just about includes the "hombre" of couplets 1 and 4, who in each case has something to lean on or something that leans on him (a baguette, a child) and thereby vouchsafes his humanity. These six couplets are followed by four minimally identified representatives of social class: a banker and a merchant (both middle class) sandwiched between a bricklayer (working class) and a pariah (outside the system). Significantly, the representatives of the middle class are seen cheating their clients, while the construction worker succumbs to a work-related accident (in a typically Vallejian procedure, the bathos of his loss is transmitted through the deadpan nonconsecutive logic of dying, and *then* not having lunch). The outcast, however much cast out of the social system, is here carefully located inside the system as the excluded remnant within it.

The three couplets that close the poem lay bare a theoretical issue that to this point has been covert: in each case the designated "someone" is the protagonist of a mini-narrative to which we have no access. This is in fact the case of *all* of the preceding couplets, although our inclination has been to see those figures as utterly encapsulated in their economic summation, without wondering about what escapes it. These final couplets, however, demand that we imagine a narrative for each one to explain what we are viewing, and thereby to restore some measure of subjectivity to their characters. We have to wonder who has died, and who is mourning them; why is someone counting on his fingers; and most significantly, why is the protagonist of the penultimate couplet cleaning a gun? Has the gun already been fired, or is this figure about to commit an atrocity?

Why is he cleaning the gun in his kitchen, which should be the space of material sustenance? As Chekhov pointed out, if a gun is mentioned at the beginning of a story, it has to go off by the end; and this gun, which appears toward the end of the poem, sheds a light back on the poem's opening, which featured a character whose baguette might look like a rifle. Bread and gun have thus been transposed, imagistically and narratively; had the rifle appeared in the first couplet, we would have taken it not as a stereotypical image of Paris but as a more ominous depiction of a soldier patrolling the space of the poem. Instead we are faced in closing with a subject at the end of his tether, reduced to violent revolt, perhaps in reaction to the catalog of iniquities that precedes his appearance.

A final point has to do with the poet's actual involvement in the scenes described rather than simply his intellectual or artistic reaction to them. If artist-figures in this poem tend to be consigned to the second line of each couplet, the third couplet covertly brings the poet into the group of modern subjects inhabiting the first lines; it describes "another [who] has entered my chest with a stick in his hand"—a more rudimentary weapon than a rifle but sufficient, nonetheless, to threaten the poet. Or, indeed, to *move* him. And the last line of the poem further shifts the formulation maintained throughout; now, instead of asking what the poet *can* do, the final line points out what the poet *cannot* do: speak for the other without screaming

This question has an unexpectedly unsettling counterpart in "Considerando en frío, imparcialmente" (Considering Coldly, Impartially). If "Un hombre pasa . . ." suggests the inappropriateness of current modes of lyric or philosophical thought for treating the common citizens of modernity, this latter poem presents a tonally unstable examination of the human, and its discourse seems strangely off-kilter for lyrical meditation:

> Considerando en frío, imparcialmente
> que el hombre es triste, tose, y sin embargo
> se complace en su pecho colorado;
> que lo único que hace es componerse
> de días;
> que es lóbrego mamífero y se peina . . .
>
> Considerando
> que el hombre procede suavemente del trabajo
> y repercute jefe, suena subordinado;
> que el diagrama del tiempo
> es constante diorama en sus medallas
> y, a medio abrir, sus ojos estudiaron

desde lejanos tiempos
su fórmula famélica de masa . . .

   Comprendiendo sin esfuerzo
que el hombre se queda, a veces, pensando,
como queriendo llorar,
y, sujeto a tenderse como objeto,
se hace buen carpintero, suda, mata,
y luego canta, almuerza, se abotona . . .

   Considerando también
que el hombre es en verdad un animal
y, no obstante, al voltear, me da con su tristeza en la cabeza . . .

   Examinando, en fin,
sus encontradas piezas, su retrete,
su desesperación, al terminar su día atroz, borrándolo . . .

   Comprendiendo
que él sabe que le quiero,
que le odio con afecto y me es, en suma, indiferente . . .

   Considerando sus documentos generales
y mirando con lentes aquel certificado
que prueba que nació muy pequeñito . . .

   le hago una seña,
viene,
y le doy un abrazo, emocionado,
¡Qué más da! Emocionado . . . Emocionado . . . [31]

The final stanza, with its emotional movement, looks and sounds like a condensation of what we expect from the lyric: to gain an insight into the human, and to be moved by the experience. This sweetened sting in its tail has dominated most readings of the poem, which take its performance of movement as an instance of lyric potency; these readings can be summed up in Alberto Escobar's comment that this poem "requires no further comment" (no es menester que añada ningún comentario) (37). And yet almost everything in it, I would suggest, undermines our expectations of the lyric. The poem looks at first sight like an examination of the human, and this question naturally draws our attention, prompting us at least momentarily to sideline the speaker's own tone and peculiar perspective. But that tone—mapped out in the initial declaration, "considering coldly, impartially"—should immediately set off some alarm bells. Does the explicit espousal of a neutral perspective not suggest that we should question its neutrality, especially in the lyric, which is supposed to have no space for it? And a second, more implicit question: should we be paying attention to the subject in this poem—the speaker—or to his object, the human subject?

We can take the second question first, because it involves what we naturally gravitate toward in reading. The poem as a whole, but especially the first three stanzas, sketches out the attributes of a human, who may be either general or particular, typical or deviant—and hence, perhaps, under investigation. This human subject is described in his physical attributes and activities; he is pegged as both a historically situated and transhistorical creature, aware of his own place in time, although most likely not thinking of himself in evolutionary terms; he is also given to gloominess, yet keeps up his personal hygiene with an eye to presenting himself in public. His main public appearance is in the workplace, where he abases himself before his employer, although he may fancy that his intrinsic worth is echoed in the opinion held of him by his superiors. But subjective affects seep into his behavior as a worker, even in his leisure time: at times he interrupts his actions in order to think, which only leads him to a feeling of despair or melancholy; at other times he steels himself to behave like a happy worker on the job, not for his own sake, but for that of productivity, becoming a good carpenter—in which we hear both an allusion to Christianity and a reference to solid construction methods, welding together spiritualism and materialism. Yet the list of his actions contains an anomaly that we tend to miss because of the formal cataloging of activities; here as elsewhere, we are tricked by a poem's form into missing its content. The person or type described not only sweats (at work) and sings (inserting a moment of leisure that either interrupts labor, or makes it joyful, as in a Vertov film), eating lunch and going to the toilet, but also *kills*—an action folded into his workday schedule. Although we might expect this to stand out as a momentous and singular event, the present tense suggests not aberration but the habitual—as if this man's work were tantamount to killing, or as though the only release from a dehumanizing workday is murder, on the same level as eating lunch or evacuating it.

And yet the speaker seems strangely oblivious to the fact that this event does not quite square with his examinee's other activities. This is our first inkling that all is not right with our mediator. It continues in his sinister poking around in this man's literal toilet products—believing that what man evacuates contains his essence—and his insistence on seeing a tautological birth certificate that proves not his subject's identity but the fact that he "was born very very small." The speaker's concern with scrutiny and documents intimates that his tone is not simply an odd lyric dispassion, but is bound up with bureaucracy; what is taking place in the poem is thus not a neutral study of the general human creature but an investigation of him, to make sure that he fits the legal, bureaucratic, or anthropological requirements to count as a member of the species or of a particular community. Yet we can never quite determine, based on the information given or the speaker's tone, whether we are dealing with a specific human subject or simply the human per se, as a juridical or philosophical construct—whether the observed human, in other words, is one standing for the many or one set apart. Nor, indeed, whether the subject under investigation is being considered as a criminal, nor even whether criminality is being treated as a deviation or as the very condition of the human. Vallejo had previously articulated these questions in a prose piece from 1923, "Muro dobleancho" (Doublewide Wall), which argued that there was no extrahuman vantage point from which to determine degrees of morality, hence "Nadie es delincuente nunca. O todos somos delincuentes siempre" (No one is ever delinquent. Or we are all always delinquent).[32] This proto-deconstructive argument—focused on the justice system's theoretical inability to judge itself—not only places all subjects within the system on the same level (suggesting that none are distinct, although all have their distinctions) but also undercuts the very possibility of a rigorous neutrality.

On this note, instead of foregrounding an observer effect—which posits a change in the behavior of a knowingly observed subject—Vallejo's poem counterintuitively and almost imperceptibly analyzes the effect of observation *on the observer*. The observed subject in this poem is taken by the logic of the observation to have no real subjectivity, whereas the observer gradually develops an emotional response to his object-understudy, in what sounds like a parody of both measuring systems and Romantic poetry (where the lyric subject swells by incorporating what he observes). After considering, considering, understanding, considering, and examining, the speaker's language is momentarily overcome by emotion—however inchoate and contradictory—which produces a spasm in the system. All of a sudden, the speaker *understands* that his subject *knows* that he loves him and hates him affectionately, although he is also indifferent to him (the grammar here suggests a reversibility of positions: the subject may also be indifferent to the speaker, *me es indiferente*). But espoused or official neutrality is not overcome so easily. In the face of this sudden emotion, the speaker takes refuge in scrutinizing documents, even putting on spectacles for the purpose, going back for one last consideration; yet he ultimately succumbs to a wave of final affection, and gestures toward his subject, throwing all professional caution to the winds—"Qué más da!" (What does it matter!)—and congratulating himself on his embrace of the other. The dispassion of the opening is thus apparently overturned by the "movement" of the last lines, and their final ellipses seem to suggest the jettisoning of words in the face of human solidarity and physical connection. But is this an accurate account of what happens at the end of this poem? As the pole shifts from observed to observer, we completely lose sight of the human subject, who is enfolded in the self-congratulatory embrace of the final stanza, without himself uttering a word. Rather than destroying the system, this looks like the apotheosis of the system: the coercive embracing of a subject, who nonetheless remains recalcitrant.

Moreover, rather than presenting the apotheosis of the lyric subject, this poem offers an ironic self-undercutting, signaling the potential complicity of the lyric with dominant systems of discourse—whether by echoing them or by ignoring them to concentrate on its own self-inflation. The 1926 poem "He aquí que hoy saludo" (Behold That Today I Salute) ironically underlines poetry's belief that it can compete with those discourses, offering alternatives by plumping up its own voice. The following stanza offers a sarcastically glib performance of poetry's faith that it has a purchase on modern discourses: urbanity, politics, the justice system, economics, geography, sociality.

> Queréis más? encantado.
> Políticamente, mi palabra
> emite cargos contra mi labio inferior
> y económicamente,
> cuando doy la espalda a Oriente,
> distingo en dignidad de muerte a mis visitas.

> *You want more? with pleasure.*
> *Politically, my word*
> *spreads charges against my lower lip*
> *and economically,*
> *when I turn my back to the Orient,*
> *I distinguish my visitors with mortal dignity.*

Vallejo's late poems demand of themselves and their readers a radical vigilance in analyzing the position and flexions of speech, whether political, civil, or poetic; it is by working inside all these modes that they offer their most cogent critical statement.[33] Lacking a mandate, his poetry goes in search of a new template—and it finds one in modern modes of discourse, corroded from the inside by their own hollowness, helped along in their destruction by the poet's parodies. Critics have noted that many of the *Poemas humanos* adopt biblical discourses—messianism, epistles, parables—to channel them in the direction of secular revolution, but much more frequent, in fact, is the corrosive mimicking of the modes of modern-day bureaucracy and parliamentary democracy. Recognizing that one of the central problems of the age was institutional rhetoric, with its ideological coercion and materially unjust effects, Vallejo begins to dismantle that rhetoric from the inside by deploying it nonsensically in the lyric.

Several of his poems from the Paris years make little tonal sense until we hear them as parodic reports to an academy, a boardroom, a courtroom, or a parliamentary session—addresses whose sanctioned form is here rendered absurd by their content.[34] "Y no me digan nada" (And Don't Say Anything to Me), for example, lays out what the laboring human (sweating blood or ink) is capable of when pushed by modernity to the limit (murder), but this comes through the voice of a disquieting speaker, who attempts to quiet the panicking voices of his audience by reassuring them that "volveremos, señores, a vernos con manzanas" (we will, gentlemen, see each other again with apples) or "sin paquetes" (without packages), without explaining the symbolic charge or even the content of those images. The speaker goes on to promise a quasi-messianic redemption, which will graft Heraclitus and Marx onto Aristotle ("la expresión de Aristóteles armada / de grandes corazones de maera, / la de Heráclito injerta en la de Marx"; the expression of Aristotle armed / with great hearts of wood, / that of Heraclitus grafted on that of Marx), entwining classical and modern theories of the res publica and its material bases. As the end of the poem intimates, however, this is not the job of the poet, whose only option in this Hölderlinian "meanwhile" is to take to his bed, looking for a weak "acento del día" (accent of the day), while retreating into his own subjectivity, summed up in an "inmensidad llorada" (wept immensity).

Similarly, "Los nueve monstruos" (The Nine Monsters) goes to great lengths to catalog the ubiquity of pain in the world—a growing pain that insinuates itself into bodies, technologies, possessions, even vegetables—only to announce in closing:

Ah! desgraciadamente, hombres humanos,
hay, hermanos, muchísimo que hacer.

Ah! unfortunately, human men,
there is, brothers, much too much to do.

This looks like an assertion that poetry, while naming and cataloging iniquities, can (only) issue a call for action, which does away with the illusion that anything can be directly accomplished by the lyric. But we miss a second irony in these lines if we do not notice that they follow directly after the question, "Señor Ministro de Salud: ¿qué hacer?" (Mr. Minister of Health: what to do?). In this light, the closing lines become either an attempt to act by putting words in the mouth of a bureaucrat—words that ultimately amount to nothing—or an empty response from that minister, pleading hopelessness.

By learning and hollowing out the modes of "his master's voice" in these poems, Vallejo maps out a much more complicated image of the poet's enmeshment in his sociopolitical environment, or of the individual's relation to his fellow mass-men. Some of the poems in this mimicking mode present themselves as perverse reports to an academy: "El hallazgo de la vida" (The Discovery of Life), for example, inflates the sensations of an individual to the level of scientific discoveries, arguing hyperbolically for the value of subjectivity in modernity. But other poems imitate the measuring or directing modes of civil society, whose attempt to organize its subjects is revealed as the mirror of social poetry; the implication is that both representational poetry and politics do violence to their subjects.

"Nómina de huesos" (Roster of Bones) offers a virtually Kafkaesque recounting of what looks like a sociological experiment, a judgment, or a punishment, inflicted on an unnamed human by a group of shadowy henchmen obeying the demands of an unidentified group. Or a modern *Ecce homo:*

> Se pedía a grandes voces:
> —Que muestre las dos manos a la vez.
> Y esto no fue posible.
> —Que, mientras llora, le tomen la medida de sus pasos.
> Y esto no fue posible.
> —Que piense un pensamiento idético, en el tiempo en que un cero permanece inútil.
> Y esto no fue posible.
> —Que haga una locura.
> Y esto no fue posible.
> —Que entre él y otro hombre semejante a él, se interponga una muchedumbre de hombres como él.
> Y esto no fue posible.
> —Que le comparen consigo mismo.
> Y esto no fue posible.

—Que le llamen, en fin, por su nombre.
Y esto no fue posible.

These staccato demands impose on the subject a series of requirements that in their more benign moments range from possible but pointless acts through illogical behavior to failures that point more to the failure of the system than to that of the "defendant" ("que le llamen, en fin, por su nombre. / Y esto no fue posible"; let them call him, finally, by his name. And this was not possible). Yet the person who is being put on trial here—ordered to perform feats that can have nothing conceivably to do with the apparent charges against him—also seems caught up in a statistical experiment. He is measured according to the logic of an abusive pseudoscience, and is revealed as being incomparable with himself while failing to make room for his familiars. The poem hints at the coercive structural analogies created by the quantifying grids of modern systems, whether statistical or juridical; civil society, in issuing its regulatory demands, reifies divisions between the subjects it is supposed to gather together, forcing them into impossible—but also potentially resistant—positions. This is not just a stumbling block for democratic systems, but a problem for poetry as it grapples with politics.[35] Vallejo's Paris poems constantly underline the shiftiness of their human subjects, who slip the bounds of the poet's classificatory systems, turning on their heel to confront him: looking back at him from a position of mute defiance, or striking the poet himself dumb.

SECTION TWO: THE CONSTITUENCY OF POETRY

One of the peculiar quandaries faced by Vallejo in composing his Paris poetry was the question of how to organize the intransigent, embraceable subjects of modernity. To do so, he turns to lists, sketching out multiple quick portraits of individual types or typical groups, offered to the reader in the form of snapshots that compose a peculiar family album of modern subjects. But the proximity of his approach to modern social science systems—typologies, data banks, and statistics—carried the dual possibility of engaging poetry with history and of falsifying the experience of the latter. Vallejo's late poetry thus finds itself walking a precarious tightrope between representation and reification.

The anaphoras that structure poems such as "Traspié entre dos estrellas"—based on the principle of the biblical Beatitudes but replacing the adjective *blessed* with *beloved*—suggest that the figures it contains are strictly comparable. However, when we look more closely at the characteristics that define them, any conventional notion of taxonomy falls to pieces.

> ¡Amado sea aquel que tiene chinches,
> el que lleva zapato roto bajo la lluvia,
> el que vela el cadáver de un pan con dos cerillas,
> el que se coge un dedo en una puerta,
> el que no tiene cumpleaños,
> el que perdió su sombra en un incendio,
> el animal, el que parece un loro,
> el que parece un hombre, el pobre rico,
> el puro miserable, el pobre pobre!

These nine lines, from the third stanza of "Traspié," map out momentary, accidental, material, and ontological portraits of the human. Among these are almost interchangeable indigent figures, who have fleas, threadbare clothing, or bare scraps of food, such as the man who "vela el cadaver de un pan con dos cerillas" (watches over the corpse of a loaf with two matches; trans. modified), in a hyper-pathetic gloss on the dancing loaves of Chaplin's *The Gold Rush*. As the list gathers speed, we move on to an animal—one whose appearance, in anticipation of Borges's Chinese encyclopedia, both defines and undermines its identity ("parece un loro"; looks like a parrot)—then to one who *looks like a man*, and whom we suspect may *be* a man, but whose material condition or moral behavior pushes him back to the ranks of the animal. From here we pass on to a "pobre rico" (indeterminately a "poor rich man" or a "rich poor man," where material and moral categories dance around one another), and finally to a "pobre pobre"—a "poor poor man"—where the repetition signals either an intensification of his condition or the poet's affective response to him, or both at once.[36] But these kinds of glimpsed figures rarely interact with one another, holding instead fast to their own idiosyncrasies, pushing themselves individually or in groups into the poet's consciousness with unsettling violence ("Ay en mi tórax, cuando compran trajes!"; Ay in my thorax, when they buy themselves a suit! [trans. modified]). And while they may be resistant parts of a social whole or body politic, these figures—as the poems never cease to remind us—are in turn made up of parts (of bodies, of objects, of moods; fingers, matchboxes, tears) that resist easy organization into a totality.

These anarchic lists corrode many of the poems from Vallejo's Paris period, from the earliest to the very latest. They are deployed to categorize not only the figures around the poet but also his own memories of objects, moods, places, and figures. The poem "Despedida recordando un adios" (Farewell Remembering a Good-Bye) offers a roster of those who have influenced the poet's thinking as he shunts them off forever. In the process, it bundles together a multiplicity of figures who are unlikely to enjoy one another's company: Saint Peters, Heraclituses, Erasmuses, Spinozas, sad Bolshevik bishops, and governors of disorder. These poems are equally stuffed full of body parts, objects, and emotions, all served up to the reader on the same platter, with no indication of how we are to connect them, or of what indeed they might mean. We have no way of knowing, for example, whether "mis cometas" (my comets) in the poem "Hablando de la leña . . . " (Speaking of Kindling . . .), appearing on the same level as the more humdrum "mis calcetines" (my socks), and "el cuerpo" (the body), are symbolic—referring to the spirit, as Paoli *(Mapas)* suggests—or simply literal, referring to events in the night sky on which the speaker pins his hopes while they mark the inexorable passing of time. At other moments, Vallejo pulls the rug out from under our attempts to make meaning, offering us in "frío del frío y frío del calor" (cold of the cold and cold of the heat; in "Despedida . . .") a tautology followed by an oxymoron, which makes us wonder whether we are dealing with a part of a whole, an intensification of the whole, or an undercutting of the whole as it incorporates its opposite. The most radical and explicit version of this play with parts is the poem "Yuntas" (Yokes), which consists of bare statements of yoked opposing terms (tears/smiles, everything/nothing, etc.) organized through a repeating structure of contradictory binary couplets, as mapped out in its opening couplet:

Completamente. Además, ¡vida!
Completamente. Además, ¡muerte!

Completely. Furthermore, life!
Completely. Furthermore, death!

In each identically structured couplet, an initial statement that declares itself all-encompassing ("completely!") is undercut by the declaration of something which exceeds its grasp ("furthermore"), and this new statement is in turn undercut by a paired line that offers up that new term's opposite. As Ferrari contends, this poem seems to perform a dismantling of dialectics, setting forth binaries that not only fail to generate a new term, but look like the parodic undermining of the poet's own faith in the ability of language to encapsulate anything at all (268–69).[37]

This gesture recalls the seriality that corroded the overall structure of *Trilce* (whose numbered poems stop somewhat arbitrarily at seventy-seven) and which occasionally reared its head within its individual poems, such as *Trilce* V, which despaired of being able to sound out the number 1 without unleashing a series that would go on to infinity.

The play with parts that structures or destructures so many of the *Poemas humanos* is to some extent a continuation of the earlier poetry's focus on fragmented languages and bodies.[38] Parts here, however, jostle not only against one another, but against any overarching principle of organization; if the poems of *Trilce* focused on friction between elements, the objects and figures that appear in the later poems are for the most part discrete, set apart, holding their own place, even when the social panorama they depict is far more crowded. Leslie Bary argues that the relation of parts to one another and to a whole in Vallejo's late poetry works to undermine any process of organization, constructing "identity and solidarity as real and necessary but also as mobile, mutable, provisional" (225). This question, in other words, has political as much as aesthetic underpinnings: what Vallejo is foregrounding, I would suggest, through the multileveled tension between parts and wholes in this poetry, is the relation between individuals (who occupy constantly shifting positions) and broader society, between isolated words and a poem's gathering meaning—or indeed its binding tone.

This quandary is depicted formally in the poetry with a remarkably light touch: through catalogs of persons, traits, actions, potentials, and affects, all teeming and entangled and never as homogeneous as their organization might suggest. As Benjamin wrote of baroque language, Vallejo's poetry—in its rendition of contemporary society—is "constantly convulsed by rebellion on the part of the elements which make it up" (*Origin* 207). This is not quite the chaotic enumeration analyzed by Spitzer in poets such as Whitman, Rilke, and Werfel, where lists produce a sense either of the ultimate integration of the whole or of its utter disintegration. The fragmentary and imperceptibly anarchic lists of Vallejo's late poetry are rather a formal rendition of the complex relation between the part and the whole, the individual and the collective, in poetry as in politics, and they demand that we hold both in sight at once, in spite of the contradictions between them.

Yet this raises immediate problems for reading this poetry, on the level of both content and form, and it points to the fraught intersection of representational politics with avant-garde aesthetics. Many of the late poems—and this is especially true of the poems generated under the impact of the Spanish Civil War—are made up of lists, which we tend to read for their overall tone without paying a great deal of attention to their constituent parts, even when those parts chafe against the organizing principle of the list. The *Poemas humanos* continually perform a kind of optical or acoustic trick, lulling us into a false sense of security which prompts us to pass over those elements in a series that do not quite fit. We find a clear example of this in "Primavera tuberosa" (Tuberous Spring), which presents a scene of gambling (an apparently metaphorical rendition of Vallejo's sense of waste in Paris), set in a framed historical moment:

Veces las del bocado lauríneo,
con símbolos, tabaco, mundo y carne

These times of the lauraceous mouthful,
with symbols, tobacco, world and flesh

The knotty image of the first line—which seems to allude to the transformative (Ovidian) power of speech or poetry, as well as to the laurels that attach to the successful poet—contrasts with the relatively straightforward statement in the second. Yet the list in this line is itself anything but straightforward. If tobacco is a contingent accessory—to gambling or to producing poetry—the world and the flesh that follow it both radically expand and contract the scene, in a baroque telescoping that introduces a metaphysical dimension without entirely erasing the material body. And what about those symbols? Do they refer to the three elements that follow—standing outside the list as its governing principle—or are they part of it, just one more of the accessories of life, an invariant ideal held onto as everything else passes by or is gambled away? Or is the poet-gambler simply showing us his hand, revealing the ace—symbolism—always hidden up his sleeve?

As the *Poemas humanos* shift between elements and levels of their lists, undercutting their own taxonomies, they also reveal a further tension, a mismatch between tone and content. In reading Vallejo's late poetry, we likely cling to the former, looking out for words or sentiments that we recognize and can interpret literally or symbolically, assuming that everything else fits the paradigm; the often overwhelming rhetorical structure (as in "Un hombre pasa . . . ") creates a horizon of expectations that governs the tone of our reading. This is particularly the case in those poems that fix on politics, that assume that we will count on the poet's good faith—and all the more so if we come to them equipped with the minimal knowledge that Vallejo developed an abiding, if never comfortable, commitment to Marxism in his Paris years. An outstanding example is mapped out in the first stanza of "Me viene, hay días . . . " (There Are Days, There Comes to Me . . .):

Me viene, hay días, una gana ubérrima, política,
de querer, de besar al cariño en sus dos rostros,
y me viene de lejos un querer
demostrativo, otro querer amar, de grado o fuerza,
al que me odia, al que rasga su papel, al muchachito,
a la que llora por el que lloraba,
al rey del vino, al esclavo del agua,
al que ocultóse en su ira,
al que suda, al que pasa, al que sacude su persona en mi alma.
Y quiero, por lo tanto, acomodarle
al que me habla, su trenza; sus cabellos, al soldado,
su luz, al grande; su grandeza, al chico.
Quiero planchar directamente
un pañuelo al que no puede llorar
y, cuando estoy triste o me duele la dicha,
remendar a los niños y a los genios.

The very first words announce that this poem is concerned with both desire and politics, and we inevitably conflate the two, assuming that we are about to read a manifesto for solidarity and empathy. Yet the poem actually gets stuck from the start at the limits of its own desire: the speaker longs to kiss not his other but tenderness itself, falling in love with his own intermittent emotion. And after this opening salvo, the poem immediately starts zigzagging to such a dizzying extent that we seize on whatever we can recognize—love for one's most resistant neighbor, someone crying or unable to cry, a child—all of which are enfolded in the speaker's overwhelming desire. But in the process, we read too quickly over what looks like a symbol in the middle of this list ("the king of wine, the slave of water"), without considering that a master-slave dynamic does not quite apply here. Meanwhile, the speaker's intentions themselves look honorable, because he repeatedly reiterates his desire to love and help his neighbor; yet we have to wonder what good it would do to iron a handkerchief for one who cannot cry (trying to prompt him with accessories?), or indeed how happy either the interlocutor or the soldier would be to have the poet play with his hair.

These gratuitous acts in fact have a touch of malevolence to them, as becomes more apparent in the second stanza:

Quiero ayudar al bueno a ser su poquillo de malo,
y me urge estar sentado

a la diestra del zurdo, y responder al mudo,
tratando de serle útil en .
lo que puedo, y también quiero muchísimo
lavarle al cojo el pie,
y ayudarle a dormir al tuerto próximo.

These verses cast the poet as a bit of a pest. His responses to adverse
conditions (left-handedness, muteness, one-eyedness) initially look supplementary or complementary: standing in for a left-handed man's right
hand; responding to the mute to reassure him that his communications
are successful; washing a cripple's unused foot to keep it comfortable.
Yet the speaker's desire to act as a prosthetic also has counterproduc-
tive effects: by sitting at that right hand, he signals an imbalance more
than he corrects one; he speaks *to* rather than *for* the mute; and he
resolves a final problem with an inappropriate answer. The speaker's
desired desire is running amok here, satisfying itself with off-key responses: racing from condition to condition with apparently the best
intentions in the world, he ceaselessly misunderstands them and their
possible solutions (later in the poem he expresses a contrary desire to
"cuidar a los enfermos enfadándolos"; take care of the sick [by] annoying them). Yet carrying out all these desires will, he suggests in closing,
allow him to be "bueno conmigo / en todo" (good to myself / in everything). The problem with this and other late poems is that—because of
Vallejo's Marxist credentials, and our general reliance on poetry's good
faith—we want them to be good-natured, and we therefore pass too
easily over their "poquillo de malo."

The very organization of the series here, gathered under the rubric of
neighborly goodwill, also makes us miss something else that is crucial in
the poem: it consists entirely of hypotheses, driven by the intensely con-
voluted knottiness of the speaker's subjectivity. For as the first stanza
maps out quite clearly, this poem does not express a desire *per se* but a
desire to desire, which doubles the excessiveness and fictitiousness of its
gestures while shedding doubt on the nature and functioning of desire
itself, not to mention its possible political reach, in a gesture toward
the other that cannot help turning into self-reflection; care for the other
here is first and foremost care for the self. In a further twist, the speaker's desire is intermittent, comes from afar rather than from within, is
explicitly performative, and involves some violence—a "querer amar,
de grado o fuerza" (desire to love, willingly or by force), "al borde
célebre de la violencia / o lleno de pecho el corazón" (at the celebrated
edge of violence, / or my heart full of chest). All of these supplementary

observations make the poem's central lines—which should be (and have been made) extractable as a statement of local and global solidarity—wincingly ironic, a self-celebration masquerading as self-abnegation:

> ¡Ah querer, éste, el mío, éste, el mundial,
> interhumano y parroquial, provecto!

> *Ah to desire, this one, mine, this one, the world's,*
> *interhuman and parochial, mature!*

The delicate entanglement of parts and wholes in the *Poemas humanos* raises a practical and theoretical problem with regard to quotation and extraction, which can too easily simplify the "statements"—and the qualification is important here—being made by the poems. When I earlier quoted the speaker's bewailing of "la cantidad enorme de dinero que cuesta el ser pobre" (the enormous amount of money it costs to be poor; my trans.) ("Por ultimo . . . "; "Finally . . . "), I neglected to mention two things. First, there is a syntactical quibble in this line, which can also be read as "the enormous amount of money that the poor person costs," which radically shifts the focus of the complaint. Second, the poem as a whole presents a speaker who delights not only in paradoxes, but in his own amorality, which places him—at least momentarily—on the side of the corrupt: "el oro que robarta yo a mis víctimas, / ¡rico de mí, olvidándolo!" (the gold I robbed from my victims, / how rich I am in forgetting it! [trans. modified]). In reading this poetry, in other words, we have to be constantly on the lookout for contradictions between their statements—and often, between words and their tonal frame. These kinds of lists play against our expectations not because none of their components fit the bill but because *some* of them do—which leads us to pass far too easily over the ones that do not. At the same time, tone zigzags from sincerity to irony and back again so quickly that we can miss the shift even in those rare instances where we can pinpoint the modes.

Tone is surprisingly least stable of all in those poems that deal directly with politics, that reflect on the lyric's capacity to summon a mood or rouse to action. The poem "Ande desnudo en pelo el millonario!" (Let the Millionaire Walk Naked, Stark Naked!), for example, whips up its rhetoric through a series of seven long exclamations, each one containing multiple demands of its own, hammering out a series of lyric calls for what looks like a social revolution with distinctly biblical undertones. It imagines the overturning of current conditions, so that those who currently have everything should be left with nothing, while the destitute can earn their just rewards. But as in the case of

"Telúrica y magnética"—discussed in the introduction—the poem's shouted lines are too frenzied to be sustainable. More fundamentally, the content of the demands does not match the tone, nor do those demands quite mesh. Several of the calls are directed toward people who can act ("luchad por la justicia con la nuca, / igualaos"; fight for justice with your nape, / make yourselves equal), but many simply utter nonsensical desires ("hilo a los horizontes portátiles"; thread for the portable horizons), while the occasional line shouts out surprisingly for continuity ("muchos años de clavo al martillazo"; many years of nail for the hammer stroke). Some of the exhortations, such as that of the title, turn prevailing conditions on their head; others exaggerate them to such an extent that—going back to the modes of *Trilce*—the negative becomes positive and lack becomes abundance, as in "dése al mísero toda su miseria" (give to the wretched man all his wretchedness). But the majority follow their own illogical lyric logic: from fictions of poetic genesis ("sea la codorniz"; let the quail be) through what looks like an impenetrable symbol ("cúmplase el leopardo entre dos robles"; let the leopard between two oaks be fulfilled) to the actual cancellation of poetic power, and hence of this very poem: "no me hagáis caso" (pay no attention to me). After all of these urgent exhortations, the poem ends in an abrupt self-interruption which suggests that not even the poet is fully committed to his speech: "Me llaman. Vuelvo" (They're calling me. I'll be back).

If the elements in this list of calls do not quite add up to a program, the poem's progressively self-ironizing tone also squares uneasily with a political or pedagogical voice for the lyric (directed to a collective), or with conventional notions of the lyric as an emanation of subjective feeling. And as we immediately recognize on reading this poetry, tone is only half the battle; what we also have to grapple with, and in much more oblique ways, is the arrangement of words or phrases, which tend to be strung together in series whose elements are far more heterogeneous than their homogenizing formal organization suggests. This might seem to point to a collage technique—the emblem of non-organic art, as Peter Bürger argues, whose meaning lies in its lack of a totalizing meaning and whose parts are interchangeable or eliminable. Yet Vallejo polemically insisted that "un poema es una entidad vital mucho más orgánica que un ser orgánico en la naturaleza" (a poem is a far more organic vital entity than an organic being from nature) (*ACC* I: 346) and that nothing could be cut out of a poem. This demands that we exercise an analogous caution in reading; to quote from these poems often entails a violence that separates words from their tonal context, giving them an entirely new—and often much too easy—meaning, sidestepping the complexity at the heart of Vallejo's obliquely political poetic practice.

The recent discovery of some of the manuscripts for Vallejo's later poetry suggests that the accommodation of specific words was often the guiding impulse of the poem, which is almost unimaginable from the standpoint of their apparently political undertow, and it sheds a completely new light on Vallejo's attitude to both poetic experiment and selection of contents. As Juan Fló revealed, at least four of the dated poems from 1937 were initially constructed from a set of words listed down the right-hand side of the margin, crossed out as they were incorporated into each poem, always in the same verse where they had first appeared. Remarkably, the words themselves are often quite banal, not at all characteristic of Vallejo's language (as Fló notes, only one of them features a body part); they also have little connection among themselves, and are usually not the determining words in the poem. Stranger still, not all of them survived through the various stages of correction that came afterward. In the most startling example, the word *"sociedad"* (society) in the poem "Transido, salomónico, decente" (Racked, Salomonic, Decent) was originally the chemical element "molibdeno" (molybdenum), which, aside from the completely different lexical register, refers to a soluble element rather than the (social) fluid into which it sinks. Fló provocatively connects Vallejo's practice here to earlier currents of experiments with poetry (17), such as Novalis's meditation on the sense that can be generated almost mathematically by the combination of random words, which comes close to the language games we saw in *Trilce*.[39]

We might also see this as part and parcel of a fantasy of generative speech that appears several times in these late poems. Importantly, this is usually connected not to the poet's own language but to that of heroic historical figures such as the Bolshevik of "Salutación angelica" (Angelic Salutation), of whom the marveling poet proclaims, "Vi que en tus sustantivos creció yerba" (I saw that grass grew in your nouns), or the miners of "Los mineros salieron de la mina" (The Miners Came out of the Mine), for whom he wishes, "Crezcan la yerba, el liquén, la rana en sus adverbios!" (May grass, lichen, and frogs grow in their adverbs!) Yet the poet's own procedure, generating unpredictable words and images out of developing structures, often comes close to this fantasy of *autotelos*. Deleuze commented that Beckett "makes language grow from the middle, like grass" (11), but Vallejo's language, in its attempt to fit in as much content and sensory pleasure as possible, grows from all sides and in indeterminate directions at once. In this, and specifically in this particular image, his late poetry also harkens back to Whitman, whom Vallejo was reading carefully in Paris, and who haunts the entirety of his poems from these years; the early prose poem "Cesa el anhelo . . . " (Longing ceases . . .) counterbalances the shouting of a city with the image of a statue in whose palm a *brizna de yerba* (leaf of grass) has suddenly grown.

Vallejo further multiples meaning through processes of erasure that maximize the punning potential of certain words. "De disturbio en disturbio" (From Disturbance to Disturbance), for instance, describes the speaker's profile playing a "terrifying role" *(papel espeluznante)*, which recalls the photograph at the base of "Piedra negra sobre una piedra blanca." Yet the original version had the phrase "papel de línea espeluznante," which points not to a "role" but to *lined paper,* the material on which the poet writes out his "disturbances." The juxtaposition of the two versions reveals an unexpected double meaning that asserts the specificity of the poet's role as being that of recording, even if what he records is his own profile, which cuts across the paper's lines in unorthodox ways. And speaking of pictures and their portability, Vallejo's linguistic procedure very occasionally makes its rationale relatively transparent. In "Salutación angelica," he attributes a Bolshevik's ease of travel or transnational appeal to the fact that he carries "un pasaporte en blanco en tu sonrisa" (a blank passport in your smile), a clear inversion of the recognizably modern experience of having a blank smile in one's passport photo.

The *Poemas humanos* contain still more radical poems that constitute a kind of compositional experiment, radically separating words from tone. Tone in these poems is frequently only an effect of punctuation, and is usually exclamatory; even those poems that begin with questions, such as "Hablando de la leña, callo el fuego?" (Speaking of Kindling, Do I Silence Fire?), turn into a series of exclamations, laying bare poetry's desire for answers, producing only further exhortations: "¡Pregunta, Luis; responde Hermenegildo!" (Ask, Luis! Respond, Hermenegildo!). Other poems are nothing but content, consisting of series of isolated words lacking an ostensible frame. The most notorious examples are the poems "La paz, la abispa, el taco, las vertientes . . . " (The Peace, the Wasp, the Shoe Heel, the Slopes . . .)—whose five stanzas are organized around different grammatical categories, such as nouns and adjectives—and "Transido, salomónico, decente" (Racked, Solomonic, Decent)—structured around a sequence of verb tenses. Although the layout of each poem seems to rule out any possible narrative, their too loudly announced procedure actually helps us to decode them quite easily. In the case of the first poem, which seems to present a scene at a funeral, the poem's meaning becomes the lack of meaning that inheres with the loss of the subject, which survives only in fragmented form among the mourners. The second poem explicitly attaches itself to a subject caught in the grip of an impossible decision after an apparent insult, who, despite all his cogitation, ultimately renounces action and slides into oblivion, canceling out his own personality.[40]

Yet *Poemas humanos* also contains poems of an unusually searing subjectivity, which contain a mesmerizing reflection on the relation between words and tone in a poem. "Hoy me gusta la vida mucho menos" (Today I Like Life Much Less), for example, may initially look like a simple examination of the speaker's mood at a particular moment, but it raises increasingly complex questions about tone in poetry. To begin with, whether the lyric describes an emotion or attempts to provoke one, and not in its reader—as we might expect—but in the writer. Such poems take the question of tone seriously, treating it as performative rather than as merely descriptive or, indeed, fictitious. In other words, and in quite uncanny ways, the speaker in Vallejo's late poetry is often literally subjected to his own tone—which rouses him or depresses him, and which often ends up producing a strain that we can hear in his own acts of voicing.

> Hoy me gusta la vida mucho menos;
> pero siempre me gusta vivir, ¡ya lo decía!
> Casi toqué la parte de mi todo y me contuve
> con un tiro en la lengua detrás de mi palabra.

The slightly abashed assertion of the first line is directly offset by a statement meant to put the speaker's and our minds at rest: "pero siempre me gusta vivir" (but I always like to live), which sets up an opposition between life as theoretical abstraction and life as practical process—an opposition of reason and sense concretized in the line "noches de tacto, días de abstracción" (tactile nights, abstracted days) in "Quedéme a calentar la tinta en que me ahogo" (I Stayed on to Warm up the Ink in Which I Drown). But this counterbalance is immediately undercut by the clause at its tail, "ya lo decía." This can mean either "I've often said it," or more problematically, "I was just saying so," which entails that the poet is reassuring himself by citing his own reassurance in the very same line, which makes the poem fold in upon itself. The following verses are similarly unsettling: whether the speaker is suggesting that *just now* he almost uttered an enormity (cast typically in physical rather than purely verbal terms) or is referring to a previous and almost shattering existential moment, the fact remains that he has restrained or contained himself, and more bewilderingly, is telling us so, announcing that he is pulling back from full articulation. We are faced, then, in this opening, with a tonally charged assertion that contradicts itself, that admits that something has been left unsaid, although it tries to deflect the poet's and our attention from that unvoiced word.

The next two stanzas of the poem map out moments from the speaker's life: they alternate between snapshots of his life in Paris—wearing a vest and trousers, sitting in a café looking at chestnut trees—and memories of his family in Peru, set contrapuntally against a present tense self-touching and self-saying, which is either habitual or performative: "hoy me toco el mentón en retirada" (today I touch my chin in retreat), "yo me digo" (I tell myself), "y diciendo . . . " (and saying . . .), "y repitiendo . . ." (and repeating . . .). The fourth stanza offers a startling recapitulation of the words we have seen so far in the poem, suddenly bereft of the context that had fleshed them out:

> Dije chaleco,
> todo, parte, ansia, dije casi, por no llorar.

The poet here pulls back the skin of the poem, revealing not a lyric skeleton but a verbal tool kit, undercutting the illusion that his tone had attempted to sustain, leaving behind only words. Yet in the very moment when the truth of the lyric utterance is undercut by showing its hand, a more truthful tone emerges. If *anxiety* is the one word in this list that had not previously been uttered, and is revealed as the word that was *almost uttered,* this makes the poem's self-observation a shattering but also successful voicing of the one word that matters.[41] Its articulation here catapults the speaker into the most directly autobiographical statement of bodily and mental pain that we find in Vallejo's late poetry:

> Que es verdad que sufrí en aquel hospital que queda al lado
> y está bien y está mal haber mirado
> de abajo para arriba mi organismo.

Laying bare its contents, the poem reveals that its own words make its optimistic tone a sham, only to redirect that tone toward a devastating articulation of words of truth. But just for a moment: what reasserts itself in the final stanza is a desperate restatement of a positive tone, attempting to reinstate itself by claiming a hollow victory over celebratory words, whose hysterical repetition nonetheless turns them into pure sounds of pain:

> porque, como iba diciendo y lo repito,
> ¡tanta vida y jamás! ¡Y tantos años,
> y siempre, mucho siempre, siempre, siempre!

Words themselves threaten to disappear in the poem "Y si después de tantas palabras . . . " (And If after So Many Words . . .); their sheer quantity cannot guarantee their survival. The poem peters out in an undecidable register: "Entonces . . . ¡Claro! . . . Entonces . . . ¡ni palabra!" (Then . . . Of course! . . . Then . . . Not a word!), which suggests that no words will be left to mark the failure of discourse, but also—on a supremely ironic note—that the lyric should not speak of what might come to pass, for fear of bringing it about. In the very first poem of *Los heraldos negros,* language had capitulated before pain, because the latter was ineffable; here the suggestion is that poetry has become pointless, although it persists in the self-delusion of its own power. This seems to mark the absolute breakdown of the lyric in the face of Vallejo's growing historical pessimism in 1936. It seems to be the last of the undated poems of Vallejo's Paris period, suggesting that at this point, he saw no way out of the impasse between lyric impotence and historical inevitability.

SECTION THREE: "POETRY DATES FROM TODAY"[42]

What rescues the lyric, for Vallejo and for dozens of his contemporaries, is the Spanish Civil War, and in a way that differed utterly from earlier cataclysms. World War I had produced fragmentary or personal lyrics bearing witness to its effect on individual subjectivities—Wilfred Owen, Siegfried Sassoon, Georg Trakl—and had then prompted Dada's wholesale attack on the civilized lyric in the face of mangled bodies and cultures. But the Spanish Civil War, instead of shutting down the possibilities of articulation, suddenly opened up two new horizons: the rousingly spontaneous gathering of local and international volunteer soldiers in Spain to resist the rise of fascism, and the equally spontaneous production of what Vallejo calls a "popular epic," emblematized both in direct collective action and in literature—such as the anthology *Romancero de la guerra de España,* consisting of hundreds of anonymous ballads (*ACC* II: 960–64). Meanwhile, many of the writers who found themselves in Spain in 1936–37—whether as fighters (George Orwell), diplomats (Pablo Neruda), or participants in the Second International Writers' Congress for the Defense of Culture in summer 1937 (some two hundred from twenty-eight countries, including Vallejo)— produced their own accounts of the resistance battle in Spain and what it meant for both politics and art. Several poets took this as an opportunity to foreground the newly popular inspiration of their poetry, as evidenced in the titles of their collections: Miguel Hernández's *Viento del pueblo* (Wind of the People), Rafael Alberti's *El poeta en la calle* (The Poet in the Street). Others turned the lyric into a mode of rabid witnessing, banishing the aestheticist modes of previous poetry. Neruda's manifesto-like poem "Explico algunas cosas" (I Explain a Few Things), for example, begins with a challenge to the reader, "Preguntaréis: Y dónde están las lilas?" (You will ask: and where are the lilacs?), followed by the trenchant response, "Os voy a contar todo lo que me pasa" (I'm going to tell you all that is happening to me), and after a luminous evocation of his previous life in a market town in Madrid, it launches into a furious description of destruction, which has sent that life to ground.[43] But after a catalog of scenes of violence, the poem turns this conflagration into a series of images of potential resistance:

> pero de cada casa muerta sale metal ardiendo
> en vez de flores, [. . .]
> pero de cada nino muerto sale un fusil con ojos
>
> *but from each dead house comes burning metal*
> *instead of flowers, [. . .]*
> *but from each dead child comes a gun with eyes*

And rather than abandoning a faith in poetry, Neruda's poem culminates in a chilling performance of formal power, which shapes a newly urgent role for the lyric:

> Venid a ver la sangre por las calles;
> venid a ver
> la sangre por las calles;
> venid a ver la sangre
> por las calles!
>
> *Come and see the blood in the streets;*
> *come and see*
> *the blood in the streets;*
> *come and see the blood*
> *in the streets!*

Vallejo's response to the Spanish Civil War took a more tentative and self-critical tack.[44] Over the course of 1937 he wrote a series of prose articles addressing the war from a number of different angles, which—for a time at least—sidelined the question of poetry, focusing instead on the practicalities of economic organization and on the need to rethink Latin America's relation to its former colonial master (ACC II: 965–66).[45] In a rhapsodic but unpublished article from early 1937 (ACC II: 960–64), Vallejo hailed the spontaneous, collective, and anonymous actions of the Spanish volunteer soldiers as an unprecedented event in history, claiming that in their self-motivated and horizontal organization they differed radically from the unknown soldier so iconic to World War I, who had acted out of national duty and in deference to political and military leaders. By contrast, Vallejo casts the action of these new masses (made up of *transeúntes* rather than professional or conscripted fighters) as a reflex response, beyond ideology—the absolute apotheosis of a human instinct for self-preservation in the face of a violent attack from within or outside the system. Moving beyond nationalism and rejecting coercive governance, the mass appeared to be constituting itself as truly sovereign.[46]

In the article "Las grandes lecciones culturales de la guerra española" (The Great Cultural Lessons of the Spanish War) (ACC II: 957–59) Vallejo finally took on the question of the war's aesthetic ramifications, mapping out what he saw as three possible options for the progressive writer: noncommitted writing, whose intense humanism harbored a revolutionary charge (Shakespeare, Goethe, Balzac); committed left-wing writing, which tended to overestimate its immediate power; and the productions of writers who threw themselves into the trenches but also managed to mediate and transmit the aspirations of their fellow fighters in their writing. It is significant in this last example that Vallejo neither cancels the role of literature nor reduces it to direct representation; instead, he pushes for a writing that will outlast its immediate moment, that will remain explosive in the future—a writing both urgent and durable.

This play between the present moment and a sense of future history also entails a confrontation between speech and writing that is staged repeatedly in the Spanish Civil War sequence.[47] In a 1937 letter, Vallejo noted that "las cosas hay que tratarlas de viva voz, para que resulten" (things have to be worked out through talking, person to person) (CC 452), whereas writing, as he repeatedly insisted, could only have a distant effect, which was incalculable in the present.[48] But this incalculability was the most potent political aspect of writing: what did not exhaust itself in present-tense immediacy could have unforeseeable future effects, keeping writers and writing in a productive state of tension, turning their words into weapons that cut not just into the present but into the future as well. "Los responsables de lo que sucede en el mundo somos los escritores, porque tenemos el arma más formidable, que es el verbo" (It is we as writers who are responsible for what happens in the world, for we have the most formidable weapon, which is the word) (*ACC* II: 970). And the history for which writers were responsible had to be in the future tense.

But this was far from an avowal of poetry's lack of responsibility to the present. Vallejo's Spanish Civil War sequence does engage directly with several of the most recent battles, although not so much to present them as news as to mediate them for what can be mined from them in the future; poetry is here not "news which stays news," as Pound memorably put it, but news for the future, in a more Benjaminian mode. The collection also occasionally allows itself to imagine a utopia (Ortega, *Teoría poética*), as in the much-anthologized "Masa" (Mass), which marks the demise of an individual fighter, resurrected through the coming together of every last human on earth in a rigorously all-encompassing collective vision; or the "Pequeño responso a un héroe de la República" (Short Prayer for a Loyalist Hero), which envisions a book sprouting from the cadaver of a soldier; or even poem III on Pedro Rojas, who lived "en representación de todo el mundo" (as a representative of everyone), and whose corpse was found to be "lleno de mundo" (full of world), where "world" marks at once an internationalist vision and a common humanity grounded in the body. But at times the poet's voice sounds a warning: in poem XIV, for example, Vallejo addresses his exclamations to Spain in a series of cautions—although as we have grown to expect from his exclamations, the poem's content here consists of a string of contradictory and quite surprising calls:

¡Cuídate de tus héroes!
¡Cuídate de tus muertos!
¡Cuídate de la República!
¡Cuídate del futuro! . . .

Beware of your heroes!
Beware of your dead!
Beware of the Republic!
Beware of the future! . . .

In what would eventually become the closing poem of the series, the poet adopts a different, more intimate, more hesitant tone. Addressing the "niños del mundo" (children of the world), and suggesting that the war may not have the hoped-for outcome, he repeatedly hedges his warning with the caveat "—digo, es un decir—" (—I'm saying, I'm only saying—; my trans.). Casting Spain as a mother or teacher caught up in her own worries, he appeals to her children to lower their voices: "bajad la voz, el canto de las sílabas, el llanto / de la materia" (lower your voice, the song of the syllables, the wail / of matter). The call is not for no action but for no violent speech—or for no excessive hope in the possibilities of speech. Or, perhaps, for no poetry. What keeps Vallejo's poetry on the move in this collection is its constant self-critique: measuring itself against events in the process of their unfolding, it continually suggests not that it may be not enough but that it is in fact too much. And yet in its very excessiveness, it finds a reason for keeping on murmuring.

The opening poem of the collection, styled as a first response to the Spanish Civil War, directly stages the role of the poet in the face of this historical commotion. But although it foregrounds his feelings of uselessness, it does not take the somber tack we might expect. In fact there is almost a liberating euphoria to its frenzied unsettlement, as the poet does not quite take a backseat to the direct actors of history but instead rushes around them, trying to find a new place for himself in relation to them and their actions:

> Voluntario de España, miliciano
> de huesos fidedignos, cuando marcha a morir tu corazón,
> cuando marcha a matar con su agonía
> mundial, no sé verdaderamente
> qué hacer, dónde ponerme; corro, escribo, aplaudo,
> lloro, atisbo, destrozo, apagan, digo
> a mi pecho que acabe, al bien, que venga,
> y quiero desgraciarme;
> descúbrome la frente impersonal hasta tocar
> el vaso de mi sangre; me detengo
> [. . .]
> y, otra vez, sin saber qué hacer, sin nada, déjame,
> desde mi piedra en blanco, déjame,
> solo,
> cuadrumano, más acá, mucho más lejos,
> al no caber entre mis manos tu largo rato extático,
> quiebro contra tu rapidez de doble filo
> mi pequeñez en traje de grandeza!

What starts out as a paean to the fighter shifts to a focus on the poet:

not on his voice, however, but on his body, which contorts itself in various postures to find an adequate gesture of response. And if we focus on the solemnity of the occasion, we miss the fact that this rendition comes close to slapstick—a montage of images of shame, excitement, and, above all, commotion, as the poet's tiny body smashes itself repeatedly against the solidity and strength of the volunteer soldier. The poem rushes exuberantly and gaspingly through twelve long stanzas that try to encompass everything in the past, present, and possible future of the event, stringing together fragmentary celebrations of Spain's literary past, of its present acts of heroism, of the international volunteers who swarm into Spain; it praises the proletarian "que mueres de universo" (who dies of universe), the liberator, the peasant, the builders, the "fabulosos mendigos" (fabulous beggars) who turn lack into gain and paradoxes into possibilities. It zigzags through prophecies, exhortations, denunciations, and hopes, foreseeing the freedom of all—"del explotado y del explotador" (of the exploited and the exploiter)—and culminating in a vision of "paz indolora" (painless peace) that the poet glimpses "cuando duermo al pie de mi frente / y más cuando circulo dando voces" (when I sleep at the foot of my forehead / and even more when I go around shouting). The poet's voice presents itself here not in search of a form but raising itself in excitement; its modes, it intimates, will be fragmentary, befitting the upheaval and promise of the situation. When it settles down (at least relatively speaking) in the later poems of the sequence, it moves into quasi-religious mode, channeling the prophetic voice of the Bible, but linking spirit to matter, fusing the biblical with Marxist vindication, raging against the violence of battle and the destruction of life while intoning utopian hymns of terrestrial salvation.

Vallejo's faith in the triumph of the Republican soldiers, until the very last poem, is unwavering; but the victory he envisions—in keeping with his sensitivity to balanced binaries—is not that of one side or another but of humanity writ large, in a "lid en que ya nadie es derrotado" (combat in which no longer is anyone defeated) (IV).[49] Yet his exclamations are careful not to sidestep the horrors of war: the loss of individuals, with their typical first names and specific surnames (Pedro Rojas, Ramón Collar), or the effect of so much violence on the observer, fighter or poet:

> ¡Y horrísima es la guerra, solivianta,
> lo pone a uno largo, ojoso;
> da tumba la guerra, da caer,
> da dar un salto extraño de antropoide!

Tú lo hueles, compañero, perfectamente,
al pisar
por distracción tu brazo entre cadáveres;
tú lo ves, pues tocaste tus testículos, poniéndote rojísimo;
tú lo oyes en tu boca de soldado natural.
[. . .]
Por eso, al referirme a esta agonía,   ,
aléjome de mí gritando fuerte:
¡Abajo mi cadáver! . . . Y sollozo.
(From "X: Invierno en la batalla de Teruel"; Winter during the Battle of
Teruel)

If the fighter touches himself in embarrassment, the poet can only cry
out and weep. Both reactions together bear witness to a history experienced as at once subjective and desubjectivizing, and both of them insist
shamefacedly on their place within it.

MAKING POETRY HISTORY

Various critics have offered convincing analyses of the ways in which
España, aparta de mí este cáliz, from its title onward, fuses Vallejo's
residual Marxism with a biblical vision of human solidarity, to be
achieved not in the next world but in this one, answering metaphysics with materialism (e.g. Paoli, *"España"*). But I want to take issue
with the frequent claim that *España, aparta de mí este cáliz* marks the
culmination of Vallejo's poetics, offering him a way to conjoin his various concerns while either dissolving poetry into history or holding one
above the other. Instead, what the Spanish sequence suggests is that
poetry now has to be incessantly on the move: commenting on events
and laying bare its tangential relation to them, essaying different forms
of speech (shouting, shaping, metaphorizing, literalizing). Even more
significantly, *España. . .* comprises only fifteen poems out of a total
of at least sixty-seven that Vallejo composed between September and
December 1937, and the other fifty-two poems—many of which I have
referred to in this chapter—have little explicit connection to history.
Although the first poem from this dated group went into the Spanish
Civil War cycle, the chronology shows Vallejo hopping back and forth
between these two kinds of compositions. Clearly Vallejo did not know
for a time that he was writing a sequence on the Spanish Civil War. As
Hart has demonstrated, some poems—such as "El acento me pende del
zapato" (My Accent Hangs from My Shoe; trans. modified)—began in

one paradigm only to migrate into the other, moving fluidly between history and subjectivity, obliquely revealing their enmeshment.

The poems *not* focused on Spain have their own relation to contemporary history and its inhabitants, and most strikingly, their tone shifts under the impact of the war. Not, as we might expect, in the direction of sobriety but rather toward slapstick depictions and affectionately mocking modes of address, often with an undertow of anguish. These poems depict the poet himself in frenetic motion, galvanized by a sudden confidence in his place in history, even when the foreshortened span of his actions leaves him with a sense of barely moving. The Baroque conceit which reduces temporal existence to a single gasp is translated via more modern techniques of film into a spatial image of running on the spot, as in the case of the subject of "Va corriendo, andando, huyendo . . . " (He Goes Running, Walking, Fleeing . . .) who, for all his motion, is frozen "parado de tanto huir" (standing from so much fleeing; my trans.).

And at the moment of Vallejo's reborn faith in history and the place within it of the lyric, the tone of his poems becomes not more serious but more playful. This becomes clear when we compare the undated (but likely early 1930s) poems on modern subjects—focused on marked historical agents, such as Bolsheviks, Peruvian miners, agricultural and industrial laborers, and the unemployed—with those dated poems that address the poet's average fellow men. The tone of the former tends toward the reverential, revolutionary, almost messianic, but the latter have notes of distinct irreverence, as they cajole and tease their addressees. If the earlier Paris poems presented an uneasy face-off between the poet and his subject, the later ones are confident in the poet's place in the poem, casting him as addressing his others in tones of aggressive seductiveness and salty sociability: "¿Y bien? ¿Te sana el metaloide pálido?" (Well? Does the Pallid Metalloid Heal You?) This particular poem, in its efforts to jolt its addressee into revolt, echoes the earlier "Parado en una piedra" (Standing/Unemployed on a Stone), but rather than taking any capacity for resistance as a given, it suggests that its complacent human subject can only be prodded into action by insults. Addressing his subject as a slave—and later, mixing respect with mockery, as "Señor esclavo" (Mr. slave)—the speaker launches into an acutely ironic speech—"en la mañana mágica / se ve, por fin, / el busto de tu trémulo ronquido" (on the magic morning / the bust of your tremulous snore / is seen, at last)—to needle his addressee into rebellion.

But where did this leave the poet, who "habl[a] solo" (speaks to himself)—like the solitary filmgoer of "Esto / sucedió entre dos párpados" (This / Happened between Two Eyelids) who continually mimics in real life the "resbalón" (slip; explicitly related to slapstick through a mention of bananas) he sees intermittently on-screen—and who has to wrestle not just with his subjects for representation, but with his misbehaving tools? Vallejo summed up these concerns in the extraordinary sonnet "Intensidad y altura" (Intensity and Height), whose title ironically attempts to fit poetry into practical forms of measurement (height and density), and whose content presents the repeated stymieing of the poet's attempts at self-articulation.

> Quiero escribir, pero me sale espuma,
> quiero decir muchísimo y me atollo;
> no hay cifra hablada que no sea suma,
> ni pirámide escrita sin cogollo.
>
> Quiero escribir, pero me siento puma,
> quiero laurearme, pero me encebollo.
> No hay toz hablada, que no llegue a bruma,
> no hay dios, ni hijo de dios, sin desarrollo.
>
> Vámonos, pues, por eso, a comer yerba,
> carne de llanto, fruto de gemido,
> nuestra alma melancólica en conserva.
>
> ¡Vámonos! ¡Vámonos! Estoy herido;
> vámonos a beber lo ya bebido,
> vámonos, cuervo, a fecundar tu cuerva.

The poet's efforts to speak or write either turn into too much matter (a reef, a puma) or evanesce with no lasting residue (foam, mist); at the same time, he has no hope of reining in his utterances—because one figure inevitably leads to others and forges a whole—nor any way to begin from a zero point, because any construction has to begin not from but *with* emptiness. The poet is therefore trapped between the weight of the past and the incalculable indeterminacy of a future, the solidity of matter and the ephemerality of the spirit—and poetry, in the midst of it all, remains incalculable in its forms and effects. This is both a reflection on poetry in a particular historical moment and a critique of its determination to aim for an adequate image.

What the sonnet offers in place of a compensatory or integrative sequence of metaphors is a series of quite charming absurdities, which nonetheless deal with utterly serious questions that I have been mapping throughout this book: the relation between poetry and the present, a self-deprecating portrait of the artist, an attention to bodily processes, the orchestration of art around emptiness, a call to action. The poem's most memorable line, "quiero laurearme, pero me encebollo" (I want to laurel myself, but I stew in onions), wittily cancels Ovidian possibilities of salvationary metamorphosis (Daphne turning into a laurel tree) but also any hope of institutional success (becoming a poet laureate). Instead, the speaker becomes a bathetically domestic object—even if the onion, which in the kitchen harmonizes well with *laureles* or bay leaves, has just as layered a construction as those pyramids, and, moreover, a denser core.

The poem's tercets, rather than rejecting these previous images as inoperative, recapitulate the domestic or quite humdrum object as the only basis for action. If there is nothing new under the sun, no way to articulate a radically new voice—the central concerns of the European avant-gardes—and no sense in producing a new object, the only possible procedure involves recycling, which turns the guano poetics of *Trilce* into active politics. In this poem, rather than focusing on what comes out of the body, Vallejo reconsiders what might go into it: his answer is a program for self-cannibalization, suggesting that the human subject nourish itself with lack and suffering, eating its own "carne de llanto, fruta de gemido, / nuestra alma melancólica en conserva" (flesh of sobs, fruit of wailing, / our melancholy soul in preserves; trans. modified).

In the tercets there is an important shift from self-analysis to collective action among an indistinct group of addressees ("nosotros"), suggesting that this is a program not just for poetry but for politics as well. And the enigmatic raven who closes the poem is not just a recapitulation of other allegorical birds in Vallejo's poetry. It also connects back to a tradition of the lyric, and in particular, the carefully constructed poems of Edgar Allen Poe (Buxó, *César Vallejo* 97), whose transatlantic translation by Baudelaire effectively jump-started modern poetry. But if in the poem's last lines, collective bodily action replaces individual poetic effort, this does not entirely cancel out the role of poetry. It is, after all, lyric form that converts stagnation and description into an excited call to movement: the five-times-repeated "¡Vámonos!" (Let's go!)—four of which are in the last tercet—transforms a carpe diem from its more usual prophecy of destruction into an energetic call to action.[50]

The poem "Sermón sobre la muerte" (Sermon on Death)—which seems to be the last poem Vallejo ever composed—examines the conditions under which such action is to be achieved. Styling itself as an address to an audience, it nonetheless emphasizes the tension between writing and speaking that also underlay "Intensidad y altura," twice mentioning the *pupitre* (desk) at which a sermon is preproduced, but also the *púlpito* (pulpit) from which it is orally delivered. Like so many other poems from Vallejo's late period, its modes are ostensibly biblical, but it intermittently channels the bureaucratic in its concern with determining current conditions—summed up in the mind-boggling observations, "se hacen menester sermón y almendras" (there is a need for sermons and almonds; my trans.) and "sobran literalmente patatas" (there are literally too many potatoes). Calculating counterposed lacks and abundances, this poem surveys life from the vantage point of death, and hence, unsurprisingly, is markedly focused on endings; it begins with the words "Y, al fin" (And, finally) and inquires into the goals of both directed actions and life itself, suggesting in a Baroque conceit that the only product of life is death, just one more fruit in a still life.

But if the poem seems to be concerned with final meaning—extracted teleologically at its endpoint—it is equally focused, as is the end of "Intensidad y altura", on generation. One term begets another in this poem less through sense (symbolic resonance) than through sound and semantic parallels: the aurally connected opposites *pupitre-púlpito*, but also *loco-lovo-cordero-sensato-caballísimo* (mad, wolve [sic], lamb, sensible, most utmost horse), which gives an uncanny sense to sound, making it a generative impulse that strings together both words and tone: from lyric madness (loco) we come to a misspelled but almost homophonic wolf (lovo), from there to the lamb he preys on (cordero), on to a momentary awareness of the hidden word "cuerdo" (wise), which leads us to "sensato" (sensible) and finally back to a different animal entirely *(caballísimo)*. This clearly brings us back to the earlier modes of *Trilce*, its gathering of sense in and around sound, with occasional detours to chase echoes of other words. What connects it to the later poetry is its focus on the individual who speaks to a collective, yet who inevitably sinks into himself as he justifies his authority to speak to or for others. As so often in Vallejo, this question is brought back to the body, its organs, and its senses, which are made the ineradicable ground for rescuing the self and others:

> defenderé mi presa en dos momentos,
> con la voz y también con la laringe,
> y del olfato físico con que oro
> y del instinto de inmovilidad con que ando,
> me honraré mientras viva—hay que decirlo.

I will defend my catch in two moments,
with my voice and also with my larynx,
and of the physical smell with which I pray,
and of the instinct for immobility with which I walk,
I'll be proud while I'm alive—it must be said.

That "hay que decirlo" overwrites the more tentative or wavering "entre el decirlo / y el callarlo" (between saying it / and silencing it) of
España . . . IX, and it rescues poetry for history, as a necessary mode
of witnessing. What it witnesses is the body, but also the voice, and the
determined inscription of both in action, in ways that defy expectations
or orchestrate paradoxes (an immobile walking, an oration grounded
in smell—melding kinaesthetic and synaesthetic modes). Most significantly, this poem offers a final instance of positioning—or rather, of its
avoidance, proclaiming instead a constant shiftiness. In an unusually
clear closing statement, Vallejo asserts not a fixed artistic or political
position but rather an unfixability that sounds at once lyric, historical,
and political:

porque, al centro, estoy yo, y a la derecha
también, y, a la izquierda, de igual modo.

because, at the center, am I, and to the right,
also, and, to the left, in equal measure. (My trans.)

Dividing his own figure into three parts, or multiplying that figure three
times, Vallejo offers a Gance-like triptych that radically expands the
panorama in which he and his writings can be viewed, which is what I
have been attempting throughout this book. This final statement offers
a montage of three different views of the poet—which we might divide,
as I have done in these last two chapters, between the prose writer,
the lyricist, and the average man—which reflect one another in a hall
of mirrors, capturing some of what surrounds him in the process, and
which bears on and determines his shifting affiliations and self-articu-
lations. But importantly, that simultaneous montage does not offer a
linear narrative, a filmic progression through positions. Instead it leaves
us with a final image of the poet in constant motion, moving not from
one position to another but between them, elaborating multiple attachments in a process of constant self-critique. His poetry demands just as
much of us as readers: that we, like Vallejo and his lyric, stay shifting,
contingent, measured, and always out of place.

Conclusion

Poetry and Crime

La poesía es un atentado celeste

Poetry is a heavenly crime

—Vicente Huidobro

Readings of Vallejo have tended to present him as exceptional: in his context, in his approach to language, in his difficulty, and in his struggles with local and international modernity. My approach throughout this book, by contrast, has been to work against any such notion of his exceptionality. To fully understand the challenges of his writings, it is crucial to read him in connection with his contemporary avant-gardes in their various media (poetry, sculpture, theater), with the mass medium of film, with the larger cultural panoramas of both Latin America and Europe, and with unfolding political discourses in both arenas. Vallejo never cuts himself off from the world. His poetry constantly depicts him standing on a threshold or out in the open, calling out to passersby; in a rare instance when he presents himself inside a room, that room contains a map of other spaces ("Ello es que el lugar donde me pongo . . . "; "It Happens That the Place Where I Put On . . . "). His writing patterns his engagement with the world in the contortions of its own forms and in the pathos of its contents, and it demands that we treat it as fundamentally enmeshed with its contemporary moment.

I have also been attempting to dismantle another notion of exceptionality: this time attached to poetry itself, which tends to be approached as a discourse set apart from other forms of social utterance. As Pascale Casanova puts it, New Criticism–derived readings tend to concern themselves with the "*how* of a literary text" rather than with "the question of *why* it exists in this form," and in the process, they "reduce textual analysis to unraveling an enigma exclusively on the basis of the materials provided, as in detective novels, by the text itself" (*Beckett* 27). Poetry continues to invite this approach, because it looks like a self-sufficient artifact, or indeed a locked room—a *stanza,* in the sense teased out by Giorgio Agamben *(Stanzas).* But the most productive kind of criticism, like the most probing detective, knows that this room is never completely sealed off from the outside. Baudelaire, the first determined poet of the modern street, translated not only Poe's poetry but also his "Murders in the Rue Morgue," clearly drawn to the question of how a seemingly impermeable space is not just structured by the space around it but is in fact a passage through it. And for all its apparent hermeticism, Vallejo's poetry is continually invaded by other bodies, other voices, other rooms.

Intriguingly, the intersection between poetry, the locked room, and detective fiction is at the center of two Latin American novels of the 1990s in which Vallejo plays an enigmatic yet crucial role: *La pesquisa* (The Investigation) (1994), by the Argentinean Juan José Saer, and *Monsieur Pain* (1999), by the Chilean Roberto Bolaño. Both authors are best known as novelists, although each one considered himself a poet and experimented with fusing the genres of poetry and prose in unusual ways. Bolaño began his career writing neo-avant-garde poetry in the 1970s (thematized in *Los detectives salvajes;* The Savage Detectives), and included poet-figures in most of his subsequent novels; Saer repeatedly toyed with the idea of writing a novel in verse, and gave his single collection of poems the telling title *El arte de narrar* (The Art of Narration). Each author, moreover, repeatedly associated poetry with crime, committed by, to, or around the poet: Bolaño's *De noche en Chile* (By Night in Chile) hinges on the activities of the murderous sky-writing poet Carlos Wieder, while his *Amuleto* (Amulet) features a female poet who becomes a near-witness to a coup d'etat while locked in a university bathroom; Saer's short story "La recepción en Baker Street" (Reception in Baker Street) sketches out a plan for a crime novel in verse.

If many of their other writings draw upon poetry's oblique, intermittent, or fragmentary ways of witnessing history, in *The Investigation* and *Monsieur Pain* Saer and Bolaño both summon Vallejo himself to the witness stand—in the latter as a victim, and in the former as an implicit investigator, working within modernity to expose its crimes.

Their respective invocations point to divergent if complementary readings of Vallejo—as a central figure in Latin American poetics but a still-marginal figure in the broader Western panorama of the modern lyric. Saer's oblique reference to his poetry makes it clear that half a century after his death, Vallejo had become a central icon of the Latin American poetic tradition—an intimate, intransigent counterpart to the gigantism and grandiloquence of Pablo Neruda. But for Bolaño, Vallejo continues to emblematize the precarious life of a poet in the modern metropolis; *The Savage Detectives* contains a brief sketch of a group of Peruvian poets eking out a miserable living in Paris in the 1970s, clearly patterned on Vallejo's experience.

Saer's *The Investigation* tells two parallel stories: first, that of a serial killer in Paris, whose crimes are pinned on a character apparently ill-disposed to commit them; second, that of a literary enigma in Argentina, involving the discovery among a late poet's papers of a prose manuscript (a crime against his own strict adherence to the lyric) which bears the title of an early Vallejo poem, "En las tiendas griegas" (In the Greek Tents). In Bolaño's *Monsieur Pain,* meanwhile, a practitioner of alternative medicine is commissioned to prevent the death of Vallejo; the poet's unremitting death, which occurs slowly and effectively "off-camera"—literally in another room—turns the novel's pale protagonist into an investigator. In both novels, investigators have little access to the materials (a text and a body) that need to be examined. The manuscript at the heart of Saer's novel is kept sealed in a folder inside a plastic envelope in a locked box in a decaying house, presided over by its presumed author's daughter; in Bolaño's narrative, Vallejo wastes away in a room that the narrator is barred from entering by a shadowy conspiracy of doctors.

In these two novels, in other words, Vallejo's writings and his body are literally encrypted. But although both novels hinge on his recognizable figure, his appearance in each one is in fact tangential and elliptical. In Saer's novel, he appears only as the source for the *title* of the mysterious manuscript, which is moreover drawn from a little-anthologized poem from Vallejo's first collection, *Los heraldos negros*. In Bolaño's novel, Vallejo literally disappears from view, at an agonizing remove from the central character called upon to investigate his ongoing death. Nonetheless, his minimal appearance in each one speaks volumes about both authors' readings of his poetry, condensing their thoughts about the place of poetry in history, about the relation between form, content, and space of utterance. Both novels present a narrative that tries, and ultimately fails, to make sense of the events they recount; and in both, the form of poetry hovers just outside the frame as the potential key to the story. Both might therefore have taken as their epigraph T. S. Eliot's lines, "We had the experience but missed the meaning, / And approach to the meaning restores the experience / but in a different form."[1] The narrators of both novels are too blinded by their faith in narrative to investigate *poetry's* meaning; no one pays any attention to the role played by Vallejo's poetry in the stories in which they are involved. For Bolaño's Monsieur Pain, Vallejo is simply another body to be treated, his attention drawn more by the person requesting that attention—the young widow, Madame Renaud—than by an obscure Latin American poet, who writes in a language he cannot understand and whom he never thinks to read. For Saer's Argentinean conversation partners, focus falls on assessing the unlikely attribution of a prose manuscript to their poet-mentor, never raising the question of why the manuscript's title might be drawn from Vallejo, and from a minor poem at that.

To shift the metaphor slightly, this is also a question of frames: of frame-stories, but also frames for modern stories. Modernist writing, Fredric Jameson argues, is grounded in the multiplication of frames for the modern subject: the local context in which experience unfolds, but also a distant context, where local modernity has its real roots in the exploitation and importation of raw materials (other subjects, other matters). The European subject, in this account, develops—unwittingly—within two simultaneous frames that do not visibly overlap, one of which may be entirely hidden from view ("Modernism"). For subjects on the peripheries of Western modernity, however, these two frames are equally palpable, and the pressure on Latin American writers from independence onward is to connect to both frames at once, without losing sight of the specific demands of either one. As is evident in the polemic with which I opened this book, this pressure frequently leads to a polarization between writers taken as subscribing to either a Latin Americanist or a European worldview. But it more often manifests itself in the situation of an individual writer, as is the case of Vallejo, who engages with both European and Latin American aesthetics, and demands to be read in relation to both cultural contexts at once. The challenge of a renewed modernist studies must be to realize that this cross-cultural relation is a two-way street.

The Investigation is itself a frame-tale, although it formally inverts its contents, so that the actual frame-tale (a gathering of friends in Argentina) is folded into what seems to be the central story (a media-saturated crime in Paris). And the novel explicitly invokes an antagonism between close-up and distant views of Latin America. Not only is it evenly divided between the Parisian and Argentinean narratives—subtly mimicking the form of Cortázar's *Rayuela* (Hopscotch)—but it hinges on a struggle for control of the story: between the narrator, Pichón Garay, an Argentinean who has been installed in Europe for twenty-odd years, and his old friend Tomatis, who remained in Argentina during the dirty war. Their battle over the central narrative is directly a question of responsibility to what Saer calls a "zone"—demarcated by aesthetics, but also by politics. Tomatis seems to win the battle on the level of ethics: having stayed in Argentina through its recent turbulent history, he indirectly witnesses the disappearance of Pichón's twin brother, El Gato, and it falls to him to deal on practical terms with the aftermath. But Pichón's failure to return home, as the narrative intimates, is an equally important emotional consequence of a traumatic personal and national history, and his different relation to Argentina is therefore recast as a question of perspective. This is spelled out in the summary of the manuscript at the center of the novel: a story within a story within a story. That internal narrative, *In The Greek Tents,* concerns two different views of the Trojan war: by a dedicated old soldier who is too close to events to perceive them clearly, and by a recently arrived younger soldier who has had far greater access to news of battles circulating on the streets of Athens. This split perspective directly invokes not only Cortázar's claims, but Benjamin's distinction between two kinds of storyteller—one who stays at home to report on events, one who travels in order to bring news home—which is also at the center of the outer story, attempting to make sense of a serial killer's crimes in a world in which experience, repackaged as media-processed information, is both hermetically sealed and quickly out of date.

Two further questions are simultaneously at stake here: on the one hand, the ability to discern the truth of events based on interpretation (reading the newspapers or television reports—an updated version of Poe's "Mystery of Marie Roget"—or reading the manuscript); on the other, the capacity to determine authorship, whether of a story, a novel, or a crime. The crime is in effect threefold: Pichón's abandonment of his twin brother and of his homeland for a comfortable life in Paris; the poet's abandonment of poetry to write a prose narrative; and the serial killer's abandonment of his moral code in favor of a violence through which he turns his victims—like a diligent literary critic— literally inside out. And Vallejo, who appears here as himself a frame—giving a title to the internal narrative—is a figure for indirect modes of witnessing, for a simultaneous relation to the local and the international, and for an image of violence being done to bodies and minds under the pressures of consumer capitalism. Although the novel in which he appears is naturally written in prose, as is the manuscript at its displaced center, the lingering presence of Vallejo's poetry in the manuscript's title hints at an abiding sense that the lyric's sidelined and framed discourse contains a secret history of history itself: of violence done to the body, and of the violence of the body's flailing attempts to understand the history in which it is enmeshed.

Bolaño's novel, by contrast, presents us with a narrator who knows nothing of Vallejo's poetry and who experiences him only as a decaying body wracked by hiccups. Those hiccups, like the *bulla* (din) of *Trilce* I, might be a symbol of the interruption—and ultimately, the silencing— of poetry; or conversely, they might be a condensation of its modes of speech, heard as involuntary spasms of the vocal chords, pointing to a rottenness or an arrhythmia in the body politic. Vallejo's slow death in this novel—like the interwar history that flashes up in his own poetry and prose—is glimpsed only intermittently, paralleled by a film screened at a certain point in the novel whose narrative is ominously elliptical, and which characters admit to have understood only in parts, despite repeated viewings. That film, like Vallejo's late poetry, offers tantalizing views of history in the course of its unfolding, but its form obscures any facile comprehension of its content.

But another form of form in Bolaño's novel is space: the realignment of European powers in the lead-up to the second world war, leading to transnational conspiracies to which the pro–Spanish Republic Peruvian poet arguably falls victim. As geographical alliances becomes more tightly knit, the novel's various characters are squeezed into a succession of cramped spaces: stairwells, hospital rooms, restaurants, warehouses. Their physical constraints mimic not only the closing-in of what in retrospect becomes a historical inevitability, but the form of poetry itself, its condensed containment of personal and historical pressures that are barely understood, yet are emotionally and physiologically sensed by the body. That body, in this novel, belongs to the poet Vallejo; the reader's task, through the stand-in Monsieur Pain, is to get as close as possible to the poetic corpus without deadening its pulse. Vallejo's death is the direct result of his doctors' refusal to cut into his body—a body in pain, evoked in the translinguistic play of the novel's title—but it is also the indirect consequence of Monsieur Pain's withholding of bodily contact: unlike the surgeon who, as Benjamin argues, emblematizes the modern interpreter of both history and its texts, Pain the mesmerist holds his hand at a distance from the dying Vallejo's forehead during their single encounter. He does no violence to Vallejo's body, but he also fails to connect with that body, and he gains no sense at all of the body of his poetry, leading directly to the death of both.

My attempt in this study, conversely, has been to cut into Vallejo's poetic corpus from a variety of different angles, showing the ways in which its body processes a surrounding modernity through momentary engagements with a series of different debates and contexts. Vallejo's poetry insistently presents figures, body parts, feelings, and landscapes that stand alongside each other, rubbing up against one another, erasing the dividing line that separates one from the other. Serving, in his own words, as an "intelligent screen," Vallejo affords us a glimpse of the frictional interplay between Europe and Latin America, through his writing's simultaneous attachment to these two contexts, which are so rarely juxtaposed. This split-screen vision, mapped out in the self-critical movements of his poetry and prose, offers an invitation to rethink the parameters of a properly international lyric modernity.

Translations of Poems

All translations are from Clayton Eshleman's Complete Poetry of César Vallejo.
My occasional modifications of the translations are signaled by the use of square brackets.

Telluric and Magnetic

    Sincere and utterly Peruvian mechanics
that of the reddened hill!
Soil theoretical and practical!
Intelligent furrows: example: the monolith and its retinue!
Potato fields, barley fields, alfalfa fields, good things!
Cultivations [integrated by] an astonishing hierarchy of tools
and which integrate with wind the lowings,
the waters with their deaf antiquity!

    Quaternary maize, with opposed birthdays,
I hear through my feet how they move away,
I smell them return when the earth
clashes with the sky's technique!
Abrupt molecule! Terse atom!

    Oh human fields!
Solar and nutritious absence of the sea,
and oceanic feeling for everything!
Oh climates found within gold, ready!
Oh intellectual field of cordilleras,
with religion, with fields, with ducklings!
Pachyderms in prose when passing
and in poetry when stopping!
Rodents who peer with judicial feeling all around!
Oh my life's patriotic asses!
Vicuña, national
and graceful descendant of my ape!
Oh light hardly a mirror [away] from shadow,
which is life with the period and, with the line, dust,
and that is why I revere [it], climbing through the idea to my skeleton!

    Harvest in the epoch of the spread pepper-tree,
of the lantern hung from a human temple
and of the one unhung from a magnificent barrel!
Poultry-yard angels,
birds by a slip-up of the cockscomb!
[Guinea-pig (girl or boy)] to be eaten fried
with the hot pepper from the templed valleys!
(Condors? Screw the condors!)

    Christian logs by the grace of
a happy trunk and a competent stalk!
Family of lichens,
species in basalt formation that I
respect
from this most modest paper!
Four operations, I subtract you
to save the oak and sink it in sterling!

Slopes caught in the act!
Tearful [Auchenids], my own souls!
Sierra of my Peru, Peru of the world,
and Peru at the foot of the globe: I adhere!
Morning stars if I aromatize you
burning coca leaves in this skull,
and zenithal ones, if I uncover
with one hat doff, my ten temples!
Arm sowing, get down and on foot!
Rain based on noon,
under the tile roof where indefatigable
altitude gnaws
and the turtle dove cuts her trill in three!
Rotation of modern afternoons
and delicate archaeological daybreaks[!]
Indian after man and before him!
I understand it all on two flutes,
and I make myself understood on a quena!
As for the [rest], they can jerk me off! . . .

Trilce II

    Time Time.

Noon dammed up in night damp.
Bored pump in the cell block bailing out
time time time time.

    Was Was.

Cocks song on scratching in vain.
Mouth of the bright day that conjugates
was was was was.

    Tomorrow tomorrow.

The repose in being still warm.
The present thinks keep me for
tomorrow tomorrow tomorrow tomorrow.

    Name Name.

[What's it called what urts us?
It's called Thesame which suffers from a]
name name name namE.

Communion

Fair queenly one! Your veins are the ferment
of my ancient nonbeing and of the black
champagne of my life!

Your hair is the undiscovered rootlet
of the tree of my vine.
Your hair is the strand from a miter
of fantasy that I lost!

Your body is the bubbly skirmish
of a pink Jordan;
and it ripples, like a beatific whip
that would have put the viper of evil to shame!

Your arms create a thirst for the infinite
with their [chaste Hesperides] of light,
like two white redeeming roads,
two dying wrenchings of a cross.
And they are molded in the unconquered blood
of my impossible blue!

Your feet are two heraldic larks
eternally arriving from my yesterday!
Fair queenly one! Your feet are the two tears
I choked back, descending from the Spirit
one Palm Sunday when I entered the World,
already forever distant from Bethlehem!

Babel

Sweet [home without style], built
with a single blow and with a single bit
of [iridescent] wax. And in the home
she damages and [fixes]; at times she says
"The hospice is nice; no need to look further!"
[And] other times she [bursts] into tears!

Trilce V

Dicotyledonous group. From it [overture
petrels], propensities for trinity,
finales that begin, ohs of ayes,
[you'd think them] rhinestoned with heterogeneity.
Group of the two cotyledons!

Let's see. [Let's let that] be without being more.
Let's see. [Let's not] let it transcend outwards,
[it should] think as if it's not being listened to,
[it should] chrome and not be seen.
And not [glissée into the grand] collapse.

The created voice rebels and doesn't want
to be meshwork, [nor love].
Let the newlyweds be newlyweds in eternity.
So don't strike 1, which will echo into infinity.
And don't strike 0, which will be so [silent],
that it will wake [1 up and set it on its feet].

Ah bicardiac group.

Trilce LI [My trans.]

That's not so. I was just kidding,
that's all. That's it. Otherwise,
you're also going to see
how much it's going to hurt me to have been like that.

That's not so. Shush.
It's okay now.
Like other times you do the same to me,
that's why I've been that way to you.

Me, who checked so many times to see if
you were really crying,
because other times you were only
pouting sweetly;
me, who never dreamed that you'd believe them,
I was won over by your tears.
That's okay.

But now you know: none of it was true.
And if you keep on crying, okay then!
Next time I won't even see you when you play.

Trilce XLII

[Just wait. I'm about to tell you all
everything. Just wait until
this headache subssides. Just wait.]

Where have you left yourselves
that you're never needed?
No one's needed! Very good.

[Rose, come in from the top floor.
I'm a child. And once again rose:
you don't even know where I'm going.]

Is the death star reeling?
Or [is it] strange sewing machines
inside the left side.
[Just] wait a moment more.

No one has seen us. Pure
search for your waist.
Where have your eyes popped [to]!

[Penetrate] reincarnated [in] the parlors
of western crystal. Exact
music plays almost a pity.

I feel better. Without fever, and fervent.
Spring. Peru. I open my eyes.
Ave! Don't leave. God, as if suspecting
some ebbless flow [ow].

[Whack in the face], the curtain sweeps
nigh the prompt-boxes.

Acrisia. Tilia, go to bed.

Trilce XIII

I think about your sex.
My heart simplified, I think about your sex,
before the ripe daughterloin of day.
I touch the bud of joy, it is in season.
And an ancient sentiment dies
degenerated into brains.

I think of your sex, furrow more prolific
and harmonious than the belly of the Shadow,
[even if Death were to conceive and bear child]
from God himself.
Oh Conscience,
I am thinking, yes, about the free beast
who takes pleasure where he wants, where he can.

Oh, scandal of honey of the twilights.
Oh mute thunder.

Rednuhtetum!

Trilce IX

I sdrive to dddeflect at a blow the blow.
Her two broad leaves, her valve
opening in succulent reception
from multiplicand to multiplier,
her condition excellent for pleasure,
all readies truth.

I strive to ddeflect at a blow the blow.
To [please her], I transasfixiate Bolivarian asperities
at thirty-two cables and their multiples,
hair for hair majestic thick lips,
the two tomes of the Work, constringe,
and I do not live absence then,
        not even by touch.

I fail to teflect at a blow the blow.
We will never saddle the torose Trool
of egotism or of that mortal chafe
of the bedsheet,
since this here woman
        —how she weighs being general!

And female is the soul of the absent-she.
And female is my own soul.

Ostrich

Melancholy, pull out your sweet beak [already],
don't [feast your fast] on my [wheatfields] of light.
Melancholy, enough! [How] your daggers drink
the blood my blue leech would suck out!

Do not finish off the fallen woman's manna;
I want some cross to be born of it tomorrow,
tomorrow when I have no one to turn my eyes to,
when the coffin opens its great sneering O.

My heart is a [pot] sprinkled with [bitterness],
There are other old birds who graze inside it;
Melancholy, stop drying up my life,
and bare your woman's lip . . . !

Trilce XXVI

Summer knots three years
that, beribboned with [carmine] ribbons, at full
          sob,
chariot the rusty indices
of moribund alexandrias,
of cuzcos moribund.

Alvine knot undone, one leg there,
the other even further,
          torn off,
          pendulous.
Undone knot of the sinamayera's
lacteal glands,
good for brilliant alpacas,
for a coat of feather useless,
arms more legs than arms!

So the end shows color, like everything,
like a drowsy chick hopping
from the cracked shell,
into light eternally pullet.
And so, after the ovum, shouldering fours,
          [already for what] sorrow.

Those fingernails ached
tautening their own asylum fingers.
From then on they grow inward,
          die outward,
          and in between neither come nor go,
          neither come nor go.

The fingernails. An ardent crippled ostrich runs,

from lost souths,
an arrow into the blind strait
          of fused breasts.

   In the heat of a point
of VIGOROUS humble obliquity,
the greek jack of diamonds turns into
a swarthy jack of islands,
a coppery jack of lakes
facing moribund alexandria,
cuzco moribund.

Trilce I

   Who's making all that racket, and not even letting
the islands [that go on remaining] make a will.

   A little more consideration,
as it will be late, early,
and easier to assay
the guano, the simple fecapital ponk
a brackish gannet
toasts unintentionally,
in the insular heart, to each hyaloid
     squall.

   A little more consideration,
and liquid muck, six in the evening
     OF THE MOST GRANDIOSE B-FLATS.

   And the peninsula stands up
[on the back], muzziled, imperturbable,
on the fatal balance line.

Trilce XXV

Thrips uprear to adhere
to joints, to the base, to napes,
to the underface of numerators on foot.
Thrips and thrums from lupine heaps.

As the lee of each caravel, unraveled
without Americanizing, snorts loudly,
plow handles give way in calamitous spasm,
with a puny pulse unfortunately given
to blowing its nose on the back of its wrist.
And the most high-pitched sopraneity
tonsures and hobbles itself, and gradually
ennazals toward icicles
of infinite pity.

Spirited loins wheeze hard
on bearing, dangling from musty breastplates,
cockades with their seven colors
below zero, from the guano islands
to the guano islands.
Thus the dirty honeycombs in the open air of little
faith.
Thus the hour of the rounds. Thus the one with a detour
to future planes,
when the innanimous gerfalcon reports solely
failed silence-deserving crusades.

Then thrips end up adhering
even in trapdoors and in rough drafts.

Black Stone on a White Stone

I will die in Paris in a downpour
on a day I can already remember.
I will die in Paris—and [it's nothing to run from]—
maybe a Thursday, like today, in autumn.

Thursday it will be, because today, Thursday,
as I prose these [verses], I've [put on my humeri
badly], and never like today have I turned
with all my [path], to see myself alone.

César Vallejo has died, they [all] beat him
without him doing anything to them;
they gave it to him hard with a stick and hard

[also] with a rope; witnesses are
the Thursdays and the humerus bones,
the solitude, [the downpour, the pathways] . . .

A Man Walks by with a [Loaf of Bread] on His Shoulder

A man walks by with a [loaf of bread] on his shoulder
Am I going to write, after that, about my double?

Another sits, scratches, extracts a louse from his armpit, kills it
How dare one speak about psychoanalysis?

Another has entered my chest with a stick in his hand
To talk then about Socrates with the doctor?

A cripple walks by [giving his arm to a child]
After that I'm going to read André Breton?

Another trembles from cold, coughs, spits blood
Will it ever be [right] to allude to the deep Self?

Another searches in the muck for bones, rinds
How to write, after that, about the infinite?

A bricklayer falls from a roof, dies and no longer eats lunch
To innovate, then, the trope, the metaphor?

A merchant cheats a customer out of a gram
To speak, after that, about the fourth dimension?

A banker falsifies his balance sheet
With [what cheek does] one cry in the theater?

An outcast sleeps with his foot behind his back
To speak, after that, to anyone about Picasso?

Someone [attends] a burial sobbing
How then to become a member of the Academy?

Someone cleans a rifle in his kitchen
How dare one speak about the beyond?

Someone goes by counting [on] his fingers
How to speak of the [non-I] without screaming?

Considering Coldly, Impartially

Considering coldly, impartially
that man is sad, coughs and, nevertheless,
takes pleasure in his reddened chest;
that the only thing he does is to be made up
of days;
that he's a gloomy mammal and combs his hair . . .

　Considering
that man proceeds softly from work
and reverberates boss, sounds employee;
that the diagram of time
is a constant diorama on his medals
and, half-open, his eyes have studied
since distant times
his famished mass formula . . .

　Understanding without effort
that man pauses, occasionally, thinking,
as if wanting to cry,
and, subject to lying down like an object,
becomes a good carpenter, sweats, kills,
and then sings, eats lunch, buttons himself up . . .

　Considering too
that man is truly an animal
and, nevertheless, upon turning, hits [me in the] head with his sadness . . .

　Examining, finally,
his discordant parts, his toilet,
his desperation, upon finishing his atrocious day, erasing it . . .

　Understanding
that he knows I love him,
that I hate him with affection and, in short, am indifferent to him . . .

　Considering his general documents
and scrutinizing with a magnifying glass that certificate
that proves he was born very tiny . . .

　I make a gesture to him,
he approaches,
and I hug him, and it moves me.
[So what!] It moves me . . . moves me . . .

Roster of Bones

They demanded shouting:
—Let him show both hands at once.
And this was not possible.
—Let them, while he's crying, take the measure of his steps.
And this was not possible.
—Let him think an identical thought, in the time that a zero remains useless.
And this was not possible.
—Let him do something crazy.
And this was not possible.
—Between him and another man similar to him, let a crowd of men like him interpose themselves.
And this was not possible.
—Let them compare him with himself.
And this was not possible.
—Let them call him finally by his name.
And this was not possible.

[There Are Days, There Comes to Me] an Exuberant, Political Hunger . . .

[There are days, there comes to me] an exuberant, political hunger,
to desire, to kiss tenderness on both its faces,
and there comes to me from afar a demonstrative desire,
another desire to love, willingly or by force,
whoever hates me, whoever tears up his paper, the little boy,
the woman who weeps for the man who was weeping,
the king of wine, the slave of water,
whoever hid in his wrath,
whoever sweats, whoever passes by, whoever shakes his person in my soul.
And I desire, therefore, to adjust
the braid of whoever talks to me; the soldier's hair;
the light of the great; the greatness of the small.
I desire to iron directly
a handkerchief for whoever is unable to cry,
and, when I am sad or happiness aches me,
to mend the children and the geniuses.

I desire to help the good one become a little bit bad
and I have an urge to be seated
to the right of the left-handed, and to respond to the mute,
trying to be useful to him
as I can, and likewise I desire very much
to wash the cripple's foot,
and to help my one-eyed neighbor sleep.

Ah, desire, this one, mine, the world's,
interhuman and parochial, mature!
It comes perfectly timed,
from the foundation, from the public groin,
and. coming from afar, makes me hunger to kiss
the singer's muffler,
and whoever suffers, to kiss him on his frying pan,
the deaf man, fearlessly, on his cranial murmur;
whoever gives me what I forgot in my breast,
on his Dante, on his Chaplin, on his shoulders.

I desire, finally,
when I'm at the celebrated edge of violence
or my heart full of chest, I would desire
to help whoever smiles laugh,
to put a little bird right on the evildoer's nape,
to take care of the sick annoying them,
to buy from the vendor,
to help the killer kill—a terrible thing—
and I would desire to be good to myself
in everything.

Today I Like Life Much Less

Today I like life much less;
but I always like to live: I've often said it!
I almost touched the part of my whole and [contained] myself
with a shot in the tongue behind my word.

Today I touch my chin in retreat
and in these momentary trousers I tell myself:
So much life and never!
So many years and always my weeks! . . .
My parents buried with their stone
and their sad suffering that has not ended;
full-length brothers, my brothers,
and finally, my being standing and in a vest.

I like life enormously,
but, of course,
with my beloved death and my café
and looking at the leafy chestnut trees of Paris
and saying:
This is an eye, that one too, this a forehead, that one too . . . And repeating,
So much life and never does the tune fail me!
So many years and always, always, always!

I said vest, said
whole, part, [anxiety], I almost said, to avoid crying.
For it is true that I suffered in that hospital close by
and it is good and it is bad to have [looked at]
my organism [from toe to top].

I would like to live always, even flat on my belly,
because, as I was saying and I say it again,
so much life and never! And so many years,
and always, much always, always always!

I: Hymn to the Volunteers for the Republic

Volunteer [for Spain], civilian-fighter,
of veritable bones, when your heart marches to die
when it marches to kill with its worldwide
agony, I truly don't know
what to do, where to place myself; I run, write, applaud,
weep, glimpse, destroy, they extinguish, I say
to my chest that it should end, to good, that it should come,
and I want to ruin myself;
I bare my impersonal forehead until touching
the vessel of blood, I stop,
[. . .]
and, again, without knowing what to do, without anything, leave me,
from my blank stone, leave me,
alone,·
quadrumane, closer, much more distant,
since your long ecstatic moment won't fit between my hands,
[I smash against your double-edged speed
my tininess besuited in its greatness!]
[. . .]

X: Winter During the Battle of Teruel

[. . .] And war is utter horror, it incites,
it makes one long, eye-filled;
war entombs, fells,
[it] makes one make an odd anthropoid leap!
You smell it, companion, perfectly,
upon stepping
distractedly on your arm among the corpses;
you see it, for you touched your testicles, blushing intensely,
you hear it in your natural soldier's mouth.

Let's go then, companion;
your alerted shadow awaits us,
your quartered shadow awaits us,
noon captain, night common soldier . . .
That is why, on referring to this agony
I [distance myself] from myself shouting wildly:
Down with my corpse! . . . And sob.

Intensity and Height

I want to write, but out comes foam,
I want to say so much [and I mire];
There is no spoken cipher which is not a sum,
there is no written pyramid, without a core.

I want to write, but I feel like a puma,
I want to laurel myself, but [turn into an onion].
There's no spoken coughv which doesn't [become mist]
There's no god, or son of god, without progression.

[Let's go, then], therefore, to eat grass,
the flesh of sobs, the fruit of wailing,
our melancholy soul [in preserves].

[Let's go! Let's go! I'm wounded;
let's go and drink what's already been drunk,
let's go, raven, and fertilize your mate.]

Notes

INTRODUCTION

1. Marjorie Perloff is an interesting exception to this rule; her work makes room for both modernist and avant-garde modes, pointing implicitly in her formal analyses to the interpenetration of the two.

2. Translations are mine unless otherwise noted, with the exception of translations from Vallejo's poetry, which are taken from the *Complete Poetry of César Vallejo*. My special thanks to Clayton Eshleman for permission to reproduce them here.

3. From an article published in *Amaru* in mid-1968, reprinted in the first Diary section of *El zorro de arriba y el zorro de abajo* (21).

4. The polemic began with Cortázar's open letter to Roberto Fernández Retamar, written in Vaucluse in May 1967, published in both the Cuban magazine *Casa de las Américas* and the Argentinean *Primera Plana* later that year. Arguedas responded with an article in the Peruvian magazine *Amaru* in mid-1968, subsequently incorporated into the first Diary section of his final novel, *El zorro de arriba y el zorro de abajo*. Cortázar continued the discussion in an interview with *Life en español* in early 1969, which in turn prompted a final response by Arguedas in Lima's *El Comercio* in June of the same year. As the variety of these sites of publication suggests, what was also at stake in this debate was the relation of the nation-state to its constituent parts and to the larger continental arena, not to mention to international politics, economics, and aesthetics. For further details on the polemic, see Ostria González and Moraña.

5. For details of Chimbote's transformation in the 1960s and its depiction in Arguedas's novel, see Julio Ortega's introduction to the English translation of *The Foxes*, pp. xi–xxxi. The novel's probing of the entanglements of class, ethnic identity, nationality, and subjectivity within the frame of industrial globalization (and in particular the shipping and fisheries industries) finds provocative

parallels in the photo-essays of Allan Sekula; see, for example, *Fish Story* (1995) and *Performance under Working Conditions* (2003).

6. This polemic might seem a rehearsal of the Paris-peripheries debate that has been resuscitated in recent years by the publication of Pascale Casanova's *World Republic of Letters* (2003). In this light, a little-known article by Arguedas titled "París y la patria" (Paris and the Fatherland), published in *El Comercio* on December 7, 1958 ("Paris" 168–71), is surprisingly illuminating; Arguedas here registers his wonder on encountering unexpected bounties of nature and human diversity in the French capital, which prompts the startling realization that he has never—except in his own village—felt more at home.

7. An interesting analogue to this polemic—in a much more cordial key—is the exchange between Franco Moretti and Efraín Kristal over the organization of the world literary panorama; the results are markedly different, as Kristal notes, when we trace the movements of poetry rather than prose. Jahan Ramazani and Brent Edwards ("Genres") have both made important contributions to this debate, signaling the difficulties of reading poetry from different cultures and in different languages, beset by far greater problems of translation, probably both practical and theoretical.

8. A mestizo from a largely Spanish-speaking area, Vallejo did not speak Quechua; as I discuss in chapter 2, the Quechua terms that make their way into Vallejo's early poetry have the air of *mots rares* rather than indicating an everyday linguistic practice. For a detailed biography, see Stephen Hart's "Chronology," in Eshleman, ed., 689–703.

9. Biographers have tended to absolve Vallejo of the charge; nonetheless, an article by Hart ("Was Vallejo"), based on careful reading of documents, makes a compelling case for his involvement.

10. This mysterious death, following upon agonizing illnesses during Vallejo's early days in Paris, is the subject of Roberto Bolaño's novel *Monsieur Pain* (1999), discussed in the conclusion.

11. As Fredric Jameson has recently cautioned, we need to avoid presenting a fixed image of modernist texts, which has the effect of reifying them still further (*Modernist Papers* 4).

12. Vallejo revisits a mining community in his only novel—*El Tungsteno* (1931)—and in the unpublished play *Colacho Hermanos* (Colacho Bros.) (written 1934), later reworked as the screenplay *Presidentes de América* (Presidents of America) (1935).

13. Franco's pioneering study, *César Vallejo: The Dialectics of Poetry and Silence* (1976), adeptly intertwines formalist, historicist, and theoretical approaches; my debt to her early readings should be apparent. The past few years have seen the emergence of reinvigorated criticism of Vallejo in English, which moves illuminatingly between formal and historical analysis, some of the best examples of which are the writings of Hart, Miller, Rowe, and Sharman.

14. Translations of all poems quoted in full in the text appear in the Appendix, in order of citation.

15. It deserves note that Vallejo's new political attachment to Spain allowed him to reopen his connection to Latin America through a channel of subaltern resistance to fascism, side-stepping the thorny question of Spanish colonial his-

tory and its structural residues. Indeed, the Spanish Civil War and its new possibilities for international solidarity gave him a renewed interest in Peru's specific problems, as is evident from the chronicles he published from 1936 onward on the need for serious study of Peruvian history as groundwork for a new critical nationalism.

16. Daniel Alomía Robles had orchestrated the local tune "El cóndor pasa" (The Condor Passes) in 1916 and successfully introduced it to the world long before Simon and Garfunkel.

17. Tourism was a grounding metaphor for the internationalist projections of other Latin American avant-gardes; the Argentinean Oliverio Girondo and the Peruvian Carlos Oquendo de Amat both produced radical collections of poetry (*Veinte poemas para ser leídos en un tranvía* [Twenty Poems to Be Read on a Tram, 1922]; *Cinco metros de poemas* [Five Meters of Poems, 1928]), which referenced a series of sights on imaginary or real travels. An evident analogue in the European context is Blaise Cendrars.

18. Here I take a cue from Raymond Williams's call to "search out and counterpose an alternative tradition taken from the neglected works left in the wide margin of the century, a tradition which may address itself not to this by now exploitable because quite inhuman rewriting of the past but, for all our sakes, to a modern future in which community may be imagined again" (*Politics* 35).

CHAPTER ONE

1. Stephen Hart offers the most insightful tracing of connections between Vallejo's biography and his poetics, both in the chronology included in Clayton Eshleman's *Complete Poetry of César Vallejo* and in the short articles collected in the volume *Stumbling between 46 Stars.*

2. Vallejo's comments in his two unpublished prose notebooks, *Contra el secreto profesional* (Against the Professional Secret) and *El arte y la revolución* (Art and Revolution) are far more explicit but have to be taken with a grain of salt, because they were written during his short-lived full commitment to Marxism, and therefore involve self-readings that sit uneasily with the content and form of his actual poetry, written over a much longer period.

3. As Kamenszain puts it, "The experience of the present is what this sentiment constantly renews. That is, it is a sensibility that activates itself in synchrony with what keeps appearing in front of its very eyes. . . . [T]he core of the Vallejo poem is born and reborn. It is a millenary embryo that we read as the testimony of an experience that can only be conjugated in the present tense" (351).

4. Latin American criticism, with its strong tradition of institutional critique and interest in Marxist approaches, has been far more open to reflections on relations between poetry and history, beginning with the work of Angel Rama. For analyses of the modernista period (from the 1880s to the 1910s), see Jrade; Kirkpatrick *(Dissonant);* Molloy; Perus; and Sarlo. For earlier and later periods, see Cornejo Polar; Kuhnheim; Masiello; Ramos; Rowe; and Unruh.

5. Criticism connected with the language-writing movement has been signifi-

cantly more generous and more rigorous in its dealings with poetry, as in the work of Davidson, Perelman, or Watten.

6. An exception to this case is Whitman; see, for example, Coviello's nuanced analyses.

7. There are notable exceptions to this rule, such as David Lloyd's work on a variety of Irish poets in *Anomalous States,* which reads formal questions in the lyric as a way to think through its mediation of history. And we might note the rampant parallels between Irish and Peruvian political aesthetics around the turn of the century, such as the commitment to rescuing a minority language (Irish/Quechua) and to representing an antioligarchic, anticolonial vision of the nation. In his article "Rethinking National Marxism," Lloyd sketches out another provocative connection between Ireland and Peru, proposing James Connolly and José Carlos Mariátegui as figures for a powerful anticolonial nationalism that is not primarily industrial and is frequently linked to transnational migrant labor.

8. This quandary has a mirror image in Peruvian criticism on Vallejo, and it leaks into international readings: the desire to present Vallejo as an indigenist poet—despite the well-proven fact that he had only a smattering of Quechua words in his vocabulary—is remarkably resilient.

9. In the 1920s Mariátegui calculated the country's ethnic makeup as fourfifths indigenous, a figure that became lodged in the historical imaginary. As Jorge Coronado has recently pointed out, however, the census of 1940 lowered this number to 40 percent indigenous, although official estimates in the 1950s were once again raised to above 60 percent. What this underlines, Coronado suggests, is a lack of rigor in the conduct of censuses during this period, as well as an indeterminacy regarding ethnic categories (10).

10. My account here draws upon Heraclio Bonilla's multilayered analysis of class and ethnic tensions leading up to and beyond the War of the Pacific (182–221).

11. In its broad strokes—the expansion of journalism fed by an influx of writers from the provinces, the emergence of new forms such as the cultural weekly and the oppositional broadsheet, the interest in types and caricatures, feeding into and competing with new forms of poetry—Peru in this period shows clear parallels with the mid- to late-nineteenth-century Paris of Baudelaire and Rimbaud. Its new attention to a majority culture hitherto treated as a minority interest further links it to a more directly contemporary Dublin, captured in Joyce's *Ulysses,* published in the same year (1922) as Vallejo's second collection *Trilce.*

12. This might seem a cognate to the concept of simultaneity so central to the European avant-gardes, determined and driven by new transportation and communication technologies such as steamships, railways, film, radio, and modern newspapers (Kern). But in Peru's case, the concern was not with speed of circulation but with organizing national space, even when that space was itself subject to temporal questions—the time it took for ideas, books, or figures to travel from the metropolis to the peripheries, or for local writers to travel between cities and the provinces.

13. For instance, Mary Louise Pratt suggests that Bello's long poem "Silva a

la agricultura de la zona tórrida" "should probably be understood not simply as nostalgic or reactionary, but as a dialogic response to the commodifying, greed-glazed gaze of the English engineers" (178).

14. For an in-depth analysis of nineteenth-century poetry, see Kirkpatrick, "Poetic Exchange."

15. Roberto González Echevarría's *Myth and Archive* examines the ways in which Latin American narrative draws upon the hegemonic discourses of particular periods to map out the continent and the writer's position within it. His resonant analysis, significantly, does not touch upon poetry.

16. Mariátegui himself called attention to this problem as he prepared to trace Peruvian literary history, intimating that there was little aesthetic pleasure to be found in looking back over the past century's productions, because too many writers had been pulled away from poetry into politics.

17. The image Prada offers predates Blaise Cendrars's "Profound Today" (1917)—with its opening salvo, "I no longer know if I'm looking with my naked eye at a starry sky or at a drop of water through a microscope"—by fifteen years: "En la retorta de un químico y bajo el microscopio de un físico pasan cosas más bellas que en el cerebro de muchísimos poetas" (In a chemist's flask, under a physicist's microscope, more beautiful things happen than in the mind of many poets).

18. While it has specific Latin American accents, this is not entirely a New World phenomenon; there is a clear parallel here with post-Romantic, concordance-seeking symbolism—especially in its turn-of-the-century theosophical strain, which also made its way into Latin America, coming to some vogue among Vallejo's circles in both Trujillo and Lima (Rivero Ayllón).

19. In 1921, while hiding from the police in a country house outside Trujillo, Vallejo made a parodic detour back to occasional poetry. He submitted the "Canto a Torre Tagle" to a local competition convened to commemorate the centenary of Peru's independence; published under a pseudonym, it was awarded first place, and when the authorities later discovered the true identity of the poet—former literary misfit turned fugitive—they were unsurprisingly enraged. The poem is thus not the embarrassing throwback some critics have seen but a calculated exercise in parody and cultural provocation. As Orrego recalls, to compose the poem, Vallejo drew upon a bone-dry history of Trujillo, submitting it to zany expressive manipulations: twisting syllables into new sounds, repeating question-and-answer catalogs to the point of absurdity (*Mi encuentro* 69–70).

20. As the future APRA leader Victor Raúl Haya de la Torre recalled, however, a poetic gathering to mark the death of Darío in 1916 ended with the rally, "Darío ha muerto, ¡viva Vallejo!" (Darío is dead, long live Vallejo!), with the coda, "Chocano ha muerto, ¡muera Chocano!" (Chocano is dead, death to Chocano!) (cited in Rivero Ayllón, 19).

21. This new generation was effectively stage-managed by Prada, through his directorship of the National Library and his mentorship of a number of promising young writers.

22. For the small number of young poets who gathered around him, however, Eguren's productions constituted potent little explosions; the Lima avant-

garde turns repeatedly to this inexplicable poet in their midst, and he experienced a resurgence of critical interest in 1928 with a dossier in *Amauta*. Eguren was also a prolific photographer and painter, producing unsettling miniatures in both media which Bernabé (195) has recently connected to surrealist experimentation in Paris.

23. Living in poverty in Paris, Della Rocca de Vergalo nevertheless became associated with the era's most prominent literary writers and theorists, who signed petitions for aid to the Peruvian congress on his behalf in 1879, 1886, and 1896; none were heeded, despite featuring such names as Mallarmé, Leconte de Lisle, and Hugo. Before leaving Peru, Vergalo published a collection of poetry and a lyric drama (both in French but on indigenous themes), and in Paris he produced another volume of symbolist poetry (*Livre des Incas*, 1879) and a theoretical tract on lyric meter (*Poétique Nouvelle*, 1880), both of which put him in the forefront of lyric theorists in French, let alone Spanish. Ultimately rejected as a foreigner by the French establishment, he took off for Africa just a few years after Rimbaud, where he similarly disappeared into obscurity. Vergalo continues to be unjustly neglected by literary historians, excepting Núñez *(Letras)*.

24. This displacement in his prose coincides with the "posmodernista" turn in poetry elsewhere on the continent, such as the then-shocking incorporation of colloquial language and trivial domestic details in poems by the Uruguayan Julio Herrera y Reissig and the Mexican Ramón López Velarde.

25. This also coincides with Mariátegui's reading of Vallejo's poetry, which makes Vallejo the mouthpiece for a past resuscitated through the trope of nostalgia, as Coronado analyzes (38–41).

26. As Vicky Unruh notes, the Latin American avant-gardes were on the whole less destructive or iconoclastic than their European counterparts, largely because cultural institutions were still just getting off the ground in the early years of the century, hence not yet experienced as coercive (7).

27. Dada was also turning its back on Western civilization by harvesting a "primitive" repertoire of sounds from the peripheries. This incorporation of external models would be playfully reworked over the next few years in Latin America. The Brazilian *antropofagistas,* to take the most notorious example, reversed the process, declaring their right to cannibalize the products of Western culture. The dynamic would take on a different cast, however, in countries with an increasingly vocal and visible indigenous population, such as Peru and Mexico, as writers turned to incorporating cultural practices hitherto repressed and oppressed within the bounds of its own nation-state—signaling that the other was internal. For more on this subject, see Hedrick.

28. The article included three poems from Vallejo's *Trilce* accidentally run together as a single poem: XII ("Escapo de una finta"); XXXII ("999 calorias"), and XLIV ("Este piano").

29. This canceling of aesthetic agency has a political parallel in discourses of messianism and utopian Andeanism. In the late 1910s and early 1920s the sierra was the scene of several millenarian revolts headed by leaders who presented themselves as reincarnations of Inca emperors, giving a sense of the past vehemently reasserting itself through mediating figures in the present. The apparent inexorability of the process, grounded in repetitive myths, was grasped

in its ambivalence by the always astute Mariátegui, who wrote of the need to harness the energies of these uprisings toward revolution, consciously rather than just fatalistically (Vich 73).

30. This is a radicalization of what Kaufman sees as a central point in Benjamin's analysis of Baudelaire: the need for poetry to confront, indeed court, the possibility of its own obsolescence in modernity. Benjamin's reading may itself be said to emerge from his familiarity with Dada.

31. In this they provide a marked contrast to the Chilean Vicente Huidobro's contemporaneous attempts (also beginning in 1916) to produce new poetic products for circulation.

32. As Trotsky and Berman both note, nonetheless, the engagement with technology is often paradoxically more fervent in countries on the periphery of mechanical modernity.

33. The technical reproducibility of Futurism is caustically foregrounded by Mario de Andrade in an account of his interview with Marinetti during the latter's 1926 visit to Brazil. While Futurism had quickly gained traction among the local avant-garde (the 1922 "Semana de Arte Moderna" was originally to be called the "Semana de Arte Futurista"), Mario pours scorn on Marinetti for repeating his own points more than a decade and a half after first making them. In Mario's cutting formulation, "hablaba como una máquina" (he spoke like a machine) (Schwartz 390–91)

34. The question of automatism in Latin America differs from its European formulation through its double charge: it was seen as involving not only the mimicking of industrial forms—as was the concern in Europe (given a positive cast in Apollinaire's "one must mechanize poetry as the world has been mechanized")—but also the continuing purely formal imitation of European models.

35. Hidalgo's "Oda al automóvil" (Ode to the Automobile) is itself a weak revision of Marinetti's manifesto—ironically (and apparently unwittingly) reclassicizing its central image through careful formal patterning (oscillating between hendecasyllables and alexandrines, with strong and intricate rhyme schemes) and a pedantically literal metaphorical blazon ("El Auto es un enorme paquidermo mecánico: / su sangre es la gasolina [. . .]"; The automobile is an enormous mechanical pachyderm: / its blood is gasoline, etc.) Reproduced in Lauer, ed., *Nueve libros*.

36. Poetry thus becomes an analogue to the newspaper, offering a multifaceted, polyphonic image of the present instant, replacing experience with information, and grounding the text in a shared common knowledge of modern international chaos. The hybrid Futurist Manifesto—part prosaic program, part lyrical narrative—was aptly published on the front page of *Le Figaro*.

CHAPTER TWO

1. For explorations of this uneasy fit, see Sharman, "Semicolonial."

2. For an in-depth analysis of *posmodernismo*'s twofold exaggeration and domestication of *modernista* modes, see Gwen Kirkpatrick's *Dissonant Legacy of Modernismo*.

3. This is a more complex notion of lyric responsibility than the easy incar-

nation posited in "Nostalgias imperiales I": "Y lábrase la raza en mi palabra / como estrella de sangre a flor de músculo" (the race takes shape in my word, / like a star of blood on the surface of muscle), even if the latter begins to propose a crucial conjunction of language and bodies.

4. As Tom Gunning insists, "One cannot understand modernity without penetrating its passion for images. Images fascinate modern consciousness obsessively, and this modern sense of images comes from a belief that images can somehow deliver what they portray" ("Whole World" 30).

5. This raises an interesting question about whether the modern is best experienced by eyes or ears—examined by Georg Simmel in his 1903 essay, "The Metropolis and Mental Life."

6. Similarly, in *Ulysses,* Stephen Dedalus's attempt to speak founders against the voices learned from literary history and the everyday noises reaching him from outside—"*A shout in the street,* Stephen said, shrugging his shoulders" (28).

7. As Bakhtin notes, the speaker "does not expect passive understanding that, so to speak, only duplicates his own idea in someone's mind. Rather, he expects response, agreement, sympathy, objection, execution, and so forth" (*Speech* 69). And "when constructing my utterance, I try actively to determine this response; moreover, I try to act in accordance with the response I anticipate, so this anticipated response, in turn, exerts an active influence on my utterance" (95).

8. There is no actual "poto de chicha" in *Los heraldos negros,* although "Nostalgias imperiales I" features both a "poyo con tres potos" (a stone bench with three gourd pots) and an "eucaristía de una chicha de oro" (Eucharist of golden chicha [maize alcohol]), which Eguren seems to combine unconsciously. In any case, the blasphemy of the latter image would have been far more shocking to the average reader than the tonal disruption on which Eguren fixes.

9. Walter Benjamin insisted on the importance of environmental noise in modern poetry if it was to connect with its context; he therefore advocated writing in a café, taking conversations as a backdrop but also as a texture for the lyric ("Writer's Technique").

10. Vallejo's practice here presents an illuminating coincidence with practices of avant-garde collage, which not only posited the simultaneous availability of all artistic options (canceling hierarchies and traditions) but also actively combined clashing styles within individual artworks.

11. As Wittgenstein writes in the *Tractatus* (1921), "the limits of my language mean the limits of my world"; just as relevant is Jean-Luc Godard's suggestive recasting of this in *Two or Three Things I Know about Her* (1967): "the limits of my world mean the limits of my language."

12. José Coronel Urtecho's 1926 "Oda a Rubén Dario" deploys many similar techniques, from collages of voices, languages, tones, and colloquialisms to rhetorical non sequiturs and demythifying references to culture, accompanied by the sounds of sandpaper, drums, and whistles.

13. Yurkiévich argues that Vallejo deals in montage rather than collage because the fragments that he incorporates are not quite ready-mades. Yet those

discourses are marked so much more by style than by content that invocations of those styles themselves function as found objects.

14. This seems a more plausible translation than Eshleman's "Hesperidian castes."

15. Orality is often associated with salesmanship—of the self or of objects—in Vallejo's Peruvian poetry (e.g., "La de a mil" and *Trilce* XXXII's *bizcochero*), in a striking contrast with other Latin American avant-gardes that foreground the written signs of advertising in the modern city. For further theoretical thoughts on the lyric as self-advertising, see Riley, *Words* 28–29.

16. Numerous anecdotes point to Vallejo's obsession with mutilating the words of well-known poems and songs, repeating them to such an extent that their sense wears down, moving beyond the familiar into nonsense. See, for example, Espejo 60.

17. Orrego also played a crucial role in encouraging Vallejo to take the risks of *Trilce;* even if his critical comments on the collection link it back to the question of representation—albeit through form more than content—his conversations with Vallejo were focused on radical experiments in language. As Vallejo attested in this same letter: "Del diálogo crepitante, de la fricción encendida de tus palabras con mi corazón, surgieron muchas chispas que, luego tomaron carne poética definitiva en mi sensibilidad y que, sin embargo, son completamente mías" (That crackling dialogue, that heated friction between your words and my heart, gave off so many sparks which later took on definitive poetic form in my sensibility, and which are yet entirely mine) (*Mi encuentro* 47). Orrego played Eckermann to Vallejo's Goethe; his own philosophical writings took a backseat to his encouragement of the young poet, almost ironically signaled in the title of the collection of aphorisms he published in the same year as *Trilce, Notas marginales.*

18. Prada had sounded an important battle cry on behalf of a new generation in his 1888 speech at the Politeama: "¡Los viejos a la tumba, los jóvenes a la obra!" (44–47) (Old men to the grave, and young men to the task at hand! *Free Pages* 50). Moreover, literature's language, Prada argued—in a nod to Wordsworth—needed to track between the technical and the colloquial, the high and the popular (29–30; *Free Pages* 22).

19. Vallejo had arrived in Lima in early 1917, and two of the earliest figures he sought out for published interviews were Prada and Eguren. His interview with the latter put him romantically in mind of "el dolor y el genio incomprendido de Verlaine, de Poe, de Baudelaire" (the pain and uncomprehended genius of Verlaine, of Poe, of Baudelaire). However, in an infamous later confession to Ciro Alegría, Eguren admitted that he did not *understand* Vallejo, less for his difficulty than for his "vulgar" aesthetic choices, such as the use of colloquial expressions.

20. Ortega summarizes *Trilce*'s critical history as a "caso elocuente de lectura, sobrelectura y mala-lectura, y esta extraordinaria diversidad interpretativa no implica sólo la variedad de perspectivas de leer, sino que dice algo sobre la naturaleza de esta poesía, sobre el carácter de su apelación comunicativa" (an eloquent case of readings, over-readings and bad readings; this extraordinary interpretive diversity points not only to a wide variety of reading approaches,

but says something about the nature of this poetry, about the way it calls to communication) ("Prologue" 11).

21. Ortega's edition of *Trilce* is invaluable for the serious reader of Vallejo. Aside from its excellent introduction to the collection, it follows each poem with a summary of different critical readings, pointing to the diversity of interpretations that can be generated by this poetry; each summary is in turn rounded out by Ortega's own comments.

22. Bakhtin in his later writings gestures toward a limited dialogism for the lyric, considering "self-objectification (in the lyric, in the confession etc.) as self-alienation and, to a certain degree, a surmounting of the self." "By objectifying myself (by placing myself outside)," he continued, "I gain the opportunity to have an authentically dialogic relation with myself" (*Speech* 122).

23. I am here taking two specific cues from Carrie Noland's work on poetry. First, her suggestion that "the quintessentially lyric moment [is] the moment when the lyric subject is forced to divulge that its voice is not entirely its own" (9); and second, her call for "an alternative understanding of the lyric and of its relation to history, an understanding that may allow us to reread lyric poems in relation to the 'internal dialogism' that characterizes their verbal texture" (17).

24. As Susana Reisz puts it, "lo que habla en el poema es la escritura de Vallejo y, en ella y a través de ella, un concierto de voces naturales e impostadas que articulan un mosaico de palabras propias y ajenas" (what speaks in the poem is Vallejo's writing and, in it and through it, a concert of natural and assumed voices which compose a mosaic of voices of his own and others) (*Teoría literaria* 221).

25. We might note here that *Trilce*'s focus on potentiality—invoking a future for its shape-shifting objects and memories—is a new addition, missing from *Los heraldos negros*.

26. It is striking, however, that Pablo Neruda's *Residencia en la tierra* (1925-32) also begins with a sound, and moreover one that is separated from its vehicle—a pealing bell.

27. Heinrich von Kleist's short essay "On the Gradual Production of Thoughts Whilst Speaking" advocates talking out loud to arrive not at the formulation of an idea but at the idea itself. "The French say 'l'appétit vient en mangeant' and this maxim is just as true if we parody it and say 'l'idée vient en parlant.'" And this thinking aloud is best done in company: "It is a strangely inspiring thing to have a human face before us as we speak; and often a look announcing that a half-expressed thought is already grasped gives us its other half's expression" (405–9). Barthes makes a similar argument in *The Grain of the Voice*, although his understanding of oral phrasing is more fixed upon a relation to the other than upon the self: "when we speak, when we 'expose' our thoughts as they are put into words, we consider it worthwhile to express aloud the inflections of our search; because we are wrestling with language out in the open, we make sure that our discourse 'takes,' 'consists,' that each step of this discourse is legitimated by the previous step; in a word, we want a straight-forward delivery and we show off the signs of this filiation in due form; hence all those *buts* and *therefores* in our public speech, all those repetitions or explicit denials. It isn't that these little words have great logical value; they are,

if you like *expletives* of thought. . . . [W]e want our interlocutor to listen to us; we revive his attention with meaningless interpellations . . . appeals, modulations . . . through which a body seeks another body" (4, 6).

28. To cite Barthes once more: "the amorous subject draws on the reservoir (the thesaurus?) of figures, depending on the needs, the injunctions, or the pleasures of his image-repertoire. . . . No logic links the figures, determines their contiguity: the figures are non-syntagmatic, non-narrative; . . . they stir, collide, subside, return, vanish with no more order than the flight of mosquitoes. . . . [T]he lover speaks in bundles of sentences but does not integrate these sentences on a higher level, into a work; his is a horizontal discourse: no transcendence, no deliverance, no novel (though a great deal of the fictive)" (*Lover* 6–7).

29. As Barthes notes, fragmentary discourse yields up a peculiar kind of sense: "Figures take shape insofar as we can recognize, in passing discourse, something that has been read, heard, felt. . . . A figure is established if at least someone can say: *'That is so true! I recognize that scene of language'* " (*Lover* 4).

30. I provide my own translation of this poem in the Appendix, cited here in fragments.

31. More than a poem, this sounds like a *bolero*, whose generic conventions alert us immediately to the lover's complaint, the form of which is more important than the content. I am grateful to Arcadio Díaz Quiñones for suggesting this, and to several graduate students for corroborating it.

32. My slight modifications of Eshleman's translation are signaled in the text below in square brackets.

33. The autobiographer Rousseau in fact makes an appearance in the collection, although he is significantly denied the peace of mind needed to compose his confession by interrupting voices in XXII: "Don Juan Jacobo está en hacerío, / y las burlas le tiran de su soledad, / como a un tonto" (Mr Jean Jacques is in the black books, / and the jeers draw him out of his solitude, / like a fool).

34. Vallejo had encountered Samain's writings through Enrique Diez Canedo's 1913 anthology of French poets. He might also have assimilated him through his readings of the Uruguayan poet Julio Herrera y Reissig, who was himself accused of plagiarizing Samain in the early 1900s—a case this poem might be referencing obliquely.

35. The figure of the mother is oddly omnipresent in avant-garde statements and practices in Peru. Valdelomar ceaselessly wrote to his mother from Italy, asking her to provide him with memories of Pisco, as well as the objects that might evoke them, and dedicated his stories to her. Carlos Oquendo de Amat may have cast his *Cinco metros de poemas* (Five Meters of Poems) (1927) as a montage of film, fruit, and advertising ("abre este libro como quien pela una fruta"; open this book as you would peel a piece of fruit), but he dedicates the poems not to modernity but to maternity and the infancy it nurtures: "estos versos inseguros como mi / primer hablar dedico a mi madre" (these verses, as insecure as my / first words, I dedicate to my mother). For Barthes, "the writer is someone who plays with his mother's body . . .: in order to glorify it, to embellish it, or in order to dismember it, to take it to the limit of what can be

known about the body: I would go so far as to take bliss in a *disfiguration* of the language" (*Pleasure* 37; emphasis in original).

36. To cite Butler, "language appears to be motivated by a loss it cannot grieve, and to repeat the very loss that it refuses to recognize," or as she paraphrases Kristeva: "the materiality of the spoken signifier, the vocalization of sound, is already a psychic effort to reinstall and recapture a lost maternal body; hence, these vocalizations are temporarily recaptured in sonorous poetry which works language for its most material possibilities. . . . To the extent that the referential impulse of language is to return to that lost originary presence, the maternal body becomes, as it were, the paradigm or figure for any subsequent referent. . . . Every effort to signify encodes and repeats this loss" (69–70).

37. Vallejo foregrounds this potent ambiguity in the wordplay of a later poem, where a "cuerpo" that we would expect to be "solitario" is instead "solidario" ("Epístola a los transeúntes" [Epistle to the Passersby], in *Poemas humanos*).

CHAPTER THREE

1. Jorge Monteleone tracks the migration of the swan through poems by Baudelaire, Mallarmé, Darío, and Lihn, signaling the ways in which its reference encrypts allusions to contemporary histories.

2. González Martínez's sonnet replaces the swan with Minerva's owl; his line "Tuércele el cuello al cisne" is itself a reworking of Verlaine's 1874 "Art poétique," with its call to wring the neck of rhetoric. My thanks to David Lloyd for calling my attention to this.

3. Vallejo repeatedly offers the quill as an instrument of writing, steering clear of more modern instruments such as the typewriter, thus avoiding the question of media determination which is fundamentally important for his avant-garde contemporaries in Latin America and Europe.

4. Although the Charioteer is a constellation in the northern hemisphere, it is visible from Peru. I thank Tsevi Mazeh for confirming this point.

5. A similar play with perspective—fingertips blotting out celestial bodies—appears in Juan José Saer's startling short story "Manos y planetas" (Hands and Planets), 187–88.

6. Franco also points to Vallejo's rematerializing of metaphysics; poem XIX, she notes, creates a deity "who can only be spoken of in language which derives from the material world [and who] cannot reveal a beyond but only 'clear up' the given" (*Dialectics* 84). Nonetheless, Franco reads this falling back into matter as a source of disillusionment in Vallejo's poetry, whereas I want to suggest that it serves as the determined ground for a newly materialized aesthetic.

7. "The workings of Michelangelo with the stone are of a piece, quite literally so, with the seeming exertions of the captive within it: both of them would summon the power required for the composing of a self otherwise lost to the material from which it might be formed" (xvi).

8. The poem explicitly rejects harmony, played out through the close homonym "ammonia," in the line "amoniácase casi el cuarto ángulo del círculo" (the fourth angle of the circle ammoniafies almost). But there is an extra res-

onance—uncovered by my student Meghan Schoen—that connects harmony back to procreation: ammonia takes its name from the fertility god Amun, who is in fact further referenced in the "ortivos nautilus" (ortive nautili) of the second stanza (nautili are descended from the now-extinct ammonites). There is a possible further twist here that takes us back to the constellation of XXVI. As Joanna Aizenberg explained to me, the northern-southern hemispheric divide is inscribed in nautili's very reproductive organs; these form mirror images of one another across the equator, which renders mating impossible. For a dense reading of this poem through the lens of Benjaminian allegory, see von Buelow.

9. Octavio Paz underlines the persistence of Romantic structures of fusion and organicism in Latin American *modernista* and avant-garde writing, part of the continuing imperative of self-representation in recently postindependence nations (148).

10. Vallejo's fragmentation of the body runs counter to explanatory statements made by his earliest commentators. Orrego, for instance, insisted on the poetry's capacity to put back together what is fractured by modern mentalities and modes of living, making his case precisely through the figure of the body: "Él hace síntesis constructiva, nosotros anatomía disgregadora. . . . Él percibe la vida trémula y agitada, en toda su vehemencia funcional, nosotros la percibimos como clasificación, es decir, como cadáver" (He performs constructive synthesis, while we perform anatomical dissections. . . . He perceives tremulous and agitated life in all its functioning vehemence, while we perceive it through classifications, i.e. as a cadaver) (*Mi encuentro,* 20). Orrego's reading gets *Trilce*'s procedure backward: it is precisely by taking things apart, through dissection, that Vallejo can offer a much richer account of the enmeshment of bodies, objects, times, and places with one another and with the language used to approach them—and thereby a different assessment of the lyric's relation to history.

11. This might be seen as a reworking of the world-upside-down motif of Baroque dystopian prose, for example, Quevedo's *Sueños* (Dreams), which casts figures scrambling for their missing body parts on the Day of Judgment only to find that they have reassembled themselves incorrectly.

12. As Jean Franco specifies, "in Vallejo's poetry, the part is not simply used for the whole for the sake of verbal economy but in order to stress certain functions" (*Dialectics* 109), functions that are experiential and emotional as well as purely physiological.

13. This fact alone should problematize notions that Vallejo's lot is with Andean culture; like Valdelomar—who actually did grow up on the coast, in the town of Pisco—Vallejo sets his sights on the sea, whereas the return to the family home in the sierra is always a failure.

14. Despite the minimal archaeological work that had yet been done in 1910s and 1920s Peru, this practice was well documented, and it seems no coincidence that Prada should have referred to modern journalism's capacity to "trepana[r] los cráneos más duros" (trepan the hardest skulls) (cited in López Lenci 35).

15. In terms of representation (here a speaking *of* as well as a speaking *for,* prefiguring the statement in Neruda's 1950 Canto General, "Yo vengo a hablar por vuestra boca muerta"; I come to speak through your dead mouth),

the subject is not only multiple but also marked—culturally and racially—by a term already in circulation among *indigenista* writers and intellectuals. One immediate reference is *Raza de bronce* (The Bronze Race) (1919), the foundational indigenist novel by the Bolivian Alcides Arguedas; an earlier example of the epithet's literary consecration is the poem "La raza de bronce" (1902) by Amado Nervo—a poet much admired by Vallejo—which imagined the lyric subject interrogating a spectral procession of pre-Columbian heroes.

16. Some poems do seem more carefully positioned than others, given their apparent proposition of a metapoetics: the first and last, but also those at *Trilce*'s midpoint, which—at least in the case of XXXVIII—suggests that the collection is about to swallow its contents, Scheherazade-like.

17. Vallejo's revisiting here of his earlier abstract title (in a poem published in the Spanish avant-garde journal *Alfar*) parallels Francis Picabia's return to the painting that marked his move away from representation to abstraction (*Udnie*, 1913) in *I See Again in Memory My Dear Udnie* (1914) (see Rothman); artist and poet both return to the scene of their crime against the referent. Vallejo and Picabia became friends after his arrival in Paris, and in a 1925 newspaper article Vallejo gleefully noted that a journalist had declared his *Trilce* to be far more radical than Picabia's abstract paintings (*ACC* I: 170).

18. As David Lloyd signaled to me, the "sol peruano" conjoins Marx's insistence on money as base metaphor with Derrida's focus on the sun as the grounding term for metaphorical systems. It also references the centrality of the sun to Incan cosmology and notions of sovereignty.

19. *Trilce* V seems to ironize the system of exchange into which Latin America was inducted by Columbus (whose traces are found in the "petrels" that he wrongly took to indicate the closeness of land); here offshoots of a vegetable organism are taken to be "avaloriados" (rhinestoned), whereby a misspelling invests baubles—*abalorios*—with "valor."

20. Richard Terdiman traces the movement of metaphor between language and matter in relays between economic and literary circuits; by a happy coincidence, the example he chooses—Diderot's encyclopedia entry on silver—focuses on the example of a Peruvian mine (*Body* 84–109).

21. In XLVIII, numbers and coins take on concrete and animated form; the coins with which the speaker plays act like bodies—shouting, urinating, multiplying, mirroring themselves—but they also behave like the figure on which their current designation depends; as Coyné wittily noted, "el que se llame 'sol' el peso peruano determina el incendio de la primera estrofa" (the fact that the Peruvian unit of currency is called the sol [sun] produces the fire of the first stanza) (217).

22. In this simultaneously regenerative and hollowing syntax, Vallejo comes uncannily close to Wallace Stevens, whose Snowman, in the 1923 collection *Harmonium,* "nothing himself, beholds / Nothing that is not there and the nothing that is."

23. Criticism has begun to foreground pain's privileged position in the poetry to such an extent that, as Hart notes, "Vallejo es ya considerado como el poeta *del* dolor" (Vallejo is now considered *the* poet of pain; "César Vallejo" 152), which Ortega connects to the agonizing experience of time in *Trilce*

(*Teoría* 49–59). Rowe *(Ensayos)* offers some exquisite readings of pain's effect on language in Vallejo's poetry while also pointing to its generative potential.

24. This echoes the stultifying repetition of II, in which the slowly passing, identical days under the indifference of the prison clock prompt the despondent question, "Qué se llama cuanto heriza nos? / Se llama Lomismo que padece / nombre nombre nombre nombrE" (What's it called what urts us? / It's called Thesame which suffers from / a name a name a name a namE; my trans.)

25. As Butler notes, "matter (*material* and *hyle*) is neither a simple, brute positivity or referent nor a blank surface or slate awaiting an external signification, but is always in some sense temporalized" (31). Similarly, Raymond Williams points to the occluded human imprint on a nature ideologically repurposed as separate and pristine, insisting instead that "the idea of nature contains, though often unnoticed, an extraordinary amount of human history" ("Ideas" 67)—which is particularly important to trace, as Jennifer French notes (6–7), in landscapes subjected to neocolonial depredation. Thus in the case of Latin American matter, given the long history of its reading and use by the metropolis—discussed below—the need to pay sustained and specific attention to geopolitical histories impresses itself upon us; my argument through this chapter therefore runs counter to Francine Masiello's erasure of historical traces from Latin American matter in her otherwise compelling recent article, "La naturaleza de la poesía." For further important studies of Latin American landscapes and their refraction in literature—local and international—see González Echevarría; Kaempfer; Pratt.

26. I am grateful to Paul Firbas for calling my attention to this phenomenon. Andrés Zamora has recently explored the coincidence of Renaissance cartographic practices and the rise of European liberal humanism with the "excrementalization" of the New World.

27. The most succinct statement is Roberto González Echevarría's article "Modernidad, modernismo y nueva narrativa," which argues that the artificiality of Spanish American *modernismo* derives from its trafficking in luxury items received from Europe, disconnected from both processes of production and primary needs.

28. Bonilla offers a trenchant analysis of this neocolonial relation; see pp. 34–105.

29. "Con simplificación empobrecedora suele considerarse nuestra poesía, y la de todo el tercer mundo, como inevitablemente referencial, como explícitamente testimonial" (Through an impoverishing simplification, our poetry—indeed that of the entire third world—tends to be thought of as inevitably referential, as explicitly testimonial in its impulse) (Yurkiévich, *Confabulación* 149).

30. This may also be a further allusion to an ostrich, reputed to be able to eat embers.

31. Or a figure for food's relationship to the lyric in general; a hungry Leopold Bloom reflects on the ways in which food determines not just physical but poetic well-being: "I wouldn't be surprised if it was that kind of food you see produces the like waves of the brain the poetical. For example one of those policemen sweating Irish stew into their shirts you couldn't squeeze a line of poetry out of him. Don't know what poetry is even. Must be in a certain mood" (*Ulysses* 136).

32. I am indebted to Richard Stamelman for suggesting this connection.

33. Reading Vallejo with Bataille (24) once again: "To halfheartedness, to loopholes and desires that reveal a great poetic impotence, one can only oppose a black rage and even an incontestable bestiality; it is impossible to get worked up other than as a pig who rummages in manure and mud uprooting everything with his snout—and whose repugnant voracity is unstoppable."

34. The Incas considered guano a more precious commodity than gold—emphasizing its use value rather than its exchange value—and forbade any-one to disturb the birds that produced it, under pain of death (Skaggs 4). For Humboldt in Peru, see Núñez and Petersen; for further histories of guano, see Gootenberg; Cadava.

35. As Cerna Bazán succinctly notes, "En contraste con las plasmaciones en moneda de la forma dinero, que se desprenden de lo sensorial en grado sumo para ser dignas representantes de la riqueza social (Marx), el acercamiento al excremento guano, esa sustancia tan abrumadoramente material, nos impone su presencia a través de los sentidos, especialmente el olor y el tacto. . . . En esa calabrina-mercancía simple el sujeto encuentra todavía la mayor cercanía a su cuerpo, y así a su trabajo y a su tiempo" (194–95) (Whereas money is turned into coins and thereby pulled as far away from the sensorial as possible in order to become a worthy representative of social wealth (Marx), the excrement *guano*, an imposingly material substance, asserts its presence through our senses, particularly smell and touch. . . . Through this simple fecapital merchandise, the subject is brought ever closer to his own body, and thereby also to his labor and his time).

36. My reading of these poems refers to the original rather than Eshleman's translation, which takes some (necessary and often productive) liberties. The poetry of *Trilce* abounds in semantic as well as syntactical ambiguities, and in-dividual words often shift meaning radically depending on the discursive thread or semantic system one chooses to privilege. Thus a word such as "testar" in the first poem's opening stanza can be related to witnessing, evaluation, legal discourse, all of which are invoked elsewhere in the poem, but a more arcane meaning also relates it to a practice of wine fermentation, which is further echoed in the "toast" of the second stanza and which reconnects to the larger thematic of fermentation in the poetry itself. This kind of multiplication of in-terpretive possibilities sometimes leaves the reader worried that she is barking up the wrong tree, but it also explains why *Trilce* is so enduringly entertaining to read.

37. The poem may be concerned with the experience of frustrated defeca-tion within the prison confines (Espejo; Coyné), with a preemptive rejoinder to critics (Neale-Silva), with the mode of its own composition (MacDuffie), or with the insignificance of the individual before the species (Franco, *Dialectics*); but each of these readings is at least equally feasible, because all depend on the arbitrary interpretation of what they perceive as a hermetic code, a modern-day *trobar clus* (Buxó). Rather than attempting to "translate" the poem into univo-cal, intelligible discourse, my reading tries to show that this attempt is in fact precluded by the very indeterminacy of the statements composing the poem, and focuses instead on the dynamic it reveals at work.

38. Durling elucidates the digestive metaphor by tracing it back to classical rhetoric (61–62): "Latin *digero* meant properly to force apart, to separate, hence to distribute. . . . Applied to mental activity, *digero* meant especially to set in order. Cicero says that subject matter must be distributed among the different parts of a speech: one digests it. Quintilian says questions must be digested, or set in order. For any expression to take place, a prior digesting must take place."

39. At the end of the poem, the object is importantly unaccompanied by its counterpart—noise—and this is signaled in the very choice of the enclitic *-se* form. Were the pronoun in its usual position, we would hear not only "se para" but also "separa," implying a second presence.

40. A number of different semantic clusters are invoked here that overlap in curious ways: geographical features, time, evaluative processes, body parts, and also—more curiously—a series of words related to wine: "testar," "calabriar," and, more festively, "brindar."

41. Leopold Bloom wonders whether statues in the library also have private parts, worrying about what happens to goddesses after drinking the nectar of the gods: "Lovely forms of women sculpted Junonian. Immortal lovely. And we stuffing food in one hole and out behind: food, chyle, blood, dung, earth, food: have to feed it like stoking an engine. They have no. Never looked. I'll look today" (*Ulysses* 144–45).

42. This might also, of course, be a reference to Vallejo's travels by boat between Trujillo and Lima, both of which have guano islands just off their ports.

43. The relationship between excrement and language is echoed in the rhetorical grandstanding of the newspaper office in *Ulysses* (108): "We mustn't be led away by words, by sounds of words. We think of Rome, imperial, imperious, imperative". . . . "What was their civilization? Vast, I allow: but vile. *Cloacae*: sewers. . . . The Roman, like the Englishman who follows in his footsteps, brought to every new shore on which he set his foot . . . only his cloacal obsession. He gazed about him in his toga and he said: *It is meet to be here. Let us construct a watercloset.*"

44. Eshleman's comments on translating the poem sheds interesting light on *Trilce*'s procedures, here as elsewhere: "To some extent, in a poem as multidirectional as XXV, certain word choices become compromises relevant to other words. For example, in line 4 *cadillos* can be translated as 'cockleburs' or as 'thrums' (warp ends, which can be associated with "unraveled" in line 5), and by selecting 'thrips' for line 1, I thus get, in line 4, 'thrips and thrums'—a sound play that may be as unusual as the sound play between the first two words in Spanish in line 1. While my translation of *Trilce* is primarily meaning-oriented, there are occasions when the sound play is so paramount that it must be given equal priority with meaning" (222). The suggestiveness of the poetry's sound is taken in fascinating directions in Wagner's "homophonic" translation of *Trilce*.

45. A tentative list is as follows: *alfar*—to rear up on hindlegs; *rebufar*—to snort; *lomos*—loins; *resoplar*—to wheeze; *portar*—to bear; *esteva*—the steering instrument of a horse-drawn carriage; *apealar*—to lasso the legs of a horse or bull; *soberbio*—"proud" or "fiery," usually applied to a horse, according to the *Diccionario de la Real Academia*; *petral*—the brace attached to the front part of

a saddle; *rondas*—surveillance on horseback, or the gathering together of heads of cattle; "rodeo."

CHAPTER FOUR

1. *El Norte,* October 3, 1924; *ACC* I: 44. Vallejo's words draw on several discrete suggestions in Darío's prose introductions to his 1905 *Cantos de vida y de esperanza* (Songs of Life and Hope) and his 1907 *El canto errante* (The Wandering Song): poetry as pedagogy, the lure of the marketplace, the pressures of history. But whereas Darío touts the ability of poetry to conquer time and space—by rising above but also incorporating them—Vallejo insists on situating his poetry in a located, historical present tense.

2. Futurism obviously lent itself to both progressive and reactionary politics, in Peru as much as in Italy or Russia; it was even adopted as a title by a conservative Peruvian political party, which ironically grounded its projects for the nation's future in the continuation of colonial structures.

3. As Coronado argues, indigenismo was not simply a rescuing of Peruvian traditions, but a sustained theoretical meditation on "how the region might, in its own way, become modern" (1).

4. If the particular charge of the Latin American avant-gardes, as Unruh has systematically studied, was the political imperative to represent new nations to themselves, this tended to take place—as Carlos Alonso suggests—under the sign not of novelty but of *futurity,* grounded in the need to offer a prophetic vision of new possibilities for the continent. As Alonso traces (6–11), novelty was both the watchword of the European avant-gardes and the principle of Europe's projections onto the New World; these dovetail in the paradoxical discourse of primitivism, understood as the recuperation of "ancient" non-Western traditions to rejuvenate Western culture. Futurity, by contrast, was the local recasting of this discourse, tethering newly independent nations not to the metropolis or to their own pasts but to what they might become.

5. In recent years Mirko Lauer has dedicated himself to collecting both isolated examples and full volumes of this poetry, which he discusses systematically in his *Musa mecánica.*

6. This is in part an accident of history. Mariátegui's sudden death in 1930 means that his comments are necessarily restricted to Vallejo's Peruvian writings and that critical history is deprived of his opinions on Vallejo's later poetry.

7. Mariátegui was in regular contact with a number of Europe-based writers during the mid- to late 1920s, who reported to him on Vallejo's abject poverty; his gesture was therefore an attempt to mitigate Vallejo's suffering by catapulting him to the prominence he felt his poetry deserved.

8. Vallejo's sidestepping of the indigenism debate is especially surprising given that in the early 1920s he had shared a room in Lima with Francisco Xandoval, who was at the time working for the newly created Ministerio de Fomento in the Sección del Trabajo y Asuntos Indígenas.

9. The series is collected in the chapter "El proceso de la literatura" (Literature in Process/On Trial) in Mariátegui's 1928 collection, *Siete ensayos de interpretación de la realidad peruana.*

10. Lambie ("Intellectuals") overstates the degree of contact and agreement between Vallejo and Mariátegui in the mid-1920s; his article is otherwise indispensable for its charting of Vallejo's political development in the context of shifting alignments and debates on the international left.

11. Vallejo composed this poem shortly after his arrival in Paris in 1923 and published it the same year in avant-garde journals in Madrid and La Coruña. A cryptic instance of self-explanation, the poem circles around a place that can never be reached or inhabited but that is nonetheless *known* by the poet, who asserts his ownership-through-knowledge almost childishly, warning others that it can only be approached after accepting conditions of propriety of his own making.

12. Serafín Delmar, for example, in *Guerrilla* (1927) accuses Vallejo of plagiarizing Russian- and Spanish-speaking poets alike, of being anachronistic, and of being, in any case, totally unknown in Latin America. Gamaliel Churata takes Vallejo to task in *Boletín Titikaka*, no. 10 (1927), in which he praises both *Trilce* and Vallejo's "interesantes y agiles informaciones parisinas" (interesting and agile Parisian notes) but criticizes the "criterio historicista primitivo" (primitive historicist criteria) and the external gaze he deploys in reading the Latin American avant-gardes. Several months later, Alfredo Rebaza Acosta hailed him as a "gran poeta—a pesar de *Trilce*" (great poet—in spite of *Trilce*). Original documents are collected in Lauer, *Polémica*.

13. However, as I discuss in chapter 6, the modes of the earlier poetry do not entirely disappear in the later work. Silva-Santisteban notes that upon receiving notice of his banishment from France for political activities in late 1930, Vallejo consoled himself by copying out *Trilce* XVI—"Tengo fe en que soy, y en que he sido menos" (I have faith that I am, and that I have been less)—giving it a title befitting the later poetry, "Requisitoria del individuo" (Summons for the Individual) (*César Vallejo: Poesía completa*, III: 303).

14. In a 1929 notebook entry, Vallejo suggests to himself a Marxist reading of *Trilce* (placing it alongside other works from the French, Russian, U.S., and Latin American avant-gardes) and a Freudian reading of his 1923 narratives, *Fabla salvaje* and *Escalas melografiadas;* it is enormously suggestive that he here ascribes conscious technique to poetry rather than to prose.

15. In 1917 Viktor Shklovsky had published the enormously influential essay "Art as Technique," whose argument for the defamiliarization of language through poetry parallels Vallejo's own experiments in *Los heraldos negros*, composed around the same time. Vallejo, however, does not seem to have been familiar with writings by the Russian formalists.

16. Vallejo's reading of Fordism through Soviet systems of industrial production brings him closer to Vertov than to Stein (for comments on these aesthetics, see McCabe and Watten). In *Man with a Movie Camera*, which Vallejo references several times in his notebooks, the rationalization of machine production does not automatize workers but gives them time to joke around on the job.

17. As Stephen Hart signals, Vallejo's argument here derives directly from Pierre Naville's 1926 polemical book, *La revolution et les intellectuels* (*Stumbling* 21–22). Mariátegui's writings on surrealism (1930) offer a more dialecti-

cal reading of the movement, tracing its beginnings in the nihilistic moment of Dada through to its eventual maturity in political commitment (*Artista* 46–52).

18. As Hart points out, however, Vallejo revised these articles for inclusion in the notebook *El arte y la revolución*, expunging any favorable references to Trotsky (*Stumbling* 22–28). See also Miller's (2002) discussion of his shifting sense of the intellectual's responsibility in these years.

19. Hart (*Stumbling* 18–39) offers a lucid account of the stages of Vallejo's political positions in the 1920s and 1930s: from the materialist vanguardism of 1925–27 through the Trotskyism of 1927–29 to a strict adherence to Stalinism and Comintern politics from 1929 to 1931. See also Lambie, "Intellectuals." Although it is difficult to trace Vallejo's movements over the subsequent five years, his intermittent chronicles show a new interest in studying both pre-Columbian history and present-day colonialism, issuing into a messianic zeal filtered through Christian communism during the Spanish Civil War in 1936–38.

20. Similarly, Vallejo's interview with a Bolshevik writer is continually interrupted by the latter's Menshevik girlfriend, who wonders why a Peruvian reporter is bothering to conduct interviews with more than one Bolshevik writer, given that all produce the same responses. Vallejo's own reply is itself hysterical: he races through a range of different explanations for her critical attitude, from economics to gender to psychoanalysis, and settles on all of them at once, as though he cannot quite dispel the doubts she raises, nor silence her dissent (*ARC* 454–56).

21. His published volume *Rusia en 1931*, nonetheless, was a tremendous commercial success, unlike any of his other publications.

22. We will see some evidence of his experiments with procedure in the manuscripts for the dated poems from 1937. Vallejo also begins to map out a sense of his own technique in writings on Vertov and Eisenstein, whose work he appreciates not only for its socialist content but also for its formal experimentation with montage, which is crucial to his poetics, as I argue in chapter 6.

23. This article connects the question of poetry's reach to issues of linguistic translation, intimating that because poetry is untranslatable, it is necessarily perceived as being restricted to the articulation of local concerns, no matter what its contents. This suspicion, which makes the generic localism of the lyric a question not just of subjectivity but of cultural repertoires, underlines Vallejo's sense that he could never properly read the poets he most admired, Whitman and Goethe. It is therefore no accident that his models for technique, as I argue in chapter 6, were not other poets but directors of silent movies: Chaplin, Eisenstein, Vertov, Gance.

24. Bazán notes that Vallejo's work for *Mundial* was a result of Mariátegui's recommendation to its editor Andrés Avelino Aramburú, who consequently sought Vallejo out on a visit to Paris (72).

25. For an in-depth analysis of this question, see my article "Mariátegui y la escena contemporánea."

26. The circle of Chaplin experts was growing by the day, as Charlie the tramp revealed himself as a hinge between emerging mass culture and the discourse of cultural critique; the years 1928–31 would see essays on Chaplin by a range of avant-garde critics of various stripes, from Xavier Abril and Maria Wi-

esse in Peru through Philippe Soupault and other assorted surrealists in France to Benjamin, Kracauer, Adorno, and Arnheim in Germany.

27. Interpreting Peruvian history (in tandem with discoveries by the archaeologist Luis Valcárcel) for a European audience would lead Vallejo to some contradictory, even self-alienating statements. On a number of occasions he rhetorically attempted to sidestep the role of "native informant" by aligning himself with a "civilized" European public (e.g., *ACC* II: 950).

CHAPTER FIVE

1. Jorge Puccinelli has found 37 articles in *El Norte* (Trujillo), 127 in *Mundial* (Lima), and 41 in *Variedades* (Lima), as well as scattered chronicles in other Latin American (Mexican, Cuban, Costa Rican, Colombian, and Argentinean) newspapers and sporadic pieces in French, Spanish, Italian, German, and Russian periodicals (*ACC* I: xlvii). Any study of Vallejo's chronicles is indebted to his remarkable detective work.

2. As I discuss in chapter 6, Vallejo did compose at least forty-seven poems between 1923 and 1936 (some in prose, some in free verse, others in metrical form), and sixty-seven more in late 1937, fifteen of which he organized into the sequence *España, aparta de mí este cáliz*.

3. The exceptions are Puccinelli, Chang-Rodríguez, Orrillo, McDuffie, Cisneros, Podestá, Miller, Rowe, and Carrasco; the last four in particular aim to connect Vallejo's chronicles to the shifting modalities of his poetry but also to the broader panorama of international modernity and its structuring discourses. As for the question of genre, important studies of the *modernista* chronicle are found in González, Rotker, and Ramos. The avant-garde chronicle, as a genre practiced by numerous writers, has yet to receive sustained attention.

4. As Podestá points out (23, 31–32), Vallejo's journalistic eye is usually trained on the literary proletariat rather than on a struggling working class per se; he therefore offers few portraits of truly marginal figures such as we find in the writings of Orwell and the photo-texts of Brassai, although these kinds of figures will come to haunt his later poetry.

5. "Total War, Modernism, and Encyclopedic Form," talk delivered at Harvard University's Modernism seminar, October 14, 2008.

6. As a myth of Parisian rebirth, this is notably self-effacing: an encounter with a Spaniard turns Vallejo into an indistinct and out-of-place type. We might contrast it with the story told by the Guatemalan Miguel Angel Asturias of his own self-discovery in Paris just a year later: after being interpellated by a Sorbonne anthropology professor as "Maya," he abandoned his determination to enter Parisian intellectual life as a sophisticated foreigner in favor of a self-presentation as an indigenous informant, of greater interest to the European intelligentsia (Henighan 44).

7. The poem "Luna Park," by Vallejo's compatriot Abraham Valdelomar, offers a similar reading of Paris in 1913. Drawn by both a passing woman and his "sudamericana curiosidad" into a newly inaugurated amusement park, he stumbles first onto what looks more like a medieval dance of death than the

expected cosmopolitan whirl, and second, into a model native village, featuring a "tribu de salvajes," a funhouse-mirror reflection of his own outsider status which put the observer at risk of turning into the observed. His condemnation, however, is directed not at the organizers of the colonialist exhibit but at the natives themselves, who have "allowed" themselves to be captured and put on display, willfully handing their descendants over to cultural dissolution and perversion by civilization. Bernabé (130) suggests that the encounter enables Valdelomar to adopt a Latin American gaze equidistant from both Eurocentrism and indigenism.

8. As Evelyne Penia Fodor commented to me, this account echoes Vallejo's reading of Lima as a circus on his arrival there from Trujillo, as mapped out in *Trilce* XIV.

9. Vallejo develops the metaphor in an article written two months later, after he has begun to realize the extent to which Latin America is invisible to Europe. The virulently sarcastic piece, "Cooperación" (*El Norte,* February 26, 1924; *ACC* I: 41–43), sets the pieties of transatlantic solidarity against the reality of systematic indifference, finishing with the defiant declaration, "Bajo Imperio! Aquí estamos los bárbaros" (Hey late Empire! The barbarians are here). Depicting a Latin America poised to defeat Europe, it borrows from accounts of boxing matches, alluding to the Argentinean Luis Firpos's recent close call for the world heavyweight title against the American Jack Dempsey, who had previously unseated French champion Georges Carpentier.

10. This Latin American disappointment at Paris—giving the sense that not the experiencing subject but the very experience is out of date—is itself a recognizable performance; it laments the loss of an experience available to the previous generation of visitors, even though it knows that that generation had registered exactly the same complaints. When the most famous Latin American chronicler of Paris, the Guatemalan Enrique Gómez Carrillo, arrived in "Lutecia" in 1900, he was so disappointed by what he found—or did not find—that he took refuge in readings of Murger (169); Vallejo, conversely, takes refuge in reading Gómez Carrillo.

11. Writing on Baudelaire's mid-nineteenth-century Paris, Benjamin points to the proliferation of conspirators in marginal artistic culture (*Writer* 46–52). Their numbers had not diminished eighty years later. Brassai invites us to "penetrate this other world, this fringe world, the secret, sinister world of mobsters, outcasts, toughs, pimps, whores, addicts, inverts" found in "one of those seemingly ordinary bars in Montmartre, or [in] a dive in the Goutte-d'Or neighborhood. . . . Conversation ceases. The owner looks you over with an unfriendly glance. The clientele sizes you up: this intruder, this newcomer—is he an informer, a stool pigeon?" (n.p.).

12. Benjamin, Gutiérrez-Girardot, and Gluck offer important accounts of bohemia and of the flâneur's ambiguous place in it.

13. "The experience of visual and linguistic strangeness, the broken narrative of the journey and its inevitable accompaniment of transient encounters with characters whose self-presentation was bafflingly unfamiliar, raised to the level of universal myth this intense, singular narrative of unsettlement, homelessness, solitude, and impoverished independence. . . . The life of the

émigré was dominant among the key groups, and they could and did deal with each other. Their self-referentiality, their propinquity and mutual isolation, all served to represent the artist as necessarily estranged, and to ratify as canonical the works of radical estrangement" (34–35).

14. Puccinelli (xxi) examines the implicit equation Vallejo draws between his own experiments in writing and those of Satie in music; at other moments he aligns himself with Conrad, Juan Gris, Picasso, and Chaplin (discussed below) while distancing himself from the artistic and/or political dogmatism of Vicente Huidobro and Diego Rivera, at least until late 1927.

15. In his early years in Paris Vallejo attempted to forge an acquaintance with a number of resident experts in art, science, and politics, publishing occasional interviews with figures such as French Prime Minister Raymond Poincaré or the scientist Charles Henry; his most fruitful acquaintance was with the pro-Cubism art critic Maurice Raynal, whose series of little books on modern artists (e.g., Zadkine, Archipenko, Picasso, Gris) introduced Vallejo to contemporary painting and sculpture.

16. Asturias claims to have arrived in Paris on Bastille Day, 1924; the date of arrival, which appears to be a fiction, connects his rebirth abroad to a revolution (Henighan 43). It is noteworthy that neither Asturias nor Vallejo refer to one another, despite their coinciding in Paris between 1924 and 1933; given Asturias's greater insertion in French culture, their paths may rarely have crossed.

17. The early 1926 chronicle/prose poem, "El hallazgo de la vida" (The Discovery of a Lifetime) (ACC I: 213–14), brings together a focus on the horizon with the image of being "un extranjero en la tierra" (a foreigner on earth), having to learn all systems of bodily and linguistic gestures anew, in an oblique continuation of the modes of Trilce.

18. Vallejo's failure to return home makes this a truncated heterology, in Michel de Certeau's sense; instead of reinserting himself into Peruvian culture, he moves through a series of shifting affiliations with other cultural options—the Harlem Renaissance, Soviet aesthetics, and finally the deterritorialized international possibilities associated with the Spanish Civil War.

19. I take this formulation from Amos Segala's comment on Asturias's experience in Paris (cited in Henighan, 59). Henighan also makes the important point that many young intellectuals "left for Paris in search not only of European culture but of other Spanish Americans. The city developed into the best place in the world for a Spanish American artist to feel out the contours of his identity, testing his experiences and intuitions against those of writers and intellectuals from fraternal countries. . . . The Parisian séjour changed in nature, evolving into a period of months or years spent reading, writing, discussing and accumulating experiences rather than a permanent renunciation of Spanish America. . . . The fact of living in Paris, therefore, came to seem less like a betrayal than it might have done to progressive intellectuals of the previous generation" (39).

20. Vallejo's approach anticipates Stein's parodic anthropology in Paris France, although Stein's claim, "Not to know the well known in Paris does not argue yourself unknown, because nobody knows anybody whom they do not know" (11), is underwritten by her ironic confidence that anybody who is worth knowing knows her, because they are known by her.

21. The somewhat unsavory Sux, as Juan Domingo Córdoba reports (144), at one point offered to publish Vallejo's poetry under his own (better-known) name and to split the proceeds.

22. In 1930 Vallejo became a regular contributor to the short-lived oppositional Spanish weekly *Bolívar*, edited by his Peruvian friend Pablo Abril de Vivero, and over the next couple of years he published sporadically in left-wing Madrid newspapers—*La Voz, Estampa,* and *Ahora*—in adddition to contributing occasional pieces to the Buenos Aires journals *Claridad* and *Nosotros* and possibly some anonymous articles to *L'Humanité.* Very few articles between 1931 and 1938 have been found, with the exception of a series of essays in some French publications—*Germinal, Beaux-Arts,* and *L'Amérique*—that significantly focus on Peru, concentrating on its political and social formations and its still-rudimentary historical and archaeological studies.

23. Ironically, it was largely through his Madrid associates that Vallejo remained in touch with Peru; the Madrid-based Abril de Vivero and the Spanish surrealist Juan Larrea both visited Lima in the late 1920s, where they brought themselves up to date on recent culture and politics. Larrea was also beginning to establish himself as an important archaeological collector, and in 1933 he mounted a Paris exhibition of artifacts he had brought back from Peru; by helping him with the catalog, Vallejo began to delve into his own underexplored national history. See Núñez ("Vallejo") for accounts of Vallejo's disconnection from home amid 1930s political upheavals.

24. Vallejo also contributed a markedly xenophobic article on Asian immigration to Peru to the periodical *L'Europe nouvelle* in 1925, merging an insistence on Peru's Latinate history and future with a complaint about both the dilution of the indigenous population and the flow of capital out of the country. His response to what he perceives as a national problem is a call for greater European immigration (*ACC* I: 140–49).

25. After much negotiation through Abril de Vivero, who was working for the Peruvian consulate in Spain, Vallejo was granted a stipend to study law in Madrid in 1925, which led to a series of desultory trips south to collect the funds (and various maneuvers to have them collected by Spanish friends instead), until he finally abandoned the grant in late 1927.

26. As this community moved in the direction of a commitment to socialism, it began to be beset by internal fractures. In 1928 a split within the Peruvian party APRA (with various cells abroad) prompted Vallejo's Paris cell to align itself with Mariátegui; just two years later Vallejo was preparing his own attack on Mariátegui's group (to be published in the Madrid periodical *Bolívar*), which he hurriedly retracted upon hearing news of the latter's death (*CC* 380). This incident undermines Lambie's largely unsupported argument ("Intellectuals") about the impact of Mariátegui's mid-1920s writings on Vallejo's political development.

27. To judge from comments by Julio Cortázar ("Carta") and Ángel Rama ("Literature") in the 1960s and 1970s, this situation did not greatly change in the intervening half century. The disciplinary structure of Latin American studies, in its practical insistence on national or regional divisions, still makes little room for the study of intellectual and artistic exchanges between areas.

28. As Vallejo is careful to point out, however, this does not mean that Latin America was an empty space or "new continent," as it tended to be understood by the European avant-gardes, but rather that it lacked a proper understanding of its own history at the national and intracontinental levels. Citing the recent example of studies and traveling exhibitions by the Peruvian archaeologist Luis Valcárcel and by Mexican and Argentinean folkloric theater groups, he called for further rigorous study and sharing of knowledge, so that individual countries might begin to understand their own histories and forge connections with the rest of the continent (ACC I: 222–25).

29. In his administrative job at the newspaper bureau at 11, avenue de l'Opéra, Vallejo enjoyed brief acquaintances with visiting Latin American dignitaries but always as their subordinate, looking after their children, proofreading their writings. Nonetheless, the bureau's collection of journals allowed him to keep minimally up to date on contemporary Latin American events.

30. Vallejo's determination to separate Paris from the nation-state to which it nominally belongs leads him to posit its greater affinity with any town in Latin America than with a provincial town in France, if only because of Latin America's cultural colonization by Paris (ACC II: 579–80).

31. Michael North offers a compelling counterpoint between machine imaginaries in Keaton's 1928 The General and Vertov's 1929 Man with a Movie Camera, suggesting that contemporary responses to the machine in ideologically opposed spaces are not as divergent as we might think (27–52).

32. Vallejo nonetheless points to Cubism's capacity for resistance (ACC II: 632), as it continues to demand an effort on the part of the consumer, educating the public up to its level. He thus offers a glimpse of the possible humanization of the commercial world; as he suggests vis-à-vis the machine, ideology resides not in a form or a technology but in the uses that are made of it.

33. Vallejo notes that the phenomenon of surmenage in the modern city tends to be examined along psychological and sensorial lines (the training of the body to cope with the expansion of stimuli, analyzed by Simmel and Benjamin); however, he insists that this also has an economic basis, which had yet to be taken properly into account (ACC II: 698–99).

34. Rowe (179) and Pérez de Tudela (56) both note that Vallejo's chronicles replace the sound-centered modes of his earlier poetry with an accent on sight; each suggests that his chronicles operate according to visual montage, which offers a parallel to Dos Passos's camera eye. I would add, however, that Vallejo's interest in the way stories circulate—from eye to mouth to mouth—retains a focus on what is heard and how it is expressed.

35. As Puccinelli notes, Vallejo's style in his chronicles shifts quickly from a reproduction of the abstruse language of his earlier poetry—the mot rare—to a concern with finding the mot juste, in its double sense of precision and justice. Citing Conrad's preface to A Personal Record (1912), "Give me the right word and the right accent and I will move the world!" Vallejo declares in 1925, "Al apogeo desenfrenado y ciego de la palanca de Arquímedes, al entusiasmo groseramente positivo que ha parido el aeroplano bombardeante y el asfixiante gas de las batallas, menester es que suceda el apogeo del verbo, que revela, que une, y nos arrastra mas allá del interés perecedero y del egoísmo" (The un-

bridled and blind apogee of Archimedes' lever, the grossly positive enthusiasm produced by the bomber-plane and by choking chemical warfare, must both be followed by the apogee of the word—which reveals, which unites, and which pulls us beyond ephemeral interest and egotism) (*ACC* I: 123).

36. Armstrong's contextualized reading of Loy's manifesto (106–29) underlies my reading of body culture and its international context in Vallejo's chronicles.

37. This division, in Vallejo's chronicles, is similarly played out between reason and madness, which he celebrates in reviews of outsider-art exhibitions held in Paris in the mid-1920s, countering the rationalization of the body (its training toward heightened productivity) with its spontaneous, nonsensical gestures. This interest in the potential of madness brings him surprisingly close to the surrealist aesthetic politics that he attacks elsewhere (*ACC* I: 526–28).

38. Robert Kaufman ("Marx against Theory") offers a brilliant reading of the metrical version of this poem as, precisely, a meditation on how to marry politics to form.

39. Although the bodies of his early chronicles on sport are often female—as in the case of fashion, women's bodies more directly reveal the changing forms of modernity, if only because they more quickly attract the male gaze—his interest in the desexualized female bodies that perform Nordic gymnastics allows him to congratulate himself on his newly "modern" and de-eroticized ability to see beyond gender (*ACC* I: 250; II: 660). This suggests that it is sport more than Marxist theory or Soviet doctrine that prepares him to appreciate ungendered laboring Bolshevik bodies.

40. Elsewhere he calls for a deprofessionalization of sport, to produce consciously "sporting men" rather than sportsmen; his praise for Lindbergh crossing the Atlantic in civilian clothing rather than in uniform sets sport at an oblique angle to his running commentary on fashion (*ACC* I: 490).

41. As Klein notes, the Parisian revue was a "translation, poetic and militant at the same time, of a first, as yet unwitting thrust towards an international subculture, product of a deculturation-acculturation process, which soon overtook the whole of the Western world" (182). Vallejo's chronicles coincided with its heyday, when it reached a total of about 17,000 seats; with the advent of sound cinema and the expansion of radio technology, its popularity subsided, and most music halls were turned into movie theaters (185).

42. Buoyed up by—and somewhat envious of—the great popular success of black music in Paris, which he saw as analogous to the folkloric grounding of Satie and Stravinsky, Vallejo began calling for serious study and international tours of Latin American music, beginning with the whistling pots of Nazca and moving through history to contemporary experiments by the Peruvian Daniel Alomía Robles, the Brazilian Heitor Villalobos, and the Mexican Julián Carrillo (*ACC* I: 224).

43. Vallejo here coincides directly with the theories and practices of a new generation of Afro-Caribbean and *negrista* poets, such as Nicolás Guillén and Luis Palés Matos, who were themselves in dialogue with members, texts, and performances of the Harlem Renaissance.

44. It deserves mention that from the late 1920s, as Vallejo moved away from newspaper chronicles toward direct reportage (in his two books on the So-

viet Union), he also began to dabble in drama. The gap in his biography—little is known about his life from the early 1930s until his death in 1938—is largely filled with theater; he produced a handful of plays during that time, predominantly under the influence of Soviet examples, but managed to get none of them staged, despite Lorca's advocacy in 1932 (when Lorca was writing *Bodas de sangre,* revising *Don Perlimplín,* and working on *El público,* which he also had difficulty staging). The plays are outside the scope of this book; I refer the reader to Podestá's unsurpassed study. But Vallejo also toyed with the idea of making movies; in 1929 he attempted (again with no luck) to have his prose work *Hacia el reino de los Sciris* turned into a film and later produced a screenplay-sketch of his own play *Colacho Hermanos* under the title *Presidentes de América;* meanwhile, his short play *Charlot contra Chaplin* or *Dressing Room* focuses on one of the foremost figures of the international screen, like Lorca's 1928 playlet, *El paseo de Buster Keaton.*

45. Vallejo sets Shaw and Pirandello alongside one another in several chronicles (e.g., "La conquista de París por los negros" [The Black Conquest of Paris], *Mundial* 287, December 11, 1925; *ACC* I: 170–72), pointing to the differences between them but thereby also the possibility of equally productive approaches to the same question through traditional and avant-garde aesthetics; his juxtaposition of Debussy and Satie follows a similar schema ("El más grande músico de Francia" [France's Greatest Musician]; *ACC* I: 255–61).

46. Vallejo's 1926 poem "Me estoy riendo" (I Am Laughing) contains surprising references to the Jewish exodus from Egypt—coinciding with attempts to connect pre-Columbian culture to findings in Egyptian and Greek archaeology, with an added emphasis on the pain of exile.

47. It must be noted that through his ongoing defense of artistic autonomy—in drama as in other art forms—Vallejo criticizes agit-prop artworks being produced by East and West alike; hence his direct rejection in late 1927 of calls by both Diego Rivera (*ACC* I: 518–19) and Víctor Raúl Haya de la Torre (*ACC* I: 328; II: 645) for the increased politicization of the artist. Political beliefs, he repeatedly claimed, should manifest themselves organically, through all facets of human sensibility. Thus "el poeta socialista no ha de ser tal solamente en el momento de escribir un poema, sino en todos sus actos, grandes y pequeños, internos y visibles, conscientes y subconscientes y hasta cuando duerme y cuando se equivoca o se traiciona" (the socialist poet should be a socialist not only at the moment of writing a poem, but in all his acts, small and large alike, internal and visible, conscious and unconscious, even in sleeping and making mistakes and betraying himself) (*ACC* II: 653).

48. For a dazzling reading of the interruptive interplay of theater and film in these years, see George Baker, *The Artwork Caught by the Tail,* 289–337.

49. One of the only dissenting voices belongs to the Bolivian Alcides Arguedas, who complained that silent cinema was inculcating complacency, leaving global publics happier to watch Chaplin—and his domestic disputes—than to learn about other countries (such as Bolivia) (*Etapas* 343).

50. This narrative of stymied silence is somewhat disingenuous: even the earliest screenings of film in Peru featured live orchestras, meaning that silent film was never quite free of sound; and *Ben Hur* (1925) itself predated Vitaphone technology (1927).

51. By the early 1930s, however, Vallejo had developed a keener sense of film's critical potential; in a series of articles on Peru for *Germinal* in 1933, he mentions having seen documentary films on contemporary life in various parts of the global south—India and the Congo—and calls for a similar documenting of social conditions in Peru (*ACC* II: 904).

52. A trenchant parody of this appears in chapter 6 of *Ulysses,* in which Bloom muses on the possibility of keeping deceased relatives alive in memory through technological reproduction: "Have a gramophone in every grave or keep it in the house. After dinner on a Sunday. Put on poor old greatgrandfather. Kraahraark! Hellohellohello amawfullyglad kraark awfullygladaseeagain hellohello amawf krpthsth" (93).

CHAPTER SIX

1. Yurkiévich is one of the only critics to insist on this aspect of Vallejo's late poems ("Aptitud"). He does so by shifting attention away from a reductive statement of their themes and back to the reader's experience of reading the poetry; he demonstrates the ways in which it repeatedly pulls the reader up short, unsettling any interpretive comfort—but also any excessive solemnity—in the process of sense-making. His short article sketches out several of the points that I draw out more extensively in what follows. Roy Andersson's *Songs from the Second Floor* (2000) offers a provocative translation of this poetry's discomforting political and social humor into film.

2. In signaling this, I am diverging from Franco's argument that the *Poemas humanos* offer an "allegory of the poverty of individualism" ("Vallejo" 46). Although the individuals who appear in the late poetry are for the most part interchangeable, often represented by the poet himself, this seems rather a comment on the leveling of modernity—experienced at the material as much as at the ideological or sociological level—than on the narcissism of the individual. Vallejo's emphasis throughout is on the discrete, if necessarily similar, subjectivities that make up a collective.

3. In a journal entry from 1937 in the notebook *Contra el secreto profesional,* Vallejo hints at the relation between selfishness and altruism as steps in a necessary dialectic, which he relates to a broader dialectic of objectivity and subjectivity. Vallejo also makes the somewhat playful claim in this short piece that he has moved dialectically beyond dialectical laws (*ERC* 533).

4. At least two poems are still missing, both referred to in the notebook *Contra el secreto profesional*—"Mi autorretrato" (My Self-Portrait) and a poem containing the dialectical line "ser poeta hasta el punto de no serlo" (to be a poet up to the point of not being one).

5. Vallejo's Paris poetry was first published in 1939—by his widow, Georgette de Vallejo, and the Peruvian scholar Raúl Porras Barrenechea—under the title *Poemas humanos;* the collection included all of the prose, metrical, and free verse poems that he composed between 1923 and 1938, including the sequence *España, aparta de mí este cáliz,* which Vallejo had clearly arranged as a separate collection and which was published by Republican soldiers in Barcelona in 1939. In a 1968 facsimile edition, Vallejo's widow redivided the collection

into three parts: prose poetry, metrical and free verse poetry, and the Spanish Civil War sequence. Meanwhile, the Spanish poet Juan Larrea, who had been a close friend of Vallejo's during several stretches of his time in Paris, proposed dividing the European poems into two separate collections: *Nómina de huesos* (Roster of Bones) for the undated poems and *Sermón sobre la barbarie* (Sermon on Barbarism) for the dated poems. Given that no title can be ascribed with any certainty to the late poetry, several critics have simply suggested referring to the entirety as the *Poemas de París,* or the *Posthumous Poems.* However, as Paoli notes (26), the title *Poemas humanos* has an emotional appropriateness that explains its staying power among readers.

6. In a 1931 interview, Vallejo mentioned that he was producing a collection of poetry under the suggestive title *Instituto Central de Trabajo* (Central Institute of Labor). From late 1935 through early 1936, he tried several times to interest the Spanish poet José Bergamín—who had been involved with the second edition of *Trilce* in Madrid—in publishing a new collection of his poetry but received no response, despite Rafael Alberti's intervention (CC 439, 441, 443). Hart suggests that this may have been because Bergamín was occupied at the time with publishing Federico García Lorca's collection *Poeta en Nueva York* (Poet in New York) but points out that, in any case, the total of new poems Vallejo had written to that date would not have exceeded thirty-four, barely enough to justify publication as a collection ("The Chronology" 613–17).

7. Analogues might be the shift from the cinema of attractions to a narrative cinema (Strauven); Mariátegui's reading of surrealism as the maturity of Dada (*Artista* 42–45) or of narrative as what results when the Russian Revolution has time to catch its breath and write over the more breathless poetry of its first moments (161); Disney's recasting of animation as concerned with "life" rather than simply with motion (North 75).

8. Recent critical works by Stephen Hart and William Rowe come closer to this model, offering angled and fragmented views—or *cuts*, to use Rowe's film-inflected term—of Vallejo's writing.

9. Vallejo had begun to experiment with lyrical prose while in Peru, publishing two blocks of narrative shortly after *Trilce*: the short stories of *Escalas melografiadas* (Melographed Scales), and the novella *Fabla salvaje* (Savage Fable).

10. After the formalization of the genre in Baudelaire's experiments—collected posthumously in the 1869 collection, *Le Spleen de Paris. Petits Poèmes en Prose*—a number of Latin American *modernista* poets (such as Rubén Darío and Julián del Casal) used prose poetry to signal the disjunctions between aesthetic and bourgeois modernity. Their prose poems tended to set the poet in conflict with the norms of the changing social systems within which he found it impossible to operate, but they also contrasted his figure with the multiple anonymous passersby who made up the crowds of the urban city, not to mention with the new patrons for art; central to this prose poetry is an ironic comparison between the lyric poet's values and his environment, which rendered those values and his mission inoperative. Paradoxically, those same poets were frequently commissioned to write newspaper chronicles, which must therefore be seen as standing in heightened tension with their prose poems.

11. Vallejo's cultural politics were explicitly antipopulist; an artist such as Picasso, he claimed, did not descend to the level of the public, but educated the public taste to meet him. *ACC* II: 631.

12. Sonya Stephens argues that "in making available different meanings and in staging oppositional discursive relationships in a genre which is itself dependent on contrasting formal modes, the *Petits Poèmes en prose* constitutes a textual encounter representative of the dysfunctional social and linguistic encounters it stages" (22). Indeed Vallejo's poem looks like a parodic reworking of Baudelaire's "L'Etranger" (The Stranger), which casts a speaker interrogating a lyric poet, resulting in an unsolvable clash of discourses and value systems; here, by contrast, all distinction between poet and fellow man is canceled.

13. Translations from the French on this page are my own.

14. As Eric Trudel pointed out to me, however, the first half of the first example cleaves carefully to the form of the French alexandrine's first hemistich—accented on the third and sixth syllables and followed by a pause—whereas the second follows looser Spanish syllabic rules.

15. My reading here is indebted to insights by Barry McCrea and Thangam Ravindranathan.

16. These blows are a repetition of the "golpes" of *Los heraldos negros,* when Vallejo still had faith that poetry might not be able to say something directly, yet could convey it indirectly. As Tamara Kamenszain signals, "that foundational first line will return blow-by-blow in all of Vallejo's poetry: life delivers blows in the space between the most impersonal ("hay," there are) and most personal ("yo no sé," I don't know), punching holes in the calcification of sense" (350).

17. In these same years, Vallejo toyed with the idea of writing a poem that would simply announce his current state of health and personal affairs (*ERC* 531)—a "defetishization" of lyric language as Rowe puts it ("César" 182), denying poetry any kind of transcendence.

18. This personal insertion was an afterthought; the first version referred to a prison in Madagascar.

19. Juan José Saer's "imaginary treatise," *El río sin orillas* (The River without Banks), offers a version of this point in its fourth section, cast as a response to Adorno's question of how to write poetry after Auschwitz. The pivotal scene hinges on a paradoxically vicarious form of subjectivity experienced by the speaker as he watches an indigent local woman wade in a river; feeling her sensations in his own body, he develops a sense of sympathy or empathy at a distance, or better, a telepathy, which does not merge their subjectivities—the woman remains radically other in terms of gender, class, and race—but prompts an experience of bodily parallels.

20. Another poem that builds directly on a Christian formula is "Traspié entre dos estrellas," whose structure plays on the Beatitudes (see Paoli 51–82).

21. This gesture takes place in a poem that alludes to the larger question of postcolonial speech, as the speaker admits that he suffers "del lenguaje directo del león" (from the direct language of the lion), which Darío's politicized symbolism had made coterminous with Spanish. Yet the poet also manages to speak through that former master's voice, by seizing on a shared cultural tradition.

The poem's final line, with its mock-epic "sonriendo de mis labios" (smiling from my lips), alludes to the tautologically physical language of emotion of medieval Spanish epics such as the *Poem of the Cid* (e.g., the formula "llorando de sus ojos"; crying from his eyes), and thereby finds a way to bring emotion back to the body. What makes this more complicated is that the metropolitan context in which Vallejo speaks is mismatched: France rather than Spain. He thus speaks from a position of double marginality, writing back to the wrong empire in the language of another colonial master, speaking a language still marginalized in official Western discourse, which, as Molloy argues (372), is endemic to the situation of the Latin American writer.

22. This sudden separation of bodies—or better, hierarchization of the poet's voice and the other's body—seems connected to the poet's fall into thought, whose abstraction (as we will see in the poem "Un hombre pasa. . ."; A Man Walks By . . .) risks alienating the poet from his own physicality: "de tanto pensar no tengo boca"; from so much thinking I have no mouth ("Viniere el malo . . . "; Were the Evil One to Come . . .).

23. The best-known argument for radical lyric subjectivity as a dialectical engagement with the world is of course Theodor Adorno's "Lyric Poetry and Society," but the question has also been raised from more concretely historical angles; see, for example, Alan Filreis's analysis of Wallace Stevens's unsuspected wavering between modernism and social poetry, or Luis García Montero's introduction to the collection *Hace falta estar ciego* (One Needs to Be Blind), which insists that any assertion of autonomy is necessarily grounded in a sense of the poet's own historicity and of the genre's shifting historical place (1–21).

24. I am alluding here to Simon Jarvis's useful paraphrase of Schopenhauer's notion of "blurting-out": "a moment at which a loss of control over a language which it is precisely the poet's art to master, to turn into an instrument, appears to testify to some specific emotional or intellectual (and necessarily and quite trivially material, historical and particular) pressure which makes that instrumentalism break down" (8).

25. Jarvis foregrounds Wordsworth's attempts to expand materialist thinking's economistic framework by incorporating subjectivity in its various modes of expression: need, desire, pleasure (4–5). The same thought underlies Vallejo's rejection of Gide's call for a cancellation of need and suffering, on the basis that these were necessary components of human experience (*ERC* 471).

26. The most notorious Latin American example of such a representational poetics is Neruda's *Canto general* (1950), which assures exterminated indigenous populations that the poet comes "a hablar por vuestra boca muerta" (to speak through your dead mouth), and convokes them, impossibly, to speak through him: "Acudid a mis venas y a mi boca. / Hablad por mis palabras y por mi sangre" (Come to my veins and my mouth. / Speak through my words and my blood).

27. Cornejo Polar addresses this question from the angle of ethnic rather than universalist politics, arguing that the first generation of indigenists—his examples include Vallejo and Mariátegui—necessarily found themselves in the position of writing for those who could not read them.

28. Vallejo in fact did all in his power to find a job at a factory during his

early years in Paris, as he insisted in a 1924 letter that underlined his repugnance for lyric bohemia (CC 72).

29. This conjoined figure reaches back to the poem "Ágape," from *Los heraldos negros,* which cast the poet on his doorstep advertising his offerings to passersby; in the Paris poetry, by contrast, the poet no longer has anything to offer.

30. As Paoli notes (22), the poem anticipates Brecht's 1949 "An die Nachgeborenen" (To Posterity): "Was sind das für Zeiten, wo / ein Gespräch über Bäume fast ein Verbrechen ist / weil es ein Schweigen über so viele Untaten einschließt!" (Ah what an age it is / when to speak about trees is almost a crime / For it is a kind of silence about injustice! [trans. H. R. Hays]). Vallejo's target here, however, is manifestly professional artistic languages rather than everyday language.

31. The poem may be familiar to readers from a different context. In an article under the poem's title in the *New Left Review* in 2002, Efrain Kristal responded to Franco Moretti's novel-based account of international literary history by drawing attention to the understudied role of poetry as a carrier of culture. After mapping out the importance of poetry in nation- and continent-building discourses in Latin America, Kristal drew attention to the unsuspected influence of Vallejo's poetry—and this poem in particular—on one of the central texts of late European modernism, Beckett's *Waiting for Godot.* I would add, however, that the traces of Vallejo's poem in Lucky's speech (sidelined, unattended to, hysterical) suggest not the centrality of poetry but its continuing marginality, now understood positively as a mad discourse that interrupts and punctuates but remains outside narrative, theatrical, or theoretical inquiries into history and the human.

32. Although this squares with Vallejo's Marxist reading of the imperfect human, and with his many Paris chronicles on the criminal justice system, it actually predates his immersion in Marxism by several years. And the question of a conjoined criminal and social justice system, for Vallejo, needed to situate itself beyond ideology; hence in a late 1927 article, which notes the widespread outcry through the West at the execution of Sacco and Vanzetti, he draws attention to the cases of those who have no party affiliation and whose plight therefore goes unregistered.

33. Michael Palmer describes the lyric deconstruction of an extraliterary code as a "politics that *inheres,*" as opposed to a more practical but less complex political poetry; his respective examples for these two modes are Vallejo and Neruda. "Politics seems a realm of power and persuasion that would like to subsume poetry (and science, and fashion, and . . .) under its mantle, for whatever noble or base motives. Yet if poetry is to function—politically—with integrity, it must resist such appeals as certainly as it resists others. . . . Poetry is profoundly mediational and relative and exists as a form of address singularly difficult to prescribe or define" (643).

34. Jonathan Culler ("Why Lyric?") attacks the critical attempt to deduce the situation of the lyric subject, arguing that this quasi-autobiography leads us to miss questions of intertextuality. But in some of Vallejo's late poems, which adopt voices at variance with what we expect from the lyric subject, it is only

by imagining a situation for the speaker that we can explain his peculiar use of language, pinpointing the ways in which he is drawing upon different reservoirs of discourse.

35. Vallejo's lyric analysis here differs importantly from contemporaneous essays by Benjamin and Kracauer: where their target, for pressing historical reasons, is fascist politics, Vallejo's critique of parliamentary democracy—before his immersion in Marxism—is inordinately prescient.

36. This last figure also takes us back to the first poem of Vallejo's first collection, "Los heraldos negros," where the repeated adjective "el hombre, pobre, pobre!" (poor, poor man!) was a marker of existential pathos and of the poet's affective response.

37. As Manfred Engelbert suggested to me, however, this is also a *performance* of a dialectic, caught in constant forward movement, never resting on its laurels.

38. Dianna Niebylski (19) contends that metonymy becomes a crucial structural principle in Vallejo's late poetry; as this book's underlying argument should make clear, however, this is the case through all stages of his writing. What marks the difference between the earlier and later poetry, as Franco signaled, is Vallejo's new focus on the individual as a member of a collective, although what complicates this still further, I would argue, is his intermittent focus on the division between the poet and his fellow modern citizens.

39. We might also consider the procedure in light of Dada sound poetry, and in particular, Hugo Ball's "confession" that on performing his nonsense verses onstage at the Cabaret Voltaire while dressed as a "magic bishop," his determination to banish any meaning from his utterances was undercut by his growing feeling that he was ceremoniously "intoning" the words, giving the performance a mystical aura for audience and performer alike (70–71).

40. Interestingly, this poem reworks and empties out a sonnet by the Spanish Golden Age poet Lope de Vega, "Desmayarse, atreverse, estar furioso" (To faint, to dare, to be furious), whose adjectives and verbs were connected by the practice of love: "esto es amor: quien lo probó lo sabe" (this is love; he who has known it knows it).

41. I offer "anxiety" here in place of Eshleman's "yearning."

42. Blaise Cendrars, from *Panama, Or the Adventures of My Seven Uncles* (1918).

43. Translations are taken from *Spain in Our Hearts*, trans. Donald D. Walsh (New Directions, 2005).

44. Andrés Trapiello repeats Larrea's account of some tension between Neruda and Vallejo in these years, centering on the question of commitment; while Neruda's newfound interest in politics led him to raise his voice quite dramatically in poetry and in public, Vallejo—who had been studying Marxism for at least eight years when the Spanish Civil War broke out—retained his usual moderation and reflectiveness (354). This contrast in modes is equally apparent in their poetry.

45. Vallejo's letters from the period show a suddenly more active interest in bringing himself up to date with the current political situation at home, whereas

his most recent articles—before the outbreak of war in Spain—had focused on the pre-Columbian past.

46. Vallejo does not mention it here, but aside from their bodily action, fighters for Spain were also producing their own literary responses to the event, and from an inordinately provocative antinationalist position; if Spain's past was the province of Franco's Nationalists, the Republican resistance managed to draw on its cultural tradition in the form of the ballad, producing hundreds of *romances* circulated as flyers and from mouth to mouth along the trenches.

47. For an in-depth consideration of orality in the collection, see Buxó, "Vallejo"; conversely, Jrade ("César Vallejo's *España*") offers a fascinating account of the figure of writing in the sequence.

48. Several of the most perceptive critical readings of *España* . . . have focused on Vallejo's continuing play with oral forms; see in particular Buxó, "Vallejo"; and Ortega, "Proceso".

49. As Lambie ("Intellectuals") convincingly argues, however, the issues Vallejo raises in the collection have a rigorously historical grounding in fractures on the Spanish left from 1936 through mid-1937.

50. Buxó (*César*) reads this poem as an "anti-poetics," pointing to the triumph in it of life over literature, of ethics over aesthetics, although he does not acknowledge that that triumph is only given shape—and a shifting, illusory shape at that—through the mediation of literary form. He also shows a reluctance to grant any place in this poem to ephemeral or bathetic moments of the everyday life supposedly being championed; thus he suggests that Higgins's connection of the onion in stanza 2 with cooking is an example of the kind of problematic "free association" generated by Vallejo's poetry—despite the several other references to kitchen items in the poem, such as "conserva" (jam/pickle) and, indeed, "laurel," which is also a humble bay leaf.

CONCLUSION

1. These lines do in fact form the epigraph to a slightly earlier novel by the Argentinean Ricardo Piglia, *Respiración artificial* (Artificial Respiration) (1980).

Bibliography

WORKS BY CÉSAR VALLEJO

Artículos y crónicas completas. 2 vols. Ed. Jorge Puccinelli. Lima: Pontificia Universidad Católica del Perú, 2002. Abbreviated as *ACC.*

Correspondencia completa. Ed. Jesús Cabel. Lima: Pontificia Universidad Católica del Perú, 2002. Abbreviated as *CC.*

Ensayos y reportajes completos. Ed. Manuel Miguel de Priego. Lima: Pontificia Universidad Católica del Perú, 2002. Abbreviated as *ERC.*

Poesía completa. 4 vols. Ed. Ricardo Silva-Santisteban. Lima: Pontificia Universidad Católica del Perú, 1997.

Narrativa completa. Ed. Antonio Merino. Madrid: Akal, 2007.

Teatro completo. 2 vols. Ed. Enrique Ballón Aguirre. Lima: Pontificia Universidad Católica del Perú, 1979.

Trilce. Ed. Julio Ortega. Madrid: Cátedra, 1993.

TRANSLATIONS

The Complete Poetry: A Bilingual Edition. Ed. and trans. Clayton Eshleman. Berkeley: University of California Press, 2007. Abbreviated as *CE.*

Trilce. Ed. and trans. Michael Smith and Valentino Gianuzzi. Exeter: Shearsman Books, 2005.

Trilce [Homophonic Translation]. Trans. James Wagner. New York: Calamari Press, 2005.

WORKS CITED

Adorno, Theodor. "Lyric Poetry and Society" [1957]. *Notes to Literature* I. Ed. Rolf Tiedemann. Trans. Shierry Weber Nicholson. New York: Columbia University Press, 1991. 37–54.

Agamben, Giorgio. *Infancy and History: The Destruction of Experience*. Trans. Liz Heron. London: Verso Books, 1993.

———. *Stanzas: Word and Phantasm in Western Culture*. Trans. Ronald L. Martínez. Minneapolis: University of Minnesota Press, 1993.

Aguilar, Gonzalo. "El lugar de Latinoamérica en la teoría de la vanguardia." *Fronteras literarias en la literatura latinoamericana*. Buenos Aires: Instituto de Literatura Hispanoamericana, 1996. 111–20.

Alonso, Carlos. *The Burden of Modernity*. Oxford: Oxford University Press, 1998.

Althusser, Louis. "Ideology and Ideological State Apparatuses." *Lenin and Philosophy and Other Essays*. Trans. Ben Brewster. New York: Monthly Review Press, 1971. 127–86.

Apollonio, Umbro, ed. *Futurist Manifestos*. Boston: MFA Publications, 2001.

Aquézolo Castro, Manuel, ed. *La polémica del indigenismo*. Lima: Mosca Azul, 1988.

Arguedas, Alcides. *Etapas de la vida de un escritor*. La Paz, 1963.

———. *Raza de bronce*. Buenos Aires: Losada, 1945 [1919].

Arguedas, José María. *El zorro de arriba y el zorro de abajo*. Ed. Eve-Marie Fell. Nanterre: Colección Archivos, 1990 [1969].

———. "Entre el quechua y el castellano." *Aproximaciones a César Vallejo*. Ed. Angel Flores. New York: Las Américas, 1975. 187–88.

———. *The Fox from Up Above and the Fox from Down Below*. Ed. Julio Ortega. Trans. Frances Barraclough. Pittsburgh: Pittsburgh University Press, 2000.

———. "París y la patria." *Katatay* 1:1–2 (June 2005): 168–71.

Armstrong, Tim. *Modernism, Technology, and the Body*. Cambridge: Cambridge University Press, 1998.

Arroyo Reyes, Carlos. "Abraham Valdelomar y el movimiento colonidista." *Cuadernos hispanoamericanos* 557 (1996): 83–95.

Attridge, Derek. *Poetic Rhythm: An Introduction*. Cambridge: Cambridge University Press, 1996.

Baker, George. *The Artwork Caught by the Tail: Francis Picabia and Dada in Paris*. Cambridge: MIT Press, 2007.

Bakhtin, Mikhail. *Rabelais and His World*. Trans. Helene Iswolsky. Bloomington: Indiana University Press, 1984.

———. *Speech Genres and Other Late Essays*. Trans. Vern McGee. Ed. Caryl Emerson and Michael Holquist. Austin: University of Texas Press, 1996.

Ball, Hugo. *Flight Out of Time: A Dada Diary*. Trans. Ann Raimes. Ed. John Elderfield. New York: Viking, 1974.

Ballón Aguirre, Enrique. "La escritura poetológica: César Vallejo, cronista." *Lexis* 6:1 (1982): 57–98.

Barthes, Roland. *The Grain of the Voice*. Trans. Linda Coverdale. New York: Hill & Wang, 1985.

———. *A Lover's Discourse—Fragments*. Trans. Richard Howard. New York: Hill & Wang, 1994.

———. *The Pleasure of the Text*. Trans. Richard Howard. New York: Farrar, Straus & Giroux, 1975.

————. *Sade, Fourier, Loyola.* Trans. Richard Miller. Baltimore: Johns Hopkins University Press, 1997.

Bary, Leslie. "Counterhegemonic Subjectivities in Cesar Vallejo and Oswald de Andrade." *Modernism and Its Margins.* Ed. Anthony Geist and José Monleón. New York: Garland, 1999. 215–27.

Basadre, Jorge. *Equivocaciones: ensayos sobre literatura penúltima.* Lima: Librería Studium, 1988 [1928].

Bataille, Georges. *Visions of Excess: Selected Writings, 1927–1939.* Trans. Alan Stoekl. Minneapolis: University of Minnesota Press, 2001.

Bazán, Armando. *César Vallejo: dolor y poesía.* Buenos Aires: Mundo America, 1958.

Baudelaire, Charles. *Selected Writings on Art and Literature.* Trans. P. E. Charvet. New York: Penguin, 1993.

Benjamin, Walter. "Surrealism. The Last Snapshot of the European Intelligentsia" [1929]. *Selected Writings.* Vol. 2: 1927–34. Ed. Michael Jennings, Howard Eiland, and Gary Smith. Cambridge, MA: Harvard University Press, 1999. 207–21.

————. "The Author as Producer." *Selected Writings.* Vol. 2: 1927–34. Ed. Michael Jennings, Howard Eiling, and Gary Smith. Cambridge, MA: Belknap Press, 1999. 768–83.

————. *The Origin of German Tragic Drama.* Trans. John Osborne. London: Verso, 1998.

————. "The Storyteller: Observations on the Work of Nikolai Leskov." *Selected Writings.* Vol. 3: 1935–38. Ed. Howard Eilings and Michael W. Jennings. Cambridge, MA: Belknap Press, 2006. 143–66.

————. "The Work of Art in the Age of Its Technological Reproducibility." *Selected Writings.* Vol. 3: 1935–38. Ed. Howard Eilings and Michael W. Jennings. Cambridge, MA: Belknap Press, 2006. 101–33.

————. *The Writer of Modern Life: Essays on Charles Baudelaire.* Ed. Michael Jennings. Cambridge, MA: Belknap Press, 2006.

————. "The Writer's Technique in Thirteen Theses" [1928]. *One-Way Street and Other Writings.* Trans. Edmund Jephcott and Kingsley Shorter. Verso: London, 1992. 458–59.

Berman, Marshall. *All That Is Solid Melts into Air.* New York: Penguin, 1988.

Bernabé, Mónica. *Vidas de artista: bohemia y dandismo en Mariátegui, Valdelomar y Eguren (1911–1922).* Rosario: Beatriz Viterbo; Lima: Instituto de Estudios Peruanos, 2006.

Beutler, Gisela, and Alejandro Losada, eds. *César Vallejo: Actas del Coloquio Internacional Freie Universität Berlin, 1979.* Tübingen: Niemeyer, 1981.

Birkenmaier, Anke. *Alejo Carpentier y la cultura del surrealismo en América Latina.* Madrid: Iberoamericana; Frankfurt: Vervuert, 2006.

Bolaño, Roberto. *Monsieur Pain.* Barcelona: Anagrama, 1999.

Bonilla, Heraclio. *Un siglo a la deriva: ensayos sobre el Perú, Bolivia y la guerra.* Lima: Instituto de Estudios Peruanos, 1980.

Brassai. *The Secret Paris of the 30s.* Trans. Richard Miller. New York: Pantheon, 1976.

Bürger, Peter. *The Theory of the Avant-Garde*. Trans. Michael Shaw. Minneapolis: University of Minnesota Press, 1984.

Butler, Judith. *Bodies That Matter*. New York: Routledge, 1993.

Buxó, José Pascual. *César Vallejo: crítica y contracrítica*. Mexico: UNAM, 1992.

———. "Vallejo: el estatuto oral de la epopeya." *Hispania* 72:1 (March 1989): 65–72.

Cadava, Eduardo. "The Guano of History." *Cities without Citizens*. Ed. Eduardo Cadava and Aaron Levy. Philadelphia: Slought Books, 2003. 137–65.

Carrasco, Lawrence. *Las ideas estéticas de César Vallejo*. Lima: Fondo Editorial del Pedagógico San Marcos, 2005.

Casanova, Pascale. "Literature as a World." *New Left Review* 31 (January–February 2005): 71–90.

———. *Samuel Beckett: Anatomy of a Literary Revolution*. Trans. Gregory Elliott. London: Verso, 2006.

———. *The World Republic of Letters*. Trans. M. B. deBevoise. Cambridge, MA: Harvard University Press, 2004.

Cerna Bazán, José. *Sujeto a cambio*. Lima: Latinoamericana Editores, 1995.

Certeau, Michel de. *Heterologies: Discourse on the Other*. Trans. Brian Massumi. Minneapolis: University of Minnesota Press, 1986.

Chang-Rodríguez, Eugenio. "Las crónicas posmodernistas de César Vallejo." *Inti* 36 (1992): 11–22.

Chaplin, Charles. *Charlie Chaplin: Interviews*. Ed. Kevin Hayes. Jackson: University of Mississippi Press, 2005.

Chion, Michel. *The Voice in Cinema*. Ed. and trans. Claudia Gorbman. New York: Columbia University Press, 1999.

Chocano, José Santos. *Poesía*. Ed. Luis Alberto Sánchez. Lima: Universidad Nacional Mayor de San Marcos, 1959.

Cisneros, Luis Jaime. "Una lanza por Vallejo, *chroniqueur*." *Intensidad y altura de César Vallejo*. Ed. Ricardo González Vigil. Lima: Pontificia Universidad Católica del Perú, 1993. 17–29.

Clayton, Michelle. "Mariátegui y la escena contemporánea." *José Carlos Mariátegui y los estudios latinoamericanos*. Ed. Mabel Moraña and Guido Podestá. Serie Críticas. Pittsburgh: IILI Press, 2009. 231–54.

———. "*Trilce*'s Lyric Matters." *Revista de estudios hispánicos* 42:1 (January 2008): 83–107.

Colónida: Edición facsimilar. Lima: Ediciones Copé, 1981.

Conway, Christopher. "El aparecido azteca: Ignacio Manuel Altamirano en el necronacionalismo mexicano, 1893." *Revista de crítica literaria latinoamericana* 31:62 (2005): 125–42.

Córdoba Vargas, Juan Domingo. *César Vallejo del Perú profundo y sacrificado*. Lima: Campodónico, 1995.

Cornejo Polar, Antonio. *Escribir en el aire: ensayo sobre la heterogeneidad cultural en las literaturas andinas*. Lima: Latinoamericana Editores, 2003.

Cornejo Polar, Jorge, and Carlos Iván Degregori, eds. *Vallejo: su tiempo y su obra. Actas del Coloquio Internacional: Universidad de Lima, agosto 25–28 de 1992*. 2 vols. Lima: Universidad de Lima, 1994.

La coronación de José Santos Chocano. Lima, 1922.

Coronado, Jorge. *The Andes Imagined: Indigenismo, Society, and Modernity.* Pittsburgh: University of Pittsburgh Press, 2009.

Cortázar, Julio. "Carta abierta a Roberto Fernández Retamar" [1967]. *Obras críticas.* Buenos Aires: Alfaguara, 1994. III:29–43.

———. "Julio Cortázar: un gran escritor y su soledad." *Life en español,* 7 April 1969: 43–55.

Coviello, Peter. "Intimate Nationality: Anonymity and Attachment in Walt Whitman." *American Literature* 73:1 (March 2001): 85–119.

Coyné, André. *César Vallejo.* Buenos Aires: Nueva Visión, 1968.

———. *Medio siglo con César Vallejo.* Lima: Pontificia Universidad Católica del Perú, 1999.

Culler, Jonathan. *The Pursuit of Signs.* Ithaca: Cornell University Press, 1981.

———. "Why Lyric?" *PMLA* 123:1 (January 2008): 201–6.

Cussen, Antonio. *Bello and Bolívar: Poetry and Politics in the Spanish American Revolution.* Cambridge: Cambridge University Press, 1992.

Damon, Maria, and Ira Livingston. *Poetry and Cultural Studies: A Reader.* Urbana: University of Illinois Press, 2009.

Davidson, Michael. *Ghostlier Demarcations: Modern Poetry and the Material World.* Berkeley: University of California Press, 1997.

Dawes, Greg. "Más allá de la vanguardia: teoría estética de César Vallejo." *Revista de crítica literaria latinoamericana* 32:63–64 (2006): 67–85.

Deleuze, Gilles. *Essays Critical and Clinical.* Trans. Daniel W. Smith and Michael A. Greco. Minneapolis: University of Minnesota Press, 1997.

De Man, Paul. *Blindness and Insight: Essays in the Rhetoric of Contemporary Criticism.* Minneapolis: University of Minnesota Press, 1971.

Derrida, Jacques. "'Eating Well,' or The Calculation of the Subject." In *Points . . . : Interviews, 1974–94.* Ed. Elisabeth Weber. Trans. Peggy Kamuf et al. Stanford: Stanford University Press, 1995. 255–87.

———. "White Mythology." *Margins of Philosophy.* Trans. Alan Bass. Chicago: University of Chicago Press, 1982. 207–72.

Dolar, Mladen. *A Voice and Nothing More.* Cambridge, MA: MIT Press, 2006.

Durling, Robert. "Deceit and Digestion in the Body of Hell." *Allegory and Representation.* Ed. Stephen Greenblatt. Baltimore: Johns Hopkins University Press, 1981. 61–93.

Edwards, Brent. "The Genres of Postcolonialism." *Social Text* 78:22 (Spring 2004): 1–15.

———. *The Practice of Diaspora: Literature, Translation, and the Rise of Black Internationalism.* Cambridge, MA: Harvard University Press, 2003.

Eisenstein, Sergei. *Film Form.* Trans. Jay Leyda. New York: Harcourt, 1977.

Ellmann, Richard. *James Joyce.* New York: Oxford University Press, 1982.

Escobar, Alberto. "Lecturas de Vallejo: mitificación y desmitificación." *César Vallejo: Actas del Coloquio Internacional Freie Universität Berlin, 1979.* Ed. Gisela Beutler and Alejandro Losada. Tübingen: Niemeyer, 1981. 19–40.

Espejo Asturrizaga, Juan. *César Vallejo: itinerario del hombre, 1892–1923.* Lima: Seglusa, 1989.

Fabre, Michel. *La rive noire: Les écrivains noirs américains à Paris, 1830–1955*. Marseille: A Dimanche, 1999.

Ferrari, Américo. "Sobre algunos procedimientos estructurales en los *Poemas humanos*." *En torno a César Vallejo*. Ed. Antonio Merino. Madrid: Júcar, 1988. 267–91.

Filreis, Alan. *Modernism from Right to Left: Wallace Stevens, the Thirties, and Literary Radicalism*. Cambridge: Cambridge University Press, 1994.

Flaubert, Gustave. *Letters* II. Ed. Francis Steegmuller. Cambridge, MA: Belknap Press, 1980.

Fló, Juan, and Stephen Hart, eds. *César Vallejo: autógrafos olvidados*. London: Tamesis; Lima: Pontificia Universidad Católica del Perú, 2003.

Forgues, Roland. *La espiga miliciana*. Lima: Horizonte, 1988.

———. "La utopía social de César Vallejo." *Perú en su cultura*. Ed. Daniel Castillo Durante. Lima: Prom Perú, 2001. 101–9.

Franco, Jean. *César Vallejo: The Dialectics of Poetry and Silence*. Cambridge: Cambridge University Press, 1976.

———. *Critical Passions: Selected Essays*. Ed. Kathleen Newman and Mary Louise Pratt. Durham: Duke University Press, 1999.

French, Jennifer. *Nature, Neocolonialism, and the Spanish American Regional Writers*. Dartmouth: University Press of New England, 2005.

Freud, Sigmund. *General Psychological Theory*. New York: Touchstone, 1991.

Gallo, Rubén. *Mexican Modernity: The Avant-Garde and the Technological Revolution*. Cambridge, MA: MIT Press, 2005.

García Montero, Luis. Prologue. *Hace falta estar ciego: poéticas del compromiso para el siglo XXI*. Ed. José M. Mariscal and Carlos Prado. Madrid: Visor, 2003.

Girondo, Oliverio. "Carta abierta a *La Púa*" and *Veinte poemas para ser leídos en el tranvía* [1922]. *Obra completa*. Ed. Raúl Antelo. Madrid: Archivos, 1999.

Gluck, Mary. *Popular Bohemia: Modernism and Urban Culture in Nineteenth-Century Paris*. Cambridge, MA: Harvard University Press, 2005.

Gómez Carrillo, Enrique. *Treinta años de mi vida*. Guatemala: Editorial José de Pineda Ibarra, 1974.

González, Aníbal. *La crónica modernista hispanoamericana*. Madrid: Porrúa, 1983.

González Echevarría, Roberto. "Modernidad, modernismo y nueva narrativa." *Revista interamericana de bibliografía* 30 (1980): 157–63.

———. *Myth and Archive: A Theory of Latin American Narrative*. Cambridge: Cambridge University Press, 1990.

González Prada, Alfredo. "Carta acerca de Abraham Valdelomar y el movimiento *Colónida* (11/26/1949)." *Colónida: edición facsimilar*. Lima: Ediciones Copé, 1981.

González Prada, Manuel. *Free Pages and Other Essays: Anarchist Musings*. Trans. Frederick H. Fornoff. Oxford: Oxford University Press, 2003.

———. *Pájinas libres*. Ed. Luis Alberto Sánchez. Lima: PTCM, 1946.

———. "La poesía" (1902). *Obras*. Lima: Ediciones Copé, 1985. I:333–44.

Gootenberg, Paul. *Imagining Development: Economic Ideas in Peru's "Ficti-*

tious Prosperity" of Guano, 1840–1880. Berkeley: University of California Press, 1993.

Gumbrecht, Hans Ulrich. *In 1926: Living at the Edge of Time.* Cambridge, MA: Harvard University Press, 1997.

Gunning, Tom. "Modernity and Cinema: A Culture of Shocks and Flows." *Cinema and Modernity.* Ed. Murray Pomerance. New Brunswick: Rutgers University Press, 2006. 297–315.

———. "'The Whole World within Reach': Travel Images without Borders." *Virtual Voyages: Cinema and Travel.* Ed. Jeffrey Ruoff. Durham: Duke University Press, 2006. 25–41.

Gutiérrez Girardot, Rafael. *Modernismo: supuestos históricos y culturales.* Mexico: Fondo de Cultura Económica, 1988.

Harrington, Joseph. *Poetry and the Public Sphere: The Social Form of Modern U.S. Poetics.* Middletown: Wesleyan University Press, 2002.

Hart, Stephen. "César Vallejo: 'chchascapca nanain' (dolor de una estrella)." *Vallejo: su tiempo y su obra. Actas del Coloquio Internacional, Universidad de Lima, agosto 25–28 de 1992.* Ed. Jorge Cornejo Polar and Carlos Iván Degregori. Lima: Universidad de Lima, 1994. II:152–61.

———. "The Chronology of César Vallejo's *Poemas Humanos:* New Light on the Old Problem." *Modern Language Review* 97:3 (July 2002): 602–19.

———. "Chronology of Vallejo's Life and Works." *The Complete Poetry: A Bilingual Edition.* Ed. and trans. Clayton Eshleman. Berkeley: University of California Press, 2007. 689–703.

———. *Stumbling between 46 Stars.* London: Centre of Vallejo Studies, 2007.

———. "Vallejo in Between: Postcolonial Identity in *Poemas Humanos.*" *Romance Studies* 19:1 (June 2001): 17–27.

———. "Was Vallejo Guilty as Charged?" *Latin American Literary Review* 26: 51 (1998): 79–89.

Hart, Stephen, and Jorge Cornejo Polar. *César Vallejo: A Critical Bibliography of Research.* London: Boydell & Brewer, 2002.

Henighan, Stephen. *Assuming the Light: The Parisian Literary Apprenticeship of Miguel Ángel Asturias.* Oxford: Legenda, 1999.

Hills, Elijah Clarence, ed. *The Odes of Bello, Olmedo, and Heredia.* New York: Putnam & Sons, 1920.

Irby, James E. "Visions of the Heroic: Martí, Darío, Mistral." *Studies in Honor of Enrique Anderson Imbert.* Ed. Nancy Abraham Hall and Lanin A. Gyurko. Newark: Juan de la Cuesta, 2003. 141–61.

Jameson, Fredric. "Modernism and Imperialism." *Nationalism, Colonialism, and Literature.* Ed. Seamus Deane. Minneapolis: University of Minnesota Press, 1990. 43–66.

———. *The Modernist Papers.* London: Verso, 2007.

Jarvis, Simon. *Wordsworth's Philosophic Song.* New York: Cambridge University Press, 2007.

Jitrik, Noe. *Las contradicciones del modernismo: productividad poética y situación sociológica.* Mexico: El Colegio de Mexico, 1978.

Joyce, James. *Finnegans Wake.* London: Penguin, 1976.

———. *Ulysses.* New York: Vintage, 1986.

Jrade, Cathy L. "César Vallejo's *España, aparta de mí este cáliz:* The Struggle between Two Modes of Discourse." *Hispanic Journal* 18 (Spring 1997): 125–34.

———. *Modernismo, Modernity, and the Quest for Spanish American Literature.* Austin: University of Texas Press, 1998.

Kaempfer, Alvaro. "Economías de redención: 'La agricultura de la zona tórrida' (1826), de Andrés Bello." *Modern Language Notes* 122 (2007): 272–93.

Kahn, Douglas. *Noise, Water, Meat: A History of Sound in the Arts.* Cambridge, MA: MIT Press, 1999.

Kamenszain, Tamara. "To Attest by Oxymoron: The César Vallejo Case." Trans. Mónica de la Torre. *Review: Literature and Art of the Americas* 40:2 (2007): 349–53.

Kaufman, Robert. "Adorno's Social Lyric, and Literary Criticism Today: Poetics, Aesthetics, Modernity." *The Cambridge Companion to Adorno.* Ed. Tom Kuhn. Cambridge: Cambridge University Press, 2004. 354–75.

———. "Marx against Theory (Much Ado about Nothing—And Poetry)." Forthcoming.

Keizer, Garret. "Specific Suggestion: General Strike." *Harper's Magazine,* October 2007.

Kenner, Hugh. *The Pound Era.* Berkeley: University of California Press, 1971.

Kern, Stephen. *The Culture of Time and Space, 1880–1913.* Cambridge, MA: Harvard University Press, 1983.

Kirkpatrick, Gwen. *The Dissonant Legacy of Modernismo.* Berkeley: University of California Press, 1989.

———. "Poetic Exchange and Epic Landscapes in Nineteenth-Century Latin America." *Literary Cultures of Latin America: A Comparative History.* Ed. Djelal Kadir and Mario Valdés. Oxford: Oxford University Press, 2004. 173–87.

Klein, Jean-Claude. "Borrowing, Syncretism, Hybridisation: The Parisian Revue of the 1920s." Trans. J. Barrie Jones. *Popular Music* 5 (1985): 175–87.

Kleist, Heinrich von. "On the Gradual Production of Thoughts Whilst Speaking." *Selected Writings.* Ed. and trans. David Constantine. London: Dent, 1997. 405–9.

Kracauer, Siegfried. *The Mass Ornament.* Trans. Thomas Levin. Cambridge, MA: Harvard University Press, 2005.

Krauss, Rosalind. *The Originality of the Avant-Garde and Other Modernist Myths.* Cambridge, MA: MIT Press, 1986.

Kristal, Efrain. "'Considering Coldly . . .': A Response to Franco Moretti." *New Left Review* 15 (May–June 2002): 61–74.

Kuhnheim, Jill. *Spanish American Poetry at the End of the Twentieth Century.* Austin: University of Texas Press, 2004.

Lambie, George. "Intellectuals, Ideology and Revolution: The Political Ideas of César Vallejo." *Hispanic Research Journal* 1:2 (June 2000): 139–69.

———. "Vallejo and the End of History." *Romance Quarterly* 49:2 (Spring 2002): 126–43.

Laporte, Dominique. *History of Shit.* Trans. Nadia Benabid and Rodolphe el-Khoury. Cambridge, MA: MIT Press, 2000.

Lauer, Mirko. *La polémica del vanguardismo, 1916–28*. Lima: Universidad Nacional Mayor de San Marcos, 2001.

———. *Musa mecánica: máquinas y poesía en la vanguardia peruana*. Lima: Instituto de Estudios Peruanos, 2003.

———, ed. *Nueve libros vanguardistas*. Lima: Virrey, 2001.

Las voces múltiples. Lima: E. Rosay, 1916.

Lloyd, David. *Anomalous States: Irish Writing and the Post-Colonial Moment*. Durham: Duke University Press, 1993.

———. "Rethinking National Marxism: James Connolly and 'Celtic Communism.'" *Interventions* 5:3 (August 2003): 345–70.

López Lenci, Yasmín. *El laboratorio de la vanguardia literaria en el Perú*. Lima: Horizonte, 1999.

Lora, Juan José. "El dadaísmo y sus representantes en el Perú." *El Comercio*, 20 June 1921: 6–7.

Loureiro, Angel. *The Ethics of Autobiography*. Nashville: Vanderbilt University Press, 2000.

Loy, Mina. *The Lost Lunar Baedeker*. Ed. Roger L. Conover. New York: Farrar, Straus & Giroux, 1997.

Mariátegui, José Carlos. *El artista y la época*. Lima: Amauta, 1959.

———. *Correspondencia, 1915–30*. 2 vols. Ed. Antonio Melis. Lima: Editorial Amauta, 1984.

———. *Peruanicemos al Perú*. Lima: Amauta, 1970.

———. *Seven Interpretive Essays on Peruvian Reality*. Trans. Marjory Urquidi. Austin: University of Texas Press, 1971.

———. *Siete ensayos de interpretación de la realidad peruana*. Lima: Amauta, 1971 [1928].

Masiello, Francine. "La naturaleza de la poesía." *Revista de crítica literaria latinoamericana*, 29:58 (2003): 57–77.

Mazzotti, José Antonio. "Hacia una lectura sociocrítica de *Trilce*." *Sociocriticism* 6:11–12 (1990): 149–75.

———. "Modernismo, posmodernismo y modernidad conflictiva en el primer Vallejo." *Códice* 1 (1999): 23–31.

McCabe, Susan. *Cinematic Modernism*. Cambridge: Cambridge University Press, 2005.

McDuffie, Keith. "Rescuing the Future: César Vallejo and Postcolonial Thought." *Romance Quarterly* 49:2 (Spring 2002): 144–60.

Middendorff, E. W. *Perú: observaciones y estudios del país y sus habitantes durante una permanencia de veinticinco años*. Vol. 2: *La costa*. Trans. Ernesto More. Lima: Universidad Nacional Mayor de San Marcos, 1973.

Miller, Nicola. "To Interpret the World or to Change It? César Vallejo and the Role of the Intellectual." *Romance Quarterly* 49:3 (Summer 2002): 174–91.

———. "Vallejo, the Poetics of Dissent." *Bulletin of Hispanic Studies* 73:3 (1996): 299–321.

Molloy, Sylvia. "Postcolonial Latin America and the Magic Realist Imperative: A Report to an Academy." *Nation, Language, and the Ethics of Translation*. Ed. Sandra Bermann and Michael Wood. Princeton: Princeton University Press, 2005. 370–79.

Monroe, Jonathan. *A Poverty of Objects: The Prose Poem and the Politics of Genre.* Ithaca: Cornell University Press, 1987.

Monteleone, Jorge. "De los cisnes al pingüino (Baudelaire, Mallarmé, Darío y Lihn)." *Sesgos, cesuras, métodos.* Ed. Noe Jitrik. Buenos Aires: Eudeba, 2005. 37–44.

Moraña, Mabel. "Territorialidad y forasterismo: la polémica Arguedas/Cortázar revisitada." *José María Arguedas: hacia una poética migrante.* Ed. Sergio R. Franco. Pittsburgh: Instituto Internacional de Literatura Iberoamericana, 2006. 103–20.

More, Ernesto. *Vallejo, en la encrucijada del drama peruano.* Lima: Bendezú, 1968.

Moretti, Franco. "Conjectures on World Literature." *New Left Review* 1 (January–February 2000): 54–68.

Neruda, Pablo. *Spain in Our Hearts.* Trans. Donald D. Walsh. New York: New Directions, 2005.

"The New Lyric Studies." *PMLA* 123:1 (January 2008): 181–234.

Nicholls, Peter. *Modernisms: A Literary Guide.* Berkeley: University of California Press, 1995.

Niebylski, Dianna. "*Poemas humanos:* la afasia resuelta en un grito." *Vericuetos* 6 (1992): 14–24.

Nochlin, Linda. *The Body in Pieces.* New York: Thames & Hudson, 1994.

Noland. Carrie. *Poetry at Stake: Lyric Aesthetics and the Challenge of Technology.* Princeton: Princeton University Press, 1999.

North, Michael. *Machine-Age Comedy.* New York: Oxford University Press, 2008.

Núñez, Estuardo. *Las letras de Francia y el Perú.* Lima: Universidad Nacional Mayor de San Marcos, 1997.

———. "Vallejo y el Perú: los difíciles años treinta." *Intensidad y altura de César Vallejo.* Ed. Ricardo González Vigil. Lima: Pontificia Universidad Católica del Perú, 1993. 59–64.

Núñez, Estuardo, and Georg Petersen G. *El Perú en la obra de Alexander von Humboldt.* Peru: Librería Studium, 1971.

Orrego, Antenor. *Mi encuentro con César Vallejo.* Bogotá: Tercer Mundo, 1989.

———. "Palabras prologales." Alcides Spelucín, *El libro de la nave dorada.* Trujillo: Ediciones El Norte, 1926. 13–34.

Orrillo, Winston. *César Vallejo: periodista paradigmático.* Lima: Universidad Nacional Mayor de San Marcos, 1998.

Ortega, Julio. Prologue to critical edition of *Trilce.* Madrid: Cátedra, 1993.

———. *Teoría poética de César Vallejo.* Providence: Del Sol, 1986.

Ostria González, Mauricio. "La polémica Arguedas-Cortázar treinta años después." *Crisis, apocalipsis y utopías.* Ed. R. Canovas and R. Hozven. Santiago: Pontificia Universidad Católica de Chile, 2000. 423–28.

Palmer, Michael. "The Flower of Capital" [1979]. *Manifesto: A Century of Isms.* Ed. Mary Ann Caws. Lincoln: University of Nebraska Press, 2001. 642–44.

Paoli, Roberto. "España, aparta de mí este cáliz." *César Vallejo.* Ed. Julio Ortega. Madrid: Taurus, 1974. 347–72.

————. *Mapas anatómicos de César Vallejo*. Florence: d'Anna, 1981.

Paz, Octavio. *Los hijos del limo: del romanticismo a la vanguardia*. Barcelona: Seix Barral, 1974.

Perelman, Bob. *The Marginalization of Poetry: Language Writing and Literary History*. Princeton: Princeton University Press, 1996.

Pérez de Tudela, Rocío Oviedo. "La imagen diagonal: de lo cinemático en César Vallejo." *Anales de literatura hispanoamericana* 32 (2003): 53–70.

Perloff, Marjorie. *The Futurist Moment*. Chicago: University of Chicago Press, 1986.

Perus, Francoise. *Literatura y sociedad en América Latina*. Mexico: Siglo Veintiuno, 1976.

Piglia, Ricardo. *The Absent City*. Trans. Sergio Waisman. Durham: Duke University Press, 2000.

Podestá, Guido. *Desde Lutecia: anacronismo y modernidad en los escritos teatrales de César Vallejo*. Berkeley: Latinoamericana Editores, 1994.

Poggioli, Renato. *The Theory of the Avant-Garde*. Trans. Gerald Fitzgerald. New York: Harper & Row, 1971.

Poirier, Richard. *The Performing Self*. New Brunswick: Rutgers University Press, 1992.

Pratt, Mary Louise. *Imperial Eyes: Travel Writing and Transculturation*. London: Routledge, 1992.

Puccinelli, Jorge. "César Vallejo a través de sus artículos y crónicas." *ACC I*: xv–xl.

Puchner, Martin. *Poetry of the Revolution: Marx, Manifestos, and the Avant-Gardes*. Princeton: Princeton University Press, 2006.

Rama, Ángel. "Literature and Exile." *The Oxford Book of Latin American Essays*. Ed. Ilan Stavans. Oxford: Oxford University Press, 1998.

————. *Los poetas modernistas en el mercado económico*. Montevideo: Universidad de la República, 1968.

Ramazani, Jahan. *The Hybrid Muse: Postcolonial Poetry in English*. Chicago: University of Chicago Press, 2001.

Ramos, Julio. *Divergent Modernities: Culture and Politics in Nineteenth-Century Latin America*. Ed. and trans. John D. Blanco. Durham: Duke University Press, 2001.

Read, Justin. "Solar Currency: The Monetary Policy of Vallejo's *Trilce*." Forthcoming.

Reisz, Susana. "Entre el modermismo y las vanguardias: Dialogismo y polifonía anárquica en *Trilce* de César Vallejo." *¿Qué es el modernismo? Nuevas encuestas, nuevas lecturas*. Ed. Richard Cardwell and Bernard McGuirk. Boulder: Society of Spanish and Spanish-American Studies, 1993. 355–70.

————. *Teoría literaria: una propuesta*. Lima: Pontificia Universidad Católica del Perú, 1987.

Riley, Denise. *Words of Selves: Identification, Solidarity, Irony*. Stanford: Stanford University Press, 2000.

Rivero Ayllón, Teodoro. *Itinerario de un poeta alucinado: Vida y obra de Francisco Xandóval*. Trujillo: Trilce Editores, 1997.

Rosenberg, Fernando. *The Avant-Garde and Geopolitics in Latin America*. Pittsburgh: University of Pittsburgh Press, 2006.

Rothman, Roger I. "Between Music and the Machine: Francis Picabia and the End of Abstraction." *Tout-Fait: The Marcel Duchamp Studies Online Journal* 2:4 (January 2002): n.p.

Rotker, Susana. *The American Chronicles of José Martí: Journalism and Modernity in Spanish America.* Trans. Katherine Semmler and Jennifer French. Hanover: University Press of New England, 2000.

Rowe, William. "César Vallejo en París: las velocidades de lo moderno." *De márgenes y silencios: homenaje a Martin Lienhard.* Ed. Annina Cerlici and Marilia Mendes. Madrid: Iberoamericana; Frankfurt: Vervuert, 2006. 177–90.

———. *Ensayos vallejianos.* Berkeley: Latinoamericana, 2006.

———. *Hacia una poética radical.* Rosario: Beatriz Viterbo, 1996.

———. "When Was Peru Modern? On Declarations of Modernity in Peru." *When Was Latin America Modern?* Ed. Nicola Miller and Stephen Hart. New York: Palgrave, 2007. 121–45.

Saer, Juan José. *Cuentos completos (1957–2000).* Buenos Aires: Planeta, 2001.

———. *The Investigation.* Trans. Helen Lane. London: Serpent's Tail, 1999. [Translation of *La pesquisa.* Buenos Aires: Seix Barral, 1994.]

———. *El río sin orillas: Tratado imaginario.* Madrid: Alianza, 1991.

Said, Edward. *The World, the Text, and the Critic.* Cambridge, MA: Harvard University Press, 1983.

Salomon, Noël. "Algunos aspectos de lo 'humano' en *Poemas humanos.*" *Aproximaciones a César Vallejo.* Ed. Angel Flores. New York: Las Américas, 1975. II:191–230.

Sánchez, Luis Alberto, ed. *Chocano: poesía.* Lima: Universidad Nacional Mayor de San Marcos, 1959.

———. *Valdelomar o la belle époque.* Mexico: Fondo de Cultura Económica, 1969.

Sarlo, Beatriz. *Una modernidad periférica: Buenos Aires, 1920 y 1930.* Buenos Aires: Nueva Visión, 1988.

Scarry, Elaine. *The Body in Pain.* New York: Oxford University Press, 1985.

Schwartz, Jorge, ed. *Las vanguardias latinoamericanas: Textos programáticos y críticos.* Mexico: Fondo de Cultura Económica, 2002.

Schwartz, Marcy. *Writing Paris: Urban Topographies of Desire in Contemporary Latin American Fiction.* Albany: SUNY Press, 1999.

Sekula, Allan. *Fish Story.* Dusseldorf: Richter Verlag, 1995.

———. *Performance under Working Conditions.* Ed. Sabine Breitwieser. Vienna: Generali Foundation, 2003.

Sharman, Adam. "Semicolonial Times: Vallejo and the Discourse of Modernity." *Romance Quarterly* 49:3 (Summer 2002): 192–205.

———. *Tradition and Modernity in Spanish American Literature: From Darío to Carpentier.* New York: Palgrave, 2006.

Shattuck, Roger. *The Banquet Years.* New York: Random House, 1968.

Shotter, John. "Seeing Historically: Goethe and Vygotsky's 'Enabling-Theory Method.'" *Culture and Psychology* 6:2 (2000): 233–52.

Siegel, Jerrold. *Bohemian Paris: Culture, Politics, and the Boundaries of Bour-*

geois Life, 1830–1930. Baltimore: Johns Hopkins University Press, 1999.

Simmel, Georg. "The Metropolis and Mental Life" [1903]. The Sociology of Georg Simmel. Ed. and trans. Kurt Wolff. New York: Free Press, 1964.

Skaggs, Jimmy M. The Great Guano Rush: Entrepreneurs and American Overseas Expansion. New York: St. Martin's Press, 1994.

Spitzer, Leo. La enumeración caótica en la poesía moderna. Trans. Raimundo Lida. Buenos Aires: Coni, 1945.

Stein, Gertrude. Paris France. New York: Charles Scribner's Sons, 1940.

Stephens, Sonya. Baudelaire's Prose Poems: The Practice and Politics of Irony. New York: Oxford University Press, 2000.

Stovall, Tyler. Paris Noir: African-Americans in the City of Light. Boston: Houghton Mifflin, 1996.

Strauven, Wanda, ed. The Cinema of Attractions Reloaded. Amsterdam: Amsterdam University Press, 2006.

Tapscott, Stephen, ed. Twentieth-Century Latin American Poetry: A Bilingual Anthology. Austin: University of Texas Press, 1996.

Terdiman, Richard. Body and Story: The Ethics and Practice of Theoretical Conflict. Baltimore: Johns Hopkins University Press, 2005.

———. Discourse/Counter-Discourse. Ithaca: Cornell University Press, 1985.

Trapiello, Andrés. Las armas y las letras: Literatura y guerra civil (1936–39). Barcelona: Peninsula, 2002.

Trotsky, Leon. Literature and Revolution. Ed. William Keach. Trans. Rose Strunsky. Chicago: Haymarket, 2005 [1923].

Unruh, Vicky. Latin American Vanguards. Berkeley: University of California Press, 1994.

Valdelomar, Abraham. Obras completas. 4 vols. Ed. Ricardo Silva Santisteban. Lima: Ediciones Copé, 2001.

Vallejo, Georgette de. Vallejo, allá ellos, allá ellos, allá ellos! Lima: Zalvac, 1978.

Vich, Cynthia. Indigenismo de vanguardia. Lima: Pontificia Universidad Católica del Perú, 2000.

Von Buelow, Christiane. "Vallejo's Venus de Milo and the Ruins of Language." PMLA 104:1 (1989): 41–52.

Watten, Barrett. The Constructivist Moment: From Material Text to Cultural Poetics. Middletown: Wesleyan University Press, 2003.

Weiss, Jason. The Lights of Home: A Century of Latin American Writers in Paris. New York: Routledge, 2003.

Williams, Raymond. "Ideas of Nature." Culture and Materialism: Selected Essays. London: Verso, 2005. 67–85.

———. The Politics of Modernism. London: Verso, 2007.

Wood, Michael. "Yeats and Violence." London Review of Books, August 14, 2008.

Yurkiévich, Saúl. "Aptitud humorística en Poemas humanos." Hispamérica 567 (1990): 3–11.

———. "En torno de Trilce." César Vallejo. Ed. Julio Ortega. Madrid: Taurus, 1974. 245–64.

———. *La confabulación por la palabra*. Madrid: Taurus, 1978.

Zamora, Andrés. "La utopia excremental de Juan Goytisolo, escritor latino-americano: aneras de defecar(se) en la cultura occidental." *Heterotropías*. Ed. Carlos Jáuregui and Juan Pablo Dabove. Pittsburgh: IILI Press, 2003. 351–71.

Zubizarreta, Armando. *Perfil y entraña de* El caballero Carmelo. Lima: Universo, 1968.

Index

TEXT
10/13 Sabon Open Type

DISPLAY
Sabon Open Type

COMPOSITOR
Modern Language Initiative

TEXT PRINTER AND BINDER
Odyssey Press, Inc.